The Ultimate Deception

By

Frank L. Caw, Jr.

ISBN: 0-7596-4037-8

This book is printed on acid free paper.

1stBooks - rev. 9/15/02

"But thou, O Daniel, shut up the words, and seal the book, even to the time of the end... for at the time of the end shall be the vision."

— The prophet Daniel

Internet Website Address: http://www.frankcaw.com

Internet e-Mail Address: frank@frankcaw.com

This book is dedicated to the loving memory of my late wife, Debbie, who went to be in the presence of God on October 23, 1997, and who was so instrumental in helping me to prepare for my ministry during those many long, difficult years.

— Table Of Contents —

— Introduction —

There are many endtime prophecies in the Bible we can understand now for the very first time — extraordinary prophecies that detail an incredible array of apocalyptic events! Some of these events will include astounding military conflicts in our immediate future that will set the stage for the future Final Great Deception which will surprise even Christians in many respects! When the disciples asked Jesus: "What shall be the sign of thy coming, and of the end of the age?" His immediate response was a warning: "Take heed that no man deceive you." Likewise, the apostle Paul warns that "evil men and seducers shall wax worse and worse, deceiving and being deceived." Furthermore, the apostle Paul even tells us that the initial appearance of the Antichrist will be "after the working of Satan with all power and signs and lying wonders"!

Clearly, these scriptures make it quite evident that religious and philosophical deception increasingly will flourish throughout all of the earth during the "end-times" or "time of the end." That is why you will want to know exactly what the Bible predicts for the future so you will not be confused or frightened when things do not happen the way many people thought they would happen! Because the Bible predicts that the Antichrist will appear, suddenly and unexpectedly, during a time of terror and great crisis. Then, through the use of supernatural miracles and extraordinary military prowess, he will single-handedly forge an amazing, new world of peace and security and prosperity!

But, the real danger will reside in the fact that all of these incredible benefactions will set the stage for the greatest religious deception and apostasy that the world will ever have seen! Untold numbers of lives will hang in the balance as the world is twisted and spun through a maze of brilliant deception during alternating periods of peaceful prosperity and catastrophic destruction! That is why you will want to read the startling new information available in this book.... astounding new prophecy insights gleaned from brand-new research based on a plain, sensible and literal approach to scriptural exegesis!

I. Daniel's Prophecies And Antichrist

Daniel's First Vision (Daniel 2)

More than 2500 years ago, the personal, infinite, triune God of the Christian Bible supernaturally inspired the Jewish prophet Daniel to foretell the future in a series of extraordinary visions. Although each vision foretold the same, basic series of future events and developments, each one added new, additional insight as each new revelation unfolded. Accordingly, this correlation of historical and futuristic events within these visions is very important because it eliminates all reasonable doubt concerning the accuracy of our interpretation based upon the mathematical laws of probability. A chart portraying this harmony of the visions is located at the end of this chapter.

Daniel's first vision — a vision actually seen by Nebuchadnezzar, but interpreted by Daniel — involves a huge and horrific-looking image shaped into an immense man-like form:

Daniel 2:31-48

31 Thou, O king, sawest, and behold a great image. This great image, whose brightness was excellent, stood before thee; and the form thereof was terrible.

32 This image's head was of fine gold, his breast and his arms of silver, his belly and his thighs of brass,

33 His legs of iron, his feet part of iron and part of clay.

34 Thou sawest till that a stone was cut out without hands, which smote the image upon his feet that were of iron and clay, and brake them to pieces.

35 Then was the iron, the clay, the brass, the silver, and the gold, broken to pieces together, and became like the chaff of the summer threshingfloors; and the wind carried them away, that no place was found for them: and the stone that smote the image became a great mountain, and filled the whole earth.

36 This is the dream; and we will tell the interpretation thereof before the king.

37 Thou, O king, art a king of kings: for the God of heaven hath given thee a kingdom, power, and strength, and glory.

38 And wheresoever the children of men dwell, the beasts of the field and the fowls of the heaven hath he given into thine hand, and hath made thee ruler over them all. Thou art this head of gold.

39 And after thee shall arise another kingdom inferior to thee, and another third kingdom of brass, which shall bear rule over all the earth.

40 And the fourth kingdom shall be strong as iron: forasmuch as iron breaketh in pieces and subdueth all things: and as iron that breaketh all these, shall it break in pieces and bruise.

41 And whereas thou sawest the feet and toes, part of potters' clay, and part of iron, the kingdom shall be divided; but there shall be in it of the strength of the iron, forasmuch as thou sawest the iron mixed with miry clay.

42 And as the toes of the feet were part of iron, and part of clay, so the kingdom shall be partly strong, and partly broken.

43 And whereas thou sawest iron mixed with miry clay, they shall mingle themselves with the seed of men: but they shall not cleave one to another, even as iron is not mixed with clay.

44 And in the days of these kings shall the God of heaven set up a kingdom, which shall never be destroyed: and the kingdom shall not be left to other people, but it shall break in pieces and consume all these kingdoms, and it shall stand for ever.

45 Forasmuch as thou sawest that the stone was cut out of the mountain without hands, and that it brake in pieces the iron, the brass, the clay, the silver, and the gold; the great God hath made known to the king what shall come to pass hereafter: and the dream is certain, and the interpretation thereof sure... (KJV)

Daniel states specifically that the "head of gold" represents Nebuchadnezzar, king of the Babylonian Empire. (Dan. 2:36-38). In ancient times, a king and his kingdom were viewed synonymously with each other — which helps us to understand why Babylon and Nebuchadnezzar represent each other in this vision. Likewise, history will readily confirm that the "arms of silver" represent the dual-nature of the Medo-Persian Empire, and that the belly of brass symbolizes the Grecian Empire of Alexander the Great. The "legs of iron" represent the dual nature prevalent during much of the history of the ancient Roman Empire.

"The fourth kingdom shall be strong as iron." This simply means that the Roman Empire was to be a very powerful and mighty empire; it has nothing to do with the form of government employed by the Romans. For instance, there is no basis for the theory that iron in this prophecy represents centralized government. Instead, it means precisely what it says. Just as iron represents strength, so likewise did the Roman Empire possess incredible strength and durability as a powerful governing force of longevity.

What do the ten toes of the image represent? The following passage provides the answer: "Whereas thou sawest the feet and toes, part of potter's clay (weak parts; Dan. 2:42), and part of iron (strong parts; Dan. 2:42), the kingdom (Roman Empire) shall be divided..." (Dan. 2:41).

Does not this passage reflect the actual outcome of events when the Roman Empire finally did collapse? Even a cursory glance at world history will show that the Roman Empire never fell before another world empire as did the others, but instead, split into a number of kingdoms and political entities which now form the modern-day countries of Europe and Asia Minor and northern Africa. Likewise, some of these countries — represented by the iron in the toes — have been strong and independent nations, while some of the other countries — represented by the clay in the toes — have exhibited weakness, thereby leading to their conquest at times by stronger neighboring countries who would change their boundary lines.

"They shall mingle themselves with the seed of men: but they shall not cleave one to another..." This phrase simply means that the political leaders and Royal families in many of these countries would attempt to forge political alliances with one another, sometimes even through inter-marriages between their families, but never would there be any lasting confederations or alliances among them. Although demonic activity on and above the earth will explode in frequency and intensity during the very last days before Christ's Return, this particular passage does not address that issue because the subject matter clearly and singularly centers on the ten toes — as the complete immediate context of the phrase shows.

Many commentators have theorized that the ten toes of the image represent the revival of a modern-day Roman Empire where all the nations of Europe merge into a monolithic union or structure of some type, i.e., a United States of Europe. However, this theory, as it usually is presented, does not give us the most accurate picture possible. For instance, Daniel predicted there would be numerous attempts to reunite into a revived Roman Empire, but that in each case "they (would) not cleave one to another, even as iron is not mixed with clay." (Dan. 2:43). History has proven this prophecy correct. Although there have been many attempts to re-create the Roman Empire, they all have been unsuccessful or short-lived.

That is why Daniel 2:44 states that the individual countries (kings; toes) are still in existence at the time when God establishes His literal Kingdom on earth, thus proving these countries will retain their national identity and political sovereignty to a certain extent even during the "last days." This is confirmed in Revelation 13:1 which shows each of the ten horns (i.e., the modern Roman Empire countries) wearing a crown of power and authority after the Rapture has taken place at a time when the Antichrist is universally acknowledged as invincible because of his war-making prowess and satanic powers. So apparently, even though these countries will form the nucleus of his world empire, they also will retain significant political sovereignty.

Accordingly, it is important to note that it is the man, Antichrist, who produces the empire, not an empire which appoints a leader as many people suppose. Revelation 17 states that the beast (Antichrist) and the ten horns receive their power simultaneously, and that they will retain this power for only a short period of time. That is why it is so significant that there have been very determined efforts recently to unify Europe even though the geographical boundary lines for the ten horns and the European Union do not coincide with each other.

Since the majority of the nations comprising the European Union once were a part of the Old Roman Empire, and nothing is said in this prophecy which would preclude them from confederating with neighboring countries who never were, it is reasonable to suppose that the European Union is important, prophetically. For instance, it could be important in the sense that it is preparing people in that part of the world — philosophically and politically and economically — for their country's participation as member states in the new confederacy or empire which the Antichrist will inspire. Additionally, so as to further enhance and smooth preparations for entry into the empire of Antichrist, the European Union has even created a ready-made organizational mechanism which could quickly be adapted to the new circumstances of the moment. Therefore, the stage is now set and awaiting the appearance of the Antichrist at which time the prophesied "last days" empowerment of the "ten horns" will begin:

Revelation 17:12-13
12 And the ten horns which thou sawest are ten kings, which have received no kingdom as yet; but receive power as kings one hour with the beast.
13 These have one mind, and shall give their power and strength unto the beast. (KJV)

Daniel continues by stating that a stone "cut out without hands" will strike the symbolic image, causing it to crumble. Since all of the symbolic image will be intact and standing at that future point in time, the ten-horn countries and all of the other countries which once comprised the various world empires portrayed by this image will not only be in existence, but will be rich and powerful as well. The stone (the "chief cornerstone," our Lord and Saviour, Jesus Christ) will then grow into a "mountain" (i.e., kingdom; empire) covering all of the earth. We are informed that this means God will establish an eternal Kingdom which will smash the sovereignty of all earthly kingdoms, thus making every country throughout the world subject to the rulership of God. (Dan. 2:44, 45).

Daniel's Second Vision (Daniel 7)

Many years after interpreting the vision which Nebuchadnezzar had seen, Daniel experiences an extraordinary vision of his own in which he views four powerful animals — a lion, a bear, a leopard, and a terrible, non-descript beast boasting ten horns — as they rise up from the sea amidst the blowing of mighty, boisterous winds. After considering some of the more extraordinary aspects and stipulations associated with this vision, however, it becomes obvious that this vision, too, must be taken symbolically because a literal meaning would be impossible and non-sensical.

Accordingly, we note first that the passage, Daniel 7:17, stipulates that these four "great beasts" are four great kingdoms which "shall arise out of the earth." A more accurate translation, however, such as *Young's Literal Translation Of The Bible*, translates this verse as: "These great beasts, that are four, are four kings, they rise up from the earth..." Furthermore, a consultation with *Strong's Hebrew-Greek Dictionary* confirms that Young was correct in rendering this passage to read "rise" rather than "shall arise." The proper translation in this case is important because some have tried to say that all four beasts can appear only after the time of Daniel and Babylon since Daniel was told that all four beasts "shall arise" — which, by implication, supposedly means after the Babylonian Empire ceased to exist. If this were true, it might be easier to argue that the first beast could not represent Babylon — although there still would remain the problem of explaining why Babylon, in the first vision, was also the first empire portrayed in the sequence of world empires. However, a more accurate translation clearly eliminates any such possible concern by allowing us to harmonize and correlate all of the elements portrayed within the first three visions which were given to Daniel or interpreted by him.

It is important to note, also, that some parts of Daniel's visions which were futuristic for Daniel are now fulfilled history from our perspective. God (wisely) launched into prophecies concerning the "last days" from the springboard of "empire-history" in order to give us a time-space-historical reference point from which we could properly interpret the end-time prophecies. Furthermore, a complete understanding of all the visions in their entirety was reserved for the "end-times." That is why Daniel was confused by the second and third prophecies when they added important details and information not found in the first vision. However, this practice of gradual or progressive revelation is quite typical of how God operated in biblical times. For instance, God's plan of salvation through Christ increasingly was revealed down through the centuries of time, starting with Adam and Eve with their very limited knowledge, to the epistles and Revelation with their sophisticated and comprehensive view of things.

Daniel 7:1-7

1 In the first year of Belshazzar king of Babylon Daniel had a dream and visions of his head upon his bed: then he wrote the dream, and told the sum of the matters.

2 Daniel spake and said, I saw in my vision by night, and, behold, the four winds of the heaven strove upon the great sea.

3 And four great beasts came up from the sea, diverse one from another.

4 The first was like a lion, and had eagle's wings: I beheld till the wings thereof were plucked, and it was lifted up from the earth, and made stand upon the feet as a man, and a man's heart was given to it.

5 And behold another beast, a second, like to a bear, and it raised up itself on one side, and it had three ribs in the mouth of it between the teeth of it: and they said thus unto it, Arise, devour much flesh.

6 After this I beheld, and lo another, like a leopard, which had upon the back of it four wings of a fowl; the beast had also four heads; and dominion was given to it.

7 After this I saw in the night visions, and behold a fourth beast, dreadful and terrible, and strong exceedingly; and it had great iron teeth: it devoured and brake in pieces, and stamped the residue with the feet of it: and it was diverse from all the beasts that were before it; and it had ten horns. (KJV)

"Four winds of the heaven strove upon the great sea." Winds in prophetic and symbolic passages can represent wars and conflicts and strife and judgments from God. (Dan. 8:7-13 compared with Jer. 25:32-33) (Rev. 7:1-3). Likewise, in prophecy, "sea" or "water" can symbolize the masses of mankind or the nations of people on the earth. (Rev. 13:1) (Rev. 17:1, 15).

The first animal or beast (lion) represents Babylon. Just as gold represented Babylon in the first vision because it is chief among metals, so likewise was the lion selected to symbolize Babylon in the second vision because it is king of the animal world. As further evidence, the details given concerning the lion correspond precisely to those given describing the reign of Nebuchadnezzar. For instance, the eagle's wings identify the beast as Babylon because Babylon is compared to an eagle in other scriptures. (Jer. 48:40) (Ezek. 17) (Hab. 1:6-8). Since Nebuchadnezzar carved out a vast empire for himself in just a few short years, the eagle wings denote the swiftness of his military conquests. We also observe active symbolic imagery that portrays the plucking of the lion's eagle wings before it is lifted from the earth and forced to stand upon its feet as a man with a man's heart. This obviously correlates with Daniel 4 which describes how the proud and regal Nebuchadnezzar was struck down by God through seven years of insanity until he acquired the humility and Godly respect that allowed him to be restored to sanity again as a man.

The second beast in appearance is a bear reminiscent of a large species of bear inhabiting the mountains of Media. It is intended to symbolize Medo-Persia because of their shared reputation for cruelty and blood-thirstiness and robbery and plundering. (Isa. 13:16-18) (Jer. 51:48-56).

The symbolic action associated with the two sides of the bear demonstrates how both Medes and Persians formed this vicious empire even though one side is emphasized to illustrate the strength and vitality of the Persians over the Medes. As confirmation of our interpretation, we noted earlier that the two silver arms in Daniel's first vision also represented the dual nature of the Medo-Persian Empire. Likewise, in a similar manner, Daniel's third vision in Daniel 8 also depicts the supremacy of the Persians over the Medes when it portrays one of the two horns on the Medo-Persian ram rising higher than the other horn, thereby illustrating how Cyrus the Persian rose up in power after the reign of Darius the Mede while becoming the more powerful of the two. Hence, there is complete harmony and agreement within all three of these visions by Daniel. However, in Daniel's second vision, we are given additional information about Persia when it uses three ribs in the mouth of the bear to signify additional territory beyond the boundary lines of the Babylonian Empire which was conquered by Medo-Persia.

A leopard is universally known for its amazing swiftness, so when that imagery is enhanced with the addition of four wings rather than two, as in the case of the symbolic lion which represented Nebuchadnezzar, it creates a hybrid image quite capable of symbolizing the incredible quickness with which Alexander the Great conquered the then-known world. Likewise, after the sudden, premature death of Alexander the Great, the Grecian Empire was divided among four of his generals, depicted by the "four heads" of the leopard. Not surprisingly, once again, symbolism associated with this vision is reminiscent of the symbolism pictured in one of the other visions of Daniel, namely, his third vision in Daniel 8, whereby four horns are seen emerging from the head of the Grecian goat immediately after the great horn, Alexander the Great, is broken.

Next we encounter the fourth beast which is described simply as non-descript because it was so powerful and dreadful and terrible that it defied description. Rome was "diverse from all the others" in the sense that it was a republic in nature while all of the previous empires were dictatorships. However, this major, fundamental difference between it and the other world empires did not prevent Rome from ruling its conquered subjects with an iron hand — which explains why iron is mentioned once again as a fundamental characteristic of Rome just as it was before in Daniel's first vision.

The ten horns? Daniel states that they represent "ten kings." As noted several times already, the details of Daniel's visions seem to match and correlate with each other in perfect harmony, and in the first vision the ten toes of the image represented the modern-day countries which emerged from the area of the old Roman Empire. Accordingly, this would seem to imply that the ten horns also represent the modern Roman countries. Although there are more than ten such countries, ten can represent an approximate or unknown or round number in prophetic and symbolic passages as the following scriptures attest:

Jude 1:14
14 And Enoch also, the seventh from Adam, prophesied of these, saying, Behold, the Lord cometh with ten thousands of his saints, (KJV)

Daniel 7:10
10 A fiery stream issued and came forth from before him: thousand thousands ministered unto him, and ten thousand times ten thousand stood before him: the judgment was set, and the books were opened. (KJV)

Revelation 2:10
10 Fear none of those things which thou shalt suffer: behold, the devil shall cast some of you into prison, that ye may be tried; and ye shall have tribulation ten days: be thou faithful unto death, and I will give thee a crown of life. (KJV)

Revelation 5:11
11 And I beheld, and I heard the voice of many angels round about the throne and the beasts and the elders: and the number of them was ten thousand times ten thousand, and thousands of thousands; (KJV)

A United States of Europe before the initial appearance of the Antichrist? Based on what we have learned already regarding the symbolism in Daniel's visions, there would have been five beasts pictured in this vision rather than four if a new and successive empire had been destined to replace the old Roman Empire. Accordingly, just as the four heads of the leopard portray the four-fold division of the Grecian Empire when it folded after the death of Alexander the Great, so likewise do the tens horns of the beast symbolize the numerous political subdivisions of the Roman Empire after it collapsed. However, as we saw earlier, even though these modern Roman countries will retain some degree of political sovereignty up until the time of Armageddon, they will unite into a confederacy of sorts at the same time the Antichrist comes to power because they "receive power as kings one hour with the beast" and "give their power and strength unto the beast" by becoming the core nucleus of his world empire which eventually will encompass all the nations of the world.

Daniel 7:8, 19, 20, 23, 24

8 I considered the horns, and, behold, there came up among them another little horn, before whom there were three of the first horns plucked up by the roots: and, behold, in this horn were eyes like the eyes of man, and a mouth speaking great things.

19 Then I would know the truth of the fourth beast, which was diverse from all the others, exceeding dreadful, whose teeth were of iron, and his nails of brass; which devoured, brake in pieces, and stamped the residue with his feet;

20 And of the ten horns that were in his head, and of the other which came up, and before whom three fell; even of that horn that had eyes, and a mouth that spake very great things, whose look was more stout than his fellows.

23 Thus he said, The fourth beast shall be the fourth kingdom upon earth, which shall be diverse from all kingdoms, and shall devour the whole earth, and shall tread it down, and break it in pieces.

24 And the ten horns out of this kingdom are ten kings that shall arise: and another shall rise after them; and he shall be diverse from the first, and he shall subdue three kings. (KJV)

"Shall devour the whole earth." When interpreting phrases such as "whole earth" or "whole world" or "all the world" in the Bible, we must understand that an absolute, strict literal interpretation of such phrases sometimes are modified in their meaning by contextual considerations, including other scriptural passages. In this instance, Rome never actually ruled over the entire global planet as we know it today, but the Roman Empire did conquer and dominate virtually all of the entire world known to Western Civilization at that point in time. Likewise, in a similar manner, Babylon (Dan. 2:38) and Greece (Dan. 2:39) also ruled over their known worlds during their respective times in history. (Compare: Romans 1:8; Romans 10:18; Col 1.23; etc.) However, in Revelation 13, when it is said the Antichrist will rule over the whole world and that people from every nation and tongue will worship him as god, it is very likely that the phrase "whole world" means precisely that because people living at that future point in time obviously will understand it as such.

Sometime during the existence of these modern-day Roman countries, a "little horn" suddenly and unexpectedly appears among them. (Dan. 7:8). Because horns throughout scripture represent the power and authority inherent in kingdoms or countries, this "little horn" quite logically represents a small, new kingdom or a small, new country. However, in this instance, the little horn also represents a strong-man leader or dictator because Daniel very quickly ascribes human attributes to the little horn country, attributes such as "a mouth speaking great things." For that reason, it would seem this tiny, new country and the man associated with it appear together simultaneously in a manner which suggests that it is the man who causes the little horn country to spring into existence. Bible students generally call this man the Antichrist, and it is during the lifetime of this person that the Battle of Armageddon takes place, thereby leading to the subsequent establishment of God's eternal Kingdom on earth. (Dan. 7:14).

"Three of the first horns plucked up by the roots." Currently, there are two plausible interpretations for the national identity of these three horns. The first possibility involves the three East European countries of Hungary, Rumania and Bulgaria. They are alluded to specifically in this vision because they are the Roman Empire countries which have been dominated by the Russian communist empire. Although, for the moment, they appear to be somewhat independent despite the fact that national communists still play a dominant role in their national politics and security functions of government, for whatever reason they very possibly will be "plucked up" or liberated by the Antichrist during his initial rise-to-power — if the Antichrist conquers the military forces of Russia.

However, the most probable explanation for the above scriptural passage involves the current war on organized terrorism and the more obvious sponsors and supporters of organized terrorism, i.e., Syria, Iraq and Iran. Because in light of the horrific terrorist attacks against the United States last year on September 11, 2001, and the emerging threat to civilization that is posed by radical Islamic terrorist groups and Iraqi and

Iranian weapons of mass destruction, it seems very likely that the world can reach the level of terror necessary to justify the creation of a new world empire by Antichrist without necessarily facing a military crisis provoked by Russian aggression. Therefore, since the United States apparently plans to attack Iraq in the near future (as of September 13, 2002) in order to eliminate its weapons of mass destruction, we either must run into unforeseen military problems, or Iraq and its terrorist allies preemptively strike first, or we lose the national will to mount an effective military campaign against Iraq, or some other scenario develops! But, somehow or other, circumstances will evolve so that it becomes necessary for the Antichrist to appear suddenly to rescue the world from terror and destruction or the threat thereof.

However, the above scenarios do not necessarily preclude Russian military aggression from also playing a significant role in the terror equation that triggers the rise of Antichrist. Therefore, since the Antichrist will control all the nations of the world just after the Rapture takes place, and since he will be the chief prince of (Magog) Russia years before Armageddon occurs, these scriptural considerations imply one of two possible scenarios for the immediate future of Russia. Either the power-hungry hard-liners in Russia voluntarily relinquish political control over their country after devoting many long years to secretive and massive preparations for a war with the United States, or they decide to embark on a journey of military adventurism in hopes of restoring the glory of the former Soviet Empire.

Thus, it is very possible that if a major military conflagration between Iraq and the United States begins, several other hostile parties will jump into the fray on the side of Iraq if and when Iraq attacks Israel as part of its response strategy. For instance, the Hizbullah terrorists in southern Lebanon reportedly have deployed over 10,000 Katushya rockets along the Lebanese-Israeli border for use against Israel at the most strategic moment. Likewise, Syria and Iran and the Palestinian terrorists supposedly are poised to attack Israel when significant hostilities commence between Iraq and the United States. Furthermore, radical Islamic terrorists could launch another round of devastating terrorist attacks against Europe and/or the United States. Then finally, it is quite possible that Russia will exploit the military expansionist opportunities that a catastrophic series of Middle East wars probably would create. So, without any question, all of these developments would add immeasurably to the sense of terror and fear that will envelop the world. Accordingly, it appears very likely that the three horns will represent the countries of Israel, Syria and Iraq because these three countries were also once a part of the old Roman Empire, and they apparently will be subdued militarily by the Antichrist when he first rises to power.

Thus, it is important to know that several biblical scriptures predict that Israel will be subdued by the Antichrist during his initial ascendancy to power. As for Syria and Iraq, however, the Bible only says that these two countries will become a part of the empire of Antichrist; it does not say whether they will do so voluntarily, or whether they will be conquered militarily by the Antichrist. But, we should note that biblical scriptures do predict that the Antichrist will conquer numerous armies during his initial appearance as he "waxes exceeding great" in a southern and eastern direction, and that he will "destroy wonderfully" through the use of supernatural power derived from Satan. Furthermore, both of these countries — along with Iran, Saudi Arabia and Afghanistan — are major sponsors and supporters of organized terrorism out of the Middle East. So, at this point, they appear to be likely candidates for military conquest by the Antichrist when he suddenly appears to rescue the world from a horrific wave of terrorism and/or Middle East wars and/or Russian military aggression. Therefore, if the Antichrist subdues Syria and Iraq when he conquers Israel, the identity of the three horns will have to be ascribed to these three countries.

Moreover, the sudden appearance of Antichrist to rescue the world from the horrific threat of terrorism and catastrophic wars will be so unexpected and amazing that the Roman Empire countries (ALL ten horns) will voluntarily "GIVE their power and strength unto the beast (Antichrist)." (Rev. 17:13). Please note that NONE of the ten horns are forced to swear allegiance to Antichrist; they very willingly pledge their loyalties to him of their own free will!. That is why when Daniel says that the little horn will "subdue" three of the ten horns, he must mean that by subduing them, the Antichrist actually liberates them completely so that they are able to pledge their allegiance to him when the remaining ten horns do so as pictured in Revelation 17.

"Behold, in this horn were eyes like the eyes of man." This descriptive phrase probably denotes more than just mere human intelligence. Other scriptures we will survey later clearly attribute satanic and supernatural power to the Antichrist, so this also could be a veiled reference to such power. Furthermore, it is even possible that he will have very unusual-looking eyes in a literal sense. Just to serve as an example, for instance, Walid Jumblatt, Druze politician and warlord in southern Lebanon, has very large and unusual-looking eyes which I noticed immediately when he first came to my attention in the Fall of 1983 during the Lebanese Civil War. More than once it was reported that newsmen were talking about his extraordinary cunning in maneuvering politically and militarily to achieve more power and influence than what his small army ordinarily would warrant. Of course, only time will tell for certain if he will prove to be the Antichrist.

"And a mouth speaking great things." The Antichrist will demonstrate extraordinary powers of persuasion and oratorical skills while boldly proclaiming his creative and amazing solutions for world and regional problems. Therefore, when he begins to enforce and inspire conditions of world peace and security and prosperity during a time of great crisis and terror, there should be no problem in understanding why most people will become mesmerized by this man. Obviously he will be a very impressive and charismatic person with tremendous powers of persuasion.

Daniel 7:25 gives us additional insight: "And he (Antichrist) shall speak great words against the most High.... and think to change times and laws..." In other words, Antichrist will boldly defy God while advocating his own standard of morals and values for society. No decent standard or sensible norm will be safe from attack or immune to criticism. Accordingly, from the very outset, there never will be any pretense on his part at being very sympathetic toward Israeli Jews or Bible-believing Christians, nor will he ever pretend to be the Jewish Messiah as some people suppose — especially since Israel will be one of the very first countries he attacks when he first rises to power. (Dan. 8:9). Instead, he will begin soon after his initial appearance to criticize and defy traditional Christian beliefs and values, and then immediately after the Rapture, even become quite willing to kill anyone who proclaims their faith in Christ. Later, he will even violate the sanctity of the sacred Holy of Holies room in a rebuilt Jewish Temple while proclaiming himself the god of gods.

I John 4:3

3 And every spirit that confesseth not that Jesus Christ is come in the flesh is not of God: and this is that spirit of antichrist, whereof ye have heard that it should come; and even now already is it in the world. (KJV)

II John 1:7

7 For many deceivers are entered into the world, who confess not that Jesus Christ is come in the flesh. This is a deceiver and an antichrist. (KJV)

I John 2:18, 22

18 Little children, it is the last time: and as ye have heard that antichrist shall come, even now are there many antichrists; whereby we know that it is the last time.

22 Who is a liar but he that denieth that Jesus is the Christ? He is antichrist, that denieth the Father and the Son. (KJV)

In these passages, not only are we told that a specific, unique personage called "antichrist" will appear some day, but that since the inception of Christianity, there always have been people who have denied that the historic Jesus Christ is God manifested in the flesh, or as noted in I John 2:22, that both God the Father and God the Son are the true God in Heaven. These people, too, are "little" antichrists in a manner of speaking. So, while we are warned against the heresy these people teach, we also are given further insight as to exactly what the Antichrist will advocate, and how the Bible itself actually defines the word "antichrist."

Since *Merriam-Webster's Collegiate Dictionary* defines the prefix "anti" as meaning "one that is opposed," this means that the Antichrist will be opposed (to the true God in Heaven). As we noted in the paragraph above while commenting on I John 2:22, the Bible says that Antichrist will deny the true God in Heaven, i.e., the personal, infinite, triune God of Christianity. This is completely consistent with Daniel when he says in Daniel 7:25 that the Antichrist "shall speak great words against the most High," and in Daniel 11:36-37 where he states that the Antichrist will "magnify himself above every god, and shall speak marvellous things against the God of gods... nor regard any god: for he shall magnify himself above all." This, then, is how we should define the word "antichrist" because that is how the Bible defines it.

That is why it is wrong to think that the Antichrist ever will pretend to be the Jewish Messiah — even when he first appears as a savior who rescues the world from apparent imminent destruction. Instead, the Antichrist will deny both God the Father and God the Son while proclaiming himself to be a god above all. Therefore, it is not a coincidence that the popular New Age Movement teaches we can achieve godhood and extraordinary powers of the mind through "higher consciousness" techniques or "cosmic Christ consciousness." Thus, the historical evidence proving the true identity of Jesus is ignored by these people and their followers, and He is relegated to the status of just another ordinary psychic seer.

"Whose look was more stout than his fellows." Although Antichrist will originate from a tiny, brand-new country, he and his small army of soldiers will accomplish incredible military feats which will astound the whole world. His military prowess will seem so impressive and amazing, and his small nation will seem so fierce and violent and ruthless compared to neighboring countries, that they will very quickly acquire a reputation for fierceness and invincibility. That is why, immediately after the Rapture in Revelation 13, we are told that the whole world marvels at the military prowess of the Antichrist when everyone proclaims, "Who is like unto the beast? who is able to make war with him?"

"And he (Antichrist) shall be diverse from the first (i.e., the ten horns; the modern Roman Empire countries)." The year 1989 proved to be an amazing watershed in international politics, marking an extraordinary upsurge in the democratic spirit throughout the world which has continued to grow in strength and influence during subsequent years since then. In stark contrast, however, from the very moment his ascendancy to power first begins, the Antichrist will exercise absolute dictatorial control over the newly-independent country from which he will originate before eventually extending his rulership over the whole world (Rev. 13:4-8).

Daniel 7:8-11

8 I considered the horns, and, behold, there came up among them another little horn, before whom there were three of the first horns plucked up by the roots: and, behold, in this horn were eyes like the eyes of man, and a mouth speaking great things.

9 I beheld till the thrones were cast down, and the Ancient of days did sit, whose garment was white as snow, and the hair of his head like the pure wool: his throne was like the fiery flame, and his wheels as burning fire.

10 A fiery stream issued and came forth from before him: thousand thousands ministered unto him, and ten thousand times ten thousand stood before him: the judgment was set, and the books were opened.

11 I beheld then because of the voice of the great words which the horn spake: I beheld even till the beast was slain, and his body destroyed, and given to the burning flame. (KJV)

"Thrones were cast down." This phrase in verse 9 could also be translated as "set down" or "put in place." Likewise, the heavenly scene described in verses 9 and 10 is pictured in much greater detail in Revelation 4 and 5 where the judgment throne of God is set up and surrounded by the thrones of the "24 elders."

It is instructive to note that Daniel's narrative describing endtime earthly events is interrupted by verses 9 and 10 which portray events in Heaven immediately after Christians have been "Raptured" or "caught-up" to Heaven. Therefore, verses 8 and 11 establish a precise time-frame which tells us when the Rapture will take place relative to events on earth. More specifically, verse 8 portrays a series of earthly events which conclude with the little horn Antichrist "speaking great things." The next two verses, i.e., verses 9 and 10, then describe various events which take place in Heaven immediately after the Rapture. Then, verse 11 picks up where it left off in verse 8 by resuming its narration of the exact same earthly activity (i.e., "the voice of the great words which the horn spake"). Without question, this interruption in the continuity of the narrative establishes the fact that Antichrist will begin his ascendancy to power before the Rapture occurs. The context of this passage also indicates that the Rapture will occur before persecutions are initiated against the tribulation saints, thus further confirming that the Rapture is pre-tribulation in nature.

Daniel 7:12

12 As concerning the rest of the beasts, they had their dominion taken away: yet their lives were prolonged for a season and time. (KJV)

This would seem to indicate that the various empire beasts (i.e., the modern-day countries which once comprised these empires) will enjoy a resurgence in power and wealth and influence during the "last days" immediately prior to the Rapture. This resurgence in power and affluence is corroborated by Daniel 2:45 which states that all of the symbolic image pictured in Daniel's first vision is standing upright (i.e., powerful and wealthy) at the time God breaks the power of the various world empire countries. However, even though He breaks their power and sovereignty, He does allow them to survive and enter into His new, literal Kingdom on earth, an eternal Kingdom which will replace all earthly kingdoms. In Revelation and other passages throughout the Bible, we are told that this process will occur on a gradual basis during the Millennial Reign of Christ on the earth.

Daniel 7:13-27

13 I saw in the night visions, and, behold, one like the Son of man came with the clouds of heaven, and came to the Ancient of days, and they brought him near before him.

14 And there was given him dominion, and glory, and a kingdom, that all people, nations, and languages, should serve him: his dominion is an everlasting dominion, which shall not pass away, and his kingdom that which shall not be destroyed....

17 These great beasts, which are four, are four kings, which shall arise out of the earth.

18 But the saints of the most High shall take the kingdom, and possess the kingdom for ever, even for ever and ever.

19 Then I would know the truth of the fourth beast, which was diverse from all the others, exceeding dreadful, whose teeth were of iron, and his nails of brass; which devoured, brake in pieces, and stamped the residue with his feet;

20 And of the ten horns that were in his head, and of the other which came up, and before whom three fell; even of that horn that had eyes, and a mouth that spake very great things, whose look was more stout than his fellows.

21 I beheld, and the same horn made war with the saints, and prevailed against them;

22 Until the Ancient of days came, and judgment was given to the saints of the most High; and the time came that the saints possessed the kingdom.

23 Thus he said, The fourth beast shall be the fourth kingdom upon earth, which shall be diverse from all kingdoms, and shall devour the whole earth, and shall tread it down, and break it in pieces.

24 And the ten horns out of this kingdom are ten kings that shall arise: and another shall rise after them; and he shall be diverse from the first, and he shall subdue three kings.

25 And he shall speak great words against the most High, and shall wear out the saints of the most High, and think to change times and laws: and they shall be given into his hand until a time and times and the dividing of time.

26 But the judgment shall sit, and they shall take away his dominion, to consume and to destroy it unto the end.

27 And the kingdom and dominion, and the greatness of the kingdom under the whole heaven, shall be given to the people of the saints of the most High, whose kingdom is an everlasting kingdom, and all dominions shall serve and obey him. (KJV)

"And they shall be given into his hand until a time and times and the dividing of time." This passage simply states that people who become Christians after the Rapture ("tribulation saints") will be persecuted for a certain period of time by the Antichrist. Other scriptural passages clarify this period of time as lasting for three and one-half years. (Rev. 12:6) (Rev. 12:14) (Rev. 13:5) (Dan. 12:7).

Daniel's Third Vision (Daniel 8)

Daniel's third vision initially involves two animals, a ram and a goat, which Daniel later identifies as representations of the ancient Persian and Grecian empires. (Dan. 8:20, 21). The remainder of Daniel's vision, however, clearly delineates events which will happen during the "time of the end," a very vital point clearly stated and emphasized in four different verses within this same passage of scripture. (Dan. 8:17, 19, 26, 27). Therefore, this vision should not be dismissed lightly as an ancient fulfilled prophecy with little relevance to endtime prophecy analysis as some are inclined to do. Instead, this prophecy should be given its due consideration for the extraordinary information and insight which can be gleaned from its words. Accordingly, here is what Daniel saw in his third vision:

Daniel 8:3-14, 17, 19-26

3 Then I lifted up mine eyes, and saw, and, behold, there stood before the river a ram which had two horns: and the two horns were high; but one was higher than the other, and the higher came up last.

4 I saw the ram pushing westward, and northward, and southward; so that no beasts might stand before him, neither was there any that could deliver out of his hand; but he did according to his will, and became great.

5 And as I was considering, behold, an he goat came from the west on the face of the whole earth, and touched not the ground: and the goat had a notable horn between his eyes.

6 And he came to the ram that had two horns, which I had seen standing before the river, and ran unto him in the fury of his power.

7 And I saw him come close unto the ram, and he was moved with choler against him, and smote the ram, and brake his two horns: and there was no power in the ram to stand before him, but he cast him down to the ground, and stamped upon him: and there was none that could deliver the ram out of his hand.

8 Therefore the he goat waxed very great: and when he was strong, the great horn was broken; and for it came up four notable ones toward the four winds of heaven.

9 And out of one of them came forth a little horn, which waxed exceeding great, toward the south, and toward the east, and toward the pleasant land.

10 And it waxed great, even to the host of heaven; and it cast down some of the host and of the stars to the ground, and stamped upon them.

11 Yea, he magnified himself even to the prince of the host, and by him the daily sacrifice was taken away, and the place of his sanctuary was cast down.

12 And an host was given him against the daily sacrifice by reason of transgression, and it cast down the truth to the ground; and it practised, and prospered.

13 Then I heard one saint speaking, and another saint said unto that certain saint which spake, How long shall be the vision concerning the daily sacrifice, and the transgression of desolation, to give both the sanctuary and the host to be trodden under foot?

14 And he said unto me, Unto two thousand and three hundred days; then shall the sanctuary be cleansed....

17 So he came near where I stood: and when he came, I was afraid, and fell upon my face: but he said unto me, Understand, O son of man: for at the time of the end shall be the vision....

19 And he said, Behold, I will make thee know what shall be in the last end of the indignation: for at the time appointed the end shall be.

20 The ram which thou sawest having two horns are the kings of Media and Persia.

21 And the rough goat is the king of Grecia: and the great horn that is between his eyes is the first king.

22 Now that being broken, whereas four stood up for it, four kingdoms shall stand up out of the nation, but not in his power.

23 And in the latter time of their kingdom, when the transgressors are come to the full, a king of fierce countenance, and understanding dark sentences, shall stand up.

24 And his power shall be mighty, but not by his own power: and he shall destroy wonderfully, and shall prosper, and practise, and shall destroy the mighty and the holy people.

25 And through his policy also he shall cause craft to prosper in his hand; and he shall magnify himself in his heart, and by peace shall destroy many: he shall also stand up against the Prince of princes; but he shall be broken without hand.

26 And the vision of the evening and the morning which was told is true: wherefore shut thou up the vision; for it shall be for many days. (KJV)

After Alexander the Great died suddenly and prematurely, his empire was split into four independent kingdoms by his four top generals, each of whom selected one of the new kingdoms to govern. Hence the symbolic "four notable ones" which appear after the "great horn" of the "goat" is "broken." Then an unspecified period of time goes by until the "little horn" or "fierce king" appears. This man (Antichrist) "prospers" in his plans for a while, but eventually he is destroyed "without hand" and God's Kingdom is established for eternity.

Daniel 8:8, 9

8 Therefore the he goat waxed very great: and when he was strong, the great horn was broken; and for it came up four notable ones toward the four winds of heaven.

9 And out of one of them came forth a little horn, which waxed exceeding great, toward the south, and toward the east, and toward the pleasant land. (KJV)

The context of this verse shows the "little horn" Antichrist originating from one of the four divisions of the Grecian Empire which emerged following the death of Alexander the Great. Almost immediately, the little horn, representing both a tiny, new country and the personage of Antichrist, waxes "exceeding great" very quickly as it conquers in a southern and eastern direction. Please note that the "pleasant land" (Israel; Palestine; Dan.11:16, 41; Ezek. 20:6, 15; Psalms 106:24; Jer. 3:19; Zech. 7:14) is mentioned specifically as one of the first countries attacked by the Antichrist in his initial rise to power, thereby precluding any reasonable possibility that he might pretend to be the promised Messiah to the Jews. The fact that the scriptural evidence also clearly indicates that the Antichrist will originate from the country of Lebanon decreases that possibility even more so.

Sometimes it is said that the "little-horn" Antichrist will come from one of the "four winds of heaven" toward which the four goat horns sprout. However, aside from the contextual implication that the action in this passage centers on the four notable horns, logic dictates that if the little horn truly was suppose to appear from one of the "four winds of heaven," meaning anywhere on earth, then it would have been pointless even to mention the Persian and Grecian empires in this vision! This interpretation is bolstered considerably by the fact that the fourth vision in Daniel 11 portrays the Antichrist as originating from the Syrian dynasty which emerged from the four-fold split of the Grecian Empire after Alexander the Great died. Obviously this point only confirms our view that the little horn will come from one of the four goat horns, not one of the four winds of heaven.

Likewise, many commentators have taught that the "little horn" is Antiochus Epiphanes, the Syrian ruler who desecrated the Jewish temple by placing a sow in it and forcing the Jews to worship it. This desecration, it is alleged, is the "transgression of desolation" mentioned in verse 13. But that alternative explanation is highly improbable for several reasons:

1. Daniel makes reference to an "abomination of desolation" in two other scriptural passages that are associated with the Antichrist. (Dan. 9:27) (Dan. 12:11). Therefore, in order to be consistent, it seems likely that Daniel 8:11-14 also refers to the abomination of desolation that will be perpetrated by the Antichrist. This is especially true because, as we will see shortly, the 2300 days in which the sanctuary will be desecrated while the daily sacrifices are abolished actually should be translated as 2300 evenings and mornings, for a total of 1150 days. Since this prophecy

has never yet been fulfilled precisely as Daniel predicted, it still remains a future prophecy.

2. After warning the Jews about the "abomination of desolation, spoken of by Daniel the prophet," Jesus continued his discourse regarding other signs which also would signal the imminence of His Return, thereby indicating contextually that Daniel's prophecy was an end-time event. (Matt. 24) (Mark 13) (Luke 21). Please note that Jesus never alluded to the possibility that Daniel's prophecies involving an abomination had already been fulfilled by Antiochus Epiphanes. Instead, He based His prophecy on the assumption that Daniel had prophesied about only one such desecration with any future prophetic significance. Therefore, the little horn in Daniel 8 must refer to the future actions of the Antichrist.

3. There is an amazing, consistent harmony and correlation among the various individual elements of the visions given to Daniel. For instance, the Persian Empire was symbolized by two arms of silver in Daniel 2, two sides of a bear in Daniel 7, and two horns of a ram in Daniel 8. Likewise, the Grecian Empire was symbolized by a trunk of brass in the first vision, a leopard with four heads in the second vision, and a goat with four horns in the third vision. In like manner, then, since the "little horn" in Daniel's second vision represents Antichrist, logical consistency demands an identical meaning in Daniel's third vision. To say otherwise clearly defies the mathematical laws of probability as a careful analysis of the information presented in the chart, *Harmony Of Daniel's Visions*, located at the end of this chapter, will show.

4. Daniel emphasizes several times throughout his third vision that the vision is intended primarily for the "time of the end." (Dan. 8:17, 19, 26, 27). Nevertheless, sometimes it is said that "the time of the end" in this prophecy really only refers to a period of time which took place soon after the Persian and Grecian empires had faded into oblivion. But if that were true, then we would have to question what Daniel could have said for some people to believe him when he clearly and distinctly stated several times that the vision was for the endtimes. In other words, if Daniel really had wanted to indicate that his vision was for the time of the end, then what could he have said otherwise that would have been more convincing? We must not throw away our dictionaries or forget the rules of grammar and logic if we are going to get very far in our scriptural quest for truth. Therefore, it seems highly probable that the symbolic "little horn" in this vision, as in the previous vision, is associated with "end-time" events, not

ancient history.

5. Finally, as we will see later, Daniel's third vision repeats the same pattern that was established in the two previous visions when they presented explanations for key elements of the prophecies after their initial presentation. Accordingly, in this third vision, just as verses 20 and 21 explain that the ram and the goat represent Persia and Greece, so likewise does verse 23 describe the "little horn" in verse 9 as the "fierce king" who is prophesied to display some very specific and supernatural abilities and actions. For instance, it is predicted that the little horn will possess miraculous supernatural power from Satan which will enable him to conquer his enemies with astounding results, then destroy people through the practice of deceit and peace and prosperity, then destroy the holy people while proclaiming himself to be a god, and then ultimately be destroyed by God "without hand." Furthermore, verses 10 and 11 say that the little horn will magnify himself as a god, and even will cause some of the stars or evil angels to fall to the earth. Quite obviously Antiochus Epiphanes did not even come close to fulfilling all of these fantastic prophecies! So, we must conclude that Antiochus Epiphanes was not the little horn or fierce king prophesied by Daniel if we interpret words in the Bible in the same sensible manner we would in any other book.

Before continuing with our analysis, we can summarize by saying there are numerous scriptures which clearly indicate the Antichrist will originate from somewhere within the modern-day areas which once comprised the ancient Roman and Grecian and Assyrian empires, and that an additional scriptural passage even states that the Antichrist will originate from somewhere within the area of the old Syrian dynasty. Accordingly, the only modern countries which meet all of these scriptural requirements are the modern-day countries of Lebanon and Syria. However, some of the scriptures also stipulate that the country of origin for the Antichrist must be a very small and brand-new country. In fact, they stipulate that this country, whose political leader will be the Antichrist, must first spring into existence at the very same time the Antichrist first begins his ascendancy to world prominence and power because the "little horn" symbolism portrayed in these scriptures represents both the man, Antichrist, and his political kingdom or country.

So, in other words, the scriptures very strongly suggest that the Antichrist will declare independence for a very tiny, brand-new country immediately before creating a new world empire over which he will rule.

Therefore, we can narrow our focus down even further to somewhere within the area of Lebanon when additional scriptural requirements are also considered. That is why it is my contention that Walid Jumblatt and his fierce Druze mountain people are the primary candidates for becoming the scriptural "little horn" due to a variety of compelling circumstances in Lebanon that conform to a number of scriptural mandates.

Daniel 7:7, 8

7 After this I saw in the night visions, and behold a fourth beast, dreadful and terrible, and strong exceedingly; and it had great iron teeth: it devoured and brake in pieces, and stamped the residue with the feet of it: and it was diverse from all the beasts that were before it; and it had ten horns.

8 I considered the horns, and, behold, there came up among them another little horn, before whom there were three of the first horns plucked up by the roots: and, behold, in this horn were eyes like the eyes of man, and a mouth speaking great things. (KJV)

This passage indicates that Antichrist will originate from somewhere within the area that once was dominated by the Romans because the "little horn" (Antichrist) appears among the "ten horns" (modern Roman countries) of the "fourth beast" (Roman Empire). Since the little horn appears after the ten horns are already in existence, it must represent a very small country that is relatively recent in origin rather than an old country, or otherwise it would have been counted as one of the original "ten horns."

Likewise, because horns throughout scripture represent the power and authority inherent in kingdoms or countries, this "little horn" quite logically represents a small kingdom or a small country. However, in this instance, the little horn also represents a strong-man leader or dictator because Daniel very quickly ascribes human attributes to the little horn country, attributes such as "a mouth speaking great things." For that reason, it would seem this tiny country, and the man associated with it, appear together simultaneously in a manner which suggests that it is the man who causes the little horn country to spring into existence. Therefore, since this small country must appear simultaneously with the man, Antichrist, it must, in fact, be a brand-new country that does not even exist yet at this point in time.

Daniel 8:8, 9

8 Therefore the he goat waxed very great: and when he was strong, the great horn was broken; and for it came up four notable ones toward the four winds of heaven.

9 And out of one of them came forth a little horn, which waxed exceeding great, toward the south, and toward the east, and toward the pleasant land. (KJV)

This passage clearly indicates that the "little horn" will originate from one of the four kingdoms which were carved from the collapsing Grecian Empire soon after Alexander the Great died. Bearing in mind we previously demonstrated that Antichrist will also originate from a small, new country within Roman territory, a comparison of maps portraying the Roman and Grecian empires will show that the only area shared in common by both empires was the country of Greece and the Middle East area.

However, Antichrist not only originates from both the Roman and Grecian empires, but Old Testament prophets frequently referred to him as "the Assyrian," too. (Isa. 10:5, 6) (Isa. 10:20-34) (Isa. 14:24-27) (Isa. 19) (Isa. 23:13) (Isa. 27:12, 13) (Isa. 30:18-33) (Isa. 31:4-9) (Micah 5:3-15) (Micah 7:7-20). Therefore, all of these scriptures indicate he also will originate from somewhere within the area that once comprised the ancient Assyrian Empire. Accordingly, a comparison of maps portraying the former territories of the Assyrian, Grecian and Roman empires will show that only Egypt, Lebanon, Syria, Iraq and Jordan were once a part of all three of these world empires. So, the Antichrist must originate from a small, new country that will spring into existence within the area of one of these Middle East countries.

Finally, a careful analysis of Daniel 11 will show that the first thirty-four verses in Daniel's fourth vision use the designation "King of the North" when referring to various Syrian Kings from the old Syrian dynasty in that period of ancient history. (See footnotes for Chapter 11 in *Dake's Annotated Reference Bible*.) But, the exploits and attributes ascribed to the "King of the North" for the remainder of that chapter obviously can apply only to the Antichrist! (Dan. 11:35-45). Accordingly, we must conclude that the Antichrist will originate from somewhere within the Syrian dynasty which emerged from the four-fold split of the Grecian Empire after Alexander the Great died. However, as previously noted, since the "little horn" must be a very small, new country, this automatically eliminates an old, established country such as Syria from consideration. But, since Lebanon was once a part of the old Syrian dynasty, a tiny new country within its borders would satisfy all scriptural requirements.

Therefore, the above scriptural requirements necessitate that the country of origin for the Antichrist must be a tiny, new country located somewhere within the area of Lebanon and Syria. However, additional considerations narrow the probabilities down even further to southern Lebanon:

1. The "little horn" must be a very tiny country in comparison to neighboring countries throughout the old Roman Empire area. Furthermore, the little horn must be a brand-new country which springs into existence just as the Antichrist begins to wax "exceeding great" in a southern and eastern direction because the man and the country are very closely identified with each other in scripture. Accordingly, these scriptural requirements alone eliminate most of the possibilities within the area under consideration, thus making our task much easier. Given the current political realities within both Syria and Lebanon, it seems much more likely that a small, new country will appear within Lebanon, rather than Syria.

This is due primarily to the fact that Syria has been a relatively strong and stable country over the last couple of decades — although there is an element of doubt now that President Hafez Assad died recently. However, in Lebanon we see ongoing domination of the country by the Syrians while various political and religious factions oppose each other on a variety of issues. Likewise, Israel recently withdrew its military troops from southern Lebanon, thereby permitting the Hizbullah terrorists to take control of the area since the government in Beirut refuses to send troops to establish law and order. Apparently, the government would rather see the region plagued by anarchy and chaos rather than do anything that would include repressing Hizbullah violence against Israel. Meanwhile, Iran and Iraq and Syria have all been quite active in the area in their efforts to supply the Hizbullah terrorists with massive amounts of weapons and rockets and military supplies for eventual use against Israel.

Then finally, to further complicate matters, the Lebanese factions have begun to challenge the presence of Syria in Lebanon because Lebanese autonomy has become a very popular public issue in recent months. Not surprisingly, it did not take very long for Lebanese Druze warlord and popular politician Walid Jumblatt to capitalize on this rising tide of popular sentiment by becoming a leading critic of the Syrian occupation in Lebanon. Emotions ran so high that Syria even felt compelled to deploy many of its military troops temporarily into the Chouf mountain region where Jumblatt and his Druze people live. After all, how could Syria know that they were forcing a military confrontation with the man who probably will become the Antichrist? Then later, the Lebanese military arrested more than 250 opposition activists, including many prominent opposition leaders, for opposing the Syrian army occupation! However, it did not take very long for both Cardinal Sfeir and Druze leader Walid Jumblatt to lead widespread criticism against this crackdown — prompting the military to release most of the activists whom they had just arrested!

Moreover, Jumblatt's new stature as a national leader — marked by accomplishments such as the reconciliation he negotiated between the Druze and Christians, the various political alliances he has formed across the entire political spectrum, and his rapidly expanding base of support among the Druze in Syria and Palestine — have all helped to earn him a new regional role in affairs-of-state. Now that Syria has taken direct control of the Lebanese military in response to the rising unrest throughout Lebanon against its occupation, this represents yet another reason why Jumblatt — who very possibly will be the Antichrist — could soon declare independence for a tiny, brand-new Druze country within Lebanon! There will be no other way to break the shackles of oppression and domination that the Syrian military is imposing upon Lebanon!

2. Antichrist will originate from a fierce, warlike people. Daniel states that the country of Antichrist will "look more stout than his fellows (ten horns; modern Roman countries)." (Dan. 7:20). Habakkuk predicts that the nation of Antichrist will be "bitter and hasty," and "terrible and dreadful." (Hab. 1:6, 7). Obviously the fierce fighting that took place during the recent Lebanese Civil War certainly lends credibility to the proposition that the Lebanese factions live up to the descriptions given by Daniel and Habakkuk. Moreover, Walid Jumblatt's Druze mountain people are noted, in particular, for their fierceness and competence in military warfare!

3. Later we will prove from various scriptures that the city of Tyre will be rebuilt by Antichrist at its original location in Lebanon, and then serve as his political capital until his demise at Armageddon. Accordingly, it is quite natural to assume that he would wish to establish

his political base somewhere within his own native country if possible — and the current village of Tyre is in southern-central Lebanon.

4. One last clue regarding this matter is found in Daniel 8:9 which states that the Antichrist will conquer armies with lightning speed while invading in a southern and eastern direction, including down into the "pleasant land" (Palestine; Israel). This statement alone puts definite limitations upon the possible location of the "little horn," and obviously it will aid greatly in the early verification of the identity of Antichrist whenever he begins his initial ascendancy to power.

At this point in time, it seems likely that the Antichrist will "wax exceeding great" in a southern and eastern direction by capitalizing on the growing tide of popular dissent and opposition throughout Lebanon against the occupation of their country by Syrian troops. Likewise, many Lebanese citizens continue to express feelings of anger and resentment over the violence and destruction and territorial violations they associate with the Hizbullah-Israeli conflict in southern Lebanon and the alleged "Israeli occupation" of the Shebba Farms area along the Israeli-Lebanese border. There also exists widespread resentment among the Lebanese against perceived Israeli mistreatment of the Palestinians in the West Bank and Gaza Strip areas. Accordingly, there appear to be several reasons why the Antichrist might fulfill biblical prophecy by driving Syrian and Israeli troops and Hizbullah terrorists out of Lebanon as he begins his quest for building a new world empire.

Daniel 8:10

10 And it waxed great, even to the host of heaven; and it cast down some of the host and of the stars to the ground, and stamped upon them. (KJV)

Young's Literal Translation renders this verse in the following manner:

Daniel 8:10

10 Yea, it exerteth unto the host of the heavens, and causeth to fall to the earth of the host, and of the stars, and trampleth them down. (YLT)

Now compare verse 10 with the same scene narrated in the book of Revelation where it portrays Satan and his fallen angels (i.e., "some of the hosts and of the stars") as they are cast out violently and banished from the heavenlies down to the earth:

Revelation 12:3-4, 7-13

3 And there appeared another wonder in heaven; and behold a great red dragon, having seven heads and ten horns, and seven crowns upon his heads.

4 And his tail drew the third part of the stars of heaven, and did cast them to the earth: and the dragon stood before the woman which was ready to be delivered, for to devour her child as soon as it was born.

7 And there was war in heaven: Michael and his angels fought against the dragon; and the dragon fought and his angels,

8 And prevailed not; neither was their place found any more in heaven.

9 And the great dragon was cast out, that old serpent, called the Devil, and Satan, which deceiveth the whole world: he was cast out into the earth, and his angels were cast out with him.

10 And I heard a loud voice saying in heaven, Now is come salvation, and strength, and the kingdom of our God, and the power of his Christ: for the accuser of our brethren is cast down, which accused them before our God day and night.

11 And they overcame him by the blood of the Lamb, and by the word of their testimony; and they loved not their lives unto the death.

12 Therefore rejoice, ye heavens, and ye that dwell in them. Woe to the inhabiters of the earth and of the sea! for the devil is come down unto you, having great wrath, because he knoweth that he hath but a short time.

13 And when the dragon saw that he was cast unto the earth, he persecuted the woman which brought forth the man child. (KJV)

"War In Heaven." The sudden, "surprise" Rapture of the "manchild" saints to Heaven immediately triggers an extraordinary war in the heavenlies, with the archangel Michael and his angels fighting against Satan and his angels in an awesome, supernatural battle of epic proportions. This mighty, final conflict in Heaven begins as Satan attempts to destroy Christian believers as they are translated or resurrected into Heaven, and its purpose is two-fold. Michael and the angels not only provide safe passage for believers as they are transported into Heaven, but Satan and his angels are cast out and banished from the heavens forever.

Daniel 8:11-14, 26

11 Yea, he magnified himself even to the prince of the host, and by him the daily sacrifice was taken away, and the place of his sanctuary was cast down.

12 And an host was given him against the daily sacrifice by reason of transgression, and it cast down the truth to the ground; and it practised, and prospered.

13 Then I heard one saint speaking, and another saint said unto that certain saint which spake, How long shall be the vision concerning the daily sacrifice, and the transgression of desolation, to give both the sanctuary and the host to be trodden under foot?

14 And he said unto me, Unto two thousand and three hundred days; then shall the sanctuary be cleansed.

26 And the vision of the evening and the morning which was told is true: wherefore shut thou up the vision; for it shall be for many days. (KJV)

Although this passage states that the Sanctuary (the rebuilt temple in Jerusalem) will be desecrated for a period of "2300 days," a more accurate translation would read "2300 evening-mornings." This is because the Hebrew word translated as "days" in this passage is actually two words: BOQER, meaning "dawn" or "morning"; and `EREB, meaning "dusk" or "evening." Accordingly, this passage should read "2300 evening-mornings" — which is how many translations do interpret it. However, since Jewish religious law requires this type of sacrifice each morning and each evening of every day, this passage actually states that 2300 such sacrifices will be abolished, and 2300 such sacrifices obviously represent a total of 1150 literal days.

"And the place of his sanctuary was cast down." The Hebrew word for "place" is MAKOWN, meaning a "fixture," i.e., a "basis; generally a place, especially as an abode." The Hebrew word for "sanctuary" in this particular passage is MIQDASH or MIQQeDASH, meaning a "consecrated thing or place, especially a palace, sanctuary or asylum." And the Hebrew word for "cast down" is SHALAK, meaning to "throw out, down or away (literally or figuratively)." Therefore, this passage probably states that the Antichrist will "throw down" or demolish the most holy part of the temple, i.e., the "Holy of Holies," the sacred inner sanctum of a three-sectioned temple.

Daniel 9:27

27 And he shall confirm the covenant with many for one week: and in the midst of the week he shall cause the sacrifice and the oblation to cease, and for the overspreading of abominations he shall make it desolate, even until the consummation, and that determined shall be poured upon the desolate. (KJV)

It is midway through the seven years of Daniel's 70th Week that the "prince that shall come" (Antichrist) will violate the terms of his seven year treaty with the Jewish nation. This violation will include the desecration of the rebuilt temple in Jerusalem and the abolishment of the twice-daily sacrifices that are necessary for adherence to Jewish Law. (Matt. 24:15) (Dan. 8:11-14) (II Thess. 2:3, 4) (Rev. 11:1, 2) (Dan. 12:11).

The following scriptural passages also give us insight regarding the desecration of the rebuilt Jewish Temple and the persecution and tribulation which the Antichrist will inflict upon the Jews for a period of three and one-half years. This great Jewish tribulation is called "Jacob's Trouble" in Old Testament scriptures, and in the New Testament, it is called the "Times Of The Gentiles." For instance, Luke 21:24 reads as follows: "Jerusalem shall be trodden down of the Gentiles, until the times of the Gentiles be fulfilled."

Therefore, the "Times Of The Gentiles" is not some mystical period of time stretching from the reign of Nebuchadnezzar until the Return of Christ as often supposed. Instead, it is simply the three and one-half years period of time during which the Jews will be subjected to tribulation while the temple is desecrated and Jerusalem is dominated by non-Jews until 2300 morning and evening sacrifices have been suspended as pre-ordained by God. This definition is even confirmed in Revelation 11:2 when it says, "it is given unto the Gentiles: and the holy city shall they tread under foot forty and two months." Accordingly, the "Times of the Gentiles" is nothing more than the latter half of Daniel's 70th Week, lasting forty-two months, during which time the rebuilt temple will be desecrated while the city of Jerusalem will be held captive by foreigners, namely Antichrist.

Revelation 11:1, 2

1 And there was given me a reed like unto a rod: and the angel stood,

saying, Rise, and measure the temple of God, and the altar, and them that worship therein.

2 But the court which is without the temple leave out, and measure it not; for it is given unto the Gentiles: and the holy city shall they tread under foot forty and two months. (KJV)

Luke 21:20-24

20 And when ye shall see Jerusalem compassed with armies, then know that the desolation thereof is nigh.

21 Then let them which are in Judaea flee to the mountains; and let them which are in the midst of it depart out; and let not them that are in the countries enter thereinto.

22 For these be the days of vengeance, that all things which are written may be fulfilled.

23 But woe unto them that are with child, and to them that give suck, in those days! for there shall be great distress in the land, and wrath upon this people.

24 And they shall fall by the edge of the sword, and shall be led away captive into all nations: and Jerusalem shall be trodden down of the Gentiles, until the times of the Gentiles be fulfilled. (KJV)

Matthew 24:15-20

15 When ye therefore shall see the abomination of desolation, spoken of by Daniel the prophet, stand in the holy place, (whoso readeth, let him understand:)

16 Then let them which be in Judaea flee into the mountains:

17 Let him which is on the housetop not come down to take any thing out of his house:

18 Neither let him which is in the field return back to take his clothes.

19 And woe unto them that are with child, and to them that give suck in those days!

20 But pray ye that your flight be not in the winter, neither on the sabbath day: (KJV)

Continuing with the next passage in our analysis of Daniel 8:

Daniel 8:23

23 And in the latter time of their kingdom, when the transgressors are

come to the full, a king.... shall stand up. (KJV)

A careful analysis of the remainder of Daniel 8 will disclose the fact that the "king" (Antichrist) appears upon the world scene immediately before the establishment of God's literal Kingdom on earth. Furthermore, many "end-time" prophecies involving Israel and Middle-East wealth and the massive proliferation of false messiahs and the onset of extreme social turmoil throughout the world have commenced their fulfillment already, and these dramatic developments represent just some of the more obvious indicators that the Return of Christ and Armageddon and the establishment of God's Kingdom are near in time. Therefore, Antichrist should begin his initial ascendancy to power within the very near future! Since verse 23 indicates that the "transgressors" exist just prior to the appearance of the Antichrist, the Soviet communists obviously represent a very plausible interpretation of the word "transgressors" in the above scriptural passage.

As further evidence, please note the opening phrase in verse 23: "And in the latter time of their kingdom." Since the Antichrist never appeared after the demise of any of the previous world empires, the "kingdom" mentioned in this passage must be in reference to the "transgressors" who also are mentioned in this very same scriptural passage. Therefore, these "transgressors" are political in nature because they have a kingdom, and they must exist after the demise of the Roman Empire, but before the appearance of the Antichrist. Since these political transgressors would not be mentioned in a prophecy that only portrays a very brief outline of world history unless they were very important, this passage must be a reference to the communist Soviet Empire.

Of course, we have always been plagued by political transgressors throughout history, but these particular transgressors represent the very ultimate manifestation of tyranny and evil and hatred! Accordingly, the prophet Habakkuk develops this theme more fully as he laments a very serious situation in the world before launching into a narrative describing the subsequent rise of Antichrist:

Habakkuk 1:1-4

1 The burden which Habakkuk the prophet did see.

2 O LORD, how long shall I cry, and thou wilt not hear! even cry out unto thee of violence, and thou wilt not save!

3 Why dost thou shew me iniquity, and cause me to behold grievance?

for spoiling and violence are before me: and there are that raise up strife and contention.

4 Therefore the law is slacked, and judgment doth never go forth: for the wicked doth compass about the righteous; therefore wrong judgment proceedeth. (KJV)

Daniel prophesies that these political transgressors will "come to the full." This was precisely the fate which apparently befell the communist Soviet Empire in 1991. Despite periodic infusions of aid and credits and technology from the Americans and to a lesser extent, the Europeans, the Soviet Empire eventually was forced to acknowledge the reality that socialism does not work very well for a number of reasons. Then, when faced by the additional threat of financing another huge round of defense armaments spending which President Ronald Reagan used skillfully and shrewdly as a bargaining chip, the Soviet Empire tasted the promise of defeat and ostensibly collapsed as a result. (I say "ostensibly" because there are very good reasons to believe that the communist hard-liners in Moscow have been engaged in frenzied and secretive preparations for a major war during the last several years, and that they still harbor dreams of restoring the Soviet Empire to its former glory.)

Concerning this time-period in world history, Jesus made the following prediction:

Matthew 24:3-6

3 And as he sat upon the mount of Olives, the disciples came unto him privately, saying, Tell us, when shall these things be? and what shall be the sign of thy coming, and of the end of the world?

4 And Jesus answered and said unto them, Take heed that no man deceive you.

5 For many shall come in my name, saying, I am Christ; and shall deceive many.

6 And ye shall hear of wars and rumours of wars: see that ye be not troubled: for all these things must come to pass, but the end is not yet. (KJV)

Luke 21:7-9

7 And they asked him, saying, Master, but when shall these things be? and what sign will there be when these things shall come to pass?

8 And he said, Take heed that ye be not deceived: for many shall come in my name, saying, I am Christ; and the time draweth near: go ye not therefore after them.

9 But when ye shall hear of wars and commotions, be not terrified: for these things must first come to pass; but the end is not by and by. (KJV)

Please bear in mind that most "end-time" conditions described as taking place during the "end of the age" may have been partially fulfilled on many occasions throughout history, but we always must look for the complete and ultimate fulfillment. Accordingly, every single aspect of a prophecy must be completely fulfilled before we really can say it has been fulfilled. On that point we should observe that sometimes people will say "wars and rumours of wars" are not a sign of the end of the world (Greek AION, meaning "age") because we always have had wars throughout most of history. Or alternatively, sometimes people will say there also were wars and rumours of wars and famine during the time-period in which the Jewish Temple in Jerusalem was destroyed by the Romans. But, Jesus intended for this passage in Matthew to be a reference to a special set of conditions and circumstances that would engulf the whole world during the "last days" (Matt. 24:3-6), and only communism and modern organized terrorism have demonstrated the ability to create dramatic and very violent trouble spots all over the world at once. This prophecy, therefore, has only been fulfilled significantly in modern times.

Jesus even warned that the very existence of the world would seem threatened by these "wars and rumors of wars and commotions (extreme social turmoil such as terrorism)." His exact words of warning were: "be not terrified." Quite obviously extraordinary circumstances must be associated with the fulfillment of this biblical prophecy. Accordingly, in my opinion, this prediction achieved a preliminary fulfillment through the "Peace Movement" of the 1980's which was encouraged and inspired by a very successful propaganda offensive launched by the Soviet Union concerning the horrors of nuclear war. Public sentiment sometimes even bordered on the hysterical.

However, most recently, the world has witnessed the apparent demise of the Soviet Empire in a possible fulfillment of the prophecy that communism would "come to the full." (Daniel 8:23). Russia even acknowledged, publicly, the existence of the poverty and inefficiency that has plagued Soviet society for many decades. Obviously the only real asset Russia has had during all of this time has been a very formidable and dangerous military capability which they have modernized significantly in recent years. Therefore, it is very possible that the communist hard-liners in Moscow will try to use their massive military capability in one, last desperate attempt to restore the former glory of the Soviet Empire. If so, that will be when the communists truly "come to the full" as Daniel predicted, and the nuclear war scare of the 1980's will have been only a preliminary fulfillment of the prophecy that world conditions would deteriorate to the point of apparent destruction. Thus, we may see the ultimate fulfillment for both of these prophecies in our immediate future when terror and panic grips the hearts of people until the Antichrist rescues the world from the horrific threat posed by organized terrorism and/or terroristic states with weapons of mass destruction and/or Russian military aggression.

Daniel 8:23, 24

And in the latter time of their kingdom, when the transgressors are come to the full, a king of fierce countenance and understanding dark sentences, shall stand up. And his power shall be mighty, but not by his own power: and he shall destroy wonderfully... (KJV)

It is when the communists "come to the full" that "a king of fierce countenance...shall stand up." This fierce-looking man is the Antichrist, and he will appear unexpectedly as the apparent answer to the hopes and prayers of people throughout the world when it will appear as if we are facing imminent destruction. Nothing will seem too difficult for this man to achieve! Although the "church-world" and "religious leaders" will seem dazed and confused while fumbling around for plausible explanations, the Antichrist will have the answers! During an extraordinary period of crisis and fear and confusion, he will mesmerize the whole world with his incredible military feats and accomplishments and enchanting oratory.

Other than from Satan, where could a man obtain this fantastic power and ability? That is what Daniel was saying in the scriptural phrases "understanding dark sentences" and "his power shall be mighty, but not by his own power." Such amazing power and super-intelligence will be satanic-inspired — as the apostle Paul likewise explains in the following scriptural passage: "Even him, whose coming (ascendancy to power and prominence) is after the working of Satan with all power and signs and lying wonders." (II Thess. 2:9).

Revelation 13:4

4 And they worshipped the dragon which gave power unto the beast: and they worshipped the beast, saying, Who is like unto the beast? who is able to make war with him? (KJV)

Daniel 11:35-39

35 And some of them of understanding shall fall, to try them, and to purge, and to make them white, even to the time of the end: because it is yet for a time appointed.

36 And the king shall do according to his will; and he shall exalt himself, and magnify himself above every god, and shall speak marvellous things against the God of gods, and shall prosper till the indignation be accomplished: for that that is determined shall be done.

37 Neither shall he regard the God of his fathers, nor the desire of women, nor regard any god: for he shall magnify himself above all.

38 But in his estate shall he honour the God of forces: and a god whom his fathers knew not shall he honour with gold, and silver, and with precious stones, and pleasant things.

39 Thus shall he do in the most strong holds with a strange god, whom he shall acknowledge and increase with glory: and he shall cause them to rule over many, and shall divide the land for gain. (KJV)

"Neither shall he regard... the desire of women... for he shall magnify himself above all." Not only will the Antichrist magnify himself above every god, but he will take no desire or delight in the beauty and attraction of women. This probably will be due to a number of factors, including self-obsession spurred on by his extraordinary supernatural power and abilities, and his personal agenda for political power and military conquests and spiritual deception. That is why there is no reason to believe he will be a homosexual as some have speculated; he will be too occupied with himself and his objectives to concern himself with base and perverted desires that would consume so much of his time and energy.

"And the king shall do according to his will." Daniel describes Antichrist as "exceeding great" (Dan. 8:9), while Alexander the Great is described simply as "very great" (Dan. 8:8). Therefore, it is reasonable to infer that the miraculous feats accomplished by the Antichrist will appear extraordinary even when compared to the fantastic military conquests waged by Alexander the Great. Other scriptures also testify to the incredible military conquests which Antichrist will achieve in fulfillment of this implied comparison. Accordingly, since Alexander the Great conquered his enemies with lightning speed, so likewise will the Antichrist. Nothing will be able to stop him or thwart his will. As John noted: "Who is able to make war with him?"

"And the king shall do according to his will." From the very beginning, the Antichrist will defy God by doing whatever he pleases. Daniel also says that he will "exalt" and "magnify" himself — statements which are reminiscent of the self-deification delusion that snared Adam and Eve in the Garden of Eden. He even will "magnify himself above every god," and be so bold as to "speak marvellous things against the God of gods." Obviously these statements seem to imply that the Antichrist, indeed, will advocate "god-hood" for everyone — just as the New Agers teach.

"Shall prosper till the indignation be accomplished." The Hebrew word for "indignation" is ZAAM, meaning "rage; fury, especially, God's displeasure at sin." Therefore, this passage simply is saying that the Antichrist will "prosper" in his plans to deceive people before the Rapture by inspiring world peace and prosperity, and then later, after the Rapture, continue to "prosper" by initiating war against Christian believers for three and one-half years. But then, after that, the Day of God's Wrath begins and the Antichrist no longer "prospers" in his plans because God's "indignation" is unleashed in the form of the Trumpet-Vial plagues, culminating in His Return at the Battle of Armageddon.

"Neither shall he regard the God of his fathers." Reference to the personal, infinite, triune God of the Christian Bible is not necessarily intended here in this passage because the letter "G" is not capitalized in the word "God" in the Hebrew. Here is how *Strong's Hebrew-Greek Dictionary* defines the word "God":

430 'elohiym (el-o-heem');

plural of 433; gods in the ordinary sense; but specifically used (in the plural thus, especially with the article) of the supreme God; occasionally applied by way of deference to magistrates; and sometimes as a superlative:

KJV— angels, X exceeding, God (gods)- dess, -ly), X (very) great, judges, X mighty.

So, the word "God" actually can be translated as "gods in the ordinary sense" or it can be rendered as "the supreme God." However, we should note, too, that the article "the" was added arbitrarily by the KJV translators because they jumped to the same conclusion that everyone else did — so the presence of the article "the" does not lend any support to the theory that this word must refer to the true God of the Bible. Accordingly, I believe it is erroneous to assume this phrase necessarily refers to the Jewish fathers of the Antichrist in an attempt to prove the Antichrist will pretend to be the Jewish Messiah. Besides, it could just as easily refer to the Islamic supreme god, Allah, if the Antichrist is a Moslem or Druze Moslem. Instead, it means precisely what it actually says, i.e., he ignores his ancestors' religion by simply declining to honor or worship the god whom his ancestors worshipped, whomever that may be. Corroboration on this point is provided in this very same passage when it continues by saying that neither will he "regard any god: for he shall magnify himself above all" before the Rapture, but that after the Rapture, he will publicly honor the "god of forces" who is none other than Satan himself:

Rev. 13:4
And they worshipped the dragon which gave power unto the beast: and they worshipped the beast, saying, Who is like unto the beast? who is able to make war with him? (KJV)

"He shall honour the god of forces." New Age thinking and Eastern mysticism probably will ascribe such power to the "universal spirit" or the "cosmic consciousness." But, those who are wise will understand that it is Satan who is the source of such abilities, not some "universal power" achieved through "higher consciousness" or a "sudden leap in evolution." However, immediately after the Rapture, everyone in the world will understand that Satan is the real reason for the incredible power and abilities of Antichrist. (Rev. 13:2, 4) (Dan. 11:39) (Hab. 1:11). Perhaps this is what II Thess. 2:3-12 means when it states that the Antichrist is "revealed" (Greek word APOKALUPTO; disclosed, uncovered, revealed) immediately after the Rapture when the Holy Spirit is "taken out of the way" (but not out of the world) as a mortally-wounded Antichrist is indwelt and possessed by Satan himself. This does not mean, though, that people will believe that Satan is evil. Instead, they most likely will think — as many people believe already — that Satan is Lucifer and that he is morally good, especially since he will have been responsible for creating world peace and prosperity through his human surrogate of instrumentality, Antichrist.

"Shall honor the god of forces." According to *Strong's Hebrew-Greek Dictionary* and Rev. Alexander Hislop, author of the classic, *The Two Babylons*, a more accurate translation of the word "forces" is "fortifications." Therefore, this phrase may be an allusion to the great rebel Nimrod, who (as documented by Hislop; pp. 30-55) can be termed "the god of fortifications." Apparently, the Antichrist will be a modern-day version of Nimrod, who was viewed in his days as an extraordinary benefactor of mankind because he taught people how to protect themselves from the wild animals by building walls around their cities, and because he was a mighty hunter of these same wild animals who were threatening to overrun the earth. But, after giving people the benefits and blessings of safety and security, he used his prestige to persuade people to rebel against God, thus beginning the great Babylonian apostasy.

"And he shall destroy wonderfully." (Dan. 8:24). When you consider the multitude of fantastic weapons now available to modern man, it certainly makes sense that the Antichrist — from a small country with a small army — would require supernatural power to achieve what the Bible predicts he will do. This is more apparent in *Young's Literal Translation*: "And wonderful things he destroyeth." Further clarification is provided in an analysis of the word "destroy." In this case, the Hebrew word translated as "destroy" is SHACHATH, meaning "to ruin." Obviously it will be a most remarkable performance. Habakkuk elaborates further:

Habakkuk 1:5-11

5 Behold ye among the heathen, and regard, and wonder marvellously: for I will work a work in your days, which ye will not believe, though it be told you.

6 For, lo, I raise up the Chaldeans, that bitter and hasty nation, which shall march through the breadth of the land, to possess the dwellingplaces that are not theirs.

7 They are terrible and dreadful: their judgment and their dignity shall proceed of themselves.

8 Their horses also are swifter than the leopards, and are more fierce than the evening wolves: and their horsemen shall spread themselves, and their horsemen shall come from far; they shall fly as the eagle that hasteth to eat.

9 They shall come all for violence: their faces shall sup up as the east wind, and they shall gather the captivity as the sand.

10 And they shall scoff at the kings, and the princes shall be a scorn unto them: they shall deride every strong hold; for they shall heap dust, and take it.

11 Then shall his mind change, and he shall pass over, and offend, imputing this his power unto his god. (KJV)

Habakkuk predicts that the Chaldean "horsemen" of Antichrist (modern-day "types" of the ancient, war-like Chaldeans) actually will "FLY as the eagle"! (Hab. 1:8). This scriptural statement obviously paints a very vivid picture of modern warfare when it portrays soldiers of Antichrist flying in military aircraft to attack their enemies! Please keep in mind that the Bible should be read and interpreted in the exact same manner as any other book! Give a plain, literal interpretation to a passage unless the context very clearly indicates otherwise or a literal interpretation does not make any sense whatsoever!

Additional evidence corroborating the identity of the Chaldeans in this passage may be seen in Isaiah 23:1, 5-9, 11, 13, 15, 17, 18 where it is stated that "the Assyrian," i.e., the Antichrist, will build the city of Tyre for the Chaldeans just before it is destroyed for seventy years. But, after that, God declares He will restore the city of Tyre so that it can serve as an eternal source of food and clothing for people who will serve Him in Jerusalem. So, obviously scripture itself plainly establishes a direct connection between Chaldeans in prophetic passages and the Antichrist and his people in Lebanon.

God begins His prophetic message to the "heathen" (i.e., the world) with the admonishment that they "regard, and wonder marvellously: for I will work a work in your days, which ye will not believe, though it be told you." In other words, world events will become so startling and spectacular, and people will become so frightened and terrified, that they will find it very difficult to believe the world was not destroyed during its time of crisis even after the Antichrist has rescued them.

"Bitter and hasty nation.... terrible and dreadful...." These descriptive phrases that are ascribed to the people of the "little horn" country are similar to those mentioned by Daniel when he predicted that the "little horn" will "look more stout than his fellows." In like manner, it is said in Daniel 8:23 that Antichrist will possess a fierce-looking appearance, most likely due to the satanic power and intelligence that will shine forth through his eyes even as it manifests itself in his overall demeanor and countenance.

"Their faces shall sup up as the east wind." Daniel said the same thing when he prophesied that the Antichrist will "wax exceeding great" in a southern and eastern direction during his initial ascendancy to power and prominence.

Habakkuk predicts that the Antichrist will "gather the captivity as the sand" because no one in the world will be able to resist him. (Hab. 1:9, 10, 17). Moreover, due to the extraordinary supernatural power imbued within him by Satan, he will literally scoff at his enemies and their modern weapons of warfare. He likewise will be a proud and arrogant man, never happy or content without the prospect of more military conquests:

Habakkuk 2:5
5 Yea also, because he transgresseth by wine, he is a proud man, neither keepeth at home, who enlargeth his desire as hell, and is as death, and cannot be satisfied, but gathereth unto him all nations, and heapeth unto him all people: (KJV)

His soldiers will "deride every strong hold: for they shall heap dust and take it." (Hab. 1:10). Until modern-day weapons utilizing a variety of high-tech chemical, biological and nuclear materials were discovered, most commentators could only assign a meaning of primitive dirt-ramparts to this passage in their attempts to interpret or decipher its message. But, now we stand on the brink of terror and destruction as terroristic states in the Middle East threaten to unleash their newly-developed weapons of mass destruction, either directly or through secretive terrorist surrogates.

The import of this prophecy was deemed so critical and vital that God commanded Habakkuk to "write the vision, and make it plain" so that teachers someday could spread its message at the appropriate time. (Hab. 2:1-3). Without question, this is very forceful and explicit language. God also stated that "the vision (was) yet for an appointed time, but at the end it (would) speak." (Hab. 2:2, 3). So, in other words, this prophecy was meant to be fulfilled during the "end-times"! As further confirmation regarding this point, we will note in a later chapter of this book that the events portrayed in Habakkuk 3 match post-Rapture events that are described in Revelation. Accordingly, this prophecy of Habakkuk, like so many others in the Bible, may have been partially fulfilled sometime in history, but the COMPLETE fulfillment is still future simply because at least one detail remains unfulfilled!

Habakkuk 2:1-4

1 I will stand upon my watch, and set me upon the tower, and will watch to see what he will say unto me, and what I shall answer when I am reproved.

2 And the LORD answered me, and said, Write the vision, and make it plain upon tables, that he may run that readeth it.

3 For the vision is yet for an appointed time, but at the end it shall speak, and not lie: though it tarry, wait for it; because it will surely come, it will not tarry.

4 Behold, his soul which is lifted up is not upright in him: but the just shall live by his faith. (KJV)

Who will the Antichrist conquer? Daniel 8:9 states that he will "wax exceeding great" in a southern and eastern direction, and that he will also invade the land of Israel. Therefore, Israel and southern Lebanon and countries east or south of Lebanon are all prime candidates for conquest. Daniel 7:8 likewise predicts that the Antichrist will subdue "three horns," most likely the countries of Israel, Syria and Iraq. Furthermore, Revelation 13:2 states that the empire of the beast (Antichrist) will include the countries which once comprised the ancient Grecian, Persian and Babylonian empires since they are characterized by the leopard, bear and lion parts of the prophetic beast. Accordingly, this revelation obviously indicates that Syria, Iraq, Iran and Afghanistan will all become a part of the world empire of Antichrist, meaning they will be conquered militarily by the Antichrist if they do not voluntarily ally themselves with him. So, in summary, the countries to watch for from a prophetic perspective would include Israel, southern Lebanon, Syria, Iraq, Iran, Afghanistan and probably Russia.

However, the Bible also declares that the Antichrist will conquer numerous armies with lightning speed, and that no one will be able to resist him as he exhibits extraordinary supernatural power in his relentless drive for more military conquests. Revelation 13 says that eventually — immediately after the Rapture — he will even exercise power and control over the whole world. Therefore, if the entire Middle East region explodes into a horrific conflagration just before the rise of Antichrist, it is very possible that countries located beyond the scope of biblical prophecy, such as India and Pakistan, will also become engaged in major warfare. Because as the level of terror and conflict intensifies, the more people will appreciate the miraculous military feats of the Antichrist.

Gog And Magog

That Ezekiel 38 portrays a Russian invasion of Israel years before the Battle of Armageddon begins is almost an article-of-faith for many people. But, in my opinion, the scriptural evidence very clearly indicates otherwise. For instance, please note that it is Gog who invades the land of Israel, not both Gog and Magog:

Ezekiel 38:2, 3

2 Son of Man, set thy face against Gog, the land of Magog, the chief prince of Meshech and Tubal, and prophecy against him,

3 And say, Thus saith the Lord God; Behold, I am against thee, O Gog, the chief prince of Meshech and Tubal. (KJV)

Moreover, it should be evident from even a cursory analysis of the text that the expressions "Gog" and "Magog" are not synonymous with each other because Gog is represented as a person (e.g., "chief prince of..." and "prophesy against him"), whereas Magog is designated as a "land." Likewise, please note verse 17 in this passage of scripture: "Thus saith the Lord God; Art thou he of whom I have spoken in old time by my servants the prophets of Israel, which prophesied in those days many years that I would bring thee against them (i.e., Israel; verse 18)." This passage clearly identifies "Gog" as the individual spoken of by the "prophets of Israel" who often prophesied he would invade Israel during the "last days"! Obviously there was only one such individual, and that person was none other than the Antichrist.

Here is how *Strong's Hebrew-Greek Dictionary* defines the terms Gog and Magog:

1136 Gog (gogue);
of Hebrew origin [1463]; Gog, a symb. name for some future Antichrist:
KJV— Gog.

3098 Magog (mag-ogue');
of Hebrew origin [4031]; Magog, a foreign nation, i.e. (figuratively) an Antichristian party:
KJV— Magog.

Clearly, once again, precisely as we observed in Ezekiel 38 itself, there is a most distinct difference between the two terms, Gog and Magog, in the Hebrew-Greek dictionary! One expression (Gog) is a symbolic name for a future antichrist (Satan), whereas the other term (Magog) is a name reserved for any foreign nation or group of people. Furthermore, this is exactly how these two terms are used in yet another prophetic passage that describes a similar situation, although contextually it takes place 1000 years after Armageddon occurs. Accordingly, in Revelation 20, we observe that the expression "Gog and Magog" is used to represent both Satan AND all of humanity who join Satan in his final rebellion against God immediately after the Millennial Reign of Christ is concluded. So, in other words, in that distant future scenario portrayed in Revelation 20, "Gog" represents Satan, and "Magog" represents rebellious people from foreign (to Israel) nations around the world:

Revelation 20:7-10
7 And when the thousand years are expired, Satan shall be loosed out of his prison,
8 And shall go out to deceive the nations which are in the four quarters of the earth, Gog and Magog, to gather them together to battle: the number of whom is as the sand of the sea.
9 And they went up on the breadth of the earth, and compassed the camp of the saints about, and the beloved city: and fire came down from God out of heaven, and devoured them.
10 And the devil that deceived them was cast into the lake of fire and brimstone, where the beast and the false prophet are, and shall be

tormented day and night for ever and ever. (KJV)

As we will confirm later, Gog (in Ezekiel 38) represents both Satan and Antichrist because they will share the same physical human body after the Rapture until near the end of Armageddon. Adequate scriptural proof concerning this matter is forthcoming in later chapters of this book. Therefore, when all of the scriptural evidence is considered very carefully, there can be no question that Gog, in Ezekiel 38, represents Antichrist fighting at the Battle of Armageddon where he meets his demise during the Second Coming of Christ.

Some translations read "Prince of Rosh" rather than "chief prince" in an attempt to imply that we should interpret this expression as meaning the "prince of Russia." However, this is absolutely erroneous because ROSH appears 456 times within the Old Testament and NEVER is it used as a proper noun! ROSH is a Hebrew word meaning chief, whereas Russia is a Finnish word meaning rowers (of a boat). There simply is no comparison or connection between these two words — words which even originate from two entirely different languages. Furthermore, the first or chief day of the Jewish calendar year is called ROSH HASHANA, thereby further proving our contention in this matter.

"And thou (Gog) shalt come from thy place out of the north parts...and will cause thee to come up from the north parts..." (Ezek. 38:15; 39:2). Sometimes it is said these two passages prove that "Gog and Magog" are from Russia because Russia lies far to the north of Israel. But, other scriptural passages in the Bible also use the word "north" to designate any invader who approaches Israel from that direction even if their country lies elsewhere in another direction. For example:

Ezekiel 26:7
7 For thus saith the Lord GOD; Behold, I will bring upon Tyrus Nebuchadrezzar king of Babylon, a king of kings, from the north, with horses, and with chariots, and with horsemen, and companies, and much people. (KJV)

Jeremiah 25:9
9 Behold, I will send and take all the families of the north, saith the LORD, and Nebuchadrezzar the king of Babylon, my servant, and will bring them against this land, and against the inhabitants thereof, and

against all these nations round about, and will utterly destroy them, and make them an astonishment, and an hissing, and perpetual desolations. (KJV)

Jeremiah 10:22

22 Behold, the noise of the bruit is come, and a great commotion out of the north country, to make the cities of Judah desolate, and a den of dragons. (KJV)

Jeremiah 4:6-7

6 Set up the standard toward Zion: retire, stay not: for I will bring evil from the north, and a great destruction.

7 The lion is come up from his thicket, and the destroyer of the Gentiles is on his way; he is gone forth from his place to make thy land desolate; and thy cities shall be laid waste, without an inhabitant. (KJV)

All of these passages portray ancient, fulfilled prophecies concerning destruction and invasion coming from the "north," thus proving our point. The context, in each case, clearly demonstrates this to be true. (See, e.g., footnotes in *Dake's Annotated Reference Bible*.)

As further verification, the countries listed by Ezekiel as being with Gog are the very same countries which comprise the empire of Antichrist:

1. According to commonly-accepted biblical scholarship, MESHECH, TUBAL, and MAGOG represent countries of northern Europe and Asia, including the various peoples of Russia. (Gen. 10). Please note that Gog (Antichrist) controls the land of Magog (Russia), and that Gog is "chief prince" of Meshech and Tubal (also Russian territory). The fact that Gog controls all of Russia simply indicates that Russia will be a part of Gog's empire at that point in time.

2. PERSIA, ETHIOPIA, and LIBYA. Persia represents modern Iran. Ethiopia was translated from the Hebrew word CUSH, which is somewhat misleading because the descendants of Cush (a grandson of Noah) populated all of black Africa, not just Ethiopia. (Gen. 10). By the same token, Libya was translated from the Hebrew word PUT (another grandson of Noah), whose descendants populated the various Arab countries of northern Africa, including Libya. (Gen. 10).

3. GOMER and TOGARMAH represent the various countries of Europe according to scholars. (Gen. 10). The phrase "and many people

with thee" represents countries which lie outside the "nucleus" area of Antichrist's empire.

Because common sense reason asserts that both Russia and Antichrist could NOT possibly control the same empire at the very same point in time, we must conclude that Russia will either be conquered by the Antichrist or it will become voluntarily submissive to the Antichrist sometime BEFORE the Rapture. Otherwise, it would not be possible for the Antichrist to fulfill biblical prophecy by controlling ALL of the world (including Russia) immediately after the pre-tribulation Rapture occurs:

Revelation 13:4, 7-8

4 And they worshipped the dragon which gave power unto the beast: and they worshipped the beast, saying, Who is like unto the beast? who is able to make war with him?

7 And it was given unto him (Antichrist) to make war with the saints, and to overcome them: and power was given him over ALL kindreds, and tongues, and nations.

8 And ALL that dwell upon the earth shall worship him... (KJV)

If you carefully and honestly compare the description of Ezekiel's battle with other scriptures describing Armageddon, it becomes quite apparent that Ezekiel's battle is the Battle of Armageddon! (Compare: Ezekiel 38:1-23; Ezekiel 39:1-20, 29; Revelation 19:11-21; Revelation 14:14-20; Zechariah 14:1-16; Zechariah 12:1-6, 9-11; Joel 3:1-17.) Please note when you read these scriptures (either in your Bible or in the seventh chapter of this book) that many major similarities can be found repeatedly throughout these passages:

1. Soldiers of Antichrist are struck with madness and fight each other.
2. Fire and brimstone rained down from Heaven; flesh of the soldiers literally consumed away.
3. Birds and animals "invited" to feast on the multitudes slain.
4. Great "shaking" of the earth; extraordinary earthquakes.
5. Winepress symbolism portraying massive slaughter.

Obviously there are many common points of similarity found in the various descriptions of Armageddon, even when you include Ezekiel 38 and 39 in the comparison. That is why there simply can be no question remaining regarding the identification of Ezekiel's battle. It sounds so similar to other passages describing Armageddon that we are forced to conclude that Ezekiel 38, in actuality, is the Battle of Armageddon.

Furthermore, Ezekiel even concludes the events described in Ezekiel 38 and 39 by stating that God NEVER will hide His face from Israel again after the battle he describes is concluded. But, this would not be a true statement if Gog really did represent Russia, thereby forcing the Battle of Armageddon to be fought at some later date. Accordingly, with that clarification in mind, please observe what God promises, very clearly and specifically, to Israel AFTER the battle in Ezekiel 38 and 39 is over:

Ezekiel 39:21-29

21 And I will set my glory among the heathen, and all the heathen shall see my judgment that I have executed, and my hand that I have laid upon them.

22 So the house of Israel shall know that I am the LORD their God from that day and forward.

23 And the heathen shall know that the house of Israel went into captivity for their iniquity: because they trespassed against me, therefore hid I my face from them, and gave them into the hand of their enemies: so fell they all by the sword.

24 According to their uncleanness and according to their transgressions have I done unto them, and hid my face from them.

25 Therefore thus saith the Lord GOD; Now will I bring again the captivity of Jacob, and have mercy upon the whole house of Israel, and will be jealous for my holy name;

26 After that they have borne their shame, and all their trespasses whereby they have trespassed against me, when they dwelt safely in their land, and none made them afraid.

27 When I have brought them again from the people, and gathered them out of their enemies' lands, and am sanctified in them in the sight of many nations;

28 Then shall they know that I am the LORD their God, which caused them to be led into captivity among the heathen: but I have gathered them unto their own land, and have left none of them any more there.

29 Neither will I hide my face any more from them: for I have poured out my spirit upon the house of Israel, saith the Lord GOD. (KJV)

The Time Element

There are several important factors we must consider very carefully when interpreting the Olivet Discourse in Matthew 24 and Luke 21. Perhaps the foremost factor is the methodology of interpretation we employ when reading and understanding the scriptures. Because if we do not understand the individual words which God is using while trying to communicate truth to us, we never will get very far in ascertaining His message.

Accordingly, please keep in mind that experiential common sense tells us the Bible should be read and interpreted in the exact same manner as any book of human origin generally is read and understood. Obviously God would appreciate the wisdom in writing His book in the same manner and style generally employed by people throughout history so as to minimize any possible confusion and honest misunderstandings! Therefore, we should give a plain, literal interpretation to a passage, in accordance with the rules of grammar and logic, unless the context very clearly indicates otherwise or a literal interpretation would not make any sense whatsoever!

Unfortunately, sometimes people say we should not follow a literal and common-sense approach to exegesis of Scripture. Instead, they say we should "spiritualize" or "allegorize" the meaning of the biblical passages we read. But, this methodological approach to interpreting God's Holy Word is erroneous and antithetical to truth for two basic reasons:

1. Since God is not the author of confusion (I Cor. 14:33), the Bible should be read and interpreted in the exact same manner as any other book! We should give a plain, literal interpretation to a passage unless the context very clearly indicates otherwise or a literal interpretation does not make any sense. To do otherwise makes it possible to argue a question mark after every statement in the Bible because everyone would have their own special way of interpreting the true meaning of words and statements! Therefore, any examination of the scriptures will be much more conducive to truth and understanding if we consistently utilize the definitions that are attached to words in everyday life and in our word dictionaries.

If we do not adhere to this methodology for ascertaining truth, then under such circumstances, how could God even hold man accountable on Judgment Day? If we were totally consistent in applying this epistemological view of knowledge to everything in life where everything was viewed on a spiritualized and subjective basis, how could we even communicate intelligibly or function in reality following such unpredictable guidelines? Everyone would have their own version of truth and understanding, and voluntary cooperation and understanding between people would be impossible. Obviously we must assume that an infinite, rational God and Creator would understand the necessity and the wisdom for realistic and objective standards while communicating to us with human words.

2. The Bible also is full of scriptural examples where the sensical literal mode of interpretation is followed. For instance, hundreds of Old Testament prophecies were fulfilled literally, thus establishing a definite precedent in which to emulate. Jesus even chided the generation of His day for their failure to recognize the prophetic signs of the time (Matt. 16:1-14), and a primary reason for this failure was their refusal to interpret literally the prophecies concerning His First Coming, more than 300 specific predictions which Jesus fulfilled with His life, death and resurrection. Therefore, I believe that wisdom and intellectual honesty mandate we avoid such error when we interpret prophecies concerning His Second Coming.

One additional point we should note before beginning our analysis of the Olivet Discourse is that even though many prophecy scriptures may have been partially fulfilled on many occasions throughout history, including the time-period in which Jesus lived, we always must look for the complete and ultimate fulfillment of every single detail in a prophecy without stretching or warping or ignoring relevant aspects of recorded history. Accordingly, every single aspect of a prophecy must be fulfilled completely before we really can say it has been fulfilled, and even then, the fulfillment must be to the fullest extent possible before we finally can say that the prophecy truly has realized its final and complete fulfillment.

As an example of how misguided some people can become when they ignore the above basic principles for interpreting biblical passages, sometimes it is alleged that the Olivet Discourse in Matthew 24 and Luke 21 was actually fulfilled near the time of Jesus. Of course, in order to make this claim, they are forced to "spiritualize" the meaning of words so that words can mean anything they wish, rather than what has been commonly agreed upon and recorded in our dictionaries. They also are forced to twist and warp and ignore many aspects of recorded history in order to make such silly, outlandish claims.

For instance, it is quite evident that the Second Coming of Christ, the

Battle of Armageddon and all of the incredible plagues described so vividly in Revelation and Old Testament passages never have happened, yet. Without any rational doubt whatsoever, there is no instance in recorded history where the whole earth was totally demolished and destroyed by a series of Trumpet-Vial plagues featuring massive amounts of fire, and gigantic pieces of hail, and huge meteorites, and widespread famine, and pestilence, and warfare, and incredible earthquakes that destroyed all of the mountains and islands and cities in the world, and where all of these catastrophes, collectively, destroyed most of the people living on the earth. Yet, some people will attempt to say otherwise, thereby illustrating the folly some people can fall into when they insist on thinking in a non-rational manner. Obviously we must avoid such grievous error.

Matthew 24:2-6

2 And Jesus said unto them, See ye not all these things? verily I say unto you, There shall not be left here one stone upon another, that shall not be thrown down.

3 And as he sat upon the mount of Olives, the disciples came unto him privately, saying, Tell us, when shall these things be? and what shall be the sign of thy coming, and of the end of the world?

4 And Jesus answered and said unto them, Take heed that no man deceive you.

5 For many shall come in my name, saying, I am Christ; and shall deceive many.

6 And ye shall hear of wars and rumours of wars: see that ye be not troubled: for all these things must come to pass, but the end is not yet. (KJV)

Luke 21:7-9

7 And they asked him, saying, Master, but when shall these things be? and what sign will there be when these things shall come to pass?

8 And he said, Take heed that ye be not deceived: for many shall come in my name, saying, I am Christ; and the time draweth near: go ye not therefore after them.

9 But when ye shall hear of wars and commotions, be not terrified: for these things must first come to pass; but the end is not by and by. (KJV)

After Jesus had prophesied that the temple would be destroyed, the disciples later asked Him, privately, when these things would happen, and what would be the signs of His Coming and of the end of the age. Evidently, as far as the disciples were concerned, their religious and cultural perspective on matters made them think that all of these things would have to be a part of the same process or series of events. They simply could not imagine any other situation or outcome because the temple was the very centerpiece of their whole earthly existence. So, from their limited perspective, when their magnificent Holy Temple was destroyed, such an event would have to signal the end of the age, too.

But Jesus chose not to divulge any additional information regarding the future destruction of the Jewish temple. Instead, He addressed their remaining questions concerning the signs that would indicate the end was near. So, it is noteworthy to observe that the very first thing Jesus did was to issue a strong warning concerning the incredible deception that would flourish throughout the earth at the time of the end. When the disciples asked Jesus: "What shall be the sign of thy coming, and of the end of the age?" His immediate response was a warning: "Take heed that no man deceive you."

In a similar vein, the apostle Paul warned that "evil men and seducers shall wax worse and worse, deceiving and being deceived." (II Tim. 3:13). Likewise, the apostle Paul even warned that the initial appearance of Antichrist will be "after the working of Satan with all power and signs and lying wonders"! (II Thess. 2:9). So clearly, these scriptures make it very evident that religious and philosophical deception increasingly will flourish throughout all of the earth during the "time of the end."

Jesus continued: "Take heed that ye be not deceived: for many shall come in my name, saying, I am Christ, and the time draweth near: go ye not therefore after them." (Luke 21:8). It is interesting to note that the New Age Movement teaches that all of us are really gods or divine-in-nature deep inside our psyches — it is just that we do not know it until we achieve "Christ consciousness" or "oneness with the universe" through "higher consciousness" techniques. In recent years they also have insisted that mankind is on the verge of a "sudden, evolutionary leap" or "transformation," and that when sufficient numbers of individuals achieve a personal transformation (i.e., a mystical, pantheistic perception of reality), then all of the world suddenly and instantaneously can make a dramatic leap forward in realizing the age-old dream of world peace, prosperity and the brotherhood of all men embodied in a "new world order." The apparent recent upsurge in freedom and democracy throughout the world, New Agers claim, is due at least in part, to this "uplifting of spiritual consciousness."

Therefore, the very first "signs" which indicate the Coming of Christ is imminent are:

1. "Many false Christs (messiahs) who deceive many." Since the late 1960's and early 1970's, millions of Americans have been caught up in a variety of Eastern religious cults! Many of these religions con people into thinking they are only techniques for relaxation and self-fulfillment, but a closer examination reveals that they actually possess all of the characteristics of a religion as set forth in a dictionary, and that they are steeped in Eastern religion methodologies designed to achieve a higher level of consciousness. Likewise, never throughout all of history have we seen the appearance of so many self-proclaimed messiahs; they literally have proliferated into the hundreds, even the thousands. Although there may have been a few false messiahs here and there down through the years, never has there been the sudden massive onslaught of false messiahs like we have today.

2. The second sign heralding the "end" which is mentioned in the Olivet Discourse is "commotions," which in the Greek means "extreme social turmoil." The endtime fulfillment of this prophetic prediction ranges from the riots and mass protests that were a hallmark of the late 1960's to the horrific onslaught of world terrorism that has plagued humanity at rapidly-escalating levels of terror and destruction and brutality ever since the early 1970's! Obviously we have addressed this matter already in an earlier section of this book.

3. "Wars and rumours of wars." Once again, without repeating material we analyzed in earlier sections of this book, please bear in mind that most "end-time" conditions described as taking place during the "end of the age" may have been partially fulfilled on many occasions throughout history, but we always must look for the complete and ultimate fulfillment. Accordingly, every single aspect of a prophecy must be completely fulfilled to the fullest extent possible before we really can say it has been fulfilled.

Incidentally, these "signs" are the only prophetic events in Matthew 24 and Luke 21 which are completely fulfilled before the Rapture; all of the events portrayed in Matthew 24:7-31 and Luke 21:10-27 parallel the events of Revelation, as we will prove later.

Luke 21:28-36

"And when these things BEGIN to come to pass (i.e., when we first see the prophetic signs involving false messiahs, wars and commotions), then look up, and lift up your heads; for your redemption (Rapture) draweth nigh. And he spake to them a parable; Behold the fig tree, and ALL the trees; When they now shoot forth, ye see and know of your own selves that summer is now nigh at hand. So likewise ye, when ye see all these things come to pass, know ye that the Kingdom of God is nigh at hand. Verily I say unto you, this generation shall not pass away, till ALL be fulfilled.

"Heaven and earth shall pass away (be changed): but my words shall not pass away. And take heed to yourselves, lest at any time your hearts be overcharged with surfeiting, and drunkenness, and cares of this life, and so that day come upon you unawares. For as a snare shall it come on all them that dwell on the face of the whole earth. Watch ye therefore, and pray always, that ye may be accounted worthy to escape (flee out of) all these things (post-Rapture events) that shall come to pass, and to stand before the son of man." (KJV)

The first thing we might observe in this scriptural passage is the promise made by Jesus that the generation which bears witness to the initial events that signal God's literal Kingdom on earth is imminently near will also see everything else happen that is prophesied in His sermon. That is why it is important to understand that when words such as "ye" or "you" are used in this passage, they are used as an editorial convenience, meaning that such words refer to the generation of believers living at the time of this prophetic fulfillment — regardless of when that fulfillment occurs — and not necessarily to the immediate audience to whom Jesus was speaking on that occasion. Obviously this is consistent with how the Bible generally is written throughout because all of God's Word is intended for the enlightenment and edification of all Christian believers, not just believers who lived during the time of Jesus and His disciples.

Likewise, when Jesus said "this generation" in the passage above, He did not necessarily mean that "this generation" absolutely had to be a reference to His immediate audience. Instead, for the same reason we noted in cases where the word "you" was used in this passage, Jesus was saying that whichever generation of believers saw these endtime signs first begin their fulfillment would be the same generation who would see everything happen, including the literal establishment of God's Kingdom on earth. This view is supported by the dictionary definition for the Greek word translated here as "this" because the Greek word could be translated properly as either "this" or "that." And if we translate the Greek word as "that" instead of as "this," then no one could possibly insist we necessarily must interpret this passage as a reference to the generation living at the time of Jesus. Here is what *Strong's Hebrew-Greek Dictionary* states:

> 3778 houtos (hoo'-tos);
> including nominative masculine plural houtoi (hoo'-toy); nominative feminine singular haute (how'-tay); and nominative feminine plural hautai (how'-tahee); from the article 3588 and 846; the he (she or it), i.e. this or that (often with article repeated):
> KJV— he (it was that), hereof, it, she, such as, the same, these, they, this (man, same, woman), which, who.

Often it is said that this parable of the fig tree should be interpreted to mean that a given generation of believers will witness the establishment of modern national Israel as the first sign of the "end" because the fig tree sometimes symbolizes Israel in the Bible. However, please note very carefully that Jesus actually said "fig tree and all the trees," obviously meaning all the trees, not just the fig tree, alone. Apparently the fig tree was mentioned in this passage, in particular, because it was very popular with the Jews at that point in time, both as a food-producing plant and as a source of shade from the hot sun.

Therefore, Jesus did not say that one particular generation would see both Armageddon and the establishment of national Israel (in 1948). Instead, the simple lesson illustrated by this parable is that just as a budding tree signals the near approach of summer, so likewise will the appearance of these "signs" signal the imminence or nearness of the Return of Christ and the subsequent establishment of God's literal Kingdom on earth. Any attempt to make this passage say anything else contrary to what is plainly stated here is a complete mistake.

In verse 28, the word "redemption" in the Greek is APOLUTROSIS, meaning the act of "ransom" in full, i.e., figuratively "riddance" or specifically Christian "salvation"; it is translated as "deliverance" or "redemption" in the Bible. Concerning this concept of "ransom in full," there is a three-fold process involved:

1) SOUL - "Christ has redeemed us from the curse of the law." (Gal. 3:13).
2) BODY - "Waiting for the adoption, to wit, the redemption of our body." (Rom. 8:23).
3) THE EARTH - "The redemption of the purchased possession." (Eph. 1:14).

In other words, "redemption" will include the restoration of everything man lost in the Garden of Eden. The redemption of the soul generally is known as "accepting Christ as Lord and Saviour"; the redemption of the body will become a reality at the time of the "Rapture" when believers are translated or resurrected to Heaven with new, immortal spirit bodies; and the redemption of the earth will be finalized after the "seven-sealed" book in Heaven is opened during a sequence of events climaxed by the Return of Christ to evict Satan from the earth.

"Take heed...lest...your hearts be overcharged with surfeiting..." The Greek word for "overcharged" is BARUNO, meaning to "burden," figuratively-speaking. The Greek for "surfeiting" is KRAIPALE, meaning "headache" from drunkenness, i.e., by implication a "debauch," and by analogy a "glut." So the message of this verse would be a warning not to burden your heart with debauchery and gluttony and drunkenness and cares of this life — a definite reference to the extraordinary prosperity which will be inspired by the Antichrist and will help him to deceive and destroy people. (Dan. 8:25).

"So that day come upon you unawares." All of the prophets of God used expressions such as "that day" to indicate the Day of the Lord, a day of darkness and gloominess and judgment. That meaning is consistent with the context of this passage. Concerning the word "unawares," the Greek dictionary defines it as meaning "non-apparent" and "unexpected," i.e., adverbially "suddenly." Thus, to an unbelieving world, everything will seem fine and dandy because there will be no apparent indication that disaster is about to strike — precisely as in the days before Noah's flood. Not surprisingly, therefore, when the Antichrist performs his incredible miracles and creates an economic paradise throughout the world, it will not be very easy to convince people that actually he is quite evil and deceptive, and that God's devastating judgments upon the earth are imminent.

"For as a snare shall it come." The Greek word for "snare" is PAGIS, and it is defined as "a trap to ensnare suddenly and unexpectedly." So, again, there is this reference to a sudden and unanticipated destruction "as in the days of Noah." But Jesus also admonished us to "watch" and "pray" so that we (as Christians) will "escape" all of these things. This word "escape" is the same one used by Paul in I Thessalonians 5:1-10 to warn that "children of darkness" would not escape or evade the day of God's wrath and judgment. But, here in this passage, Jesus teaches that Christians can avoid the chaos and destruction coming upon the world. It will be possible for them to "escape," i.e., "to flee out of" disaster and "to get safely away from danger," according to the Greek dictionary.

Jesus said no man will know "the day or the hour" of His Return. (Matt. 24:36, 42, 50). Much sensationalism, and the resultant loss of credibility for Christianity in general and prophecy in particular, could have been avoided down through the years if only people would have paid more attention to the prophetic teachings of Jesus. However, this should not deter us from ascertaining any truth that is clearly taught in Scripture.

The preceding passage (i.e., Luke 21:28-36) does, in fact, give us clues as to when God's Kingdom and the Coming of Christ are near in time. Likewise, the apostle Paul touched on this matter:

I Thessalonians 5:1-10

1 But of the times and the seasons, brethren, ye have no need that I write unto you.

2 For yourselves know perfectly that the day of the Lord so cometh as a thief in the night.

3 For when they shall say, Peace and safety; then sudden destruction cometh upon them, as travail upon a woman with child; and they shall not escape.

4 But ye, brethren, are not in darkness, that that day should overtake you as a thief.

5 Ye are all the children of light, and the children of the day: we are not of the night, nor of darkness.

6 Therefore let us not sleep, as do others; but let us watch and be sober.

7 For they that sleep sleep in the night; and they that be drunken are

drunken in the night.

8 But let us, who are of the day, be sober, putting on the breastplate of faith and love; and for an helmet, the hope of salvation.

9 For God hath not appointed us to wrath, but to obtain salvation by our Lord Jesus Christ,

10 Who died for us, that, whether we wake or sleep, we should live together with him. (KJV)

"Day of the Lord" is defined by a careful, analytical reading of various scriptures to be the "great day of God's wrath" upon the world soon AFTER the Rapture has occurred. It will last for a period of seven years during which time the seven Trumpet-Vial Plagues of fire will demolish much of the world before culminating in the Second Coming of Christ at the Battle of Armageddon. (Rev. 6:12-17) (Rev. 8:1, 2, 5-13) (Rev. 9:1-19) (Rev. 11:13-15) (Joel 2:1-11) (Joel 2:28-31) (Isa. 24:17-23) (Isa. 13:6-13) (Zech. 14:1-3) (II Peter 3:10-12) (Zeph. 1:14-18) (Amos 5:18-20) (Isa. 2:10-21). Furthermore, just as the Rapture will happen suddenly and unexpectedly without warning, so likewise will the "Day of the Lord" come "as a thief in the night" without warning precisely as this passage portrays.

"Peace and safety; then sudden destruction..." As noted later, the Antichrist will inspire a period of world peace and prosperity by which he will destroy (deceive) many. (Dan. 8:25). We also will note later that this period of world peace and prosperity will be terminated by sudden destruction immediately after the Rapture when the apocalyptic judgments of Revelation are unleashed upon the earth. Therefore, because the period of "peace and safety" in the above passage is followed immediately by "sudden destruction," it obviously correlates with the scenario associated with the Antichrist.

This view is even confirmed in the very same sentence: "Peace and safety; then sudden destruction cometh upon them, as travail upon a woman with child." Since Revelation 12 uses this very same symbolic "woman in travail" to portray the Rapture, this proves beyond any reasonable doubt that the events described in this passage should be associated within the context of the Rapture. Therefore, in essence, this passage is saying that peace and safety will be ended abruptly when the Rapture begins a process of judgment and destruction.

Paul continues by saying that since we (as Christians) are "the children of light" and "not of the night, nor of darkness," we should "not sleep as others" but should "watch and be sober." The word "watch" comes from the Greek word GREGOREUO, and it means to "keep awake" (literally or figuratively) and is sometimes translated as "vigilant." In verse 4, Paul states that because we "are not in darkness," that day (i.e., "Day of the Lord") should not overtake us as a thief.

However, in verse 3, Paul says that the children of darkness will not "escape" the "sudden destruction" which will strike the world. The word used here in the Greek for the word "escape" is EKPHEUGO — the same word we saw in Luke 21 — and, again, it means to "flee out" of danger. Accordingly, the message of this passage is a very blunt warning that non-believers will not be able to flee from the coming destruction which will occur during the Great and Terrible Day Of The Lord.

But, in contrast, God has not appointed Christians to "wrath," but to "salvation by our Lord Jesus Christ." (verse 9). It is interesting to note that the word "wrath" comes from the Greek word ORGE, and it means violent "passion" or justifiable "abhorrence," which by implication means "punishment." Accordingly, since God obviously does not "abhor" (detest) those who have accepted Christ as their personal Lord and Saviour, He has appointed or destined us "to obtain salvation." Furthermore, the word "salvation" in the Greek is SOTERIA, and it means "rescue" or "safety" in a physical or moral sense, and is translated throughout the Bible as "deliver, health, salvation, save and saving." So, obviously the dictionary definition agrees with the context of this passage in giving the word "salvation" the meaning of "rescue to safety," i.e., the Rapture.

I would like to emphasize that Paul taught that since we, as Christians, are the "children of light," we should not be caught unawares when the "Day of the Lord" approaches. In like manner, Jesus scolded the religious hypocrites of His day for their failure to discern the "signs of the times." Furthermore, the prophet Daniel said that complete understanding of his "end-time" prophecies would be "sealed till the time of the end." (Dan. 12:9) (cf. Dan. 8:17, 19, 26, 27). All of these scriptures make it clear we can know "when the hour is near."

Accordingly, since Jesus promised that one generation would see the fulfillment of all the "end-time" events described in Matthew 24 and Luke 21, we can draw some possible inferences about the general "time-frame" with which we are dealing. Unless God or modern science extends the average life-time for people living during "the time of the end," one generation's adult life-span — according to biblical scriptures — is approximately 50 years in length (Ps. 90:10) (Num. 1:2, 3). Therefore, if I am correct in saying that the first signs (i.e., false messiahs, wars and rumours of wars, and commotions) commenced their initial fulfillment during the early 1970's, then 50 years from somewhere around the early 1970's would place us somewhere in the time-period of 2020-2025 A.D. as the latest possible date for Armageddon and the establishment of God's literal Kingdom on earth. So, in other words, perhaps Armageddon will occur sometime before the year 2025 A.D. or thereabouts.

However, if Armageddon must happen sometime before the year 2025 A.D., then by biblical necessity, the approximate date of 2014 A.D. or thereabouts would be the latest possible date for the Rapture since there are at least ten and one-half years between the pre-tribulation Rapture and Armageddon. But, in view of the fact that the cities of Babylon and Tyre have yet to be rebuilt into centers of world trade and commerce, it might seem as if we could be pressed for sufficient time for everything to happen as the Bible predicts — although things could surprise us by happening very swiftly once they begin. On that point, though, perhaps it will be possible for Babylon and Tyre to continue with their accumulation of wealth and power after the Rapture even though death and destruction and tribulation and plagues will begin to strike the earth immediately after the Rapture occurs. If so, that would give us additional time for Babylon and Tyre to achieve the level of power and wealth and commercial leadership the Bible predicts they will enjoy at the time of their destruction, near the time of Armageddon itself.

On the other hand, the latest possible date for Armageddon could be pushed beyond the time-frame of 2020-2025 A.D. if the generational countdown did not begin (as I think it did) with the sudden emergence of numerous false messiahs and modern terrorism during the early 1970's. Perhaps, instead, the countdown begins as the first signs, i.e., the wars and rumors of wars and commotions, realize their ultimate fulfillment when the world becomes terrified that the end of the world truly is upon us during a future period of catastrophic military crisis (thereby prompting the rise of Antichrist). Accordingly, all things considered, it is not possible for anyone to pinpoint the exact time of His Coming; the best we can do is observe the signs carefully and scripturally in order to know, as the apostle Paul explained, when the time is near.

Harmony Of Daniel's Visions

Events	*Chapter 2*	*Chapter 7*	*Chapter 8*
Babylon	Head Of Gold	Lion	
Persia	Two Arms Of Silver	Two Sides Of Bear	Two Horns Of Ram
Greece	Trunk Of Brass	Leopard; Four Heads	Goat; Four Horns
Rome	Iron Legs	Beast	
Modern Roman Countries	Ten Toes	Ten Horns	
Rise Of Antichrist		Little Horn; Three Horns Subdued; Speaks Great Things	Little Horn; Destroys Wonderfully; Peace And Prosperity
Rapture		Saints In Heaven (Dan. 7:9-10) (Rev. 4-5)	Stars (Angels) Cast To Earth (Dan. 8:10) (Rev. 12)
Tribulation And Chaos		Tribulation Saints; Antichrist Continues To Speak Great Things	Destroy Holy People; Rebuilt Temple Desecrated
Kingdom Of God	Stone "Cut Out Without Hands" Becomes Mountain	Saints Possess Kingdom	Little Horn Destroyed "Without Hand"

II. Military Crisis In Israel

The Promise To Abraham

Thousands of years ago, God made a solemn covenant with Abraham that the Jews (the only rightful heirs of Abraham, Isaac and Jacob) would occupy the large strip of land between the river of Egypt and the great Euphrates river for ever. (See Ezekiel 47:13-23 for the borders of Israel during the Millennial Reign of Christ.) This Divine covenant promise was absolutely UNCONDITIONAL, and was made to Abraham, personally, for ETERNITY:

Genesis 15:18

18 In the same day the LORD made a covenant with Abram, saying, Unto thy seed have I given this land, from the river of Egypt unto the great river, the river Euphrates: (KJV)

Genesis 17:1-9

1 And when Abram was ninety years old and nine, the LORD appeared to Abram, and said unto him, I am the Almighty God; walk before me, and be thou perfect.

2 And I will make my covenant between me and thee, and will multiply thee exceedingly.

3 And Abram fell on his face: and God talked with him, saying,

4 As for me, behold, my covenant is with thee, and thou shalt be a father of many nations.

5 Neither shall thy name any more be called Abram, but thy name shall be Abraham; for a father of many nations have I made thee.

6 And I will make thee exceeding fruitful, and I will make nations of thee, and kings shall come out of thee.

7 And I will establish my covenant between me and thee and thy seed after thee in their generations for an everlasting covenant, to be a God unto thee, and to thy seed after thee.

8 And I will give unto thee, and to thy seed after thee, the land wherein thou art a stranger, all the land of Canaan, for an everlasting possession; and I will be their God.

9 And God said unto Abraham, Thou shalt keep my covenant,

therefore, thou, and thy seed after thee in their generations. (KJV)

Unfortunately, today, some people are teaching that the nation of Israel no longer plays a part in God's eternal plan; that it is the "church" who really is Israel, a "spiritual" type of Israel. But this false teaching clearly and directly conflicts with God's unconditional covenant promise made to Abraham. That is why, in the epistle to the Romans, it almost seems as if the apostle Paul anticipated this grievous error:

Romans 11:1, 2, 25-29
1 I say then, Hath God cast away his people? God forbid. For I also am an Israelite, of the seed of Abraham, of the tribe of Benjamin.
2 God hath not cast away his people which he foreknew. Wot ye not what the scripture saith of Elias? how he maketh intercession to God against Israel, saying,
25 For I would not, brethren, that ye should be ignorant of this mystery, lest ye should be wise in your own conceits; that blindness in part is happened to Israel, until the fulness of the Gentiles be come in.
26 And so all Israel shall be saved: as it is written, There shall come out of Sion the Deliverer, and shall turn away ungodliness from Jacob:
27 For this is my covenant unto them, when I shall take away their sins.
28 As concerning the gospel, they are enemies for your sakes: but as touching the election, they are beloved for the fathers' sakes.
29 For the gifts and calling of God are without repentance. (KJV)

Hebrews 6:13-19
13 For when God made promise to Abraham, because he could swear by no greater, he sware by himself,
14 Saying, Surely blessing I will bless thee, and multiplying I will multiply thee.
15 And so, after he had patiently endured, he obtained the promise.
16 For men verily swear by the greater: and an oath for confirmation is to them an end of all strife.
17 Wherein God, willing more abundantly to shew unto the heirs of promise the immutability of his counsel, confirmed it by an oath:
18 That by two immutable things, in which it was impossible for God to lie, we might have a strong consolation, who have fled for refuge to lay

hold upon the hope set before us:

19 Which hope we have as an anchor of the soul, both sure and stedfast, and which entereth into that within the veil; (KJV)

Hebrews 11:8, 9

8 By faith Abraham, when he was called to go out into a place which he should after receive for an inheritance, obeyed; and he went out, not knowing whither he went.

9 By faith he sojourned in the land of promise, as in a strange country, dwelling in tabernacles with Isaac and Jacob, the heirs with him of the same promise: (KJV)

Regrettably, as we saw earlier, in order to explain away such obvious and plainly-word truth, people sometimes say we should not follow a literal and common-sense approach to our analysis of Scripture. Instead, they say we should "spiritualize" or "allegorize" the meaning of the biblical passages we read. But, interpreting God's Holy Word in this manner is a clear and certain recipe for reaching erroneous conclusions about important matters. Therefore, since God is not the author of confusion (I Cor. 14:33), the Bible should be read and interpreted in the exact same manner as any other book, meaning we should give a plain, literal interpretation to a passage unless the context very clearly indicates otherwise or a literal interpretation would not make any sense. Obviously any examination of the scriptures will be more fruitful if we consistently apply the realistic definitions that are attached to words throughout everyday life and in our word dictionaries. Although literary devices such as metaphors, parables, hyperbole, symbols and figures of speech all clearly have their place in literature, we must be very careful about approaching scriptural analysis with wild abandon where everything has a hidden meaning to be deciphered or guessed.

It is important that we adhere to a rational methodology for ascertaining truth because we must assume that an infinite, rational God and Creator would understand the necessity and the wisdom for realistic and objective standards while communicating to us with human words. That is why the Bible is full of scriptural examples where the sensical literal mode of interpretation is followed. For instance, hundreds of Old Testament prophecies were fulfilled literally, thereby establishing a definite precedent in which to emulate. Jesus even chided the generation of His day for their failure to recognize the prophetic signs of the time (Matt. 16:1-14), and a primary reason for this failure was their refusal to interpret literally the prophecies concerning His First Coming, more than 300 specific predictions which Jesus fulfilled with His life, death and resurrection. Therefore, I believe that wisdom dictates we should avoid such error when interpreting prophecies concerning events associated with His Second Coming.

Sometimes it is said that the United States and Britain represent the alleged 10 "lost" tribes of Israel, and that although the tribes of Judah and Benjamin currently live in the land of Israel, they are not really heirs to the promises made by God to the ancient people of Israel. But such claims are easily refuted because members of all twelve tribes of Israel were partially regathered in the land of Israel during both Old and New Testament times, and many of the Jews living abroad in other countries were easily identifiable as belonging to all twelve tribes of Israel. (Ezra 7:7; Ezra 7:13; Ezra 7:28; Ezra 6:16; Ezra 6:21; Ezra 9:1; Ezra 10:1; Ezra 10:5; Nehemiah 7:7, 66; Nehemiah 9:1; Nehemiah 12:47; Luke 1:80; Matthew 15:24; Luke 7:9; John 1:31; John 1:47; John 3:10; John 12:13; Acts 2:22; Acts 2:36; Acts 3:12; Acts 4:8; Acts 4:10; Acts 5:21; Acts 5:35; Acts 9:15; Acts 13:16; Acts 13:24; Acts 21:28; James 1:1; Romans 11:2-5).

However, God's covenant with Israel repeating the promises He made to Abraham are conditioned on complete obedience to Him. Accordingly, God never promised that the Jews would possess the land of Israel no matter how they lived from a moral and spiritual perspective. Instead, God vowed that the Jews would live in the land of Israel only when they were obedient to His Holy Word — as clearly indicated in the following scriptural passages:

Deuteronomy 29:1

1 These are the words of the covenant, which the LORD commanded Moses to make with the children of Israel in the land of Moab, beside the covenant which he made with them in Horeb. (KJV)

Deuteronomy 30:1-10, 15-20

1 And it shall come to pass, when all these things are come upon thee, the blessing and the curse, which I have set before thee, and thou shalt call them to mind among all the nations, whither the LORD thy God hath

driven thee,

2 And shalt return unto the LORD thy God, and shalt obey his voice according to all that I command thee this day, thou and thy children, with all thine heart, and with all thy soul;

3 That then the LORD thy God will turn thy captivity, and have compassion upon thee, and will return and gather thee from all the nations, whither the LORD thy God hath scattered thee.

4 If any of thine be driven out unto the outmost parts of heaven, from thence will the LORD thy God gather thee, and from thence will he fetch thee:

5 And the LORD thy God will bring thee into the land which thy fathers possessed, and thou shalt possess it; and he will do thee good, and multiply thee above thy fathers.

6 And the LORD thy God will circumcise thine heart, and the heart of thy seed, to love the LORD thy God with all thine heart, and with all thy soul, that thou mayest live.

7 And the LORD thy God will put all these curses upon thine enemies, and on them that hate thee, which persecuted thee.

8 And thou shalt return and obey the voice of the LORD, and do all his commandments which I command thee this day.

9 And the LORD thy God will make thee plenteous in every work of thine hand, in the fruit of thy body, and in the fruit of thy cattle, and in the fruit of thy land, for good: for the LORD will again rejoice over thee for good, as he rejoiced over thy fathers:

10 If thou shalt hearken unto the voice of the LORD thy God, to keep his commandments and his statutes which are written in this book of the law, and if thou turn unto the LORD thy God with all thine heart, and with all thy soul.

15 See, I have set before thee this day life and good, and death and evil;

16 In that I command thee this day to love the LORD thy God, to walk in his ways, and to keep his commandments and his statutes and his judgments, that thou mayest live and multiply: and the LORD thy God shall bless thee in the land whither thou goest to possess it.

17 But if thine heart turn away, so that thou wilt not hear, but shalt be drawn away, and worship other gods, and serve them;

18 I denounce unto you this day, that ye shall surely perish, and that ye shall not prolong your days upon the land, whither thou passest over

Jordan to go to possess it.

19 I call heaven and earth to record this day against you, that I have set before you life and death, blessing and cursing: therefore choose life, that both thou and thy seed may live:

20 That thou mayest love the LORD thy God, and that thou mayest obey his voice, and that thou mayest cleave unto him: for he is thy life, and the length of thy days: that thou mayest dwell in the land which the LORD sware unto thy fathers, to Abraham, to Isaac, and to Jacob, to give them. (KJV)

Even a cursory analysis of Jewish history will show that every time the Jews slid into persistent and unrepentant religious apostasy, they were punished if they continued to resist collective efforts at repentance and reform. Twice they were even dispersed from their homeland, the land of Israel, after they had failed to heed repeated warnings from prophets of God! Not surprisingly, therefore, during the last two millennia, the Jews (as a nation) have not been obedient to God, so the promise of their special covenant has not been in effect due to its temporary suspension after their collective rejection of Christ Jesus as Messiah.

But, at the appropriate time, God is going to force the Jews into complete and total obedience with the terms of their ancient Mosaic covenant. Obviously this will not be an easy matter in light of the very long history of spiritual rebellion and apostasy that has marked the collective Jewish psyche. Such a drastic change in the spiritual attitude of the Jews will necessitate a very earth-shattering experience! That is the purpose of the impending catastrophic military crisis for Israel which we will arbitrarily designate as the Second Crisis!

The First Crisis

The nation Israel exists under three separate and distinct relationships: Palestine, God, and the Messiah. However, due to the very stubborn and rebellious attitude that has marked the Jewish psyche for much of their history, a return to these same three special relationships, regrettably, will have to involve three steps, each one a crisis!

The first crisis has already taken place! For centuries the Jews lived in foreign lands, relatively happy and prosperous. It took an experience as drastic and earth-shattering as the mass-murders of Hitler to instill within them the necessary desire and determination to forge a new living in a barren waste-land such as Palestine had been for so many centuries. This was the BEGINNING of the fulfillment for the following prophecy:

Ezekiel 34:11-13

11 For thus saith the Lord GOD; Behold, I, even I, will both search my sheep, and seek them out.

12 As a shepherd seeketh out his flock in the day that he is among his sheep that are scattered; so will I seek out my sheep, and will deliver them out of all places where they have been scattered in the cloudy and dark day.

13 And I will bring them out from the people, and gather them from the countries, and will bring them to their own land, and feed them upon the mountains of Israel by the rivers, and in all the inhabited places of the country. (KJV)

So far, of course, only some of the Jews throughout the world have returned to "the promised land," the land of Israel! However, a partial return of only some of the Jews first was necessary in order to prepare the land so that it could "support" naturally a mass return of all Jews. This partial return was needed because, historically, God generally works subtly and creatively within the framework of His creation whenever and wherever possible; God reserves the miraculous for the special occasions which He, in His infinite Wisdom and Knowledge, deems appropriate. For instance, God did not drop an ark down from the sky for Noah, but instead, instructed Noah to build his own ark.

So, evidently God wants us to use our God-given rationality and human abilities and initiative to accomplish most things in life for ourselves under His guidance. Otherwise, if God miraculously did everything for us, not only would we degenerate into creatures both lazy and thoughtless (in every sense of the word), but overwhelming numbers of incredible miracles would compel even the most diehard skeptic and atheist to become a "Christian." But, then, that would defeat the very purpose of God in testing humanity for these last several thousand years in His efforts to determine everyone's true spiritual attitude. That is why God has given us sufficient rational evidence within the realm of our magnificent world and universe and personal consciousness to convince the truly intellectually honest individual regarding the validity of Christianity's truth claims while still leaving it possible for the dishonest-minded to ignore the evidence at hand.

Parenthetically, a most incredible development took place during this partial return of the Jews which fulfilled an extraordinary prophecy found in Ezekiel 4:

Ezekiel 4:1-13

1 Thou also, son of man, take thee a tile, and lay it before thee, and pourtray upon it the city, even Jerusalem:

2 And lay siege against it, and build a fort against it, and cast a mount against it; set the camp also against it, and set battering rams against it round about.

3 Moreover take thou unto thee an iron pan, and set it for a wall of iron between thee and the city: and set thy face against it, and it shall be besieged, and thou shalt lay siege against it. This shall be a sign to the house of Israel.

4 Lie thou also upon thy left side, and lay the iniquity of the house of Israel upon it: according to the number of the days that thou shalt lie upon it thou shalt bear their iniquity.

5 For I have laid upon thee the years of their iniquity, according to the number of the days, three hundred and ninety days: so shalt thou bear the iniquity of the house of Israel.

6 And when thou hast accomplished them, lie again on thy right side, and thou shalt bear the iniquity of the house of Judah forty days: I have appointed thee each day for a year.

7 Therefore thou shalt set thy face toward the siege of Jerusalem, and thine arm shall be uncovered, and thou shalt prophesy against it.

8 And, behold, I will lay bands upon thee, and thou shalt not turn thee from one side to another, till thou hast ended the days of thy siege.

9 Take thou also unto thee wheat, and barley, and beans, and lentiles, and millet, and fitches, and put them in one vessel, and make thee bread thereof, according to the number of the days that thou shalt lie upon thy side, three hundred and ninety days shalt thou eat thereof.

10 And thy meat which thou shalt eat shall be by weight, twenty shekels a day: from time to time shalt thou eat it.

11 Thou shalt drink also water by measure, the sixth part of an hin: from time to time shalt thou drink.

12 And thou shalt eat it as barley cakes, and thou shalt bake it with dung that cometh out of man, in their sight.

13 And the LORD said, Even thus shall the children of Israel eat their defiled bread among the Gentiles, whither I will drive them. (KJV)

"I have appointed thee each day for a year." Normally, day means day, and year means year in the Bible as it does anywhere else. This type of plain, common-sense literal interpretation of biblical scriptures is generally the best methodology for interpretation, as we noted earlier, because it tends to minimize any confusion and misunderstandings which might otherwise be possible. That is why this methodological principle should be strictly adhered to at all times unless the context very clearly indicates otherwise, or a literal interpretation would not make any sense. However, in this particular instance, it is very plainly stated that a day should be made to represent or symbolize a year — so this passage represents an entirely different situation because, in this instance, we have explicit instruction to allow one word to represent another word. Therefore, the people of Israel and Judah were to be dispersed from their homeland and scattered throughout the nations of the world for a period of 430 years according to this passage in Ezekiel.

However, nothing like this has ever happened to the Jews throughout all of their history anytime after this prophecy was given to Ezekiel. Although some of the Jews returned to their homeland after enduring only seventy years of captivity in the land of Babylon, never have all of the Jews throughout the world ever regathered and lived in the land of Israel, and it has only been in recent, modern times that Israel has even actually regained both her national sovereignty and her capital city of Jerusalem. Therefore, apparently, other conditions apply to this prophecy so as to modify its original provisions.

The answer is found in Leviticus:

Leviticus 26:18

And if ye will not yet for all this hearken unto me, then I will punish you seven times more for your sins. (KJV)

The context of this passage portrays God making promises of blessings or punishments to the people of Israel according to how they conducted their lives in light of His commandments. Over and over again, God made it quite clear to the people of Israel that if they persisted in habitual and unrepentant sin as a nation, eventually He would lose patience with them and multiply their punishment by seven times. Not surprisingly, after several centuries of periodic and frequent bouts of disobedience on the part of Israel, the Jews were punished very severely by undergoing enforced servitude to Babylon for seventy years. (Jeremiah 25:11) (Jeremiah 29:10) (Daniel 9:2). After this initial period of punishment for seventy years was concluded, the Jews were still unrepentant, so God multiplied the remainder of their original punishment of 430 years (i.e., 430 – 70 = 360 years) by seven, resulting in 2520 years of additional punishment for the Jews. Since a biblical year is defined by the Bible as precisely 360 days in length (Dan. 7:24, 25) (Rev. 12:6, 13, 14) (Rev. 13:4-7), this meant that the 2520 biblical years of punishment would be equivalent to 907,200 days (2520 years X 360 days) during which time the Jews were to be exiled and punished by God for their sins.

Accordingly, as history shows, the Jews lost their national sovereignty and freedom to the Babylonians during the Spring or Summer of 606 B.C.. But, because of their continued disobedience and resistance to the Will of God, they even lost possession of Jerusalem when later it was destroyed in 587 B.C., nineteen years after the initial dispersion of the Jews began. Thus, we have both the servitude of the nation (as prophesied by the prophet Jeremiah) and the desolation of the city of Jerusalem (as expressed by the prophet Daniel) to consider when evaluating the impact which this 2520 year prophecy by Ezekiel had on the people of Israel. (Jeremiah 27:6-11) (Jeremiah 38:17-21) (Jeremiah 29:10) (Daniel 9:2).

Due to the very long passages of time involved, and the lack of reliable and precise historical records, we do not know exactly on what day the Jews began their initial captivity into Babylon; we only know it probably was late Spring or early Summer of the year 606 B.C.. Accordingly, a better way to calculate whether or not the 2520 biblical year prophecy by Ezekiel was ever fulfilled would be to start with the modern date of Israel's rebirth as a sovereign nation and then count backwards in time to see if we arrive at the known approximate date of Israel's initial captivity.

Since the State of Israel declared national independence on May 14, 1948, we subtract our 907,200 days of punishment as declared by Ezekiel — and with the help of Calendar Conversions, located on the Internet at http://www.genealogy.org/~scottlee/calconvert.cgi — we determine that the calendar date of July 15, 537 B.C. is the date when some of the Jews were first allowed to return to their homeland in Israel. Now, we must further subtract the seventy years of captivity from our date of July 15, 537 B.C. in order to arrive at the time when the Jewish dispersion first began. Because there are 25,200 days in seventy biblical years of time, our computations now put us at the date of July 17, 606 B.C., or the summer of 606 B.C., our original approximate target date. In other words, the Bible amazingly predicted the exact time-length in which Israel would endure servitude as a nation.

As for the city of Jerusalem itself, the Jews did not ever regain sovereign control over all of Jerusalem (after losing it in 587 B.C.) until June 7, 1967 after the Six Day War broke out when all of the Arab countries attacked the newly-formed nation of modern Israel. So, once again, starting with our date of June 7, 1967 — the day in which Israel finally regained complete sovereign control over the entire city of Jerusalem — we count backwards in time by subtracting our 2520 biblical years (i.e., 907,200 days) from our starting date, and arrive at the calendar date of August 8, 518 B.C.. Then, further subtracting our seventy biblical years of captivity (i.e., 25,200 days) from August 8, 518 B.C., we finally reach the calendar date of August 10, 587 B.C., the date when all of Jerusalem was lost to destruction and foreign domination. Although the Bible states that the Temple of Solomon was burned and destroyed on July 23-24, 587 B.C. (Jeremiah 52:12-13), if we assume that the entire city did not fall until two or three weeks later, we again achieve confirmation of a most remarkable prophetic fulfillment! Loss of sovereign control by the Jews over all of Jerusalem lasted exactly 2520 biblical years precisely as Ezekiel foretold. Obviously now that Israel has finally regained both her national sovereignty and sovereign control over all of Jerusalem, the partial return of the Jews to the land of Israel is moving along at full steam ahead!

Ezekiel 36:8

But ye, O mountains of Israel, ye shall shoot forth your branches and yield your fruit to my people of Israel; for they are at hand to come. (KJV)

Obviously this amazing prophecy foretelling the return of the Jews to the land of Israel has already been fulfilled! Land that had lain waste and unwanted for centuries suddenly began responding to the agricultural projects of the Jews once they arrived in significant numbers, thereby causing a desolate land of rocks and desert-sand to blossom forth again just as the Bible had predicted it would do. (Ezek. 34-36).

However, the Bible also predicted the continual opposition and hatred of the Palestinian Arabs toward the Jews. But, God promised He would destroy the Palestinian Arabs for two reasons: their "perpetual hatred" of the Jews, and their obsession to occupy ALL of Palestine, i.e., the land of Israel, while driving the Jews into the sea in the process.

Ezekiel 35:1-15

1 Moreover the word of the LORD came unto me, saying,

2 Son of man, set thy face against mount Seir, and prophesy against it,

3 And say unto it, Thus saith the Lord GOD; Behold, O mount Seir, I am against thee, and I will stretch out mine hand against thee, and I will make thee most desolate.

4 I will lay thy cities waste, and thou shalt be desolate, and thou shalt know that I am the LORD.

5 Because thou hast had a perpetual hatred, and hast shed the blood of the children of Israel by the force of the sword in the time of their calamity, in the time that their iniquity had an end:

6 Therefore, as I live, saith the Lord GOD, I will prepare thee unto blood, and blood shall pursue thee: sith thou hast not hated blood, even blood shall pursue thee.

7 Thus will I make mount Seir most desolate, and cut off from it him that passeth out and him that returneth.

8 And I will fill his mountains with his slain men: in thy hills, and in thy valleys, and in all thy rivers, shall they fall that are slain with the sword.

9 I will make thee perpetual desolations, and thy cities shall not return: and ye shall know that I am the LORD.

10 Because thou hast said, These two nations and these two countries shall be mine, and we will possess it; whereas the LORD was there:

11 Therefore, as I live, saith the Lord GOD, I will even do according to thine anger, and according to thine envy which thou hast used out of thy hatred against them; and I will make myself known among them, when I have judged thee.

12 And thou shalt know that I am the LORD, and that I have heard all thy blasphemies which thou hast spoken against the mountains of Israel,

saying, They are laid desolate, they are given us to consume.

13 Thus with your mouth ye have boasted against me, and have multiplied your words against me: I have heard them.

14 Thus saith the Lord GOD; When the whole earth rejoiceth, I will make thee desolate.

15 As thou didst rejoice at the inheritance of the house of Israel, because it was desolate, so will I do unto thee: thou shalt be desolate, O mount Seir, and all Idumea, even all of it: and they shall know that I am the LORD. (KJV)

"Mount Seir." "Idumea." The Arabs are descendants of Esau and Ishmael. Ishmael was the son of Abraham and Abraham's second wife, Hagar (Gen. 16), while Esau was a brother of Jacob, thus making him a grandson of Abraham. Furthermore, one of Esau's wives was a descendant of Ishmael. (Gen. 28:9). Accordingly, in prophecy, the Arabs are identified through names associated with Esau. (Deut. 2:4, 5). In Genesis 25:30 we are told how Esau disdainfully gave away his birthright for the sake of a bowl of red pottage (Hebrew HAADOM, meaning "the red pottage"), thus causing Esau to be called Edom, i.e., Red. This sad tale concerning Esau explains why Edom is also a name which is applied to the descendants of Esau. (Gen. 36:8).

"Because thou hast had a perpetual hatred." Since the time of Esau, the Arabs have harbored a hatred for their brothers, the Jews. In recent decades, they even have fought several wars which have been punctuated by periods of tense and angry relations. Although critics of Israel sometimes have accused them of being a militaristic state, obviously the very existence and survival of Israel has depended on eternal vigilance and strength. Thus, during the late 1980s, this "perpetual hatred" for the Jews was cunningly exploited by the P.L.O. in the form of the infamous Palestinian uprising, or intifatah, which began officially in December of 1987. Even though the Israelis reacted with a high degree of restraint compared to how most other governments would have reacted in a similar situation, the net effect was a steady deterioration in their image and reputation throughout the world for many years.

Of course, more recently we watched a major Middle East peace process gain momentum under the umbrella of the Oslo Accords until those accords "legally" expired on May 4, 1999. However, all interested parties involved in the "peace" process continued to express hope and optimism that a permanent peace accord between the Israelis and the Palestinians could still materialize. But, after many long months of fierce conflict between Israel and the Palestinians despite the major concessions that were offered by Israeli Prime Minister Barak during the peace negotiations, it is clear that the Palestinian Arabs simply hate and despise the Jews and the existence of national Israel — precisely as the Bible predicted! Both the Jews and the Arab world want Jerusalem and its holy sites, so just as the Bible also prophesied, the city of Jerusalem has become a major "stumbling block" for the Arabs and even the whole world. That is why the ongoing controversy and fighting over the final status of Jerusalem will help to serve as the catalyst sparking Israel's next catastrophic crisis.

"These two countries." Right now the land of Palestine is divided into two parts because the Jews live in Israel "proper" while the Palestinian Arabs occupy the West Bank area and Gaza strip within Palestine. In actuality, however, the Palestinian Arabs have been living under the auspices of a de facto central government organized and led by Arafat's Palestinian organization for the last several years. In that sense, then, there are two countries in Palestine already — although the Palestinians still aspire to official national independence in the near future regardless of the situation with Israel. Nevertheless, as incredible as it may seem, the Arabs still want all of tiny Israel despite the fact that the Arabs, collectively, have been in possession of huge chunks of land throughout the vast Middle East area for millennia.

"We will possess it." For many years, the Palestinians have been pretending that they really want only part of Israel, namely the West Bank area and Gaza region. But, according to persistent news reports from reliable sources during the last several years, media broadcasts and newspapers that cater to the Arabs have been singing a completely different tune, and reportedly, things have not changed much recently despite the existence of "peace" negotiations. Apparently, the strategy agreed upon by the Palestinian leadership was to take whatever they could get now, and then take everything else later when circumstances were more favorable. Reliable sources have even confirmed that this really has been the "unofficial" strategy of the P.L.O. and Palestinian leadership for many years now. Therefore, as noted previously, this persistent desire and obsession on the part of the Arabs to gain possession of Israel's land represents yet another dramatic biblical prophecy which has realized its modern-day fulfillment!

"Whereas the Lord was there." God's covenant promises to Israel included a prosperous and productive land. (Deut. 28:1-14). That is why whenever Palestine was fruitful and bountiful, it was because Israel was being blessed by God. But, whenever the Jews have been absent from their land because they were being punished by God for their habitual disobedience, it has been basically rocks and desert sand, thus indicating God was not there. Accordingly, when Jews first began arriving in Palestine in the early part of this century, it was a fairly desolate desert land, and very few people, even Palestinians, were actually living there. Most certainly the land of Palestine was anything but prosperous. But, all of that changed with the arrival of the Jews because God blessed them in their initiatives, helping them gradually to transform their part of Palestine into a cornucopia of agricultural and industrial wealth. Now, more than ever, the Arabs want to possess it.

Ezekiel 36:5, 8, 10, 11

Therefore thus saith the Lord God; Surely in the fire of my jealousy have I spoken against the residue of the heathen, and against all Idumea (Edom; southern Jordan; the Palestinians) which have appointed my land into their possession with the joy of all their heart, with despiteful minds, to CAST IT OUT FOR A PREY. But ye, O mountains of Israel, ye shall shoot forth your branches, and yield your fruit to my people of Israel; FOR THEY ARE AT HAND TO COME... And the cities shall be inhabited, and the wastes shall be builded...And I will settle you after your old estates, and will do better unto you than at your beginnings: AND YE SHALL KNOW THAT I AM THE LORD. (KJV)

This scriptural passage foretells a partial return of the Jews who cause Palestine to become prosperous once again after centuries of waste and decay. They are then "cast out for a prey" by the Arabs, but with the help of God they soon recapture Palestine and become even more prosperous than before! Please note, especially, that the end-result of this severe military crisis (The Second Crisis) is the collective acknowledgment of God by the Jewish people! (cf. Ezek. 35:5)

The Second Crisis

"Because thou... hast shed the blood of the children of Israel by the force of the sword in the time of their calamity." As previously noted, Moses foretold a mass return of the Jews in a prophecy several thousand years ago in which he predicted that only AFTER the Jews repented and turned back to God could they ALL return to Palestine. (Deut. 30:1-10). This fact alone explains why God is going to allow a drastic military crisis of an extraordinary nature to evolve in Palestine at the very same time anti-Semitism throughout the world intensifies. It is the only way possible to force the Jewish people into complete and sincere repentance! Their condition will become so serious that even mass extinction will appear to be very imminent; they will seem like a valley of "dry bones"! (Ezek. 37:2). Apparently, conditions will even deteriorate so badly that the unexpected restoration of Israel as a nation, after having been "cast out for a prey," will resemble a resurrection from the grave itself. Although Ezekiel 37:15-28 describes the final state or condition of Israel after Armageddon is over, the verses immediately preceding that passage apparently can be applied to both the Second Crisis and Armageddon:

Ezekiel 37:1-14

1 The hand of the LORD was upon me, and carried me out in the spirit of the LORD, and set me down in the midst of the valley which was full of bones,

2 And caused me to pass by them round about: and, behold, there were very many in the open valley; and, lo, they were very dry.

3 And he said unto me, Son of man, can these bones live? And I answered, O Lord GOD, thou knowest.

4 Again he said unto me, Prophesy upon these bones, and say unto them, O ye dry bones, hear the word of the LORD.

5 Thus saith the Lord GOD unto these bones; Behold, I will cause breath to enter into you, and ye shall live:

6 And I will lay sinews upon you, and will bring up flesh upon you, and cover you with skin, and put breath in you, and ye shall live; and ye shall know that I am the LORD.

7 So I prophesied as I was commanded: and as I prophesied, there was a noise, and behold a shaking, and the bones came together, bone to his bone.

8 And when I beheld, lo, the sinews and the flesh came up upon them,

and the skin covered them above: but there was no breath in them.

9 Then said he unto me, Prophesy unto the wind, prophesy, son of man, and say to the wind, Thus saith the Lord GOD; Come from the four winds, O breath, and breathe upon these slain, that they may live.

10 So I prophesied as he commanded me, and the breath came into them, and they lived, and stood up upon their feet, an exceeding great army.

11 Then he said unto me, Son of man, these bones are the whole house of Israel: behold, they say, Our bones are dried, and our hope is lost: we are cut off for our parts.

12 Therefore prophesy and say unto them, Thus saith the Lord GOD; Behold, O my people, I will open your graves, and cause you to come up out of your graves, and bring you into the land of Israel.

13 And ye shall know that I am the LORD, when I have opened your graves, O my people, and brought you up out of your graves,

14 And shall put my spirit in you, and ye shall live, and I shall place you in your own land: then shall ye know that I the LORD have spoken it, and performed it, saith the LORD. (KJV)

In recent years, there has been a very noticeable resurgence in anti-Semitism throughout Europe and the Middle East, and since the early days of glasnost, even in Russia and the eastern European countries. Now, as we enter into the new millennium, there are reliable news reports which indicate a dramatic upsurge in anti-Semitic violence and persecution in Russia which is expected to force huge numbers of Jews to flee to Israel and the United States in the near future! Likewise, due to a variety of factors such as the intifatah uprising by the Palestinians, shrewd diplomacy by Arafat in recent years, and growing political pressure and anti-Semitism throughout the world, the nations of earth increasingly have focused on Israel as one of the few remaining sore spots in the world. Now, very recently, due to escalating pressure to appease Arab/Muslim demands regarding the Israeli-Palestinian conflict so that they will help in the war on terrorism, the world is even becoming sharply critical of Israel. Apparently, many people believe that Israel does not have the right to defend itself against the onslaught of vicious terrorist attacks. Unfortunately, there probably is little the Israelis can do to reverse this rising tide of world-wide hostility towards them.

"Thou hast spoken against the MOUNTAINS of Israel, saying, They are laid desolate, they are given us to consume." At first glance, this appears to be a prophecy that could not possibly happen. According to various intelligence experts, Israel has maintained one of the most potent military forces in the world for the last several decades, and it was even reported during the early 1980's that the Israeli military command believed at that time it could win in a military confrontation with Russia if Russia had ever decided to invade Israel. Nor has the combined military strength of all the Arab countries ever been able to destroy Israel — although they tried to do so on several different occasions. Today, despite the militaristic posturing by Saddam Hussein in Iraq and the massive covert support given to the Hizbullah terrorists in southern Lebanon by Iran, the Arab world apparently is not very anxious to engage in a full-scale war with Israel, at least, not yet. Nor are the Palestinians in any condition to fight Israel in a direct military confrontation — no matter how much they might wish to do so. Yet, something very drastic and unexpected happens which drives the Jews out of their land.

Obadiah 10-21

10 For thy violence against thy brother Jacob shame shall cover thee, and thou shalt be cut off for ever.

11 In the day that thou stoodest on the other side, in the day that the strangers carried away captive his forces, and foreigners entered into his gates, and cast lots upon Jerusalem, even thou wast as one of them.

12 But thou shouldest not have looked on the day of thy brother in the day that he became a stranger; neither shouldest thou have rejoiced over the children of Judah in the day of their destruction; neither shouldest thou have spoken proudly in the day of distress.

13 Thou shouldest not have entered into the gate of my people in the day of their calamity; yea, thou shouldest not have looked on their affliction in the day of their calamity, nor have laid hands on their substance in the day of their calamity;

14 Neither shouldest thou have stood in the crossway, to cut off those of his that did escape; neither shouldest thou have delivered up those of his that did remain in the day of distress.

15 For the day of the LORD is near upon all the heathen: as thou hast done, it shall be done unto thee: thy reward shall return upon thine own head.

16 For as ye have drunk upon my holy mountain, so shall all the

heathen drink continually, yea, they shall drink, and they shall swallow down, and they shall be as though they had not been.

17 But upon mount Zion shall be deliverance, and there shall be holiness; and the house of Jacob shall possess their possessions.

18 And the house of Jacob shall be a fire, and the house of Joseph a flame, and the house of Esau for stubble, and they shall kindle in them, and devour them; and there shall not be any remaining of the house of Esau; for the LORD hath spoken it.

19 And they of the south shall possess the mount of Esau; and they of the plain the Philistines: and they shall possess the fields of Ephraim, and the fields of Samaria: and Benjamin shall possess Gilead.

20 And the captivity of this host of the children of Israel shall possess that of the Canaanites, even unto Zarephath; and the captivity of Jerusalem, which is in Sepharad, shall possess the cities of the south.

21 And saviours shall come up on mount Zion to judge the mount of Esau; and the kingdom shall be the LORD's. (KJV)

"In the day that the strangers carried away captive his forces... and cast lots upon Jerusalem." This prophecy allows us to make more sense out of Ezekiel's astounding predictions. It is not the Palestinian Arabs, or even all of the Arab world, who drive the Jews out of Palestine — it is the "strangers" who do so. These "strangers" who help the Palestinian Arabs regain what the Palestinians and the Arab world consider rightfully to be theirs are the military forces of the Antichrist who conquer Jerusalem during the initial rise to power by Antichrist. So, even though the Arabs never actually conquer the Israeli army themselves, they do rejoice over the plight of the Jews and stand "in the crossway" to prevent their escape during the forthcoming military disaster which will strike Israel. However, for this gleeful display of hatred and covetousness and plundering, God declares that they will be annihilated.

"In the day of their calamity." This helps us to identify the time-element involved in this prophecy. It is the same descriptive phrase used by Ezekiel for the same military crisis in Israel. It is at this point in time that the Jews are "cast...out for a prey." (Ezek. 36:5-11).

Daniel 8:9

And out of one of them came forth a little horn (Antichrist), which waxed exceeding great, toward the south, and toward the east, and toward the pleasant land (Palestine; Israel). (KJV)

The context of this verse shows the "little horn" Antichrist originating from one of the four divisions of the Grecian Empire which emerged following the death of Alexander the Great. Please note that the little horn, representing both a tiny country and the personage of Antichrist, waxes "exceeding great" very quickly as it conquers in a southern and eastern direction. This passage mentions "the pleasant land" Israel, specifically, as one of the very first countries invaded by the Antichrist because Israel always receives special attention in biblical scriptures since they are God's "chosen" people.

Daniel says in the above passage of scripture that as soon as the Antichrist appears, he will conquer armies with amazing quickness in both a southern and eastern direction. Obviously the first country east of Lebanon is Syria, and since popular opinion in Lebanon increasingly resents the presence of Syrian troops occupying their country, a new leader emerging from within Lebanon would have an excellent reason for attacking Syria. Additionally, apparent Syrian sponsorship of organized terrorism in the Middle East area provides yet another very compelling reason for subduing Syria. Nor is it very difficult to understand why he also would attack Israel upon further analysis.

For instance, the Moslems and the Druze Moslems who live in southern and central Lebanon have been friends for many years with the Palestinian Arabs who have been living and fighting in that same region. So, if the Antichrist emerged from that area, most likely he would feel a certain kinship and sympathy for the Palestinians in the West Bank area since it is obvious that Israel will never relinquish any part of Jerusalem to the Palestinians under any circumstances! This might help to explain why the Antichrist will attack Israel when he attacks Syria, although conflict between the Israelis and the Hizbullah terrorists along the Lebanese-Israeli border would obviously be a major contributing factor, also.

Obadiah 10-15

For thy violence against thy brother Jacob shame shall cover thee (i.e., Palestinian Arabs), and thou shalt be cut off forever.... in the day.... that the STRANGERS carried away captive his forces, and foreigners entered into his gates, and cast lots upon Jerusalem, even thou wast as one of them.... for the day of the Lord is near.... (KJV)

"For the Day of the Lord is near." A Second Crisis explains why Obadiah stated that the time for his events was NEAR the Day of the Lord, not DURING the Day of the Lord. (The expression "Day of the Lord" generally refers to the few years immediately prior to the Battle of Armageddon, or Armageddon itself.) However, the last few verses of Obadiah do seem to indicate this passage also applies to Armageddon and "Jacob's Trouble" (a period of three and one-half years immediately prior to Armageddon during which time the Jews are severely persecuted and led into captivity to all the nations of the earth):

Obadiah 18, 21
...and there shall not be any remaining of the house of Esau... And saviours shall come up on Mount Zion to judge the Mount of Esau; and the kingdom shall be the Lord's. (KJV)

Isaiah 34:1-13
1 Come near, ye nations, to hear; and hearken, ye people: let the earth hear, and all that is therein; the world, and all things that come forth of it.
2 For the indignation of the LORD is upon all nations, and his fury upon all their armies: he hath utterly destroyed them, he hath delivered them to the slaughter.
3 Their slain also shall be cast out, and their stink shall come up out of their carcases, and the mountains shall be melted with their blood.
4 And all the host of heaven shall be dissolved, and the heavens shall be rolled together as a scroll: and all their host shall fall down, as the leaf falleth off from the vine, and as a falling fig from the fig tree.
5 For my sword shall be bathed in heaven: behold, it shall come down upon Idumea, and upon the people of my curse, to judgment.
6 The sword of the LORD is filled with blood, it is made fat with fatness, and with the blood of lambs and goats, with the fat of the kidneys of rams: for the LORD hath a sacrifice in Bozrah, and a great slaughter in the land of Idumea.
7 And the unicorns shall come down with them, and the bullocks with the bulls; and their land shall be soaked with blood, and their dust made fat with fatness.
8 For it is the day of the LORD's vengeance, and the year of recompences for the controversy of Zion.
9 And the streams thereof shall be turned into pitch, and the dust

thereof into brimstone, and the land thereof shall become burning pitch.

10 It shall not be quenched night nor day; the smoke thereof shall go up for ever: from generation to generation it shall lie waste; none shall pass through it for ever and ever.

11 But the cormorant and the bittern shall possess it; the owl also and the raven shall dwell in it: and he shall stretch out upon it the line of confusion, and the stones of emptiness.

12 They shall call the nobles thereof to the kingdom, but none shall be there, and all her princes shall be nothing.

13 And thorns shall come up in her palaces, nettles and brambles in the fortresses thereof: and it shall be an habitation of dragons, and a court for owls. (KJV)

Ezekiel 35:14

14 Thus saith the Lord GOD; When the whole earth rejoiceth, I will make thee desolate. (KJV)

Isaiah 63:1-6

1 Who is this that cometh from Edom, with dyed garments from Bozrah? this that is glorious in his apparel, travelling in the greatness of his strength? I that speak in righteousness, mighty to save.

2 Wherefore art thou red in thine apparel, and thy garments like him that treadeth in the winefat?

3 I have trodden the winepress alone; and of the people there was none with me: for I will tread them in mine anger, and trample them in my fury; and their blood shall be sprinkled upon my garments, and I will stain all my raiment.

4 For the day of vengeance is in mine heart, and the year of my redeemed is come.

5 And I looked, and there was none to help; and I wondered that there was none to uphold: therefore mine own arm brought salvation unto me; and my fury, it upheld me.

6 And I will tread down the people in mine anger, and make them drunk in my fury, and I will bring down their strength to the earth. (KJV)

Isaiah 66:15-22

15 For, behold, the LORD will come with fire, and with his chariots like a whirlwind, to render his anger with fury, and his rebuke with flames

of fire.

16 For by fire and by his sword will the LORD plead with all flesh: and the slain of the LORD shall be many.

17 They that sanctify themselves, and purify themselves in the gardens behind one tree in the midst, eating swine's flesh, and the abomination, and the mouse, shall be consumed together, saith the LORD.

18 For I know their works and their thoughts: it shall come, that I will gather all nations and tongues; and they shall come, and see my glory.

19 And I will set a sign among them, and I will send those that escape of them unto the nations, to Tarshish, Pul, and Lud, that draw the bow, to Tubal, and Javan, to the isles afar off, that have not heard my fame, neither have seen my glory; and they shall declare my glory among the Gentiles.

20 And they shall bring all your brethren for an offering unto the LORD out of all nations upon horses, and in chariots, and in litters, and upon mules, and upon swift beasts, to my holy mountain Jerusalem, saith the LORD, as the children of Israel bring an offering in a clean vessel into the house of the LORD.

21 And I will also take of them for priests and for Levites, saith the LORD.

22 For as the new heavens and the new earth, which I will make, shall remain before me, saith the LORD, so shall your seed and your name remain. (KJV)

Isaiah 34:6, 8

...the Lord hath a sacrifice in Bozrah (a city in Edom, i.e., the Palestinian Arabs), and a great slaughter in the land of Idumea (the country of Edom)... For it is the day of the Lord's vengeance, and the year of recompenses for the controversy of Zion. (KJV)

Even a cursory analysis of the above passages in Isaiah show that the context is at the time of Armageddon. Therefore, we must conclude that the Palestinian Arabs are not completely destroyed until then.

"Cast lots upon Jerusalem." (Obadiah 11). Jerusalem is the target. Even though it belongs to the Jews historically and biblically, the Arabs want it, too. It is my understanding, however, that all Israelis, regardless of their political persuasion, are determined never to give it up to anyone. But, although God has said that Jerusalem belongs to the Jews, the Antichrist will boldly defy Him and try to give it to the Arabs instead.

Ezekiel 36:5, 8, 10, 11

5 Therefore thus saith the Lord GOD; Surely in the fire of my jealousy have I spoken against the residue of the heathen, and against all Idumea, which have appointed my land into their possession with the joy of all their heart, with despiteful minds, to cast it out for a prey.

8 But ye, O mountains of Israel, ye shall shoot forth your branches, and yield your fruit to my people of Israel; for they are at hand to come.

10 And I will multiply men upon you, all the house of Israel, even all of it: and the cities shall be inhabited, and the wastes shall be builded:

11 And I will multiply upon you man and beast; and they shall increase and bring fruit: and I will settle you after your old estates, and will do better unto you than at your beginnings: and ye shall know that I am the LORD. (KJV)

Deuteronomy 28:63-68

63 And it shall come to pass, that as the LORD rejoiced over you to do you good, and to multiply you; so the LORD will rejoice over you to destroy you, and to bring you to nought; and ye shall be plucked from off the land whither thou goest to possess it.

64 And the LORD shall scatter thee among all people, from the one end of the earth even unto the other; and there thou shalt serve other gods, which neither thou nor thy fathers have known, even wood and stone.

65 And among these nations shalt thou find no ease, neither shall the sole of thy foot have rest: but the LORD shall give thee there a trembling heart, and failing of eyes, and sorrow of mind:

66 And thy life shall hang in doubt before thee; and thou shalt fear day and night, and shalt have none assurance of thy life:

67 In the morning thou shalt say, Would God it were even! and at even thou shalt say, Would God it were morning! for the fear of thine heart wherewith thou shalt fear, and for the sight of thine eyes which thou shalt see.

68 And the LORD shall bring thee into Egypt again with ships, by the way whereof I spake unto thee, Thou shalt see it no more again: and there ye shall be sold unto your enemies for bondmen and bondwomen, and no man shall buy you. (KJV)

Verses 63-67 have been fulfilled historically. However, *Young's Literal Translation* gives us a more understandable rendering of verse 68:

Deuteronomy 28:68

68 And Jehovah hath brought thee back to Egypt with ships, by a way of which I said to thee, Thou dost not add any more to see it, and ye have sold yourselves there to thine enemies, for men-servants and for maid-servants, and there is no buyer. (YLT)

Apparently, large numbers of Jews, in a moment of desperation, will go to Egypt by way of ship. They are not sent there as slaves or prisoners; they voluntarily go there and try to sell their services as servants, but no one will take them up on their offer because the people of Egypt still consider themselves as enemies of the Jews despite their peace agreement with Israel. Thus, it is very possible that these Jews will be emigrating from Russia to Israel, and then suddenly find themselves with nowhere to go because the land of Israel will have fallen into enemy hands. Bear in mind it was estimated years ago that there probably are somewhere between one and two million Russian Jews waiting to emigrate to Israel. So, in view of recent reports that indicate anti-Semitic violence is escalating throughout Russia, emigration to Israel is becoming an urgent matter for many Russian Jews. Accordingly, the Jews now living in Russia could be a prime candidate for fulfilling this biblical prophecy. Alternatively, Jews living in Israel may fulfill this prophecy if they are forced to flee to Egypt when the Antichrist invades Israel.

It is under such drastic conditions as these that the Jews finally acknowledge God. It is then:

Ezekiel 20:33-38

Saith the Lord God.... I... will gather you out of the countries wherein ye are scattered.... with FURY poured out. And I will bring you into the wilderness of the people (a wilderness near Egypt) and there will I plead with you face to face. LIKE AS I PLEADED WITH YOUR FATHERS IN THE WILDERNESS OF THE LAND OF EGYPT, SO WILL I PLEAD WITH YOU.... And I will cause you to pass under the rod, AND I WILL BRING YOU INTO THE BOND OF THE COVENANT: And I will purge out from among you the rebels, and them that transgress against me.... and ye shall know that I am the Lord. (KJV)

Isaiah 11:11-16

11 And it shall come to pass in that day, that the Lord shall set his

hand again the second time to recover the remnant of his people, which shall be left, from Assyria, and from Egypt, and from Pathros, and from Cush, and from Elam, and from Shinar, and from Hamath, and from the islands of the sea.

12 And he shall set up an ensign for the nations, and shall assemble the outcasts of Israel, and gather together the dispersed of Judah from the four corners of the earth.

13 The envy also of Ephraim shall depart, and the adversaries of Judah shall be cut off: Ephraim shall not envy Judah, and Judah shall not vex Ephraim.

14 But they shall fly upon the shoulders of the Philistines toward the west; they shall spoil them of the east together: they shall lay their hand upon Edom and Moab; and the children of Ammon shall obey them.

15 And the LORD shall utterly destroy the tongue of the Egyptian sea; and with his mighty wind shall he shake his hand over the river, and shall smite it in the seven streams, and make men go over dryshod.

16 And there shall be an highway for the remnant of his people, which shall be left, from Assyria; like as it was to Israel in the day that he came up out of the land of Egypt. (KJV)

"Assyria." The modern-day countries which once comprised the ancient Assyrian Empire. These include Lebanon, Syria, Turkey, Iraq, and Jordan.

"Egypt." Probably the Jews who go to Egypt in ships.

"Pathros." Upper Egypt.

"Cush." Ethiopia and neighboring countries.

"Elam." Western part of Iran.

"Shinar." Ancient Babylon; Iraq.

"Hamath." Ancient city in upper Syria.

"Islands of the Sea." Idiomatic expression often used to indicate distant lands.

Immediately after the Jews repent and acknowledge God, they cross the Egyptian sea "dryshod" (just as their ancestors did centuries ago), and with God's help quickly recapture Jerusalem, destroying the military power of the Palestinian Arabs in the process. (Ezekiel 35 and 36:1-11) (Obadiah) (Isaiah 11:11-16). Please note that the Palestinian Arabs are only defeated and subdued by the Jews at this point in time; it is God who will destroy and annihilate them COMPLETELY at the Battle of

Armageddon (as previously noted). Furthermore, it is at the Battle of Armageddon that the land of the Palestinian Arabs is made "perpetual desolations." (Ezek. 35:3, 4, 7, 9, 14). Finally, when the Jews conquer the Palestinian Arabs, it is likely they will force the Arabs to go to Jordan (Edom; Idumea; city of Bozrah in southern Jordan, especially) because that is where the Arabs are living when the Lord annihilates them as punishment for their "perpetual hatred" of the Jews. (Isa. 34:1-13) (Isa. 63:1-6).

"But they shall fly upon the shoulders of the Philistines toward the west; they shall spoil them of the east together..." This passage probably means that the American military (Philistines; strangers) will help the Israelis recapture their country by providing airlift support and active military assistance and manpower. Only time will tell for sure if this is the intended meaning.

"Set up an ensign." The Hebrew word for ensign is NEC, and it means "flag" or "sail" or "generally a signal; figuratively, a token." It is possible that this could be the ancient ark of the covenant used to destroy Israel's enemies through the supernatural power of God. It is rumored, with evidence available to support such a claim, that the ark of the covenant has been hidden and guarded by Ethiopian priests down through the centuries. That possibility makes the following passage just that much more intriguing:

Isaiah 18:1-7

1 Woe to the land shadowing with wings, which is beyond the rivers of Ethiopia:

2 That sendeth ambassadors by the sea, even in vessels of bulrushes upon the waters, saying, Go, ye swift messengers, to a nation scattered and peeled, to a people terrible from their beginning hitherto; a nation meted out and trodden down, whose land the rivers have spoiled!

3 All ye inhabitants of the world, and dwellers on the earth, see ye, when he lifteth up an ensign on the mountains; and when he bloweth a trumpet, hear ye.

4 For so the LORD said unto me, I will take my rest, and I will consider in my dwelling place like a clear heat upon herbs, and like a cloud of dew in the heat of harvest.

5 For afore the harvest, when the bud is perfect, and the sour grape is ripening in the flower, he shall both cut off the sprigs with pruning hooks,

and take away and cut down the branches.

6 They shall be left together unto the fowls of the mountains, and to the beasts of the earth: and the fowls shall summer upon them, and all the beasts of the earth shall winter upon them.

7 In that time shall the present be brought unto the LORD of hosts of a people scattered and peeled, and from a people terrible from their beginning hitherto; a nation meted out and trodden under foot, whose land the rivers have spoiled, to the place of the name of the LORD of hosts, the mount Zion. (KJV)

"Beyond the rivers of Ethiopia." i.e., the land on the other side of the rivers of Ethiopia, which is, of course, Ethiopia.

"Land shadowing with wings." Possibly a reference to the fact that Ethiopia is one of the homes of the tsetse fly.

"Vessels of bulrushes." A clear reference to the papyrus plants that grew only in the vicinity of the Nile River.

"Scattered and peeled." A more accurate translation is "tall and smooth" or "tall and bronzed."

"When he lifteth up an ensign on the mountains; and when he bloweth a trumpet." It is demanded that the whole world take notice of what is happening.

"In that time shall the present (i.e., gift) be brought to the Lord...to Mount Zion." Verses 4 through 6 show that this "gift" is presented to the Lord during the end-times or time of the end. Perhaps, during the Second Crisis in the deserts between Egypt and the land of Israel, the Ethiopians will give the Ark to the Jews as a source of inspiration and Divine power to help them reclaim their land in Israel. Again, only time will tell for certain whether the Ark makes its reappearance during the Second Crisis or during the Third Crisis, Armageddon.

The appearance of the ark of the covenant during the Second Crisis could explain the following passage:

Jeremiah 3:16-18

16 And it shall come to pass, when ye be multiplied and increased in the land, in those days, saith the LORD, they shall say no more, The ark of the covenant of the LORD: neither shall it come to mind: neither shall they remember it; neither shall they visit it; neither shall that be done any more.

17 At that time they shall call Jerusalem the throne of the LORD; and all the nations shall be gathered unto it, to the name of the LORD, to Jerusalem: neither shall they walk any more after the imagination of their evil heart.

18 In those days the house of Judah shall walk with the house of Israel, and they shall come together out of the land of the north to the land that I have given for an inheritance unto your fathers. (KJV)

"Shall come together out of the land of the north." Compare:

Jeremiah 16:14-16

14 Therefore, behold, the days come, saith the LORD, that it shall no more be said, The LORD liveth, that brought up the children of Israel out of the land of Egypt;

15 But, The LORD liveth, that brought up the children of Israel from the land of the north, and from all the lands whither he had driven them: and I will bring them again into their land that I gave unto their fathers.

16 Behold, I will send for many fishers, saith the LORD, and they shall fish them; and after will I send for many hunters, and they shall hunt them from every mountain, and from every hill, and out of the holes of the rocks. (KJV)

Jeremiah 23:5-8

5 Behold, the days come, saith the LORD, that I will raise unto David a righteous Branch, and a King shall reign and prosper, and shall execute judgment and justice in the earth.

6 In his days Judah shall be saved, and Israel shall dwell safely: and this is his name whereby he shall be called, THE LORD OUR RIGHTEOUSNESS.

7 Therefore, behold, the days come, saith the LORD, that they shall no more say, The LORD liveth, which brought up the children of Israel out of the land of Egypt;

8 But, The LORD liveth, which brought up and which led the seed of the house of Israel out of the north country, and from all countries whither I had driven them; and they shall dwell in their own land. (KJV)

Jeremiah 31:7-12

7 For thus saith the LORD; Sing with gladness for Jacob, and shout

among the chief of the nations: publish ye, praise ye, and say, O LORD, save thy people, the remnant of Israel.

8 Behold, I will bring them from the north country, and gather them from the coasts of the earth, and with them the blind and the lame, the woman with child and her that travaileth with child together: a great company shall return thither.

9 They shall come with weeping, and with supplications will I lead them: I will cause them to walk by the rivers of waters in a straight way, wherein they shall not stumble: for I am a father to Israel, and Ephraim is my firstborn.

10 Hear the word of the LORD, O ye nations, and declare it in the isles afar off, and say, He that scattered Israel will gather him, and keep him, as a shepherd doth his flock.

11 For the LORD hath redeemed Jacob, and ransomed him from the hand of him that was stronger than he.

12 Therefore they shall come and sing in the height of Zion, and shall flow together to the goodness of the LORD, for wheat, and for wine, and for oil, and for the young of the flock and of the herd: and their soul shall be as a watered garden; and they shall not sorrow any more at all. (KJV)

The context for these passages clearly indicate this "Jewish return from the north" takes place after Armageddon is concluded and God's Kingdom is being established on the earth. That is why often it is taught that these Jews will be the Jews who are now living in Russia and are waiting to emigrate to Israel. However, if the Russian Jews go to Israel during, or immediately after, the Second Crisis, it would be quite natural for the Antichrist to send the "Russian Jews" back to Russia during the time of "Jacob's Trouble" immediately before Armageddon. Accordingly, that would explain the preceding passages very easily because the Antichrist could "send them back to where they came from" during the time of Jacob's Trouble when the Jews are sent into captivity to all the nations of the world.

Finally, there is no question that the dramatic fulfillment of prophecy during the Second Crisis will be quite astounding, so it is only natural to question whether the preceding passages actually deal with Armageddon, and not an earlier crisis as we are suggesting. However, a Second Crisis does eliminate the perplexing mass of contradictions noted in various prophecies concerning Israel during the "latter days." For example, there are several scriptures which state that the nations of earth gladly help the Jews return to Israel, one by one, AFTER Armageddon (Third Crisis) is over. These friendly and helpful acts of assistance obviously are peaceful in nature, and they occur after ALL military conflict has ended. (Isa. 14:2) (Isa. 27:12, 13) (Isa. 30:15) (Jer. 32:37-44) (Isa.49:22) (Isa. 66:19-21) (Jer. 16:16) (Jer. 31:6-12).

Now contrast that peaceful, individualized return of the Jews with the VIOLENT conditions surrounding the sudden, mass return of the Jews at the time of the Second Crisis when they retake the land of Israel by subjugating the Palestinian Arabs. There is no discernable way for these extreme differences to be reconciled with each other to fit the same set of circumstances. Therefore, we must conclude there are two separate and distinct returns to Israel which will be experienced by the Jews. One of them will involve a sudden, mass return of the Jews amidst very violent circumstances which conclude with the military conquest of the Palestinian Arabs, while the other Jewish return will involve a gradual return of individuals, one by one, in a very peaceful and friendly environment after all military conflict has ended and Christ, personally, has annihilated the Palestinian Arabs who will be living in southern Jordan at the time of Armageddon!

There is absolutely no doubt that Daniel 8:9 portrays the "little horn" Antichrist suddenly appearing and almost immediately waxing "exceeding great" by conquering armies with lightning speed in a southern and eastern direction, and in the "pleasant land" Israel. Therefore, this passage — by itself — establishes beyond any reasonable doubt that the Antichrist will invade Israel during his initial ascendancy to power and prominence! Accordingly, this scripture likewise necessitates a Second Crisis.

Furthermore, we know from various scriptures that the temple in Jerusalem will be rebuilt before Armageddon, and that the twice-daily Mosaic sacrifices will be observed until they are abolished by the Antichrist, three and one-half years before the Battle of Armageddon. (Matt. 24:15) (Dan. 8:11-14) (Dan. 9:27) (II Thess. 2:3, 4) (Rev. 11:1, 2). Therefore, this scriptural fact proves that the secular Jewish state of Israel will acknowledge God and conform to the terms of their ancient covenant in the near future. Obviously this collective Israeli conversion most likely will take place during the Second Crisis when God pleads with them "face to face" and brings them "into the bond of the covenant" (Ezek. 20:33-38).

Since the Jewish temple is rebuilt well in advance of Armageddon, another interesting consideration comes to mind almost immediately. Logic would dictate that the military power of the Arabs would have to be completely broken BEFORE the Jews would ever dare the rebuilding of their temple. Under no circumstances would the Arab-world allow the temple to be rebuilt over the site of their third most important shrine, Dome of the Rock, if they were in a position to prevent it. This fact, too, would seem to necessitate a Second Crisis.

We should note, however, that in recent years, there has been some speculation that the Jewish Temple actually was located on a site which was a short distance from where the Dome of the Rock is located. At this point in time, no one knows for sure just what is the truth concerning the Jewish Temple location. But the Second Crisis, especially if the ark of the covenant makes its appearance, will make it possible to build the Jewish temple wherever it belongs.

Yet another scriptural consideration involves the following passage:

Ezekiel 38:8

8 After many days thou shalt be visited: in the latter years thou shalt come into the land that is brought back from the sword, and is gathered out of many people, against the mountains of Israel, which have been always waste: but it is brought forth out of the nations, and they shall dwell safely all of them. (KJV)

Most Bible scholars and commentators agree that the contextual time-element for this passage is near the time of Armageddon. Therefore, please note that the wording of this scripture strongly implies that the Second Crisis, indeed, will have occurred sometime before then. For instance, the phrase, "Land that is brought back from the sword, and is gathered out of many people," certainly seems to describe the mass return of Jews who are gathered from many different countries throughout the world and who then collectively go back into Israel and re-take it militarily.

Parenthetically, the following phrase, "Mountains of Israel, which have been always waste," is an important and exciting indication of the time element involved! For centuries, Palestine was a barren desert land, and it has only been within the last few decades that it has begun to "blossom like a rose" due to the partial return of the Jews. Therefore, since the prosperity of the land has already begun, that means everything foretold to happen during the end-times must happen soon, or it would not be possible for this passage to say that the land of Israel has "always been waste."

"And dwelt safely have all of them," is the translation that *Young's Literal Translation* gives the last phrase of verse 8. After the Israelis regain their land during the Second Crisis, they will live in peace and security for a number of years — even after the Rapture when the rest of the world is filled with death and violence and famine and plagues. But, it is very difficult to imagine how the Israelis could live in complete peace and security, without any fear or concern for their enemies, so long as the Palestinian Arabs are nearby, hating them while coveting the city of Jerusalem and the land of Israel. That is why a Second Crisis seems so necessary.

Reading the following verse of scripture for an additional proof:

Ezekiel 38:11

And thou shalt say, I will go up to the land of UNWALLED villages; I will go up to THEM THAT ARE AT REST, THAT DWELL SAFELY, all of them dwelling without walls and having neither bars nor gates. (KJV)

This peaceful and secure situation for Israel is a repeat of what we just saw above in verse 8. A Second Crisis seems very essential to eliminating the militant threat currently posed by the Palestinian Arabs.

Yet another additional consideration:

Ezekiel 39:21-29

And the HEATHEN (nations) SHALL KNOW THAT THE HOUSE OF ISRAEL WENT INTO CAPTIVITY (during a three and one-half year period of time just before Armageddon) FOR THEIR INIQUITY (apparently the Jewish nation will have served God for a short while prior to this captivity): because they trespassed against me, therefore hid I my face from them, and gave them into the hand of their enemies.... Now will I BRING AGAIN THE CAPTIVITY OF JACOB.... THEY... TRESPASSED AGAINST ME, WHEN THEY DWELT SAFELY IN THEIR LAND.... Neither will I hide my face any more from them.... (KJV) (cf. Ezek. 36:12-38; 37:15-28.)

In the above passage, I have excerpted important portions of verses 21 through 29, some of which are highlighted further through the use of CAP letters, which briefly outline events foretold to happen in Israel during the endtimes. Please note that this passage also necessitates a Second Crisis in order to make it possible for the Jews in Israel to backslide into sin and secularism during a period of absolute peace and security.

Finally, please bear in mind that two future crises seem necessary for Israel because the singular objective for the Second Crisis will be to force the Jews into collective acknowledgement of God, while the Third Crisis (Armageddon) will end in recognition of Christ as their Messiah. (Rom. 11:25, 26) (Zech. 12:10). Accordingly, the apparent need for two different crises which involve two completely different objectives and two completely different outcomes seemingly mandates a Second Crisis event. Therefore, our only reasonable and scriptural conclusion must be that a Second Crisis will, indeed, occur! Furthermore, a return to spiritual obedience by the Jews during the Second Crisis will set the stage for a return to the Dispensation of Law (Daniel's 70th Week) which will commence three and one-half years after the Rapture when the Dispensation of Grace ends.

Daniel's 70th Week

Daniel 9:24-27

24 Seventy weeks are determined upon thy people and upon thy holy city, to finish the transgression, and to make an end of sins, and to make reconciliation for iniquity, and to bring in everlasting righteousness, and to seal up the vision and prophecy, and to anoint the most Holy.

25 Know therefore and understand, that from the going forth of the commandment to restore and to build Jerusalem unto the Messiah the Prince shall be seven weeks, and threescore and two weeks: the street shall be built again, and the wall, even in troublous times.

26 And after threescore and two weeks shall Messiah be cut off, but not for himself: and the people of the prince that shall come shall destroy the city and the sanctuary; and the end thereof shall be with a flood, and unto the end of the war desolations are determined.

27 And he shall confirm the covenant with many for one week: and in the midst of the week he shall cause the sacrifice and the oblation to cease, and for

the overspreading of abominations he shall make it desolate, even until the consummation, and that determined shall be poured upon the desolate. (KJV)

Daniel was given this vision in response to his prayerful concerns about the fate of the Babylonian Jews who supposedly would return to Jerusalem after their 70-year captivity was completed. In the Hebrew, the text literally reads "seventy sevens," NOT "seventy weeks." The Jews were familiar with a "seven" (SHABUA) of both days and years, but we are going to assume it means years because the resultant dates associated with the predicted events match secular historical records.

"To finish (put an end to) the transgression." The Hebrew word "pesha" means revolt; rebel; sin against lawful authority. It is often translated as "transgression" throughout the Old Testament. (Ps. 51:1) (Isa. 43:25; etc.). This passage states that God's ultimate objective is for Israel to put an end to all of their sins (in one day) when they are saved at the time of the Second Coming of Christ, their long-awaited Messiah. (Rom. 11:25-29) (Isa. 66:7-10) (Ezek. 36:24-30).

"To make an end of sins." Once again, this is a direct reference to all of Israel, including Jerusalem, experiencing a cleansing of all of their sins at the time of the Second Coming of Christ (Ezek. 36:24-30) (Ezek. 37:24-27) (Ezek. 43:7) (Zech. 14). God will pour out His Spirit of repentance upon all of Israel just before the Second Coming, and they will be saved as a nation in one day. (Zech. 12:10 - 3:1) (Rom. 11:25-29).

"To make reconciliation (Hebrew word "kaphar" meaning to cover; make atonement) for iniquity." This was accomplished for everyone, including Israel, by Christ Jesus on the cross at Calvary (Isa. 53) (Col. 1:20) (Col. 2:14-17) (I Peter 2:24), but Israel collectively, as a nation, rejected Jesus as their Messiah so they have not yet experienced this atonement for their sins. However, they will be fully reconciled to God at the Second Coming of Christ during the Battle of Armageddon. (Isa. 1:18-20) (Isaiah 66:7-8) (Zech. 12:10 - 13:1) (Matt. 23:37-39) (Romans 11:25-29).

"To bring in everlasting righteousness." After all of Israel's sins and transgressions have been ended through national repentance and they have experienced a complete atonement for all of their sins through Christ Jesus, their Messiah, then everlasting righteousness will be ushered in. (Isa. 9:6-7) (Isa. 12:1-6) (Dan. 2:44-45) (Dan. 7:13-14, 18, 27) (Ezek. 43:7) (Zech. 14) (Luke 1:32-33) (Romans 11:25-29) (Rev. 11:15) (Rev.

19:11 - 20:10) (Rev. 21:1 - 22:5).

"To seal up the vision and prophecy." All of this prophecy will be fulfilled completely, so it will become a closed matter.

"To anoint the most holy." The Holy of Holies, the temple and the city of Jerusalem all will be completely cleansed of past sins and sacrileges, and then the Millennial temple will be anointed. (Ezek. 40-43) (Zech. 6:12-13). This has to be the meaning intended by this passage because the expression "most holy" is never used of any person, including the Messiah; the Jews always refer to their Messiah as simply "Messiah." Furthermore, God the Father already has anointed Christ Jesus, so there is no need to anoint Him again. (Luke 22:29) (Acts 1:7) (Acts 2:36) (Phil. 2:9-11) (Heb. 1:1-3) (Rev. 11:15) (Rev. 19:11-21) (Dan. 7:13-14).

"To restore and to build Jerusalem." Actually, there were three different decrees for the restoration of Jerusalem. The first decree was given during the first year of the reign of Cyrus, king of Persia (Ezra 1:1-4; Ezra 3:8; Isa. 44:28; Isa. 45:1-4; Isa. 46:11). Cyrus reigned 9 years; then Cambyses, his son, reigned 7 years. It was during the son's reign that the work on the temple ceased. (Ezra 4:1-24).

The second decree was issued by Darius I when he confirmed the decree made by Cyrus 18 years earlier. However, although the temple in Jerusalem was finished during the sixth year of his reign, the city was not restored then. Then later, Xerxes reigned for 21 years (Dan. 11:1-3) during which time the city still was never completed.

Then finally, the third and final decree was issued by Artaxerxes, who reigned for 40 years. It was during the 20th year of his reign (445 B.C.) that he gave Nehemiah the third decree "to restore and to build Jerusalem unto the Messiah the Prince." (Dan. 9:25-26) (Neh. 2:1 - 6:19). It is from this point in time, i.e., 445 B.C., that the 70 weeks or 490 years start counting down. This is when the first segment of the 490 years (i.e., the 7 weeks or 49 years necessary for the complete restoration of Jerusalem) began. (Dan. 9:25). Likewise, although Nehemiah restored the walls in only 52 days after reaching Jerusalem, this by no means was the full restoration predicted by prophecy. The complete fulfillment of prophecy required 49 years. Therefore, the third decree to restore Jerusalem was 92 years after the initial decree was issued by Cyrus.

The "commandment to restore and to build Jerusalem" was given (Neh. 2:1-8) in 445 B.C., and Daniel says that it took "7 weeks" (49 years) for this commandment to be complied with fully. Daniel further states that "62 weeks" after the rebuilding of Jerusalem was completed, Jesus was to come as the Messiah and then "be cut off" (crucified). This means we have a total of "69 weeks" (483 years) from the commandment to the "official" presentation of Jesus as Messiah on Palm Sunday, April 6, 32 A.D.. (Luke 19:38-44).

This date of April 6, 32 A.D. is determined in the following manner. By employing a lunar calendar count (as implied by other scriptures; Dan. 7:24, 25; Rev. 12:6, 13, 14; 13:4-7), and starting with the date March 14, 445 B.C. (cf. Neh. 2:1), these 483 "years" are calculated as follows. 69 "Weeks" x 7 years x 360 days = 173,880 days; 173,880 days from March 14, 445 B.C. gives the date of April 6, 32 A.D.. (See *Evidence That Demands A Verdict* by Josh McDowell, pgs.180, 181.)

Daniel 9:26

26 And after threescore and two weeks shall Messiah be cut off (i.e., crucified), but not for himself: and the people (i.e., people who lived within the old Roman Empire) of the prince that shall come (i.e., Antichrist, the prince) shall destroy the city (i.e., Jerusalem) and the sanctuary (i.e., the Jewish Temple; fulfilled by the Romans in 70 A.D.); and the end thereof shall be with a flood, and unto the end of the war desolations are determined. (KJV)

The Jews rejected Christ as their Messiah and so the "gospel" was given to the world, thereby beginning the Dispensation of Grace while postponing the 70th Week (which is the remainder of the Dispensation of Law which began when Moses revealed God's Laws for the nation of Israel). Furthermore, the 70th Week will remain postponed until sometime AFTER the Rapture.

Daniel 9:27

27 And he (i.e., Antichrist, the prince) shall confirm the covenant (i.e., Israel's covenant with God giving them the land of Israel) with many for one week (i.e., 7 years): and in the midst of the week he shall cause the sacrifice and the oblation to cease, and for the overspreading of abominations he shall make it desolate, even until the consummation, and that determined shall be poured upon the desolate. (KJV)

It is midway through this 70th Week that the "prince that shall come"

(Antichrist) will violate the terms of his seven year treaty with the Jewish nation. This violation will include the desecration (i.e., "make it desolate") of the rebuilt temple in Jerusalem and the abolishment of the twice-daily sacrifices so necessary for adherence to Jewish Law. (Matt. 24:15) (Dan. 8:11-14) (II Thess. 2:3, 4) (Rev. 11:1, 2) (Dan. 12:11).

"Until the consummation." Until the end of the 70th Week.

"Upon the desolate." Not upon the desolate places, but upon the Antichrist who makes the rebuilt temple desolate for three and one-half years until Armageddon. *Young's Literal Translation* makes it quite clear that it is the person, Antichrist, who is desolate:

Daniel 9:27

And he hath strengthened a covenant with many—one week, and in the midst of the week he causeth sacrifice and present to cease, and by the wing of abominations he is making desolate, even till the consummation, and that which is determined is poured on the desolate one. (YLT)

III. World Peace And Prosperity

World Economic Prosperity

The initial rise of Antichrist to world power and prominence will result in dramatic changes throughout all of society! One of the more notable developments will be the eventual establishment of a world-economy so prosperous that it will seem almost like a "golden age of prosperity" for all of humanity! But how could one man, in just a few short years, be responsible, single-handedly, for transforming the earth into a virtual economic paradise? Because Daniel states that "by PEACE shall (Antichrist) destroy (deceive, and thereby doom) many." (Dan. 8:25). According to *Strong's Hebrew-Greek Dictionary*, the Hebrew word translated here as peace is SHALVAH, and its complete, full meaning involves a condition of peace, security, prosperity, and abundance! Therefore, a more accurate translation of this passage might better read, "by extraordinary prosperity and peace shall (Antichrist) destroy many."

Accordingly, what if someone could seemingly be invincible, and thereby be in a position to enforce an absolute condition of peace and security for the world? Obviously under such conditions, the nations of earth no longer would find it necessary to spend fantastic sums of money on military capabilities, but instead, could invest their capital and people's creative energies in various economic projects and initiatives. Likewise, the continued trend toward common market arrangements among the nations (thereby setting the stage for a world common market system) would lend further support and encouragement to the expansion of world trade and commerce, a development which also would induce greater over-all prosperity. Furthermore, the growing realization and understanding throughout most of the world that free market economies are much more efficient and productive than regulated economies also holds promise of greater prosperity in the years ahead. All of these developments, therefore, if continued, could lead to a greater level of prosperity for the world in general.

The elimination of artificial trade-barriers (via a common market system) greatly enhances prosperity because it encourages everyone (individuals, regions, nations, etc.) to concentrate on whatever it is that they can produce most efficiently. Obviously if everyone is producing more efficiently and productively, then there are more material goods and services available to everyone, which is, of course, the definition of prosperity. No longer would an individual or nation expend time, energy and resources on producing something that another individual or nation could produce more efficiently because of an advantage in location, experience, availability of natural resources (thus reducing transportation costs), natural abilities, technical expertise, existing highly-specialized production facilities, more appropriate infrastructure, etc., etc..

So, as more trade barriers and regulatory restrictions are reduced or eliminated, and the government does not regulate monetary and economic activities very excessively, then increased economic prosperity for everyone must result. However, we should note also that this by no means describes the situation we have with contemporary trade treaties which attempt to control and regulate relatively freer markets in a hybrid mixture of socialism and free enterprise. Aside from the fact that these flawed treaties are designed to enhance and encourage the eventual creation of a unified political and economic world government mechanism of tyrannical proportions, they are so heavily loaded with all kinds of restrictions, stipulations and regulations that they make these treaties nothing more than systems of regulatory-style socialism which capitalize on free market principles even though they are touted as prime examples of a free market system. But, admittedly, on the other hand, such hybrid trading arrangements are much better, from an economic perspective, than are absolute trade barriers from the past.

However, a free market economy is much more productive and efficient than a highly-regulated economy for several basic reasons. For instance, it is self-evident that people tend to pursue their own self-interest according to their scale of values because no matter what a person may do, he does it because at that point in time it is most important compared to any alternatives based on circumstances and personal values and priorities. Of course, people often may make mistakes, but they always do what they think best in order to achieve their objectives. Therefore, it follows that business men generally strive to be efficient, productive and responsive to consumer wishes as much as possible in order to maximize profits, other things being equal.

In other words, no business man will try to make a "small" profit when it would be just as easy to make a "big" profit with the same degree of effort and set of circumstances. Accordingly, whenever a business man is forced to act differently than he would have preferred due to laws and regulations, he is, in essence, forced into becoming less efficient or less responsive to consumer wishes, thereby lowering the over-all level of prosperity. Obviously as more laws hamper the economy, the less prosperous the economy becomes.

Of course, some laws are necessary in order to restrain and punish forceful and fraudulent aggressions (including things such as pollution, dangerously defective products, etc.). But it is absurd to think that the collective knowledge and wisdom of a few bureaucrats and politicians is superior to the collective knowledge and wisdom of everyone embodied in the voluntary cooperation of a free market system. Likewise, government bureaucracies are usually less efficient and less responsive to consumer wishes than are private enterprises because they are not naturally regulated by the need to make a profit while meeting market competition. Anyone who has been in the real world of business knows how important these factors are in motivating people to work as hard and smart as possible.

Striving to achieve a truly free society may seem controversial or impractical to many people, but it is an ideal advocated in both the American Declaration of Independence (and supported by the U.S. Constitution) and the Christian Bible. Accordingly, one of the most important issues facing our society today is the collective decision regarding the extent to which society and government should impose their collective will on everyone through the passage of laws, regulations and taxes. Although most people never would dream of going to their neighbor's house to rob them of their property or to dictate the details of their social and economic affairs, it somehow seems proper (despite the logical inconsistency) for people to band together in the voting booth and democratically authorize the government to do so for almost any reason conceivable. The result, quite naturally, is an increasingly fragmented, envy-oriented society in which everyone legally plunders and tyrannizes everyone else.

However, it is my contention that in a pluralistic society, all social and economic relationships should be peaceful and voluntary in nature, and that each person should be left alone and free to do whatever he or she pleases so long as that person does not harm others or threaten to harm others through the use of force or fraud or theft. Although there are a few absolutely-necessary exceptions we will discuss in a moment, to disagree on this point is simply another way of saying that some people have the right to use legal or illegal methods to impose their personal viewpoints and opinions on others against their will. Therefore, I should not impose my ethic on you, nor should you try to impose your ethic on me, except in the most extreme situations involving forceful or fraudulent aggressions. Obviously this principle of non-aggression becomes especially important as we observe growing tendencies in our society, and throughout the world, to pass laws and regulations which attack the basic human rights of Christian believers in a wide variety of ways.

Furthermore, to be consistent, the prohibition against forceful and fraudulent aggressions should include both the physical and the mental. What I mean by this is that whether or not you accept the validity of the Christian Bible and its teachings concerning the moral qualities and spiritual identity of man, it can not be denied that man has always been observed as having moral motions of the conscience by which he has judged the actions of others if not always his own. Although moral standards have varied from culture to culture, certain things generally have been viewed as wrong in theory if not always in practice. Among these are non-physical violations such as libel, slander, blackmail, verbal abuse, vulgar language, and pornography. So, when I say that psychological aggressions should be prohibited, what I mean by this is that people should not be subjected to such things against their will, nor should they even be allowed at all to the extent it can reasonably be demonstrated that harm to other individuals inevitably results as a consequence. Therefore, in essence, what I am advocating for our pluralistic society is a more-consistent application of the neutral principle of non-aggression in every area of life.

One partial exception to all of this would be matters pertaining to children. Obviously parents (or society, if necessary) have a natural and God-given right to impose reasonable standards of decency and education on their children. Although parents do not have the right to subject their children to obvious physical or psychological abuse, they do have the duty and the right to impose proper values and learning. Naturally, some people might object that making children a partial exception to the principle of non-aggression violates the rule of logical consistency. But, then I would point out that no moral principle is completely autonomous to itself. Just as freedom should not be autonomous, neither should the principle of non-aggression be completely autonomous.

That is why Christians can say God is a God of love and mercy, but also a God of justice and judgment. Complexity, not contradiction, is involved in such instances. In other words, when moral laws and principles come into direct and unavoidable conflict with each other, and due to circumstances, it is impossible to comply with all of the moral principles relevant to the matter, then it is our moral duty and obligation to choose the highest level of good possible under the circumstances. Which means, of course, that we must violate one moral principle in order to make it even possible to comply with another more-important and relevant moral principle. For example, if telling a lie was the only reasonable way possible to save an innocent life from an undeserved death or murder, then obviously we should do so because the higher law (preservation of innocent life) should take precedence over the lower law (truth), as in the following biblical example:

Josh. 2:3-4
3 And the king of Jericho sent unto Rahab, saying, Bring forth the men that are come to thee, which are entered into thine house: for they be come to search out all the country.
4 And the woman took the two men, and hid them, and said thus, There came men unto me, but I wist not whence they were: (KJV)

Heb. 11:31
31 By faith the harlot Rahab perished not with them that believed not, when she had received the spies with peace. (KJV)

James 2:25-26
25 Likewise also was not Rahab the harlot justified by works, when she had received the messengers, and had sent them out another way?
26 For as the body without the spirit is dead, so faith without works is dead also. (KJV)

The preceding scriptures we have just read portray an example whereby God accounted an individual as righteous when they were forced to tell a lie in order to save the lives of innocent human beings. Now compare this example with the following one:

Exodus 1:15-21
15 And the king of Egypt spake to the Hebrew midwives, of which the

name of the one was Shiphrah, and the name of the other Puah:

16 And he said, When ye do the office of a midwife to the Hebrew women, and see them upon the stools; if it be a son, then ye shall kill him: but if it be a daughter, then she shall live.

17 But the midwives feared God, and did not as the king of Egypt commanded them, but saved the men children alive.

18 And the king of Egypt called for the midwives, and said unto them, Why have ye done this thing, and have saved the men children alive?

19 And the midwives said unto Pharaoh, Because the Hebrew women are not as the Egyptian women; for they are lively, and are delivered ere the midwives come in unto them.

20 Therefore God dealt well with the midwives: and the people multiplied, and waxed very mighty.

21 And it came to pass, because the midwives feared God, that he made them houses. (KJV)

Here is yet another example where God looked very favorably upon individuals who lied in order to save innocent human life. The midwives, in this instance, very courageously lied to the Pharaoh because it was the only practical way of saving the innocent Hebrew babies from being slaughtered. Likewise, the following passage actually portrays God instructing an innocent individual to lie so that he would not be killed unfairly and unjustly:

1 Sam. 16:1-5

1 And the LORD said unto Samuel, How long wilt thou mourn for Saul, seeing I have rejected him from reigning over Israel? fill thine horn with oil, and go, I will send thee to Jesse the Bethlehemite: for I have provided me a king among his sons.

2 And Samuel said, How can I go? if Saul hear it, he will kill me. And the LORD said, Take an heifer with thee, and say, I am come to sacrifice to the LORD.

3 And call Jesse to the sacrifice, and I will shew thee what thou shalt do: and thou shalt anoint unto me him whom I name unto thee.

4 And Samuel did that which the LORD spake, and came to Bethlehem. And the elders of the town trembled at his coming, and said, Comest thou peaceably?

5 And he said, Peaceably: I am come to sacrifice unto the LORD:

sanctify yourselves, and come with me to the sacrifice. And he sanctified Jesse and his sons, and called them to the sacrifice. (KJV)

Some people might argue that God did not really tell Samuel to lie because when Samuel told anyone that he was there to make a sacrifice to the Lord (as God instructed him to do if anyone should inquire as to why he was going to Bethlehem), he was telling the truth. But truth-telling, in its fullest, complete sense of the meaning, is not necessarily limited to the strict semantic sense of the words employed by a person, but rather, it is the impression or message which a person intends for his audience to receive when he or she is communicating ideas through words and gestures and overall demeanor.

That is why in our judicial system, a person promises to tell the truth, the whole truth, and nothing but the truth. A seemingly redundant pledge of this type is necessary because it is very possible to deceive people by giving only completely truthful statements while still withholding vital information which prevents the audience from understanding the entire situation correctly. But, sometimes, making truthful statements in order to deceive someone about the whole truth of a matter, as in the above example, is morally justifiable because they involve situations where one is forced by circumstances to choose between two evil actions or consequences in an effort to choose the highest level of good possible when no completely good options exist.

Therefore, clearly there does exist a biblical hierarchy of moral values which should govern all of our thoughts and actions in life, shaping our decisions into conformity with the revealed Divine nature of our Creator. See the following scriptural references for additional scriptural support on these matters: John 19:11; Matt. 5:19; Matt. 23:23; Acts 5:29; James 4:17; Heb. 11:17; II Kings 6:8-23; II Kings 7:5-7; Genesis 9:6; 14. Also, compare Hebrews 4:15 and I John 3:4 and II Corinthians 5:21 and I Peter 1:19 with Luke 2:44-49; and compare Leviticus 5:1 with Matthew 27:12-14.

Likewise, for the same reason, another partial exception to the principle of non-aggression involves the duty of government to protect people and their property against aggression and to settle honest disputes. In other words, forceful aggression, or the threat thereof, in the form of policemen, soldiers, courts, health and pollution officers, etc., is necessary in order to perform legitimate protective and meditative functions. Since taxes are necessary to the maintenance of protective and meditative forces, the forcible extraction of reasonable taxes, if necessary, is also justifiable. Furthermore, people even have the right, individually, to defend against any type of aggression (in an appropriate and reasonable manner that utilizes the lowest level of force or deceit or evasion possible) if the government, for whatever reason, can not or will not do so. In all of these instances, the individual and/or collective right to survival and self-defense outweighs the rule of non-aggression.

Finally, as one last example of an absolutely-essential exception, people's common sense of decency and compassion dictates that forcibly-extracted taxes also should be used to help people in health-or-life-threatening situations if no other reasonable and practical recourse (such as private charity) is available. If someone is in a position where they clearly can not help themselves even though their health or life is threatened by the lack of food, or shelter, or medical care, and so on, then again, the value of innocent human life should out-weigh the rule of non-aggression, and that person should be granted assistance. So, in summary, the ideal government in a highly diverse, pluralistic society such as ours is one which does not perpetrate aggression (via laws, regulations and taxes) except to the extent absolutely necessary for compliance with higher moral values involving the protection and preservation of innocent life, freedom and property rights.

Of course, if you are a Christian you also can appeal to the ultimate authority and source of individual rights and responsibilities, i.e., the personal, infinite, triune God of the Christian Bible. As a Christian, you can point to the pertinent evidence of history, science, ethics, values, and psychology as proof that Christianity is objective truth (e.g., see *Testing Christianity's Truth Claims* by Gordan R. Lewis; and *Evidence That Demands A Verdict* by Josh McDowell), and say that God, the Creator, is the ultimate reality and source of goodness. As such, you can say that man has tremendous value and worth because we are made in God's image and likeness, and because God loved us so much that Jesus died on the cross for our sins. (Genesis 1:27, 31; 9:6) (James 3:9) (Ps. 8:3-8) (Matt. 6:26; 22:39) (I Cor. 6:20) (I Peter 1:18, 19) (John 3:16) (Eph. 5:30, 31) (Ps. 139:14).

Accordingly, this exalted view of man (despite his morally-fallen condition) has important implications for every aspect of life, including his relationship to government. Moreover, since God is both infinite and perfectly good, we have a very firm basis for our moral values by which we can judge the actions of our government. Therefore, it is not surprising to find that the Bible very emphatically teaches that every individual has the God-given right to life, liberty, and property, and that government's primary function is simply "to execute wrath upon him that doeth evil" (John 10:10) (III John 2) (II Corinthians 3:17) (James 1:25; 2:12) (Galatians 5:1; 6:7) (Romans 8:21) (Luke 19:12-26) (Matthew 7:12; 16:27; 25:14-30) (Gen. 1:26-28; 9:1-7) (Exodus 20:12-17) (Revelation 22:12) (cf. Titus 3:1 and Romans 13:1-10 and I Peter 2:13-14 and Luke 20:25 with Acts 5:29). Although, for now, we may have to fight for these rights (in an appropriate manner), at least, ultimately, they are not dependent upon the whims and passions and appetites of government officials and voting majorities.

It was generally this philosophical "world-view" of reality that prompted our Founding Fathers in the United States to establish a very limited constitutional Republic form of government; a government which allowed people freely to pursue their own interests so long as they did not initiate force or fraud or thievery against others. To paraphrase Thomas Jefferson: "The primary function of government is simply to restrain people from injuring one another, but otherwise leaving them free to regulate their own pursuits in life."

Accordingly, we can say it is wrong when people use the government to plunder and rob others — and this is precisely what happens whenever taxpayers and consumers and employers are forced by law to support tariffs, subsidies, loans, benefits, guarantees of any type, monopolies, charities, pensions, wage and price controls, insurance programs, and so on, from which others benefit. Therefore, any law which benefits some people at the expense of others — a law which takes any type of property from some people and gives it to others to whom it does not belong — is wrong and should be abolished as quickly as possible unless it functions as a last-resort or "safety-net" type of welfare program.

That is why we also can say it is wrong for the government (and the banking system) to counterfeit money — which is precisely what is does whenever it inflates (increases) the quantity of money and credit in our country in order to help pay for its vast array of socialistic spending programs. It is wrong, first of all, because it results in more dollars competing for the goods and services available in our economy, thus bidding prices upward (assuming all other factors remain constant).

Obviously whoever gets the new money first benefits at the expense of everybody else.

In other words, money and credit inflation cause price inflation which, in turn, dilutes the value of your money and redistributes that lost value to those people who first receive the new money. Monetary and credit inflation also are wrong because they create malinvestments (i.e., misguided investments) due to significant distortions in the price mechanism which serves as the information center for a free market economy. Although it is true that in the early stages of monetary and credit inflation, a false economic boom will occur, eventually — just like a drug addict — larger and larger doses will be needed just to get the same degree of stimulation. Therefore, false inflationary prosperity not only results in the creation of long-term economic problems, but is financed through the subtle transfer and theft of personal wealth via inflation.

It is very possible that the Antichrist will achieve a quick economic prosperity for the world through this immoral method. It is even quite plausible when you consider the fact that there is considerable political pressure already for a massive redistribution-of-wealth from the "richer" countries to the "less fortunate" ones. Obviously the current trend toward a global money system, if realized, would greatly facilitate such an endeavor because if the world becomes united, economically, and standardized on one currency or monetary unit, then all that would be required to effect massive transfers of wealth would be the creation of new "credit money" in centralized computers. So if, and when, we attain a "cashless" society, whereby all buying and selling is transacted through one giant computer system, it could be achieved quite easily. In other words, it would be a very easy matter for the Antichrist to play "Santa Claus" to the world-at-large!

This type of mind-set helps to explain the meaning of Daniel 11:39: "...and he (Antichrist) shall cause them to rule over many, and shall divide the land for gain." *Strong's Hebrew-Greek Dictionary* sheds additional light on the interpretation of this passage. The word "divide" in the Hebrew is CHALAQ, and it means "to be smooth" figuratively, and by implication to mean "apportion" or "separate" in the sense of "distribute, divide, flatter." The Hebrew word for "land" is ADAMAH, and it means "soil, ground, earth." The Hebrew for "gain" is MeCHIYR, and it means "price, payment, wages." Therefore, the implication of flattery seemingly is involved in this distribution of land and natural resources by Antichrist.

Sometimes it is said that Daniel 11:24 speaks along these same lines concerning the Antichrist:

Daniel 11:24

24 He shall enter peaceably even upon the fattest places of the province; and he shall do that which his fathers have not done, nor his fathers' fathers; he shall scatter among them the prey, and spoil, and riches: yea, and he shall forecast his devices against the strong holds, even for a time. (KJV)

However, the evidence would seem to indicate otherwise. For example, *Dake's Annotated Reference Bible* offers very detailed and convincing explanations in support of an ancient historical fulfillment for Daniel 11:1-34. Likewise, all of Daniel's fourth vision involves literal language only; there is no obvious indication that any symbolism is employed anywhere throughout the vision. Accordingly, there is no apparent justification for taking some of the verses in this passage and giving them a symbolic interpretation in order to lead into the Antichrist.

If we were to interpret this vision so that the Antichrist actually made his initial appearance in verse 20 of this passage, then the fourth vision would contradict other passages in the Bible concerning the exploits and projected history of Antichrist. For example, verse 20 allegedly describes the initial rise of Antichrist and his "deadly wound" as mentioned in Revelation 13: "Then shall stand up in his estate a raiser of taxes in the glory of the kingdom: but within few days he shall be destroyed, neither in anger nor in battle." The Hebrew word used here for the word "glory" is HEDER, meaning "honour," and it is used figuratively for the city of Jerusalem, so it could be a reference to the Syrian ruler, Seleucus IV, who died a short time after he sought to plunder God's Temple in Jerusalem. Likewise, the Hebrew word translated as "kingdom" in this phrase is defined by *Strong's Hebrew-Greek Dictionary* as simply "a rule" or "dominion" of any type, as shown in the following excerpt from Strong's dictionary:

4438 malkuwth (mal-kooth'); or malkuth (mal-kooth'); or (in plural) malkuyah (mal-koo-yah');

from 4427; a rule; concretely, a dominion:

KJV— empire, kingdom, realm, reign, royal.

So, the phrase "in the glory of the kingdom" could easily be translated correctly as "in the honour of dominion," meaning "in God's temple in His Holy City of Jerusalem." Furthermore, the Hebrew word for "destroyed" is SHABAR, meaning "to burst" literally or figuratively. One of the dictionary definitions for the word "burst" is "to fill or cause to swell to the point of breaking open," which could be a possible reference to the assassination of Seleucus IV by poison. The phrase, "neither in anger, nor in battle," likewise, is a probable reference to the aforementioned assassination by poison. Accordingly, in light of these various considerations, we must conclude it is highly probable that this passage is a reference to the poison assassination of the Syrian ruler, Seleucus IV, after he violated the Temple of God in Jerusalem.

In contrast, the Antichrist will not be destroyed soon after he invades Israel during his initial rise-to-power. (Dan. 8:9). But, when he is "wounded to death" after the Rapture, he only is healed of a "deadly wound," not actually killed and then brought back to life and incarnated by Satan. Although Satan is a powerful being, I am unaware of any evidence that would prove he actually has the power to "raise the dead."

Another problem for this theory is found within the very next verse: "And in his estate shall stand up a vile person, to whom they shall not give the honour of the kingdom: but he shall come in peaceably, and obtain the kingdom by flatteries." This passage describes perfectly the manner in which Antiochus Epiphanes managed eventually to become King. (See *Dake's Annotated Reference Bible*). However, regarding the Antichrist, other biblical scriptures teach that soon after the Rapture when Satan occupies the physical body of Antichrist, Satan immediately will find himself in possession of Antichrist's "empire" by virtue of his shared occupancy. Likewise, the whole world will worship both Satan and Antichrist at that point in time (Rev. 13:4), so for both of these reasons, there will be no need for Satan to attempt the acquisition of an empire through flattery.

Furthermore, because peace will be taken from the world immediately after the Rapture (Rev. 6), Satan obviously would be precluded from "coming in peaceably" to obtain a kingdom in a world that will be without peace at that point in time. It also would be impossible for him to "enter peaceably even upon the fattest places of the province" because, once again, there will not be any peace in the world after the Rapture, nor will there be any prosperity or "fattest places" in the world after the Rapture (except in Israel until the middle of Daniel's 70th Week).

"And he shall forecast his devices against the strong holds." Some commentators give this passage an interpretation that attributes extraordinary power to either the "forecasting" or the "devices." But the Hebrew word for "forecast" is CHASHAB, meaning to "weave" or "interpenetrate," or figuratively, to "conspire" or "plot." Likewise, the Hebrew word for "devices" is MACHASHABAH or MACHASHEBETH, meaning "contrivance, i.e., a texture, machine," or abstractly, "intention" or "plan" (meaning a plot or a plan, depending on whether it is bad or good). In other words, to "plot a plan."

Matthew 24:37-39

For as the days of Noe (Noah) were, so shall the coming of the Son of man (Rapture) be. For as in the days that were before the flood they were eating and drinking, marrying and giving in marriage (peace and prosperity and normal, everyday living) UNTIL the day that Noe (Noah) entered the ark. And knew not until the flood came, and took them all away; SO SHALL ALSO the coming of the son of man be. (KJV)

In other words, peace and prosperity will prevail everywhere throughout the world (and not just in the United States) UNTIL the Rapture takes place! This passage is further verified by Revelation 6 where once again we observe that peace and prosperity are TAKEN from ALL of the WORLD by the four horsemen, immediately AFTER the Rapture. Quite obviously peace and prosperity would have to be existent before they could be taken away, and for those who would maintain that we have peace and prosperity now, I am sure that a substantial percentage of earth's population would give you argument in light of the many dozens of wars and conflicts currently taking place throughout various regions of the world. Accordingly, there must be a period of peace and abundance and prosperity and security everywhere in the world without any evidence of active military conflict before these passages can be fulfilled completely. Additional corroboration on this point can be seen in the following scriptures.

The apostle Paul warned us there would be "peace and safety; THEN sudden destruction...as travail upon a woman with child." (I Thess. 5:3). Because Revelation 12 employs this very same symbolism of a woman travailing with child to describe the Rapture, it is quite apparent that this passage in I Thess. 5:3 states that "sudden destruction" and "a woman travailing with child" occur together simultaneously or almost simultaneously. Therefore, this passage clearly teaches that a period of peace and safety will prevail throughout the world UNTIL both the Rapture and sudden destruction happen at about the same point in time.

As further confirmation, Jesus warned Christians who would be living during the "last days" to pray that they would be accounted worthy to ESCAPE (*Strong's Hebrew-Greek Dictionary*: EKPHEUGO; to get free from, to get safely away from danger, to flee out of) all these things (post-Rapture events described in Luke 21:10-27)." (Luke 21:36). Therefore, in view of all of this scriptural evidence, we must conclude that peace and prosperity will prevail throughout the world UNTIL the Coming of Christ, starting with the Rapture, ushers in a cataclysmic period of devastating destruction for the whole world.

The City Of Babylon

Revelation 18:1-24

1 And after these things I saw another angel come down from heaven, having great power; and the earth was lightened with his glory.

2 And he cried mightily with a strong voice, saying, Babylon the great is fallen, is fallen, and is become the habitation of devils, and the hold of every foul spirit, and a cage of every unclean and hateful bird.

3 For all nations have drunk of the wine of the wrath of her fornication, and the kings of the earth have committed fornication with her, and the merchants of the earth are waxed rich through the abundance of her delicacies.

4 And I heard another voice from heaven, saying, Come out of her, my people, that ye be not partakers of her sins, and that ye receive not of her plagues.

5 For her sins have reached unto heaven, and God hath remembered her iniquities.

6 Reward her even as she rewarded you, and double unto her double according to her works: in the cup which she hath filled fill to her double.

7 How much she hath glorified herself, and lived deliciously, so much torment and sorrow give her: for she saith in her heart, I sit a queen, and am no widow, and shall see no sorrow.

8 Therefore shall her plagues come in one day, death, and mourning, and famine; and she shall be utterly burned with fire: for strong is the Lord God who judgeth her.

9 And the kings of the earth, who have committed fornication and lived deliciously with her, shall bewail her, and lament for her, when they shall see the smoke of her burning,

10 Standing afar off for the fear of her torment, saying, Alas, alas, that great city Babylon, that mighty city! for in one hour is thy judgment come.

11 And the merchants of the earth shall weep and mourn over her; for no man buyeth their merchandise any more:

12 The merchandise of gold, and silver, and precious stones, and of pearls, and fine linen, and purple, and silk, and scarlet, and all thyine wood, and all manner vessels of ivory, and all manner vessels of most precious wood, and of brass, and iron, and marble,

13 And cinnamon, and odours, and ointments, and frankincense, and wine, and oil, and fine flour, and wheat, and beasts, and sheep, and horses, and chariots, and slaves, and souls of men.

14 And the fruits that thy soul lusted after are departed from thee, and all things which were dainty and goodly are departed from thee, and thou shalt find them no more at all.

15 The merchants of these things, which were made rich by her, shall stand afar off for the fear of her torment, weeping and wailing,

16 And saying, Alas, alas, that great city, that was clothed in fine linen, and purple, and scarlet, and decked with gold, and precious stones, and pearls!

17 For in one hour so great riches is come to nought. And every shipmaster, and all the company in ships, and sailors, and as many as trade by sea, stood afar off,

18 And cried when they saw the smoke of her burning, saying, What city is like unto this great city!

19 And they cast dust on their heads, and cried, weeping and wailing, saying, Alas, alas, that great city, wherein were made rich all that had ships in the sea by reason of her costliness! for in one hour is she made desolate.

20 Rejoice over her, thou heaven, and ye holy apostles and prophets; for God hath avenged you on her.

21 And a mighty angel took up a stone like a great millstone, and cast it into the sea, saying, Thus with violence shall that great city Babylon be thrown down, and shall be found no more at all.

22 And the voice of harpers, and musicians, and of pipers, and trumpeters, shall be heard no more at all in thee; and no craftsman, of whatsoever craft he be, shall be found any more in thee; and the sound of a millstone shall be heard no more at all in thee;

23 And the light of a candle shall shine no more at all in thee; and the voice of the bridegroom and of the bride shall be heard no more at all in thee: for thy merchants were the great men of the earth; for by thy sorceries were all nations deceived.

24 And in her was found the blood of prophets, and of saints, and of all that were slain upon the earth. (KJV)

The context of this great and wealthy city is just before its destruction, near the time of Armageddon. But, obviously such wealth would take time to acquire — such a city as the one described here does not pop into existence overnight. Likewise, it is probable that such impressive wealth could be accumulated more easily in a peaceful and tranquil environment because it would be more conducive to economic trade and development. Therefore, since there will be no peace and prosperity for the world anytime AFTER the Rapture, it is reasonable to assume that Babylon will be rebuilt and accumulate most of its wealth BEFORE the Rapture occurs.

In that same vein, according to recent news reports, Saddam Hussein has already commenced rebuilding Babylon in an attempt to recapture ancient glory while discrediting Christianity — supposedly because the Christian Bible predicts that Babylon never will be rebuilt. So, on that basis, the current rebuilding of Babylon could represent the initial, literal fulfillment of a very sensational biblical prophecy that will achieve its complete and dramatic fulfillment under the rulership of the Antichrist. Therefore, we must conclude that this biblical prophecy concerning Babylon is not intended to symbolize a country or some other city as some would have us believe; instead, it is a literal city coming to life before our very eyes!

The Bible also predicts that the final condition of Babylon will be as Sodom and Gomorrah, namely complete and utter desolation as a result of massive amounts of fire and brimstone. (Isa. 13:19) (Jer. 50:40). Obviously this never has happened, yet. Additionally, according to biblical scriptures, this final cataclysmic destruction must occur near the time of Armageddon, during the great and terrible Day of the Lord, when the world will be punished for their evil amidst incredible earthquakes:

Isaiah 13:1, 4-6, 9-11, 13, 19

"The burden of Babylon, which Isaiah the son of Amoz did see... The noise of a multitude in the mountains, like as of a great people; a tumultuous noise of the kingdoms of nations gathered together (Armageddon): the Lord of hosts mustereth the host of the battle. They come from a far country, from the end of heaven, even the Lord, and the weapons of his indignation, to destroy the whole land. Howl ye; for THE DAY OF THE LORD is at hand; it shall come as a destruction from the Almighty...

"Behold, THE DAY OF THE LORD cometh, cruel both with wrath and fierce anger, to lay the land DESOLATE: and he shall destroy the sinners thereof out of it. FOR THE STARS OF HEAVEN AND THE CONSTELLATIONS THEREOF SHALL NOT GIVE THEIR LIGHT: THE SUN SHALL BE DARKENED IN HIS GOING FORTH, AND THE MOON SHALL NOT CAUSE HER LIGHT TO SHINE. AND I WILL PUNISH THE WORLD FOR THEIR EVIL... Therefore I will shake the heavens, and the earth shall remove out of her place, in the wrath of the Lord of hosts, and in the DAY OF HIS FIERCE ANGER... And Babylon, the glory of kingdoms, the beauty of the Chaldees excellency, shall be as when God overthrew Sodom and Gomorrah." (KJV)

If you will read and interpret this passage of scripture literally, it is obvious this passage states that when signs of Christ's Return are seen in the heavens, that the Babylon which once was the "glory of kingdoms" and the "beauty of the Chaldees excellency" during the reign of Nebuchadnezzar "shall be as when God overthrew Sodom and Gomorrah." In spite of this, some people still insist on interpreting the word "Babylon" in a figurative or symbolic sense, thereby getting New York City or the United States of America as the true meaning of "Babylon" in prophecy passages such as this one. They do this even though here, in this passage, it states specifically that "Babylon" is the Babylon of Nebuchadnezzar and the Chaldeans of the ancient land of Babylon, now Iraq. (Compare: Jer. 51:59-64). But, as we demonstrated earlier, there are basic, fundamental reasons why we should be interpreting biblical passages such as this one in a sensible, literal manner.

Other scriptural proofs that confirm the ancient city of Babylon will be rebuilt are as follows:

1.) Babylon will never be inhabited again after its final destruction — a prophecy which obviously has never been fulfilled, yet, since the city of Babylon is inhabited by people at this very moment. Likewise, the final destruction of Babylon must occur at the geographical location of the Babylon that was familiar to the prophet Jeremiah and Seraiah. In other words, they understood Jeremiah's prophecy as one that applied to the Babylon they knew, not to some city or country that would exist someday on the other side of the world. Furthermore, Babylon must be destroyed through violence that will sink it "into the midst of (the) Euphrates" River. Without question, the following prophecies must apply to a Babylon in our future that will be located near the Euphrates River in modern Iraq:

Isaiah 13:19-22
19 And Babylon, the glory of kingdoms, the beauty of the Chaldees' excellency, shall be as when God overthrew Sodom and Gomorrah.
20 It shall never be inhabited.... (KJV)

Jeremiah 51:29, 37, 42-43, 60-64
29 And the land shall tremble and sorrow: for every purpose of the LORD shall be performed against Babylon, to make the land of Babylon a desolation without an inhabitant.
37 And Babylon shall become heaps, a dwellingplace for dragons, an astonishment, and an hissing, without an inhabitant.
42 The sea is come up upon Babylon: she is covered with the multitude of the waves thereof.
43 Her cities are a desolation, a dry land, and a wilderness, a land wherein no man dwelleth, neither doth any son of man pass thereby.
60 So Jeremiah wrote in a book all the evil that should come upon Babylon, even all these words that are written against Babylon.
61 And Jeremiah said to Seraiah, When thou comest to Babylon, and shalt see, and shalt read all these words;
62 Then shalt thou say, O LORD, thou hast spoken against this place, to cut it off, that none shall remain in it, neither man nor beast, but that it shall be desolate for ever.
63 And it shall be, when thou hast made an end of reading this book, that thou shalt bind a stone to it, and cast it into the midst of Euphrates:
64 And thou shalt say, Thus shall Babylon sink, and shall not rise from the evil that I will bring upon her: and they shall be weary.... (KJV)

Jeremiah 50:39, 40

39 Therefore the wild beasts of the desert with the wild beasts of the islands shall dwell there, and the owls shall dwell therein: and it shall be no more inhabited for ever; neither shall it be dwelt in from generation to generation.

40 As God overthrew Sodom and Gomorrah and the neighbour cities thereof, saith the LORD; so shall no man abide there, neither shall any son of man dwell therein. (KJV)

2.) Arabs never will dwell there after its final demise. (Isa. 13:20). Neither will shepherds. (Isa. 13:20). But, both Arabs and shepherds dwell there now.

3.) The stones of Babylon never will be used again for building purposes AFTER its final destruction. (Jer. 51:26). However, they are being used now.

4.) The final overthrow of Babylon will be followed by "blessings" upon Israel, something which has not yet happened. (Isa. 13:19 through 14:8) (Jer. 50:4-7, 20).

5.) Babylon must be burned with fire, something which also has never happened, yet:

Revelation 17:16-18

16 And the ten horns which thou sawest upon the beast, these shall hate the whore, and shall make her desolate and naked, and shall eat her flesh, and burn her with fire.

17 For God hath put in their hearts to fulfil his will, and to agree, and give their kingdom unto the beast, until the words of God shall be fulfilled.

18 And the woman which thou sawest is that great city, which reigneth over the kings of the earth. (KJV)

Revelation 18:8-10, 18

8 Therefore shall her plagues come in one day, death, and mourning, and famine; and she shall be utterly burned with fire: for strong is the Lord God who judgeth her.

9 And the kings of the earth, who have committed fornication and lived deliciously with her, shall bewail her, and lament for her, when they shall see the smoke of her burning,

10 Standing afar off for the fear of her torment, saying, Alas, alas, that great city Babylon, that mighty city! for in one hour is thy judgment come.

18 And cried when they saw the smoke of her burning, saying, What city is like unto this great city! (KJV)

Revelation 19:1-3

1 And after these things I heard a great voice of much people in heaven, saying, Alleluia; Salvation, and glory, and honour, and power, unto the Lord our God:

2 For true and righteous are his judgments: for he hath judged the great whore, which did corrupt the earth with her fornication, and hath avenged the blood of his servants at her hand.

3 And again they said, Alleluia. And her smoke rose up for ever and ever. (KJV)

6.) Babylon also must be destroyed by an earthquake, which never has happened, and that earthquake must occur during the seventh plague, just before Armageddon and the Return of Christ:

Revelation 16:16-21

16 And he gathered them together into a place called in the Hebrew tongue Armageddon.

17 And the seventh angel poured out his vial into the air; and there came a great voice out of the temple of heaven, from the throne, saying, It is done.

18 And there were voices, and thunders, and lightnings; and there was a great earthquake, such as was not since men were upon the earth, so mighty an earthquake, and so great.

19 And the great city was divided into three parts, and the cities of the nations fell: and great Babylon came in remembrance before God, to give unto her the cup of the wine of the fierceness of his wrath.

20 And every island fled away, and the mountains were not found.

21 And there fell upon men a great hail out of heaven, every stone about the weight of a talent: and men blasphemed God because of the plague of the hail; for the plague thereof was exceeding great. (KJV)

7.) Babylon must be thrown down with great violence — once again, something that never has happened, yet:

Revelation 18:21
21 And a mighty angel took up a stone like a great millstone, and cast it into the sea, saying, Thus with violence shall that great city Babylon be thrown down, and shall be found no more at all. (KJV)

A survey of Babylon's history will show that it never was destroyed in the various ways just described in the above passages of scripture, and that its present condition is simply the result of continued neglect and decay throughout the last several centuries. In fact, Babylon was a populated city during the time of the apostles (I Peter 5:13), and was still existent five hundred years after Christ when the Jewish academies located there produced the Babylonian Talmud. (Compare: Jeremiah 51:59-64).

8.) The city of Babylon likewise must be destroyed "suddenly" and in "one hour" of time. (Isa. 13:19) (Jer. 50:40; 51:8) (Rev. 18:8-10, 17-19) (Isa. 47).

9.) The site of ancient Babylon will be one of the openings to the eternal "lake of fire" soon after Babylon's final destruction:

Revelation 19:2, 3
2 For true and righteous are his judgments: for he hath judged the great whore, which did corrupt the earth with her fornication, and hath avenged the blood of his servants at her hand.
3 And again they said, Alleluia. And her smoke rose up for ever and ever. (KJV)

Revelation 14:9-11
9 And the third angel followed them, saying with a loud voice, If any man worship the beast and his image, and receive his mark in his forehead, or in his hand,
10 The same shall drink of the wine of the wrath of God, which is poured out without mixture into the cup of his indignation; and he shall be tormented with fire and brimstone in the presence of the holy angels, and in the presence of the Lamb:
11 And the smoke of their torment ascendeth up for ever and ever: and they have no rest day nor night, who worship the beast and his image,

and whosoever receiveth the mark of his name. (KJV)

Isaiah 66:22-24

22 For as the new heavens and the new earth, which I will make, shall remain before me, saith the LORD, so shall your seed and your name remain.

23 And it shall come to pass, that from one new moon to another, and from one sabbath to another, shall all flesh come to worship before me, saith the LORD.

24 And they shall go forth, and look upon the carcases of the men that have transgressed against me: for their worm shall not die, neither shall their fire be quenched; and they shall be an abhorring unto all flesh. (KJV)

Isaiah 34:8-15

8 For it is the day of the LORD's vengeance, and the year of recompences for the controversy of Zion.

9 And the streams thereof shall be turned into pitch, and the dust thereof into brimstone, and the land thereof shall become burning pitch.

10 It shall not be quenched night nor day; the smoke thereof shall go up for ever: from generation to generation it shall lie waste; none shall pass through it for ever and ever.

11 But the cormorant and the bittern shall possess it; the owl also and the raven shall dwell in it: and he shall stretch out upon it the line of confusion, and the stones of emptiness.

12 They shall call the nobles thereof to the kingdom, but none shall be there, and all her princes shall be nothing.

13 And thorns shall come up in her palaces, nettles and brambles in the fortresses thereof: and it shall be an habitation of dragons, and a court for owls.

14 The wild beasts of the desert shall also meet with the wild beasts of the island, and the satyr shall cry to his fellow; the screech owl also shall rest there, and find for herself a place of rest.

15 There shall the great owl make her nest, and lay, and hatch, and gather under her shadow: there shall the vultures also be gathered, every one with her mate. (KJV)

Jeremiah 49:13, 17, 18, 33

13 For I have sworn by myself, saith the LORD, that Bozrah shall

become a desolation, a reproach, a waste, and a curse; and all the cities thereof shall be perpetual wastes.

17 Also Edom shall be a desolation: every one that goeth by it shall be astonished, and shall hiss at all the plagues thereof.

18 As in the overthrow of Sodom and Gomorrah and the neighbour cities thereof, saith the LORD, no man shall abide there, neither shall a son of man dwell in it.

33 And Hazor shall be a dwelling for dragons, and a desolation for ever: there shall no man abide there, nor any son of man dwell in it. (KJV)

Zeph. 2:8-11

8 I have heard the reproach of Moab, and the revilings of the children of Ammon, whereby they have reproached my people, and magnified themselves against their border.

9 Therefore as I live, saith the LORD of hosts, the God of Israel, Surely Moab shall be as Sodom, and the children of Ammon as Gomorrah, even the breeding of nettles, and saltpits, and a perpetual desolation: the residue of my people shall spoil them, and the remnant of my people shall possess them.

10 This shall they have for their pride, because they have reproached and magnified themselves against the people of the LORD of hosts. The LORD will be terrible unto them: for he will famish all the gods of the earth; and men shall worship him, every one from his place, even all the isles of the heathen. (KJV)

10.) The Bible also predicts that wild creatures of the desert will dwell around its desolate edges after its final and complete destruction. (Isa. 13:21, 22) (cf. Jeremiah 51:37).

11.) The "wicked woman" (Satan's Church) FLIES to the "land of Shinar" (ancient Babylon) in order to establish its new headquarters ("to build it an house"). (Zech. 5:5-11). Such a prophecy never has been fulfilled; therefore, it must represent a future fulfillment:

Zechariah 5:5-11

5 Then the angel that talked with me went forth, and said unto me, Lift up now thine eyes, and see what is this that goeth forth.

6 And I said, What is it? And he said, This is an ephah that goeth forth.

He said moreover, This is their resemblance through all the earth.

7 And, behold, there was lifted up a talent of lead: and this is a woman that sitteth in the midst of the ephah.

8 And he said, This is wickedness. And he cast it into the midst of the ephah; and he cast the weight of lead upon the mouth thereof.

9 Then lifted I up mine eyes, and looked, and, behold, there came out two women, and the wind was in their wings; for they had wings like the wings of a stork: and they lifted up the ephah between the earth and the heaven.

10 Then said I to the angel that talked with me, Whither do these bear the ephah?

11 And he said unto me, To build it an house in the land of Shinar: and it shall be established, and set there upon her own base. (KJV)

"Ephah." Was a measure of about one bushel and three pints.

"Talent of Lead." Weighed over 122 lbs., which was an extreme amount of weight for a lid covering the top of an ephah basket. Despite the weight of the lid, that still did not hold the "woman of wickedness" down, thus illustrating the power of evil.

"Two Women." It is possible that the "two women" who carry the "wicked woman" to Babylon represent two major world religions, perhaps Islam and "professing" Christianity consisting of Roman Catholicism and mainline Protestant denominations. The "wings" possibly refer to the mode of travel employed, namely air-travel by modern airplanes.

Furthermore, a careful analysis of both Revelation 17 and 18 establishes the singular fact that "Mystery Babylon" (Satan's Church) and the city of Babylon are located geographically at the exact same place near the time of their final and complete destruction:

Revelation 17:1-6, 18

"...the judgment of the great whore that sitteth upon many waters: With whom the kings of the earth have committed fornication (spiritual unfaithfulness)...and I saw a woman sit upon a scarlet coloured beast, full of names of blasphemy...And the woman was arrayed in purple and scarlet colour, and decked with gold and precious stones and pearls, having a golden cup in her hand full of abominations and filthiness of her fornication: And upon her forehead was a name written, MYSTERY, BABYLON THE GREAT, THE MOTHER OF HARLOTS AND

ABOMINATIONS OF THE EARTH. And I saw the woman drunken with the blood of saints, and with the blood of the martyrs of Jesus...And the woman which thou sawest is that great city..." (KJV)

Revelation 18

"For all nations have drunk of the wine of the wrath of her fornication, and the kings of the earth have committed fornication with her, AND THE MERCHANTS OF THE EARTH ARE WAXED RICH THROUGH THE ABUNDANCE OF HER DELICACIES... Come out of her, my people, that ye be not partakers of her sins...Therefore shall her plagues come in one day, death, and mourning, and famine; and she shall be utterly burned with fire: FOR STRONG IS THE LORD GOD WHO JUDGETH HER. And the kings of the earth who have committed fornication and lived deliciously with her, shall bewail her, and lament for her, when they shall see the smoke of her burning, standing afar off for the fear of her torment, saying, alas, alas, that great CITY Babylon, that mighty CITY! for in one hour is thy judgment come.

"And the MERCHANTS of the earth shall weep and mourn over her; for no man buyeth their merchandise any more: The merchandise of gold, and silver, and precious stones, and of pearls... and SOULS OF MEN... Alas, alas, that great CITY, that was clothed in fine linen, and purple, and scarlet, and decked with gold, and precious stones, and pearls!...And cried when they saw the smoke of her burning, saying, what CITY is like unto this great CITY!...for thy merchants were the great men of the earth; FOR BY THY SORCERIES WERE ALL NATIONS DECEIVED. And in her was found the blood of prophets, and of saints, and of all that were slain upon the earth." (KJV) (cf. Jeremiah 51:6-8)

12.) Finally, the soldiers of Antichrist must destroy Babylon with fire, very possibly with a bomb:

Revelation 17:16-18

16 And the ten horns which thou sawest upon the beast, these shall hate the whore, and shall make her desolate and naked, and shall eat her flesh, and burn her with fire.

17 For God hath put in their hearts to fulfil his will, and to agree, and give their kingdom unto the beast, until the words of God shall be fulfilled.

18 And the woman which thou sawest is that great city, which reigneth over the kings of the earth. (KJV)

Revelation 18:15-17, 21

15 The merchants of these things, which were made rich by her, shall stand afar off for the fear of her torment, weeping and wailing,

16 And saying, Alas, alas, that great city, that was clothed in fine linen, and purple, and scarlet, and decked with gold, and precious stones, and pearls!

17 For in one hour so great riches is come to nought. And every shipmaster, and all the company in ships, and sailors, and as many as trade by sea, stood afar off,

21 And a mighty angel took up a stone like a great millstone, and cast it into the sea, saying, Thus with violence shall that great city Babylon be thrown down, and shall be found no more at all. (KJV)

Middle East Wealth

"How are the things of Esau searched out! How are his hidden things sought up!" (Obadiah 6). Contextually speaking, the time-frame for this scriptural passage was established previously as the general time-period of the Second Crisis. Accordingly, this verse could very easily refer to valuable minerals, especially oil, which now belong to the descendants of Esau (i.e., Arabs). So, this passage, in essence, foretold the frenzied explorations for oil in the desert land of Esau's descendants, the Arabs.

Likewise, the visions portrayed in Daniel and Revelation strongly imply a resurgence in wealth and power for the various countries which once comprised the empires of Babylon, Greece and Persia. For example, the passage Daniel 7:11, 12 states that after the Roman "beast" (Antichrist) is destroyed, the other empire beasts also have "their DOMINION taken away: YET their LIVES (are) prolonged for a season and time." Obviously the word "dominion" used here in this passage, meaning "empire" in either a concrete or abstract manner, indicates political sovereignty and strength in contrast to a mere existence as indicated by the word "lives." This resurgence in power and affluence is corroborated by Daniel 2:45 which states that all of the symbolic image pictured in Daniel's first vision is standing upright (i.e., powerful and wealthy) at the time God breaks the power of the various world empire countries. However, even though He breaks their power and sovereignty, He does allow them to survive and enter into His new, literal Kingdom on earth, an eternal Kingdom which will replace all earthly kingdoms.

Furthermore, in Revelation we note that Daniel's symbolism concerning the various world empires also is mentioned, strongly implying again that the countries which once formed these empires comprise an important part of the future empire of Antichrist: "And the beast which I saw was like unto a LEOPARD, and his feet were as the feet of a BEAR, and his mouth as the mouth of a LION... (Rev. 13:2) (cf. Jeremiah 49:39). Therefore, all of these Middle East countries will be strong and affluent countries during the very "last days" until the Return of Christ renders them militarily impotent and politically controlled by God.

The Country Of Egypt

The prophet Jeremiah predicted the destruction of ancient Egypt, but he also promised a resurgence in wealth and power for her during the very "last days." (Jer. 46:26). That is why Egypt increasingly is playing an important role in shaping the destiny of that area of the world. Daniel even foresaw Egypt as "king of the south" during the "end times," thus symbolizing the fact that Egypt will become the leader of an important confederation of nations located in that general region. (Dan. 11:40-43). Daniel also made specific reference to the "treasures of gold and of silver, and...all the precious things of Egypt." (Dan. 11:43). Since Egypt is a relatively poor and destitute country now, these statements certainly seem to indicate a greater degree of prosperity and importance for her during the "last days"!

Daniel 11:40-45

40 And at the time of the end shall the king of the south push at him: and the king of the north shall come against him like a whirlwind, with chariots, and with horsemen, and with many ships; and he shall enter into the countries, and shall overflow and pass over.

41 He shall enter also into the glorious land, and many countries shall be overthrown: but these shall escape out of his hand, even Edom, and Moab, and the chief of the children of Ammon.

42 He shall stretch forth his hand also upon the countries: and the land of Egypt shall not escape.

43 But he shall have power over the treasures of gold and of silver, and over all the precious things of Egypt: and the Libyans and the Ethiopians shall be at his steps.

44 But tidings out of the east and out of the north shall trouble him: therefore he shall go forth with great fury to destroy, and utterly to make away many.

45 And he shall plant the tabernacles of his palace between the seas in the glorious holy mountain; yet he shall come to his end, and none shall help him. (KJV)

The prophet Ezekiel assumed the existence of this wealth and power in his prophecy when he predicted the final destruction of Egypt (just before Armageddon, according to Daniel 11:40-45). But, Ezekiel also stated that 40 years after its destruction, Egypt would become inhabited once again, but forevermore "be the basest of the kingdoms" and would "no more rule over the nations." Since Egypt never has been completely uninhabited for a period of forty years anytime after this prophecy was given, it obviously must be a prophecy which will be fulfilled near the time of Armageddon and thereafter. Ezekiel's prophecy also must be futuristic in its fulfillment because Daniel predicted power and affluence for Egypt just before the time of Armageddon. So obviously Ezekiel's prophecy has a future fulfillment when it predicts that Egypt would some day "be the basest of the kingdoms" and would "no more rule over the nations" after its final destruction near the time of Armageddon:

Ezekiel 29:1-16

1 In the tenth year, in the tenth month, in the twelfth day of the month, the word of the LORD came unto me, saying,

2 Son of man, set thy face against Pharaoh king of Egypt, and prophesy against him, and against all Egypt:

3 Speak, and say, Thus saith the Lord GOD; Behold, I am against thee, Pharaoh king of Egypt, the great dragon that lieth in the midst of his rivers, which hath said, My river is mine own, and I have made it for myself.

4 But I will put hooks in thy jaws, and I will cause the fish of thy rivers to stick unto thy scales, and I will bring thee up out of the midst of

thy rivers, and all the fish of thy rivers shall stick unto thy scales.

5 And I will leave thee thrown into the wilderness, thee and all the fish of thy rivers: thou shalt fall upon the open fields; thou shalt not be brought together, nor gathered: I have given thee for meat to the beasts of the field and to the fowls of the heaven.

6 And all the inhabitants of Egypt shall know that I am the LORD, because they have been a staff of reed to the house of Israel.

7 When they took hold of thee by thy hand, thou didst break, and rend all their shoulder: and when they leaned upon thee, thou brakest, and madest all their loins to be at a stand.

8 Therefore thus saith the Lord GOD; Behold, I will bring a sword upon thee, and cut off man and beast out of thee.

9 And the land of Egypt shall be desolate and waste; and they shall know that I am the LORD: because he hath said, The river is mine, and I have made it.

10 Behold, therefore I am against thee, and against thy rivers, and I will make the land of Egypt utterly waste and desolate, from the tower of Syene even unto the border of Ethiopia.

11 No foot of man shall pass through it, nor foot of beast shall pass through it, neither shall it be inhabited forty years.

12 And I will make the land of Egypt desolate in the midst of the countries that are desolate, and her cities among the cities that are laid waste shall be desolate forty years: and I will scatter the Egyptians among the nations, and will disperse them through the countries.

13 Yet thus saith the Lord GOD; At the end of forty years will I gather the Egyptians from the people whither they were scattered:

14 And I will bring again the captivity of Egypt, and will cause them to return into the land of Pathros, into the land of their habitation; and they shall be there a base kingdom.

15 It shall be the basest of the kingdoms; neither shall it exalt itself any more above the nations: for I will diminish them, that they shall no more rule over the nations.

16 And it shall be no more the confidence of the house of Israel, which bringeth their iniquity to remembrance, when they shall look after them: but they shall know that I am the Lord GOD. (KJV)

It is possible that the first five verses of this scripture portray an ancient, fulfilled prophecy in 570 B.C. concerning Pharaoh Hophra of

Egypt. If this is true, then in a move not without precedent, Ezekiel uses this "near-term" prophecy as a springboard for launching into a prophecy about the "end-times." We can be certain, however, that the remainder of the prophecy is futuristic because a consultation with an encyclopedia should confirm that the following predictions never have been fulfilled:

1. No man or beast is to be alive anywhere in Egypt after a time of destruction. (verse 8).

2. Egypt is to be in a state of complete desolation and waste. (verses 9 and 10). Not surprisingly, the Hebrew gives one a better understanding of the meaning intended in this passage. The Hebrew word for "desolate" is SHeMAMAH or SHIMAMAH, meaning "devastation"; figuratively "astonishment." Likewise, "waste" comes from the Hebrew word CHORBAH, meaning "drought," i.e., (by implication) a "desolation." Clearly, Egypt never has been completely devastated, perhaps even to the point of "astonishment."

3. Egypt is to be completely uninhabited for exactly 40 years. (verse 11).

4. No foot of man or beast is to touch the ground of Egypt for 40 years. (verse 11).

5. The Egyptians are to be scattered and dispersed throughout the countries of the world. (verse 12).

6. After the 40 years of waste and desolation, Egypt forevermore is to be the "basest" (Hebrew SHAPHAL, meaning "depressed," literally or figuratively) of the nations. (verses 13-15). Obviously an ancient fulfillment would make the "end-time" prophecy in Daniel 11:40-45 concerning the wealth and power of Egypt to be an impossibility.

Historically, Egypt has proven to be "a staff of reed" (i.e., not dependable) to the people of Israel during any time of trouble and distress; such will be the case during Israel's Second Crisis.

Isaiah also gives us additional information which Daniel 11:40-45 did not tell us concerning the forthcoming destruction of Egypt at the time of Armageddon. God says that He will give Egypt over to the fierce king Antichrist in the day of their terror and destruction. Then later, after the forty years of desolation throughout the land of Egypt are completed as prophesied by Ezekiel, we are told that during the Millennial Reign of Christ, "shall five cities in the land of Egypt speak the language of Canaan, and swear to the LORD of hosts..."

Isaiah 19:1-25

1 The burden of Egypt. Behold, the LORD rideth upon a swift cloud, and shall come into Egypt: and the idols of Egypt shall be moved at his presence, and the heart of Egypt shall melt in the midst of it.

2 And I will set the Egyptians against the Egyptians: and they shall fight every one against his brother, and every one against his neighbour; city against city, and kingdom against kingdom.

3 And the spirit of Egypt shall fail in the midst thereof; and I will destroy the counsel thereof: and they shall seek to the idols, and to the charmers, and to them that have familiar spirits, and to the wizards.

4 And the Egyptians will I give over into the hand of a cruel lord; and a fierce king shall rule over them, saith the Lord, the LORD of hosts.

5 And the waters shall fail from the sea, and the river shall be wasted and dried up.

6 And they shall turn the rivers far away; and the brooks of defence shall be emptied and dried up: the reeds and flags shall wither.

7 The paper reeds by the brooks, by the mouth of the brooks, and every thing sown by the brooks, shall wither, be driven away, and be no more.

8 The fishers also shall mourn, and all they that cast angle into the brooks shall lament, and they that spread nets upon the waters shall languish.

9 Moreover they that work in fine flax, and they that weave networks, shall be confounded.

10 And they shall be broken in the purposes thereof, all that make sluices and ponds for fish.

11 Surely the princes of Zoan are fools, the counsel of the wise counsellors of Pharaoh is become brutish: how say ye unto Pharaoh, I am the son of the wise, the son of ancient kings?

12 Where are they? where are thy wise men? and let them tell thee now, and let them know what the LORD of hosts hath purposed upon Egypt.

13 The princes of Zoan are become fools, the princes of Noph are deceived; they have also seduced Egypt, even they that are the stay of the tribes thereof.

14 The LORD hath mingled a perverse spirit in the midst thereof: and they have caused Egypt to err in every work thereof, as a drunken man staggereth in his vomit.

15 Neither shall there be any work for Egypt, which the head or tail, branch or rush, may do.

16 In that day shall Egypt be like unto women: and it shall be afraid and fear because of the shaking of the hand of the LORD of hosts, which he shaketh over it.

17 And the land of Judah shall be a terror unto Egypt, every one that maketh mention thereof shall be afraid in himself, because of the counsel of the LORD of hosts, which he hath determined against it.

18 In that day shall five cities in the land of Egypt speak the language of Canaan, and swear to the LORD of hosts; one shall be called, The city of destruction.

19 In that day shall there be an altar to the LORD in the midst of the land of Egypt, and a pillar at the border thereof to the LORD.

20 And it shall be for a sign and for a witness unto the LORD of hosts in the land of Egypt: for they shall cry unto the LORD because of the oppressors, and he shall send them a saviour, and a great one, and he shall deliver them.

21 And the LORD shall be known to Egypt, and the Egyptians shall know the LORD in that day, and shall do sacrifice and oblation; yea, they shall vow a vow unto the LORD, and perform it.

22 And the LORD shall smite Egypt: he shall smite and heal it: and they shall return even to the LORD, and he shall be intreated of them, and shall heal them.

23 In that day shall there be a highway out of Egypt to Assyria, and the Assyrian shall come into Egypt, and the Egyptian into Assyria, and the Egyptians shall serve with the Assyrians.

24 In that day shall Israel be the third with Egypt and with Assyria, even a blessing in the midst of the land:

25 Whom the LORD of hosts shall bless, saying, Blessed be Egypt my people, and Assyria the work of my hands, and Israel mine inheritance. (KJV)

The City Of Tyre

Ezekiel 28:11-19

11 Moreover the word of the LORD came unto me, saying,

12 Son of man, take up a lamentation upon the king of Tyrus, and say

unto him, Thus saith the Lord GOD; Thou sealest up the sum, full of wisdom, and perfect in beauty.

13 Thou hast been in Eden the garden of God; every precious stone was thy covering, the sardius, topaz, and the diamond, the beryl, the onyx, and the jasper, the sapphire, the emerald, and the carbuncle, and gold: the workmanship of thy tabrets and of thy pipes was prepared in thee in the day that thou wast created.

14 Thou art the anointed cherub that covereth; and I have set thee so: thou wast upon the holy mountain of God; thou hast walked up and down in the midst of the stones of fire.

15 Thou wast perfect in thy ways from the day that thou wast created, till iniquity was found in thee.

16 By the multitude of thy merchandise they have filled the midst of thee with violence, and thou hast sinned: therefore I will cast thee as profane out of the mountain of God: and I will destroy thee, O covering cherub, from the midst of the stones of fire.

17 Thine heart was lifted up because of thy beauty, thou hast corrupted thy wisdom by reason of thy brightness: I will cast thee to the ground, I will lay thee before kings, that they may behold thee.

18 Thou hast defiled thy sanctuaries by the multitude of thine iniquities, by the iniquity of thy traffick; therefore will I bring forth a fire from the midst of thee, it shall devour thee, and I will bring thee to ashes upon the earth in the sight of all them that behold thee.

19 All they that know thee among the people shall be astonished at thee: thou shalt be a terror, and never shalt thou be any more. (KJV)

This passage is addressed to the "king of Tyrus," but unless one indulges in very vivid hyperbole and poetic imagery, even a casual reader can discern this king most definitely is NOT human. However, if we interpret this passage literally, a methodological approach we demonstrated earlier to be valid in the vast majority of cases, the description clearly is that of Satan ruling over planet earth before his "moral fall" from grace and perfection, eons of time before the creation of Adam and Eve.

Perhaps one of the most extraordinary theological concepts in the Bible is the proposition that God created and destroyed an ancient civilization on earth eons before the time of Adam and Eve. Although the Bible says nothing about how long ago all of this took place, it does seem to indicate that a pre-Adamite society did exist at one time. If this is true, it obviously negates any possible conflict between evolutionists and creationists concerning the earth's age, because regardless of the age that true science gives to the earth, the Bible agrees. Thus, if true science ultimately proves, instead, that the earth's fossil record is simply the result of Noah's flood, as argued by many "creationist" scientists, then once again the Bible agrees. All that would be necessary for agreement would be to postulate that the destruction of the ancient pre-Adamite society was so devastating and catastrophic in nature that it completely obliterated all traces of it (a very possible scenario, incidentally).

Genesis 1:1 reads: "In the beginning God created the heaven and the earth." The word "created" was translated from the Hebrew word BARA, meaning to bring into existence, i.e., God created the world and the universe from literally nothing, from an absolutely empty vacuum. This is confirmed by Colossians 1:15-18 which reads, in part: "For by him were all things created...And he is before all things..." (cf. Hebrews 11:3; Psalms 8:3; 90:2; 95:5; 102:25; Isaiah 40:12, 22, 26, 28; 45:12, 18; 48:13.)

Genesis 1:2 reads: "And the earth was without form, and void..." According to the Hebrew, a more correct translation would read, "And the earth became waste and empty." This is based on the fact that the Hebrew word HAYAH was translated "was" in this instance, but elsewhere was translated either "became, came, came to pass, become, or come to pass" 769 times throughout the Old Testament, and it should have been translated "became" in Genesis 1:2 also. As further confirmation, *Strong's Hebrew-Greek Dictionary* defines HAYAH as meaning "become, be, come to pass, be accomplished, do, and cause," with the very critical stipuiation that it MUST always be in an emphatic sense denoting ACTION, and can never serve as a mere linking verb of a passive nature.

This very important dictionary stipulation clearly negates any arguments by critics who say that grammatical considerations dictate, in this instance, that a passive verb can be used, anyway, when translating the Hebrew word HAYAH in this passage. But, the dictionary states very emphatically that the word HAYAH must always be translated as an action verb, and never as a passive linking verb. Accordingly, this theologically-neutral definition absolutely precludes the possibility that the word "was" is the correct translation. Likewise, the phrase, "without form, and void," comes from the Hebrew words TOHUW VA BOHUW, and should have been translated as "waste and empty." Therefore, Genesis 1:2 should read, "And the earth became waste and empty," meaning that a perfect and beautiful world was made desolate and barren.

Genesis 1:3 through 2:3 and Exodus 20:8-11; 31:17 sometimes are used to prove that God literally created the entire universe in six days and that, scripturally-speaking, a pre-Adamite creation is impossible. But this is not the case at all. Whenever it is stated that God "made" the earth and the heaven, or any part thereof, it is referring to the restoration of the immediate heavens and earth sometime after the pre-Adamite destruction portrayed in Genesis 1:2. Since the word "made" is translated from the Hebrew word ASAH, meaning to make something out of already existent materials, it is in direct contrast to the Hebrew word BARA, which means literally to create from absolute nothingness as in Genesis 1:1. After Genesis 1:1, the only BARA acts of literal creation are on those occasions when God imparts life to Adam and Eve and the animals — after their physical bodies are ASAH "made" from the dust of the earth. Everything else is simply restored to its original condition or ASAH "made" from already-existent materials on earth. (See Genesis 1:3 through 2:3). This is why Genesis 2:3 states that God both "created" and "made" during the six days of Genesis 1, and why the two words are not interchangeable as some desperate critics try to argue.

Furthermore, according to Genesis 1:28, God commanded Adam and Eve to "replenish" the earth, a further indication that the earth previously was inhabited by a pre-Adamite civilization. Although *Strong's Dictionary* says that the Hebrew word for "replenish" can mean either "fill" or "refill," it is the same word used by God when He commanded Noah to refill or replenish the earth in Genesis 9:1. On that basis it is very possible that Genesis 1:28 also means "replenish" or "refill."

Some people speculate that each day of Genesis 1 represents a long period of time (e.g., a thousand years) in an attempt to harmonize their theology with the vast amounts of time supposedly demanded by science. This theory usually is based on II Peter 3:8, which states that "one day is with the Lord as a thousand years, and a thousand years as one day." In actuality, however, all that this scripture really means is that a day and a thousand years both seem very insignificant when compared to the infinite expanse of time throughout eternity. Other scriptures cited as proof for this theory usually contain a qualifying condition of some type (e.g., Ezekiel 4:1-13 allows a day to symbolize or represent a year for the express purpose of prophetic demonstration only in that one instance). Obviously such scriptures do not support the "day-age" theory.

It is my opinion that the word "day" in Genesis 1 should mean a literal day because biblical passages should always be given a literal interpretation unless the context very clearly indicates otherwise, or unless it would result in a nonsensical statement. This is made even more clear when we note that each of the days in Genesis 1 are comprised of an evening and a morning, and that they were specifically defined as literal days by God when He gave the Ten Commandments to the people of Israel. (Exodus 20:8-11; 31:14-17). So, we must not force an unnatural meaning on the word "day" in an attempt to harmonize theology and science.

Isaiah gives us additional information:

Isaiah 14:12-17

12 How art thou fallen from heaven, O Lucifer, son of the morning! how art thou cut down to the ground, which didst weaken the nations!

13 For thou hast said in thine heart, I will ascend into heaven, I will exalt my throne above the stars of God: I will sit also upon the mount of the congregation, in the sides of the north:

14 I will ascend above the heights of the clouds; I will be like the most High.

15 Yet thou shalt be brought down to hell, to the sides of the pit.

16 They that see thee shall narrowly look upon thee, and consider thee, saying, Is this the man that made the earth to tremble, that did shake kingdoms;

17 That made the world as a wilderness, and destroyed the cities thereof; that opened not the house of his prisoners? (KJV)

Here Satan is portrayed as a ruler of the nations of earth until he experiences his moral and physical fall. He "didst weaken the nations" through the use of slander against God (cf. Ezekiel 28:16, 18), eventually corrupting the hearts of people on earth and a third (Revelation 12:4, 9) of the angels. He even goes so far as to incite open rebellion against God. He then "ascend(s) above the heights of the clouds" and "ascends(s) into heaven" in order to "exalt (his) throne above the stars of God" and "be like the most High." However, he is quickly and surely "cut down to the ground" by God.

This passage above proves beyond any reasonable doubt that there were nations of people inhabiting earth at the time Satan rebelled against God, and that Satan succeeded in causing them to rebel with him. The phrase, "which didst weaken the nations," makes this quite clear. Since Satan was already a morally-fallen creature when he tempted Eve in the garden of Eden, this confirms that there was a pre-Adamite civilization on earth sometime before Adam and Eve were told to "replenish" the earth.

Ezekiel 28:15, 16, 18

15 Thou wast perfect in thy ways from the day that thou wast created, till iniquity was found in thee.

16 By the multitude of thy merchandise they have filled the midst of thee with violence, and thou hast sinned: therefore I will cast thee as profane out of the mountain of God: and I will destroy thee, O covering cherub, from the midst of the stones of fire.

18 Thou hast defiled thy sanctuaries by the multitude of thine iniquities, by the iniquity of thy traffick; therefore will I bring forth a fire from the midst of thee, it shall devour thee, and I will bring thee to ashes upon the earth in the sight of all them that behold thee. (KJV)

Here we are told that Satan was perfect from the very first day he was created by God until sin and iniquity was found in him as a result (according to Isaiah 14:12-17) of pride which came over him because of his power and beauty and importance as the leading premier angel throughout the universe. Verse 16 continues by saying that Satan was cast out of the mountain or Kingdom of God and banished from the stars of Heaven, and that someday (according to Revelation) he will be cast out permanently, forever. Verse 18 teaches that Satan and his subjects worshipped God in earthly sanctuaries or tabernacles which gave Satan the opportunity to slander God through traffick which led to his iniquity, and later, the iniquity of his earthly subjects and a third part of the heavenly angels.

That Satan became a morally-fallen creature before the creation of Adam and Eve explains why Hell originally was prepared for Satan and his angels (Matthew 25:41), and why Satan was busy tempting Eve in the Garden of Eden not very long after Adam and Eve were created. Likewise, since this rebellion by Satan took place on planet Earth, it also explains why Hell is located physically inside the Earth. (Matthew 12:40;

Ephesians 4:7-11). Disembodied beings from a pre-Adamite creation also explains the origin of demons, and why they are so interested in occupying human bodies. Anyone who would deny a pre-Adamite creation must rationally and scripturally explain these matters in some other way.

Parenthetically, it should be noted that even though Satan was physically cast out of heaven when he rebelled against God, he still has access to the throne of God (Job 1 and 2) until the time of the Rapture when he and his angels are cast out forever (Revelation 12; Hebrews 12:26-29; Haggai 2:6, 7, 21, 22).

Jeremiah 4:23-27

23 I beheld the earth, and, lo, it was without form, and void; and the heavens, and they had no light.

24 I beheld the mountains, and, lo, they trembled, and all the hills moved lightly.

25 I beheld, and, lo, there was no man, and all the birds of the heavens were fled.

26 I beheld, and, lo, the fruitful place was a wilderness, and all the cities thereof were broken down at the presence of the LORD, and by his fierce anger.

27 For thus hath the LORD said, The whole land shall be desolate; yet will I not make a full end. (KJV)

Jeremiah describes a time when the earth was "without form, and void," or as we determined earlier in Genesis 1:2, "waste and empty." But never since the creation of Adam and Eve has all of the earth been completely desolate and empty without any life whatsoever. Not even Noah's flood destroyed all of the birds and people and vegetation throughout the earth as described in this passage. (Genesis 8:10, 11). Therefore, these conditions must apply to the pre-Adamite creation at the time of its cataclysmic destruction by God.

Some people say this scripture applies only to Jerusalem (even though it specifies all of the earth and all of the cities of earth), but never has Jerusalem suffered all of these things to the degree described. Contextually speaking, Jeremiah simply was warning the people of Judah about the extreme judgment once given to all of the earth and comparing it to the lesser judgment about to descend upon Palestine, including Jerusalem. This is why verse 27 makes the following statement: "For thus hath the Lord said...yet will I not make a full end."

Some people maintain that, perhaps, Jeremiah was describing a future, chaotic condition of the world. However, this position contradicts numerous scriptures which state that people always will inhabit the earth forever. (See Genesis 8:22; 9:12, 16; 17:7, 19; II Samuel 7:24-26; Isaiah 9:6, 7; 59:20, 21; Jeremiah 31:35, 36; Ezekiel 37:24-28; Daniel 2:44; 7:13, 14, 18, 27; Zechariah 14; Luke 1:32, 33; Revelation 5:10; 11:15; 22:4, 5). So, in view of the evidence, Jeremiah 4:23-27 must refer to the earth immediately after a pre-Adamite destruction.

II Peter 3:5-7

5 For this they willingly are ignorant of, that by the word of God the heavens were of old, and the earth standing out of the water and in the water:

6 Whereby the world that then was, being overflowed with water, perished:

7 But the heavens and the earth, which are now, by the same word are kept in store, reserved unto fire against the day of judgment and perdition of ungodly men. (KJV)

According to *Strong's Hebrew-Greek Dictionary*, the Greek word translated here as the word "world" is KOSMOS, and it means "orderly arrangement" and by implication "the world, including its inhabitants, literally or figuratively." In other words, KOSMOS can, and frequently does, mean "people" or "social system." This is corroborated by at least sixty different scriptures using the word KOSMOS in such a way that it can only mean "people." For example, Matthew 5:14 says, "Ye are the light of the world," clearly meaning Christians are a witness to people, and not to the physical earth itself. Likewise, John 1:29 states that Jesus "taketh away the sin of the world," obviously meaning the sin of people, not the sin of literal earth. John 7:7 quotes Jesus as saying, "the world cannot hate you; but me it hateth," again it being evident that only people, and not a literal earth, could hate Jesus. Further confirmation on this matter may be obtained by consulting any good Bible concordance.

Accordingly, it should be noted that Noah's Flood did not completely destroy the "world," including all the people, birds, fish and animals, as stated in verse 6. But, everything in the world was destroyed completely without a trace when Satan's pre-Adamite world was destroyed by water

(Jer. 4:23-26). This view is even supported by verse 7, which states that we are living on a new earth ("the heavens and the earth, which are now"). Even further evidence is provided by verse 5: "by the word of God the heavens were of old, and the earth standing out of the water and in the water," meaning that all of the earth was not under water when it was created by God. Obviously this proves that Genesis 1 should NOT be interpreted to mean that God first created (BARA) the earth so that it was completely under water, and then later, made the "dry" land to appear during the "third" day. Instead, as the above passage states very clearly, God created the earth in such a manner that the dry land never was under the water first before becoming dry land. Thus, a pre-Adamite creation and destruction is substantiated once again by Scripture.

Romans 5:12 reads: "Wherefore, as by one man sin entered into the world, and death by sin; and so death passed upon all men, for that all have sinned." Some people use this passage to prove there was no death in the world until Adam sinned, thereby making a pre-Adamite destruction impossible. A closer analysis, however, shows that it simply means Adam brought sin and death to himself and his descendants — nothing is said about any humanoid beings who may have existed before Adam.

As noted previously, according to *Strong's Hebrew-Greek Dictionary*, the Greek word translated here as world is KOSMOS, defined as an orderly arrangement which by implication means the earth and/or its inhabitants, literally or figuratively. In other words, KOSMOS means "people" or "social system." This is corroborated by at least sixty different scriptures using the word KOSMOS in such a way that it can only mean people. Therefore, Romans 5:12 merely teaches that Adam caused sin and death to plague the world or social system of mankind, but it says nothing at all about another world or social system of beings not descended from Adam and Eve.

I Corinthians 15:21, 22 says: "For since by man came death, by man came also the resurrection of the dead. For as in Adam all die, even so in Christ shall all be made alive." Again, this passage does not disallow the creation and destruction of a pre-Adamite society; it simply says that Adam brought sin and death to humanity, and Christ brought life.

Ezekiel 28:11-19

11 Moreover the word of the LORD came unto me, saying,

12 Son of man, take up a lamentation upon the king of Tyrus, and say

unto him, Thus saith the Lord GOD; Thou sealest up the sum, full of wisdom, and perfect in beauty.

13 Thou hast been in Eden the garden of God; every precious stone was thy covering, the sardius, topaz, and the diamond, the beryl, the onyx, and the jasper, the sapphire, the emerald, and the carbuncle, and gold: the workmanship of thy tabrets and of thy pipes was prepared in thee in the day that thou wast created.

14 Thou art the anointed cherub that covereth; and I have set thee so: thou wast upon the holy mountain of God; thou hast walked up and down in the midst of the stones of fire.

15 Thou wast perfect in thy ways from the day that thou wast created, till iniquity was found in thee.

16 By the multitude of thy merchandise they have filled the midst of thee with violence, and thou hast sinned: therefore I will cast thee as profane out of the mountain of God: and I will destroy thee, O covering cherub, from the midst of the stones of fire.

17 Thine heart was lifted up because of thy beauty, thou hast corrupted thy wisdom by reason of thy brightness: I will cast thee to the ground, I will lay thee before kings, that they may behold thee.

18 Thou hast defiled thy sanctuaries by the multitude of thine iniquities, by the iniquity of thy traffick; therefore will I bring forth a fire from the midst of thee, it shall devour thee, and I will bring thee to ashes upon the earth in the sight of all them that behold thee.

19 All they that know thee among the people shall be astonished at thee: thou shalt be a terror, and never shalt thou be any more. (KJV)

As noted previously, this passage describes an immensely wise and beautiful and powerful personage who obviously must be Satan. No other creature, certainly no mere mortal, could begin to lay claim to such beauty and perfection, and supernatural wisdom, and awesome power, and fabulous wealth. Certainly no man, with the exception of Adam, was ever created by God, or allowed to enter the garden of God in Eden. Likewise, never has a mere man walked up and down in the midst of the stones of fire (stars) and the mountain of God. Only Satan could match this incredible description.

Yet verses 18 and 19 describe the exploits and destruction of a visible personage well-known and recognizable by men on the earth, namely, Antichrist! The only plausible and reasonable explanation (proven later) is that Antichrist and Satan will share the same physical human-body after the Rapture (when Satan and his angels are cast down to the earth; Rev. 12) until after the Battle of Armageddon. Apparently, therefore, the Antichrist will base his political capital in the rebuilt city of Tyre — in his native homeland, Lebanon! However, later, during the events of Armageddon, Antichrist will be destroyed and then resurrected as part of the "Second Resurrection" and immediately cast into the "lake of fire" with the False Prophet, while Satan will be chained within the "bottomless pit" for a thousand years. (Dan. 7:11) (Rev. 19:29; 20) (Isa. 14:4-11).

Briefly, we should note before proceeding with our analysis that in his prophetic writings concerning Tyre, Ezekiel mingled all of his predictions together into one batch of prophecies, some of which were intended to find their fulfillment not long after their announcement, while others were destined to be fulfilled much later during the very endtimes. Likewise, although many of his prophecies appear to have been fulfilled sometime in our history, in reality, they still require a future fulfillment simply because at least one prophetic detail never has been fulfilled, yet. Since this prophetic style was a common practice among the Old Testament prophets, it does, admittedly, make our task more difficult when sorting out the fulfilled prophecies from the futuristic prophecies not yet fulfilled.

In Ezekiel 26:3, Ezekiel prophesies that Tyre would be destroyed because God would inspire "many nations to come up against thee, as the sea causeth his waves to come up." Therefore, this passage apparently predicted that waves of invading nations would attack Tyre, and as a result, Tyre eventually would be completely conquered and destroyed.

The ancient city of Tyre was a major city-state of the Phoenicians, a people famous for their sea trade and technical skills, so it is not surprising that Tyre was a leading commercial center for the known world at that time. (Paper entitled "Is Fulfilled Prophecy Of Value For Scholarly Apologetics?" by John A. Bloom, Ph.D., 1995, which is available at http://www.trinitysem.edu/journal/prophesy.html.) While the ports and temples of Tyre were located on an island section of Tyre one-half mile off the coast (thus making it almost immune to invasion), the bulk of the city, including its manufacturing and trading facilities and food-sources were all located on the mainland. Because it was almost impossible to conquer the island segment of Tyre, it required several waves of attacking nations over a period of many long centuries before Tyre finally was annihilated and destroyed completely. (Bloom)

This process of invasion and ultimate destruction began with the initial invasion by King Nebuchadnezzar of Babylon, then in later centuries, continued with additional waves of attacks by first, Alexander the Great, then later the Muslim leader Saladin, and then finally — in 1291 A.D. — the Mamluks from Egypt who not only conquered Tyre, but completely destroyed the city as well. (Bloom) This catastrophic development, in turn, led to the area surrounding the former site of Tyre to suffer inter-sect Muslim rivalry, a major earthquake and a plague, ultimately resulting in the complete abandonment of the whole region for a very long time. (Bloom) And it was not until the 1760's that a small fishing village was established on the site of Tyre, thus fulfilling the final aspect of the ancient prophecy by Ezekiel that Tyre would become a place for the spreading of fishnets. (Bloom)

However, other prophecies concerning Tyre involve very dramatic predictions which never were fulfilled! Therefore, a future city of Tyre must be reestablished within the near future in order to fulfill these other additional prophecies as well. Then, and only then, will the oft-repeated prophecy that Tyre will be destroyed forever finally be fulfilled. Accordingly, the tremendous wealth and influence of this great future city is noted in Ezekiel 27! This particular Tyre must be a future fulfillment because ancient Tyre never attained the degree of wealth and affluence described:

Ezekiel 27:1-4, 12, 25, 27, 32-36

1 The word of the LORD came again unto me, saying,

2 Now, thou son of man, take up a lamentation for Tyrus;

3 And say unto Tyrus, O thou that art situate at the entry of the sea, which art a merchant of the people for many isles, Thus saith the Lord GOD; O Tyrus, thou hast said, I am of perfect beauty.

4 Thy borders are in the midst of the seas, thy builders have perfected thy beauty.

12 Tarshish was thy merchant by reason of the multitude of all kind of riches; with silver, iron, tin, and lead, they traded in thy fairs.

25 The ships of Tarshish did sing of thee in thy market: and thou wast replenished, and made very glorious in the midst of the seas.

27 Thy riches, and thy fairs, thy merchandise, thy mariners, and thy pilots, thy calkers, and the occupiers of thy merchandise, and all thy men of war, that are in thee, and in all thy company which is in the midst of

thee, shall fall into the midst of the seas in the day of thy ruin.

32 And in their wailing they shall take up a lamentation for thee, and lament over thee, saying, What city is like Tyrus, like the destroyed in the midst of the sea?

33 When thy wares went forth out of the seas, thou filledst many people; thou didst enrich the kings of the earth with the multitude of thy riches and of thy merchandise.

34 In the time when thou shalt be broken by the seas in the depths of the waters thy merchandise and all thy company in the midst of thee shall fall.

35 All the inhabitants of the isles shall be astonished at thee, and their kings shall be sore afraid, they shall be troubled in their countenance.

36 The merchants among the people shall hiss at thee; thou shalt be a terror, and never shalt be any more. (KJV)

Although ancient Tyre was a very famous city-state renowned for its world sea trade, it never attained the incredible wealth portrayed in the above scripture. That is why a future Tyre must be rebuilt so that all the kings of the world can become wealthy by the multitude and abundance of all her riches and treasures.

Ezekiel 26:15-21

15 Thus saith the Lord GOD to Tyrus; Shall not the isles shake at the sound of thy fall, when the wounded cry, when the slaughter is made in the midst of thee?

16 Then all the princes of the sea shall come down from their thrones, and lay away their robes, and put off their broidered garments: they shall clothe themselves with trembling; they shall sit upon the ground, and shall tremble at every moment, and be astonished at thee.

17 And they shall take up a lamentation for thee, and say to thee, How art thou destroyed, that wast inhabited of seafaring men, the renowned city, which wast strong in the sea, she and her inhabitants, which cause their terror to be on all that haunt it!

18 Now shall the isles tremble in the day of thy fall; yea, the isles that are in the sea shall be troubled at thy departure.

19 For thus saith the Lord GOD; When I shall make thee a desolate city, like the cities that are not inhabited; when I shall bring up the deep upon thee, and great waters shall cover thee;

20 When I shall bring thee down with them that descend into the pit, with the people of old time, and shall set thee in the low parts of the earth, in places desolate of old, with them that go down to the pit, that thou be not inhabited; and I shall set glory in the land of the living;

21 I will make thee a terror, and thou shalt be no more: though thou be sought for, yet shalt thou never be found again, saith the Lord GOD. (KJV)

In the preceding scripture, there can be no question that some of the prophecies portrayed represent a futuristic fulfillment involving a future city of Tyre. Granted, other prophecies in Ezekiel predicting Tyre would be thrown into the midst of the seas when it was destroyed apparently were fulfilled when the debris left over from the destruction of mainland Tyre was used by Alexander the Great to build a bridge of land out to the island fortress of Tyre. However, in the passage above, it clearly states that the waters of the ocean will come up and cover the city completely, something entirely different than having Tyre merely fall into the sea as in other prophecies. Quite obviously this prophetic prediction never has happened. Nor will it happen until near the time of Armageddon when the islands of the world will crumble into the oceans as a great final earthquake devastates the whole earth:

Revelation 16:17-21

17 And the seventh angel poured out his vial into the air; and there came a great voice out of the temple of heaven, from the throne, saying, It is done.

18 And there were voices, and thunders, and lightnings; and there was a great earthquake, such as was not since men were upon the earth, so mighty an earthquake, and so great.

19 And the great city was divided into three parts, and the cities of the nations fell: and great Babylon came in remembrance before God, to give unto her the cup of the wine of the fierceness of his wrath.

20 And every island fled away, and the mountains were not found.

21 And there fell upon men a great hail out of heaven, every stone about the weight of a talent: and men blasphemed God because of the plague of the hail; for the plague thereof was exceeding great. (KJV)

"When I shall bring thee down with them that descend into the pit, with the people of old time, and shall set thee in the low parts of the earth, in places desolate of old." It is very likely this passage concerns a future, modern city of Tyre because it is predicted that Tyre will descend down into the pit to join the people of old time, i.e., of ancient times.

Ezekiel 26:17, 21
17 And they shall take up a lamentation for thee, and say to thee, How art thou destroyed, that wast inhabited of seafaring men, the renowned city, which wast strong in the sea, she and her inhabitants, which cause their terror to be on all that haunt it!
21 I will make thee a terror... (KJV)

Although the ancient city of Tyre was renowned for its sea trade and commerce, it was never a gigantic military power which created fear and terror in people everywhere throughout the world, or even in Europe and Asia Minor. In fact, as we noted previously, down throughout history, ancient Tyre was subjected to frequent military invasions by powerful neighboring countries who always were anxious to exploit Tyre's commercial and geopolitical importance. Obviously then, this must be a reference to a future, rebuilt city of Tyre which will become the political capital of a new world leader, i.e., Antichrist, about whom the whole world will exclaim in wonder: "Who is like unto the beast? who is able to make war with him?"

Ezekiel 27:36
36 The merchants among the people shall hiss at thee; thou shalt be a terror, and never shalt be any more. (KJV)

Ezekiel 26:21
21 I will make thee a terror, and thou shalt be no more: though thou be sought for, yet shalt thou never be found again, saith the Lord GOD. (KJV)

Here are prophecies which state specifically that Tyre never will be found again. Although there is only a fishing village located there now, which is a far cry from the splendor and grandeur of ancient Tyre, nevertheless, something is still there. Since right now something can be found there, contrary to the precise wording of the above prophecies, these prophetic predictions must realize a dramatic, future fulfillment some day. There must come a time when absolutely nothing can be found there, and it will happen when the former "island" segment of Tyre is completely annihilated in the final great earthquake which will shake the whole world.

Zechariah 9:1-8

1 The burden of the word of the LORD in the land of Hadrach, and Damascus shall be the rest thereof: when the eyes of man, as of all the tribes of Israel, shall be toward the LORD.

2 And Hamath also shall border thereby; Tyrus, and Zidon, though it be very wise.

3 And Tyrus did build herself a strong hold, and heaped up silver as the dust, and fine gold as the mire of the streets.

4 Behold, the Lord will cast her out, and he will smite her power in the sea; and she shall be devoured with fire.

5 Ashkelon shall see it, and fear; Gaza also shall see it, and be very sorrowful, and Ekron; for her expectation shall be ashamed; and the king shall perish from Gaza, and Ashkelon shall not be inhabited.

6 And a bastard shall dwell in Ashdod, and I will cut off the pride of the Philistines.

7 And I will take away his blood out of his mouth, and his abominations from between his teeth: but he that remaineth, even he, shall be for our God, and he shall be as a governor in Judah, and Ekron as a Jebusite.

8 And I will encamp about mine house because of the army, because of him that passeth by, and because of him that returneth: and no oppressor shall pass through them any more: for now have I seen with mine eyes. (KJV)

In the above passage, please note that Tyre builds itself a strong hold, and heaps up huge amounts of gold and silver in its coffers. Yet, it is said that God smashes her into the sea, and destroys her with fire (at the time of Armageddon when the seventh Trumpet-Vial plague will unleash an incredibly horrific and cataclysmic earthquake that will destroy the mountains and islands and cities throughout the world). At that time, God will "encamp" about His "house" in Jerusalem because of the invading army of the Antichrist, i.e., "him that passeth by," and then no oppressor shall ever bother the land of Israel ever again. Obviously this passage requires a future fulfillment so that Tyre can gain the incredible degree of wealth and power mentioned in this scripture, and then be destroyed violently and suddenly as described.

Ezekiel states that the city of Tyre will be destroyed forever. Yet when Isaiah 23 describes this very same destruction, it concludes by predicting Tyre will be rebuilt 70 years after its destruction, and then forevermore provide food and clothing "for them that dwell before the Lord" in Jerusalem when God personally reigns over the whole earth after the Battle of Armageddon! Although these predictions would appear to be an outright contradiction, they are not. As we mentioned earlier, Tyre was, and will be, a city of two sections; part of it was, and will be, located on the "island" area that was linked to the mainland in ancient times by the use of a gigantic dirt-mound, and part of it was, and will be, located on the "real" mainland. It is the "island" segment of Tyre that will be destroyed forever during the great final earthquake occurring at the time of Armageddon when all the islands and mountains of the earth are totally destroyed. Isaiah confirms this conclusion by stating that Tyre will be destroyed near the time when Egypt is destroyed, which is just before the Battle of Armageddon (Dan. 11:40-45).

Isaiah 23:1, 5-9, 11, 13, 15, 17, 18

1 The burden of Tyre. Howl, ye ships of Tarshish; for it is laid waste, so that there is no house, no entering in: from the land of Chittim it is revealed to them.

5 As at the report concerning Egypt, so shall they be sorely pained at the report of Tyre.

6 Pass ye over to Tarshish; howl, ye inhabitants of the isle.

7 Is this your joyous city, whose antiquity is of ancient days? her own feet shall carry her afar off to sojourn.

8 Who hath taken this counsel against Tyre, the crowning city, whose merchants are princes, whose traffickers are the honourable of the earth?

9 The LORD of hosts hath purposed it, to stain the pride of all glory, and to bring into contempt all the honourable of the earth.

11 He stretched out his hand over the sea, he shook the kingdoms: the LORD hath given a commandment against the merchant city, to destroy the strong holds thereof.

13 Behold the land of the Chaldeans; this people was not, till the Assyrian founded it for them that dwell in the wilderness: they set up the

towers thereof, they raised up the palaces thereof; and he brought it to ruin.

15 And it shall come to pass in that day, that Tyre shall be forgotten seventy years, according to the days of one king: after the end of seventy years shall Tyre sing as an harlot.

17 And it shall come to pass after the end of seventy years, that the LORD will visit Tyre, and she shall turn to her hire, and shall commit fornication with all the kingdoms of the world upon the face of the earth.

18 And her merchandise and her hire shall be holiness to the LORD: it shall not be treasured nor laid up; for her merchandise shall be for them that dwell before the LORD, to eat sufficiently, and for durable clothing. (KJV)

This prophecy is not unlike many other prophecies we have discussed where we find that prophecies from different time eras can be mixed in together, as well as the fact prophecies often will realize a preliminary, partial fulfillment in ancient history, but yet also will require a final, future fulfillment simply because at least one prophetic detail never has been fulfilled. Accordingly, although ancient Tyre enjoyed a good measure of the wealth which will abound in the future Tyre, this prophecy concerning Tyre is a prediction about our immediate future.

"This people was not, till the Assyrian founded it for them that dwell in the wilderness... (but) he (God) brought it to ruin." Please note Isaiah informs us that this great city will be rebuilt by the "Assyrian." The Assyrian is none other than the Antichrist! (Isa. 10:5, 6; Isa. 10:20-34; Isa. 14:24-27; Isa. 19; Isa. 23:13; Isa. 27:12, 13; Isa. 30:18-33; Isa. 31:4-9; Micah 5:3-15; Micah 7:7-20). However, God will bring the city of Tyre to ruin near the time of Armageddon.

Isaiah 23:15, 17, 18

15 And it shall come to pass in that day, that Tyre shall be forgotten seventy years, according to the days of one king: after the end of seventy years shall Tyre sing as an harlot.

17 And it shall come to pass after the end of seventy years, that the LORD will visit Tyre, and she shall turn to her hire, and shall commit fornication with all the kingdoms of the world upon the face of the earth.

18 And her merchandise and her hire shall be holiness to the LORD: it shall not be treasured nor laid up; for her merchandise shall be for them

that dwell before the LORD, to eat sufficiently, and for durable clothing. (KJV)

If all the other prophecies involving a future city of Tyre somehow could be explained away by stretching the meaning of words, this is the one prophecy which can be viewed with absolute certainty! It can not be denied that seventy years after the final and complete annihilation of the "island" segment of Tyre, the Lord will visit Tyre and bless her exceedingly so that her merchandise will be available as food and clothing for people who will serve God in Jerusalem. Most obviously this prophecy never has been fulfilled; it must be fulfilled sometime in the future!

IV. The Occult Revival

Latter-Day Apostasy

The apostle Paul warns us that the initial appearance of Antichrist will be "after the working of Satan with all power and signs and lying wonders"! (II Thess. 2:9). When the disciples asked Jesus, "What shall be the sign of thy coming, and of the end of the age?" His immediate response was a warning: "Take heed that no man deceive you." (Matt. 24:3, 4). In a similar vein, the apostle Paul said that "evil men and seducers shall wax worse and worse, deceiving and being deceived." (II Tim. 3:13). Obviously these scriptures make it very clear that religious and philosophical deception increasingly will flourish and prevail throughout all of society during the "end-times" or "time of the end" (Dan. 12:9).

Jesus continued: "Take heed that ye be not deceived: for many shall come in my name, saying, I am Christ, and the time draweth near: go ye not therefore after them." (Luke 21:8). It is interesting to note that the New Age Movement teaches that all of us are really gods or divine-in-nature deep inside our psyches — it is just that we do not know it until we achieve "Christ consciousness" or "oneness with the universe" through "higher consciousness" techniques. In recent years they also have insisted that mankind is on the verge of a "sudden, evolutionary leap" or "transformation," and that when sufficient numbers of individuals achieve a personal transformation (i.e., a mystical, pantheistic perception of reality), then all of the world can suddenly and instantaneously make a dramatic leap forward in realizing the age-old dream of world peace, prosperity and the brotherhood of all men embodied in a "new world order." The apparent recent upsurge in freedom and democracy throughout the world, New Agers claim, is due, at least in part, to this "uplifting of spiritual consciousness."

II Thess. 2:1, 2

1 Now we beseech you, brethren, by the coming of our Lord Jesus Christ, and by our gathering together unto him,

2 That ye be not soon shaken in mind, or be troubled, neither by spirit, nor by word, nor by letter as from us, as that the day of Christ is at hand.

The phrase "day of Christ" is more-accurately interpreted by other translations such as *Young's Literal Translation* as "Day of the Lord." Likewise, *Strong's Hebrew-Greek Dictionary* will show that the English word translated here as "Christ" is not from the Greek word, CHRISTOS — which normally is used whenever the word "Christ" is intended — but from the word KURIOS. Strong defines KURIOS as follows:

2962 kurios (koo'-ree-os);
from kuros (supremacy); supreme in authority, i.e. (as noun) controller; by implication, Mr. (as a respectful title):
KJV— God, Lord, master, Sir.

So, based on references such as *Strong's Hebrew-Greek Dictionary*, the proper rendering for the phrase "day of Christ" is actually "day of the Lord," thereby allowing this passage to be consistent with the prophetic teachings found elsewhere throughout biblical scriptures. Therefore, this period of time should not be confused with the Rapture of the saints to meet the Lord in the air (i.e., "our gathering together unto him," mentioned in verse one) because the "Day of the Lord" is a period of Divine wrath and judgment upon the earth which begins immediately after the Great Tribulation and the Sixth Seal have taken place. The following scriptural passages provide very convincing proof that my proposed definition for "Day Of The Lord" is, in fact, correct:

Revelation 6:12-17
12 And I beheld when he had opened the sixth seal, and, lo, there was a great earthquake; and the sun became black as sackcloth of hair, and the moon became as blood;
13 And the stars of heaven fell unto the earth, even as a fig tree casteth her untimely figs, when she is shaken of a mighty wind.
14 And the heaven departed as a scroll when it is rolled together; and every mountain and island were moved out of their places.
15 And the kings of the earth, and the great men, and the rich men, and the chief captains, and the mighty men, and every bondman, and every free man, hid themselves in the dens and in the rocks of the mountains;
16 And said to the mountains and rocks, Fall on us, and hide us from the face of him that sitteth on the throne, and from the wrath of the Lamb:
17 For the great day of his wrath is come; and who shall be able to

stand? (KJV)

Revelation 8:1, 2, 5-13

1 And when he had opened the seventh seal, there was silence in heaven about the space of half an hour.

2 And I saw the seven angels which stood before God; and to them were given seven trumpets.

5 And the angel took the censer, and filled it with fire of the altar, and cast it into the earth: and there were voices, and thunderings, and lightnings, and an earthquake.

6 And the seven angels which had the seven trumpets prepared themselves to sound.

7 The first angel sounded, and there followed hail and fire mingled with blood, and they were cast upon the earth: and the third part of trees was burnt up, and all green grass was burnt up.

8 And the second angel sounded, and as it were a great mountain burning with fire was cast into the sea: and the third part of the sea became blood;

9 And the third part of the creatures which were in the sea, and had life, died; and the third part of the ships were destroyed.

10 And the third angel sounded, and there fell a great star from heaven, burning as it were a lamp, and it fell upon the third part of the rivers, and upon the fountains of waters;

11 And the name of the star is called Wormwood: and the third part of the waters became wormwood; and many men died of the waters, because they were made bitter.

12 And the fourth angel sounded, and the third part of the sun was smitten, and the third part of the moon, and the third part of the stars; so as the third part of them was darkened, and the day shone not for a third part of it, and the night likewise.

13 And I beheld, and heard an angel flying through the midst of heaven, saying with a loud voice, Woe, woe, woe, to the inhabiters of the earth by reason of the other voices of the trumpet of the three angels, which are yet to sound! (KJV)

Revelation 9:1-19

1 And the fifth angel sounded, and I saw a star fall from heaven unto the earth: and to him was given the key of the bottomless pit.

2 And he opened the bottomless pit; and there arose a smoke out of the pit, as the smoke of a great furnace; and the sun and the air were darkened by reason of the smoke of the pit.

3 And there came out of the smoke locusts upon the earth: and unto them was given power, as the scorpions of the earth have power.

4 And it was commanded them that they should not hurt the grass of the earth, neither any green thing, neither any tree; but only those men which have not the seal of God in their foreheads.

5 And to them it was given that they should not kill them, but that they should be tormented five months: and their torment was as the torment of a scorpion, when he striketh a man.

6 And in those days shall men seek death, and shall not find it; and shall desire to die, and death shall flee from them.

7 And the shapes of the locusts were like unto horses prepared unto battle; and on their heads were as it were crowns like gold, and their faces were as the faces of men.

8 And they had hair as the hair of women, and their teeth were as the teeth of lions.

9 And they had breastplates, as it were breastplates of iron; and the sound of their wings was as the sound of chariots of many horses running to battle.

10 And they had tails like unto scorpions, and there were stings in their tails: and their power was to hurt men five months.

11 And they had a king over them, which is the angel of the bottomless pit, whose name in the Hebrew tongue is Abaddon, but in the Greek tongue hath his name Apollyon.

12 One woe is past; and, behold, there come two woes more hereafter.

13 And the sixth angel sounded, and I heard a voice from the four horns of the golden altar which is before God,

14 Saying to the sixth angel which had the trumpet, Loose the four angels which are bound in the great river Euphrates.

15 And the four angels were loosed, which were prepared for an hour, and a day, and a month, and a year, for to slay the third part of men.

16 And the number of the army of the horsemen were two hundred thousand thousand: and I heard the number of them.

17 And thus I saw the horses in the vision, and them that sat on them, having breastplates of fire, and of jacinth, and brimstone: and the heads of the horses were as the heads of lions; and out of their mouths issued fire

and smoke and brimstone.

18 By these three was the third part of men killed, by the fire, and by the smoke, and by the brimstone, which issued out of their mouths.

19 For their power is in their mouth, and in their tails: for their tails were like unto serpents, and had heads, and with them they do hurt. (KJV)

Revelation 11:13-15

13 And the same hour was there a great earthquake, and the tenth part of the city fell, and in the earthquake were slain of men seven thousand: and the remnant were affrighted, and gave glory to the God of heaven.

14 The second woe is past; and, behold, the third woe cometh quickly.

15 And the seventh angel sounded; and there were great voices in heaven, saying, The kingdoms of this world are become the kingdoms of our Lord, and of his Christ; and he shall reign for ever and ever. (KJV)

Joel 2:1-11

1 Blow ye the trumpet in Zion, and sound an alarm in my holy mountain: let all the inhabitants of the land tremble: for the day of the LORD cometh, for it is nigh at hand;

2 A day of darkness and of gloominess, a day of clouds and of thick darkness, as the morning spread upon the mountains: a great people and a strong; there hath not been ever the like, neither shall be any more after it, even to the years of many generations.

3 A fire devoureth before them; and behind them a flame burneth: the land is as the garden of Eden before them, and behind them a desolate wilderness; yea, and nothing shall escape them.

4 The appearance of them is as the appearance of horses; and as horsemen, so shall they run.

5 Like the noise of chariots on the tops of mountains shall they leap, like the noise of a flame of fire that devoureth the stubble, as a strong people set in battle array.

6 Before their face the people shall be much pained: all faces shall gather blackness.

7 They shall run like mighty men; they shall climb the wall like men of war; and they shall march every one on his ways, and they shall not break their ranks:

8 Neither shall one thrust another; they shall walk every one in his path: and when they fall upon the sword, they shall not be wounded.

9 They shall run to and fro in the city; they shall run upon the wall, they shall climb up upon the houses; they shall enter in at the windows like a thief.

10 The earth shall quake before them; the heavens shall tremble: the sun and the moon shall be dark, and the stars shall withdraw their shining:

11 And the LORD shall utter his voice before his army: for his camp is very great: for he is strong that executeth his word: for the day of the LORD is great and very terrible; and who can abide it? (KJV)

Joel 2:28-32

28 And it shall come to pass afterward, that I will pour out my spirit upon all flesh; and your sons and your daughters shall prophesy, your old men shall dream dreams, your young men shall see visions:

29 And also upon the servants and upon the handmaids in those days will I pour out my spirit.

30 And I will shew wonders in the heavens and in the earth, blood, and fire, and pillars of smoke.

31 The sun shall be turned into darkness, and the moon into blood, before the great and the terrible day of the LORD come.

32 And it shall come to pass, that whosoever shall call on the name of the LORD shall be delivered: for in mount Zion and in Jerusalem shall be deliverance, as the LORD hath said, and in the remnant whom the LORD shall call. (KJV)

Isaiah 24:17-23

17 Fear, and the pit, and the snare, are upon thee, O inhabitant of the earth.

18 And it shall come to pass, that he who fleeth from the noise of the fear shall fall into the pit; and he that cometh up out of the midst of the pit shall be taken in the snare: for the windows from on high are open, and the foundations of the earth do shake.

19 The earth is utterly broken down, the earth is clean dissolved, the earth is moved exceedingly.

20 The earth shall reel to and fro like a drunkard, and shall be removed like a cottage; and the transgression thereof shall be heavy upon it; and it shall fall, and not rise again.

21 And it shall come to pass in that day, that the LORD shall punish the host of the high ones that are on high, and the kings of the earth upon

the earth.

22 And they shall be gathered together, as prisoners are gathered in the pit, and shall be shut up in the prison, and after many days shall they be visited.

23 Then the moon shall be confounded, and the sun ashamed, when the LORD of hosts shall reign in mount Zion, and in Jerusalem, and before his ancients gloriously. (KJV)

Isaiah 13:6-13

6 Howl ye; for the day of the LORD is at hand; it shall come as a destruction from the Almighty.

7 Therefore shall all hands be faint, and every man's heart shall melt:

8 And they shall be afraid: pangs and sorrows shall take hold of them; they shall be in pain as a woman that travaileth: they shall be amazed one at another; their faces shall be as flames.

9 Behold, the day of the LORD cometh, cruel both with wrath and fierce anger, to lay the land desolate: and he shall destroy the sinners thereof out of it.

10 For the stars of heaven and the constellations thereof shall not give their light: the sun shall be darkened in his going forth, and the moon shall not cause her light to shine.

11 And I will punish the world for their evil, and the wicked for their iniquity; and I will cause the arrogancy of the proud to cease, and will lay low the haughtiness of the terrible.

12 I will make a man more precious than fine gold; even a man than the golden wedge of Ophir.

13 Therefore I will shake the heavens, and the earth shall remove out of her place, in the wrath of the LORD of hosts, and in the day of his fierce anger. (KJV)

Zechariah 14:1-4

1 Behold, the day of the LORD cometh, and thy spoil shall be divided in the midst of thee.

2 For I will gather all nations against Jerusalem to battle; and the city shall be taken, and the houses rifled, and the women ravished; and half of the city shall go forth into captivity, and the residue of the people shall not be cut off from the city.

3 Then shall the LORD go forth, and fight against those nations, as

when he fought in the day of battle.

4 And his feet shall stand...upon the mount of Olives.... (KJV)

II Peter 3:10-12

10 But the day of the Lord will come as a thief in the night; in the which the heavens shall pass away with a great noise, and the elements shall melt with fervent heat, the earth also and the works that are therein shall be burned up.

11 Seeing then that all these things shall be dissolved, what manner of persons ought ye to be in all holy conversation and godliness,

12 Looking for and hasting unto the coming of the day of God, wherein the heavens being on fire shall be dissolved, and the elements shall melt with fervent heat? (KJV)

Zeph. 1:14-18

14 The great day of the LORD is near, it is near, and hasteth greatly, even the voice of the day of the LORD: the mighty man shall cry there bitterly.

15 That day is a day of wrath, a day of trouble and distress, a day of wasteness and desolation, a day of darkness and gloominess, a day of clouds and thick darkness,

16 A day of the trumpet and alarm against the fenced cities, and against the high towers.

17 And I will bring distress upon men, that they shall walk like blind men, because they have sinned against the LORD: and their blood shall be poured out as dust, and their flesh as the dung.

18 Neither their silver nor their gold shall be able to deliver them in the day of the LORD's wrath; but the whole land shall be devoured by the fire of his jealousy: for he shall make even a speedy riddance of all them that dwell in the land. (KJV)

Amos 5:18-20

18 Woe unto you that desire the day of the LORD! to what end is it for you? the day of the LORD is darkness, and not light.

19 As if a man did flee from a lion, and a bear met him; or went into the house, and leaned his hand on the wall, and a serpent bit him.

20 Shall not the day of the LORD be darkness, and not light? even very dark, and no brightness in it? (KJV)

Isaiah 2:10-21

10 Enter into the rock, and hide thee in the dust, for fear of the LORD, and for the glory of his majesty.

11 The lofty looks of man shall be humbled, and the haughtiness of men shall be bowed down, and the LORD alone shall be exalted in that day.

12 For the day of the LORD of hosts shall be upon every one that is proud and lofty, and upon every one that is lifted up; and he shall be brought low:

13 And upon all the cedars of Lebanon, that are high and lifted up, and upon all the oaks of Bashan,

14 And upon all the high mountains, and upon all the hills that are lifted up,

15 And upon every high tower, and upon every fenced wall,

16 And upon all the ships of Tarshish, and upon all pleasant pictures.

17 And the loftiness of man shall be bowed down, and the haughtiness of men shall be made low: and the LORD alone shall be exalted in that day.

18 And the idols he shall utterly abolish.

19 And they shall go into the holes of the rocks, and into the caves of the earth, for fear of the LORD, and for the glory of his majesty, when he ariseth to shake terribly the earth.

20 In that day a man shall cast his idols of silver, and his idols of gold, which they made each one for himself to worship, to the moles and to the bats;

21 To go into the clefts of the rocks, and into the tops of the ragged rocks, for fear of the LORD, and for the glory of his majesty, when he ariseth to shake terribly the earth. (KJV)

Obviously the above scriptural passages in Revelation which describe the “Great Day Of His Wrath” — a day ushered in by the events of the Sixth Seal, and comprised of the seven Trumpet-Vial plagues — sound remarkably similar to the descriptions of the Day of the Lord which are given in the Old Testament prophecies describing Armageddon and the period of time immediately before Armageddon. Hence the inevitable conclusion that they are one and the same. Therefore, the Day Of The Lord can NOT refer to any period of time AFTER the Millennium, but instead, it must refer to the time-period leading up to Armageddon.

II Thess. 2:3

Let no man (e.g., Antichrist) deceive you by any means: for that day (i.e., Day of the Lord) shall not come, except there come a falling away first, and that man of sin be revealed (after he has deceived). (KJV)

I Timothy 4:1

1 Now the Spirit speaketh expressly, that in the latter times some shall depart from the faith, giving heed to seducing spirits, and doctrines of devils; (KJV)

A "falling away" is translated from the Greek word APOSTASIA, which means "defection from truth," i.e., "apostasy." So, by its very definition, the word "apostasy," defined as "defection from truth," means that we are talking ONLY about people who are true believers in Christ who decide, of their own God-given freewill, to renounce or backslide or desert or abandon their faith in Christ. Obviously you must be somewhere first before you can renounce or fall away from it, so in this instance we are not talking about unbelievers, but legitimate, born-again Christians who will be taken in by the final ultimate deception which will be waged by the Antichrist through his highly-seductive "doctrines of devils."

The world Christian community of believers has always experienced a certain amount of apostasy down throughout history, and even though the modern church-world already has experienced a great deal of apostasy in many of its mainline denominations, it is only logical to assume that a very unusual amount of "backsliding" or apostatizing among Christians is intended in the fulfillment of this passage. Not only because Scripture takes special note of it as something very unusual, but also because the scriptural passage which warns us about the final falling away also implies very strongly that it will be the Antichrist who causes it to happen. That is why there is coming a day when the Bible predicts that many Christians will NOT withstand the incredible, seductive web of deception which will be spun by the Antichrist. That is why the Bible most assuredly prophesies there will be a great final apostasy among Christian believers immediately BEFORE the pre-tribulation Rapture occurs.

Such deception will be possible for many different reasons. For instance, the religious views of the Antichrist will appear to be highly credible to most people not only because He will exhibit very impressive oratory skills, but also because he will accomplish many great things for the benefit of all mankind. (Dan. 7:8) (Dan. 8:23). Among these many, varied accomplishments, most notable will be his miraculous war-making ability (Dan. 8:23, 24) (Dan. 11:35-39) (Rev. 13:4) which will enable him, single-handedly, to enforce world peace and prosperity after saving the world from apparent destruction and devastation (I Thess. 5:3) (Dan. 8:25) (Rev. 6:1-8) (Rev. 18) (Matt. 24:37-39). He also will boast extraordinary, supernatural powers of the mind in apparent attainment of the New Age ideal, i.e., a god-man endowed with "Christ consciousness." Quite naturally, he also will appeal to the baser instincts of people by promoting humanistic and mystical views such as the inherent "goodness" of people and the unlimited potential and power of the mind through "higher consciousness" techniques.

Furthermore, by claiming the knowledge of how all mankind can achieve a higher level of existence, and proving it with "power and signs and lying wonders," it will take a very strong Christian to endure the ridicule and criticism heaped upon anyone who refuses to be "scientific" and "modern" and "enlightened" and "progressive-minded." You can be sure that most people will not look very favorably upon anyone who allegedly retards or prevents the "transformation" of the world into a "much better place to live."

Only a sincere, honest-minded Christian, well-versed in matters pertaining to eschatology ("end-time" biblical prophecies) and Christian apologetics (a study of the vast amount of evidence substantiating the truth claims of Christianity), will possess the proper foundation of knowledge from which to resist the tremendous appeal this man and his religion will pose! Perhaps that is why so many Christians will backslide in the days just before the Rapture — things will not have happened the way people expect them to happen! The fact that so many Christians will backslide from their Christian faith and doctrine should give due credit to the incredible deception which Antichrist will perpetrate upon the world at large!

Daniel 8:25

And through his policy also he shall cause craft (Heb. MIRMAH; fraud, guile, treachery, deceit) to prosper...and by peace (and prosperity) shall destroy (deceive, and thereby doom) many. (KJV)

War and famine fool nobody. But if the world was to encounter a man capable of creating an economic paradise on earth while personally enforcing world peace and security, they would be easy prey to his philosophical and religious ideas. Even many Christians will be deceived! In the scriptural passage above, *Strong's Hebrew-Greek Dictionary* defines the word "craft" as meaning "fraud and guile and treachery and deceit," and the word "peace" as meaning "peace and prosperity and security and abundance." On that basis, then, the above passage actually is saying that the policies of the Antichrist will cause fraud and guile and treachery and deceit to prosper, and that the Antichrist will destroy people through peace and prosperity and security and abundance. Therefore, when placed within the context of incredible peace and security and prosperity, Satan will find it easy to deceive people, even Christians, if they are confused and misinformed or even uninformed about what is really happening. That is why it is so dangerous that currently we find ourselves in a situation where a great deal of confusion and controversy surrounds the subject of Bible prophecy, often even to the point where many Christians disdainfully ignore it altogether.

II Thess. 2:3

Let no man deceive you by any means: for that day (Day of the Lord) shall not come, except there come a falling away first, and that man of sin be revealed, the son of perdition. (KJV)

We must be very careful to distinguish the difference between the "coming" of Antichrist (II Thess. 2:9) and the "revelation" of Antichrist (II Thess. 2:3). First, he will come upon the world scene and deceive people about the nature and source of his miraculous powers, then and only then, will he be "revealed" (Greek word APOKALUPTO; revealed, disclosed, uncovered). But, once his true nature and source of power are "revealed" to the unbelieving world, the world will worship both Satan and Antichrist as the deception continues with a different focus. (Rev. 13:1-4). This extraordinary development will be possible only AFTER the Holy Spirit is taken out of the way of Satan (but not out of the world) so that He no longer hinders Satan (II Thess. 2:6-8), and it will begin immediately after the Rapture when the whole world marvels at the recovery of Antichrist after he is "wounded to death" and subsequently indwelt and possessed by Satan himself (Rev. 13:3). — "And I saw one of his heads as it were wounded to death; and his deadly wound was healed: and all the world wondered after the beast."

II Thess. 2:1-12

1 Now we beseech you, brethren, by the coming of our Lord Jesus Christ, and by our gathering together unto him,

2 That ye be not soon shaken in mind, or be troubled, neither by spirit, nor by word, nor by letter as from us, as that the day of Christ is at hand.

3 Let no man deceive you by any means: for that day shall not come, except there come a falling away first, and that man of sin be revealed, the son of perdition;

4 Who opposeth and exalteth himself above all that is called God, or that is worshipped; so that he as God sitteth in the temple of God, shewing himself that he is God.

5 Remember ye not, that, when I was yet with you, I told you these things?

6 And now ye know what withholdeth that he might be revealed in his time.

7 For the mystery of iniquity doth already work: only he who now letteth (restraineth) will let (restrain), until he be taken out of the way.

8 And then shall that Wicked (i.e., Antichrist) be revealed, whom the Lord shall consume with the spirit of his mouth, and shall destroy with the brightness of his coming:

9 Even him (i.e., Antichrist), whose coming is after the working of Satan with all power and signs and lying wonders,

10 And with all deceivableness of unrighteousness in them that perish; because they received not the love of the truth, that they might be saved.

11 And for this cause God shall send them strong delusion, that they should believe a lie:

12 That they all might be damned who believed not the truth, but had pleasure in unrighteousness. (KJV)

"Mystery of iniquity." *Strong's Hebrew-Greek Dictionary* defines the word "mystery" in the following manner:

3466 musterion (moos-tay'-ree-on);

from a derivative of muo (to shut the mouth); a secret or "mystery" (through the idea of silence imposed by initiation into religious rites):

KJV— mystery.

Likewise, the word "iniquity" is defined by Strong as:

458 anomia (an-om-ee'-ah);
from 459; illegality, i.e. violation of law or (genitive case) wickedness:
KJV— iniquity, X transgress (-ion of) the law, unrighteousness.

Accordingly, the idea here in II Thessalonians seems to be that the expression "mystery of iniquity" encompasses the whole range of evil and deceit that leads to willful spiritual blindness and religious and moral deception. Therefore, a fervent love for truth, or the lack thereof, seems to be the key element involved whenever obedience to God's laws is at stake. Traditionally, truth always has been defined as any hypothetical proposition that corresponds to reality based on factual evidence and logical consistency. That is why a careful and honest examination of the evidence reveals that the personal, infinite, triune God of Christianity is Ultimate Reality and Ultimate Truth precisely as the Christian Bible tells us.

However, since the time of the German philosopher Hegel, and especially since the early 1900's, the concept and definition of truth has undergone a radical and remarkable transformation throughout most of society due to the influence of relativistic thinking which is in sharp contrast to absolutes based upon the logic law of non-contradiction. No longer is truth often thought of as something which corresponds to reality, but rather as something which is desirable or convenient or helpful to believe in for extraneous, unrelated reasons. That is why so many people find it easier than ever before to believe in whatever they wish to believe about many different things in life, and in the case of many professing Christians, to ignore or reinterpret biblical scriptures whenever they find them unpleasant or otherwise disruptive to their lifestyle. This, then, is willful spiritual blindness; the unwillingness to seek and accept the truth — no matter what it is. Such willful spiritual blindness during the very "endtimes" is further elaborated upon within this very same biblical passage:

II Thess. 2:10-12
10 And with all deceivableness of unrighteousness in them that perish; because they received not the love of the truth, that they might be saved.

11 And for this cause God shall send them strong delusion, that they should believe a lie:

12 That they all might be damned who believed not the truth, but had pleasure in unrighteousness. (KJV)

We should note that the words "letteth" and "let" are old, archaic English words meaning "hinder," or "to hold down" in the Greek.

Accordingly, the "restrainer" or "hinderer" in this passage must represent the Holy Spirit for several reasons. First of all, the personal pronoun "he" is used in reference to the "restrainer." Since there is no obvious symbolism involved here, it is best to give this passage a consistent literal interpretation. Furthermore, it is the power of the Holy Spirit which restrains or limits the power of Satan and his minions, not the "church." Although the Bible admonishes us to be "salt" and "light" to our society and culture, and we have power and authority over Satan through the name of Jesus, that is not the same thing as actually controlling Satan externally, world-wide. Although the scriptural evidence indicates that this "restraining" influence ceases at the time of the Rapture, please note it is only said that the Restrainer is taken out of the way, but not necessarily out of the world as well. Obviously this is important to note because the Holy Spirit will continue to draw people to Christ during the Great Tribulation which follows immediately after the Rapture.

It is said that the Antichrist will sit in the rebuilt Jewish temple in Jerusalem and declare himself to be "God." However, this does not mean that he will try to pass himself off as the personal, infinite, triune Christian God of the Christian Bible, but only as a god of the New Age variety. (The letter "g" does not have to be capitalized in the Greek.) In fact, in this very same passage it is said that he "opposeth" everything associated with the true God in Heaven. Furthermore, not only does he oppose God immediately after the Rapture when he executes Christian believers for their faith in Christ, but even before the Rapture, he will advocate his own brand of morality and spirituality as confirmed in a number of passages.

For instance, Daniel 7:25 gives us additional insight: "And he (Antichrist) shall speak great words against the most High...and think to change times and laws..." So, in other words, Antichrist will boldly defy God while advancing his own standard of morals and values for all of society. No decent standard or sensible norm will be safe from attack or immune to criticism. Accordingly, from the very outset, there never will be any pretense on his part at being very sympathetic to the Jews in Israel or to Christians in general, nor will he ever pretend to be the Jewish Messiah as some people suppose — especially since Israel is one of the very first countries which he attacks when he first rises to power. (Dan. 8:9). Instead, he begins soon after his initial appearance to criticize and defy traditional Christian beliefs and values and morality, and then by the time the Rapture occurs, reaches the point where he is even quite willing to kill anyone who proclaims their faith in Christ. Later, he even has the audacity to violate the sanctity of the sacred Holy of Holies room in the rebuilt Jewish Temple while boldly proclaiming himself to be the god of gods.

II John 1:7
7 For many deceivers are entered into the world, who confess not that Jesus Christ is come in the flesh. This is a deceiver and an antichrist. (KJV)

I John 4:3
3 And every spirit that confesseth not that Jesus Christ is come in the flesh is not of God: and this is that spirit of antichrist, whereof ye have heard that it should come; and even now already is it in the world. (KJV)

I John 2:18, 22
18 Little children, it is the last time: and as ye have heard that antichrist shall come, even now are there many antichrists; whereby we know that it is the last time.
22 Who is a liar but he that denieth that Jesus is the Christ? He is antichrist, that denieth the Father and the Son. (KJV)

In these passages, not only are we told that a specific, unique personage called "antichrist" will appear some day, but that since the inception of Christianity, there always have been people who have denied that the historic Jesus Christ is God manifested in the flesh, or as noted in I John 2:22, that both God the Father and God the Son are the true God in Heaven. These people, too, are "little" antichrists in a manner of speaking. So, while we are warned against the heresy these people teach, we also are given further insight as to exactly what the Antichrist will advocate, and how the Bible itself actually defines the word "antichrist."

Since *Merriam-Webster's Collegiate Dictionary* defines the prefix "anti" as meaning "one that is opposed," this means that the Antichrist will be opposed (to the true God in Heaven). As we noted in the paragraph above while commenting on I John 2:22, the Bible says that Antichrist will deny the true God in Heaven, i.e., the personal, infinite, triune God of Christianity. This is completely consistent with Daniel when he says in Daniel 7:25 that the Antichrist "shall speak great words against the most High," and in Daniel 11:36-37 where he states that the Antichrist will "magnify himself above every god, and shall speak marvellous things against the God of gods... nor regard any god: for he shall magnify himself above all." This, then, is how we should define the word "antichrist" because that is how the Bible defines it.

That is why it is wrong to think that the Antichrist will ever pretend to be the Jewish Messiah — even when he first appears as a savior who rescues the world from apparent imminent destruction. Instead, the Antichrist will deny both God the Father and God the Son while proclaiming himself to be a god above all. Therefore, it is not a coincidence that the popular New Age Movement teaches we can achieve godhood and extraordinary powers of the mind through "higher consciousness" techniques or "cosmic Christ consciousness." Thus, the historical evidence proving the true identity of Jesus is ignored by these people and their followers, and He is relegated to the status of just another ordinary psychic seer.

Daniel 8:9

And out of one of them came forth a little horn (Antichrist), which waxed exceeding great, toward the south, and toward the east, and toward the pleasant land (Palestine; Israel). (KJV)

Daniel 8:23, 24

And in the latter time of their kingdom, when the transgressors are come to the full, a king of fierce countenance and understanding dark sentences, shall stand up. And his power shall be mighty, but not by his own power: and he shall destroy wonderfully... (KJV)

It is when the communists "come to the full" that "a king of fierce countenance...shall stand up." This fierce-looking man is the Antichrist, and he will appear unexpectedly as the apparent answer to the hopes and prayers of people throughout the world when it will appear as if we are facing imminent destruction. Nothing will seem too difficult for this man to achieve! Although the "church-world" and "religious leaders" will seem dazed and confused while fumbling around for plausible explanations, the Antichrist will have the answers! During an extraordinary period of crisis and fear and confusion, he will mesmerize the whole world with his incredible accomplishments and enchanting oratory.

Other than from Satan, where could a man obtain this fantastic power and ability? That is what Daniel was saying in the phrases, "understanding dark sentences" and "his power shall be mighty, but not by his own power." Such amazing power and super-intelligence will be satanic-inspired — as the apostle Paul likewise explains in the following scriptural passage: "Even him, whose coming (ascendancy to power and prominence) is after the working of Satan with all power and signs and lying wonders." (II Thess. 2:9).

Please note in the above scriptures that when the Antichrist begins his ascendancy to power and prominence, he immediately initiates war against his enemies, including Israel. Accordingly, there obviously will be no pretense on his part at being the promised Messiah for whom the Jews have been waiting on for countless centuries. Instead, right from the very start, he is utterly opposed to the true God in Heaven and everything associated with Him.

Daniel 11:36-39

36 And the king shall do according to his will; and he shall exalt himself, and magnify himself above every god, and shall speak marvellous things against the God of gods, and shall prosper till the indignation be accomplished: for that that is determined shall be done.

37 Neither shall he regard the God of his fathers, nor the desire of women, nor regard any god: for he shall magnify himself above all.

38 But in his estate shall he honour the God of forces: and a god whom his fathers knew not shall he honour with gold, and silver, and with precious stones, and pleasant things.

39 Thus shall he do in the most strong holds with a strange god, whom he shall acknowledge and increase with glory: and he shall cause them to rule over many, and shall divide the land for gain. (KJV)

"And the king shall do according to his will." From the very beginning, the Antichrist will defy God by doing whatever he pleases. Daniel also says that he will "exalt" and "magnify" himself — statements which are reminiscent of the self-deification delusion that snared Adam and Eve in the Garden of Eden. He even will "magnify himself above every god," and be so bold as to "speak marvellous things against the God of gods." Obviously these statements seem to imply that the Antichrist, indeed, will advocate "god-hood" for everyone — just as the New Agers teach.

"Shall prosper till the indignation be accomplished." The Hebrew word for "indignation" is ZAAM, meaning "rage; fury, especially, God's displeasure at sin." Therefore, this passage simply is saying that the Antichrist will "prosper" in his plans to deceive people before the Rapture by inspiring world peace and prosperity, and then later, after the Rapture, continue to "prosper" by initiating war against Christian believers for three and one-half years. But then, after that, the Day of God's Wrath begins and the Antichrist no longer "prospers" in his plans because God's "indignation" is unleashed in the form of the Trumpet-Vial plagues, culminating in His Return at the Battle of Armageddon.

"Neither shall he regard the God of his fathers." Reference to the personal, infinite, triune God of the Christian Bible is not necessarily intended here in this passage because the letter "G" is not capitalized in the word "God" in the Hebrew. Here is how *Strong's Hebrew-Greek Dictionary* defines the word "God":

430 'elohiym (el-o-heem');

plural of 433; gods in the ordinary sense; but specifically used (in the plural thus, especially with the article) of the supreme God; occasionally applied by way of deference to magistrates; and sometimes as a superlative:

KJV— angels, X exceeding, God (gods)- dess, -ly), X (very) great, judges, X mighty.

So, the word "God" actually can be translated as "gods in the ordinary sense" or it can be rendered as "the supreme God." However, we should note, too, that the article "the" was added arbitrarily by the KJV translators because they jumped to the same conclusion that everyone else did — so the presence of the article "the" does not lend any support to the theory that this word must refer to the true God of the Bible. Accordingly, I believe it is erroneous to assume this phrase necessarily refers to the Jewish fathers of the Antichrist in an attempt to prove the Antichrist will pretend to be the Jewish Messiah. Besides, it could just as easily refer to the Islamic supreme god, Allah, if the Antichrist is a Moslem or Druze Moslem. Instead, it means precisely what it actually says, i.e., he ignores his ancestors' religion by simply declining to honor or worship the god whom his ancestors worshipped, whomever that may be. Corroboration on this point is provided in this very same passage when it continues by saying that neither will he "regard any god: for he shall magnify himself above all" before the Rapture, but that after the Rapture, he will publicly honor the "god of forces" who is none other than Satan himself:

Rev. 13:4

And they worshipped the dragon which gave power unto the beast: and they worshipped the beast, saying, Who is like unto the beast? who is able to make war with him? (KJV)

The Antichrist will proclaim himself to be a god, but it will be as a "new-age" style of god. That is why he magnifies himself above every other god before the Rapture when he is astounding the world with his miraculous mind powers and military genius. But, after the Rapture when he is "revealed" to the world and everyone knows that his power is from Satan, he curses and blasphemes the true God in Heaven while publicly honoring the "god of forces." Likewise, it is essential to our understanding on this matter to remember that he invades Israel in his initial rise-to-power, many years before the pre-tribulation Rapture. Therefore, without a doubt, all of these things indicate there will be no pretense on his part at being the Jewish Messiah.

"He shall honour the god of forces." New Age thinking and Eastern mysticism probably will ascribe such power to the "universal spirit" or the "cosmic consciousness." But, those who are wise will understand that it is Satan who is the source of such abilities, not some "universal power" achieved through "higher consciousness" or a "sudden leap in evolution." However, immediately after the Rapture, everyone in the world will understand that Satan is the real reason for the incredible power and abilities of Antichrist. (Rev. 13:2, 4) (Dan. 11:39) (Hab. 1:11). Perhaps this is what II Thess. 2:3-12 means when it states that the Antichrist is revealed (APOKALUPTO; disclosed, uncovered, revealed) immediately after the Rapture when the Holy Spirit is taken out of the way (but not out of the world) as a mortally-wounded Antichrist is indwelt and possessed by Satan himself. This does not mean, though, that people will believe that Satan is evil. Instead, they most likely will think — as many people believe already — that Satan is Lucifer and that he is the morally good guy. Especially since he will have been responsible for creating world peace and prosperity through his human surrogate of instrumentality, Antichrist, while God will be held responsible for taking it away with His judgments upon the earth. That is why Revelation says several times that AFTER the Great Tribulation — during the Great Day Of The Lord — people on earth will curse God while refusing to repent of their sins.

"Shall honor the god of forces." According to *Strong's Hebrew-Greek Dictionary* and Rev. Alexander Hislop, author of the classic, *The Two Babylons*, a more accurate translation of the word "forces" is "fortifications." Therefore, this phrase may be an allusion to the great rebel Nimrod, who (as documented by Hislop; pp. 30-55) can be termed "the god of fortifications." Apparently, the Antichrist will be a modern-day version of Nimrod, who was viewed in his days as an extraordinary benefactor of mankind because he taught people how to protect themselves from the wild animals by building walls around their cities, and because he was a mighty hunter of these same wild animals who were threatening to overrun the earth. But, after giving mankind the benefits and blessings of safety and security, he used his prestige to persuade people to rebel against God, thus beginning the great Babylonian apostasy.

The Antichrist also will appeal to the baser instincts of man by promoting immoral sexuality, idolatry, sorceries and drugs:

Revelation 18:23, 24

23 And the light of a candle shall shine no more at all in thee; and the voice of the bridegroom and of the bride shall be heard no more at all in thee: for thy merchants were the great men of the earth; for by thy sorceries were all nations deceived.

24 And in her was found the blood of prophets, and of saints, and of all that were slain upon the earth. (KJV)

Revelation 9:20, 21

20 And the rest of the men which were not killed by these plagues yet

repented not of the works of their hands, that they should not worship devils, and idols of gold, and silver, and brass, and stone, and of wood: which neither can see, nor hear, nor walk:

21 Neither repented they of their murders, nor of their sorceries, nor of their fornication, nor of their thefts. (KJV)

Amazingly, the Bible predicts that occultism and witchcraft and drugs will become very prevalent throughout all of society in the years immediately preceding Armageddon. The word "sorceries" was used in scriptures such as Rev. 9:21 to foretell this extraordinary development because the word "sorceries" comes from the Greek word PHARMAKEIA, which means occult worship or black magic associated with the usage of drugs. Unfortunately, just like many other ungodly things, there is a growing acceptance of witchcraft and the occult in our society that would have been unthinkable not that many years ago.

Isaiah 2:10-21

10 Enter into the rock, and hide thee in the dust, for fear of the LORD, and for the glory of his majesty.

11 The lofty looks of man shall be humbled, and the haughtiness of men shall be bowed down, and the LORD alone shall be exalted in that day.

12 For the day of the LORD of hosts shall be upon every one that is proud and lofty, and upon every one that is lifted up; and he shall be brought low:

13 And upon all the cedars of Lebanon, that are high and lifted up, and upon all the oaks of Bashan,

14 And upon all the high mountains, and upon all the hills that are lifted up,

15 And upon every high tower, and upon every fenced wall,

16 And upon all the ships of Tarshish, and upon all pleasant pictures.

17 And the loftiness of man shall be bowed down, and the haughtiness of men shall be made low: and the LORD alone shall be exalted in that day.

18 And the idols he shall utterly abolish.

19 And they shall go into the holes of the rocks, and into the caves of the earth, for fear of the LORD, and for the glory of his majesty, when he ariseth to shake terribly the earth.

20 In that day a man shall cast his idols of silver, and his idols of gold, which they made each one for himself to worship, to the moles and to the bats;

21 To go into the clefts of the rocks, and into the tops of the ragged rocks, for fear of the LORD, and for the glory of his majesty, when he ariseth to shake terribly the earth. (KJV)

Zechariah 13:1-4

1 In that day there shall be a fountain opened to the house of David and to the inhabitants of Jerusalem for sin and for uncleanness.

2 And it shall come to pass in that day, saith the LORD of hosts, that I will cut off the names of the idols out of the land, and they shall no more be remembered: and also I will cause the prophets and the unclean spirit to pass out of the land.

3 And it shall come to pass, that when any shall yet prophesy, then his father and his mother that begat him shall say unto him, Thou shalt not live; for thou speakest lies in the name of the LORD: and his father and his mother that begat him shall thrust him through when he prophesieth.

4 And it shall come to pass in that day, that the prophets shall be ashamed every one of his vision, when he hath prophesied; neither shall they wear a rough garment to deceive: (KJV)

Isaiah 31:5-8

5 As birds flying, so will the LORD of hosts defend Jerusalem; defending also he will deliver it; and passing over he will preserve it.

6 Turn ye unto him from whom the children of Israel have deeply revolted.

7 For in that day every man shall cast away his idols of silver, and his idols of gold, which your own hands have made unto you for a sin.

8 Then shall the Assyrian fall with the sword, not of a mighty man; and the sword, not of a mean man, shall devour him: but he shall flee from the sword, and his young men shall be discomfited. (KJV) (Compare: Isa. 19:1-3; Isa. 47:9-12; Micah 5:10-15.)

The word "sorceries" in its modern context would include any technique that attempts to shape or change reality through any type of "mind power." Examples would include elementary forms of sorcery such as certain types of "positive thinking," and "visualization," and "guided imagery," etc.. Likewise, whenever a person blanks all rational thought from his mind through meditation (Eastern style), hypnosis, and even some types of psychotherapy, he is leaving himself vulnerable to demonic attack. Generally speaking, people ordinarily do not possess special magic or supernatural powers of the mind unless they are aided by evil demonic forces.

Some people argue for the syncretism of Christianity with psychotherapy on the basis that "all truth is God's truth." But, psychotherapy differs from true sciences such as physics and chemistry in that there is no general consensus on general principles; in fact, there are hundreds of competing theories and therapies that often contradict each other. It is true, however, that psychology is a science to the extent that it observes human nature, develops theories of learning, etc. The only conflict comes when psychology leaves its proper domain and offers advice on the moral and spiritual problems of life in contradistinction to biblical scripture. Likewise, psychological therapies are full of humanistic assumptions and presuppositions which require a most extraordinary effort in any attempt to distinguish truth from error. The practical effect in most cases, I suspect, is the inevitable blending of Christian and humanistic concepts to one degree or another.

Others argue that since we supplement our knowledge of the Bible with dictionaries, commentaries, historical records, etc., then we should also be willing to supplement biblical counseling with psychological counseling. But it is one thing to supplement our knowledge of the Bible with various objective truths gleaned from non-biblical sources; an entirely different matter to embrace unproven theories concerning man's spiritual and moral nature that either are contradictory to what the Bible teaches or not taught in the Bible at all. (See: II Peter 1:3-10; John 8:31, 32; II Tim. 3:16, 17; II Cor. 12:9, 10; Phil. 3:13, 14; 4:5-13; Ps. 46:1, 2; Col. 3; I Cor. 2:16; Gal. 5:22-24.)

The apostle Paul also predicts that every form of sin and evil will be experienced to the ultimate degree during the "last days," and that most people generally will believe whatever they wish to believe rather than believe Truth. (II Tim. 3:1-4:4) (II Thess. 2:9-12) (I Tim. 4:1-10). We should note, also, that the expression, "last days," actually can refer either to all of the time-period between the First and Second Comings of Christ (Heb.1:1) (Acts 2:16-18) (I John 2:18) (I Tim. 4:1-10), or it can simply refer to the years immediately prior to the Second Coming (II Peter 3:3-4).

However, II Tim. 3:13 makes it quite clear that "evil men and seducers shall wax worse and worse, deceiving and being deceived." Hence, the conclusion that evil and deceit will reach their ultimate degree of fulfillment immediately before the Return of Christ. (cf. Matt. 24:11, 12, 24).

I Timothy 4:1-10

1 Now the Spirit speaketh expressly, that in the latter times some shall depart from the faith, giving heed to seducing spirits, and doctrines of devils;

2 Speaking lies in hypocrisy; having their conscience seared with a hot iron;

3 Forbidding to marry, and commanding to abstain from meats, which God hath created to be received with thanksgiving of them which believe and know the truth.

4 For every creature of God is good, and nothing to be refused, if it be received with thanksgiving:

5 For it is sanctified by the word of God and prayer.

6 If thou put the brethren in remembrance of these things, thou shalt be a good minister of Jesus Christ, nourished up in the words of faith and of good doctrine, whereunto thou hast attained.

7 But refuse profane and old wives' fables, and exercise thyself rather unto godliness.

8 For bodily exercise profiteth little: but godliness is profitable unto all things, having promise of the life that now is, and of that which is to come.

9 This is a faithful saying and worthy of all acceptation.

10 For therefore we both labour and suffer reproach, because we trust in the living God, who is the Saviour of all men, specially of those that believe. (KJV)

II Timothy 3:1-17

1 This know also, that in the last days perilous times shall come.

2 For men shall be lovers of their own selves, covetous, boasters, proud, blasphemers, disobedient to parents, unthankful, unholy,

3 Without natural affection, trucebreakers, false accusers, incontinent, fierce, despisers of those that are good,

4 Traitors, heady, highminded, lovers of pleasures more than lovers of

God;

5 Having a form of godliness, but denying the power thereof: from such turn away.

6 For of this sort are they which creep into houses, and lead captive silly women laden with sins, led away with divers lusts,

7 Ever learning, and never able to come to the knowledge of the truth.

8 Now as Jannes and Jambres withstood Moses, so do these also resist the truth: men of corrupt minds, reprobate concerning the faith.

9 But they shall proceed no further: for their folly shall be manifest unto all men, as theirs also was.

10 But thou hast fully known my doctrine, manner of life, purpose, faith, longsuffering, charity, patience,

11 Persecutions, afflictions, which came unto me at Antioch, at Iconium, at Lystra; what persecutions I endured: but out of them all the Lord delivered me.

12 Yea, and all that will live godly in Christ Jesus shall suffer persecution.

13 But evil men and seducers shall wax worse and worse, deceiving, and being deceived.

14 But continue thou in the things which thou hast learned and hast been assured of, knowing of whom thou hast learned them;

15 And that from a child thou hast known the holy scriptures, which are able to make thee wise unto salvation through faith which is in Christ Jesus.

16 All scripture is given by inspiration of God, and is profitable for doctrine, for reproof, for correction, for instruction in righteousness:

17 That the man of God may be perfect, throughly furnished unto all good works. (KJV)

II Timothy 4:1-4

1 I charge thee therefore before God, and the Lord Jesus Christ, who shall judge the quick and the dead at his appearing and his kingdom;

2 Preach the word; be instant in season, out of season; reprove, rebuke, exhort with all longsuffering and doctrine.

3 For the time will come when they will not endure sound doctrine; but after their own lusts shall they heap to themselves teachers, having itching ears;

4 And they shall turn away their ears from the truth, and shall be

turned unto fables. (KJV)

Here is what Revelation has to say about the two types of churches and "Christians" prevalent during the very "last days" before the pre-tribulation Rapture occurs. First, the message to the authentic Christians who are "born-again" in Christ Jesus and are "overcomers" of the world because of their faith in Christ:

Revelation 3:6-12

6 He that hath an ear, let him hear what the Spirit saith unto the churches.

7 And to the angel of the church in Philadelphia write; These things saith he that is holy, he that is true, he that hath the key of David, he that openeth, and no man shutteth; and shutteth, and no man openeth;

8 I know thy works: behold, I have set before thee an open door, and no man can shut it: for thou hast a little strength, and hast kept my word, and hast not denied my name.

9 Behold, I will make them of the synagogue of Satan, which say they are Jews, and are not, but do lie; behold, I will make them to come and worship before thy feet, and to know that I have loved thee.

10 Because thou hast kept the word of my patience, I also will keep thee from the hour of temptation, which shall come upon all the world, to try them that dwell upon the earth.

11 Behold, I come quickly: hold that fast which thou hast, that no man take thy crown.

12 Him that overcometh will I make a pillar in the temple of my God, and he shall go no more out: and I will write upon him the name of my God, and the name of the city of my God, which is new Jerusalem, which cometh down out of heaven from my God: and I will write upon him my new name. (KJV)

"I will make them of the synagogue of Satan, which say they are Jews, and are not, but do lie." One interesting point to note is that even passages such as this one are finding a complete literal fulfillment during the very last days of the endtimes. Amazingly, there are some people who have become so obsessed with conforming their lives to the Laws of Moses in the Old Testament Covenant that they apparently have hypnotized themselves into believing they really are Jews even though they actually are Gentiles. Obviously they never have even bothered to read the book of Galatians in the New Testament very carefully or honestly.

Now, the message for "professing" Christians who are not really "born-again" in Christ Jesus:

Revelation 3:13-22

13 He that hath an ear, let him hear what the Spirit saith unto the churches.

14 And unto the angel of the church of the Laodiceans write; These things saith the Amen, the faithful and true witness, the beginning of the creation of God;

15 I know thy works, that thou art neither cold nor hot: I would thou wert cold or hot.

16 So then because thou art lukewarm, and neither cold nor hot, I will spue thee out of my mouth.

17 Because thou sayest, I am rich, and increased with goods, and have need of nothing; and knowest not that thou art wretched, and miserable, and poor, and blind, and naked:

18 I counsel thee to buy of me gold tried in the fire, that thou mayest be rich; and white raiment, that thou mayest be clothed, and that the shame of thy nakedness do not appear; and anoint thine eyes with eyesalve, that thou mayest see.

19 As many as I love, I rebuke and chasten: be zealous therefore, and repent.

20 Behold, I stand at the door, and knock: if any man hear my voice, and open the door, I will come in to him, and will sup with him, and he with me.

21 To him that overcometh will I grant to sit with me in my throne, even as I also overcame, and am set down with my Father in his throne.

22 He that hath an ear, let him hear what the Spirit saith unto the churches. (KJV)

Finally, there is one last reason why there must be a final great apostasy just prior to the Rapture. Although we will develop this theme more fully in chapter six of this book, Revelation 12 essentially entails a considerable amount of symbolism in which we observe a pregnant, sun-clad woman standing on the moon while wearing a crown of twelve stars upon her head, and travailing in great agony due to the imminent birth of her man-child. Accordingly, as we will prove later, the sun-clad woman represents the visible church of Christ who will suffer great spiritual pain immediately before the man-child Christians are Raptured to Heaven. Since we are dealing with symbolic spiritual matters in this instance, it is apparent that this travailing experience must symbolize the spiritual tribulation or final great apostasy which the church will experience just before the Rapture occurs.

However, let me hasten to emphasize that this is not the Great Tribulation. The Great Tribulation happens only after the Rapture of the true church, and it is characterized by precisely three and one-half years of mass executions of (newly-converted) Christians who will not take the mark of the beast. Before the Rapture, the Bible states repeatedly that the Antichrist will destroy (deceive) people through miracles and peace and prosperity, not physical torture. Therefore, persecution of Christians before the Rapture is spiritual and deceptive in nature; after the Rapture, it is physical and brutal in nature even though just as much deception will continue in a different form.

Sometimes it is taught that a spiritual "latter rain" during the endtimes will spark a great revival among people. (Joel 2:23, 24) (Jer. 5:24) (Hosea 6:3) (Zech. 10:1) (James 5:7). Although this is true, it will not happen before the Rapture; that period is marked only by deception and apostasy! It is only after the Rapture, during the Great Tribulation, that mass numbers of people will become saved through Christ Jesus at a time when people will dream special dreams and see visions and prophesy. (Revelation 6:12-17) (Joel 2:28-31) (Acts 2:16-21).

"A great red dragon, having seven heads and ten horns, and seven crowns upon his heads." The seven-headed dragon portrayed in Revelation 12 represents Satan, as confirmed in verse 9. This symbolic dragon is somewhat analogous to the symbolic seven-headed beast which is portrayed in both Revelation 13 and 17 — with several important differences. Whereas the seven-headed dragon represents Satan exclusively, the seven-headed beast is used to symbolize both Satan and Antichrist, a matter we will discuss more fully, later. In both symbolic images, however, the seven heads represent the seven major world empires which oppress Israel at one time or another down throughout history. Likewise, whereas the seven-headed dragon is wearing crowns on all seven of its heads, in Revelation 13, the seven-headed beast is wearing crowns on only the ten horns of the seventh head. By comparison, the seven-headed beast in Revelation 17 is not wearing any crowns at all on its seven heads and ten horns.

Revelation 17:12 indicates that the ten horns are crowned on the seven-headed beast in Revelation 13 because both the beast Antichrist and the ten-horn kings have power and authority at that point in time, whereas the seven-headed beast and the ten horns in Revelation 17 were not yet empowered at the time of John's Revelation. That is why, in Revelation 17, John said that the seven mountains or heads of the beast represent "seven kings: five are fallen, and one is and the other is not yet come, and when he cometh, he must continue a short space." (Rev. 17:10). Similarly in Revelation 17:8, "the beast that was, and is not, and yet is." Quite obviously these statements correlate perfectly with the recorded history of the seven biblical world empires! At the time John wrote Revelation, five of the seven world empires (Egypt, Assyria, Babylon, Persia, and Greece) were history, which matches the phrase "five are fallen." Rome was the existent empire at the time of his revelation, hence the phrase "and one is." Likewise, the empire of the Antichrist was future then, even as it is now at the time these words are being written, thereby matching the scriptural phrase which reads as follows: "the other is not yet come, and when he cometh, he must continue a short space."

As we will demonstrate during our analysis of Revelation, chapters 4-11 in Revelation narrate a sequential series of post-Rapture events which are parallel in time to the events portrayed in Revelation 12-16. Both accounts begin with the pre-tribulation Rapture, then correlate with each other through a long series of apocalyptic events which, in each case, culminate in the Battle of Armageddon and the Return of Christ. Furthermore, it is important to note that all of the events portrayed in Revelation 4-11 and 12-16 happen in a very specific time-frame relative to all of the other events which occur. Many of them even are numbered in their sequence of occurrence within the first parallel account. Accordingly, since all seven heads of the dragon are crowned, thereby indicating power and authority, before the manchild Christians are Raptured to Heaven, all seven biblical world empires must exist at one time or another before the Rapture. Since the seventh empire is the empire of Antichrist, it obviously has to be in existence before the Rapture can occur. Which means, of course, that the Antichrist will appear before the pre-tribulation Rapture to inspire the final great apostasy!

Mystery Babylon And The Beast

Revelation 17:1-18

1 And there came one of the seven angels which had the seven vials, and talked with me, saying unto me, Come hither; I will shew unto thee the judgment of the great whore that sitteth upon many waters:

2 With whom the kings of the earth have committed fornication, and the inhabitants of the earth have been made drunk with the wine of her fornication.

3 So he carried me away in the spirit into the wilderness: and I saw a woman sit upon a scarlet coloured beast, full of names of blasphemy, having seven heads and ten horns.

4 And the woman was arrayed in purple and scarlet colour, and decked with gold and precious stones and pearls, having a golden cup in her hand full of abominations and filthiness of her fornication:

5 And upon her forehead was a name written, MYSTERY, BABYLON THE GREAT, THE MOTHER OF HARLOTS AND ABOMINATIONS OF THE EARTH.

6 And I saw the woman drunken with the blood of the saints, and with the blood of the martyrs of Jesus: and when I saw her, I wondered with great admiration.

7 And the angel said unto me, Wherefore didst thou marvel? I will tell thee the mystery of the woman, and of the beast that carrieth her, which hath the seven heads and ten horns.

8 The beast that thou sawest was, and is not; and shall ascend out of the bottomless pit, and go into perdition: and they that dwell on the earth shall wonder, whose names were not written in the book of life from the foundation of the world, when they behold the beast that was, and is not, and yet is.

9 And here is the mind which hath wisdom. The seven heads are seven mountains, on which the woman sitteth.

10 And there are seven kings: five are fallen, and one is, and the other is not yet come; and when he cometh, he must continue a short space.

11 And the beast that was, and is not, even he is the eighth, and is of the seven, and goeth into perdition.

12 And the ten horns which thou sawest are ten kings, which have received no kingdom as yet; but receive power as kings one hour with the beast.

13 These have one mind, and shall give their power and strength unto the beast.

14 These shall make war with the Lamb, and the Lamb shall overcome them: for he is Lord of lords, and King of kings: and they that are with him are called, and chosen, and faithful.

15 And he saith unto me, The waters which thou sawest, where the whore sitteth, are peoples, and multitudes, and nations, and tongues.

16 And the ten horns which thou sawest upon the beast, these shall hate the whore, and shall make her desolate and naked, and shall eat her flesh, and burn her with fire.

17 For God hath put in their hearts to fulfil his will, and to agree, and give their kingdom unto the beast, until the words of God shall be fulfilled.

18 And the woman which thou sawest is that great city, which reigneth over the kings of the earth. (KJV)

Verse 15 states that the "water" in this scripture symbolizes or represents all of mankind. Therefore, logic dictates that both the beast and the woman dominate mankind because they both walk on top of the symbolic water.

There are several clues which help us to identify the "beast" in the above passage. Accordingly, first, please note verse 8, which reads as follows: "The beast that...shall ascend out of the bottomless pit and go into perdition." Obviously there is ONLY one individual mentioned anywhere in the Bible who meets all of these requirements, and that person is none other than Satan:

Revelation 20:1-3, 7, 10

1 And I saw an angel come down from heaven, having the key of the bottomless pit and a great chain in his hand.

2 And he laid hold on the dragon, that old serpent, which is the Devil, and Satan, and bound him a thousand years,

3 And cast him into the bottomless pit, and shut him up, and set a seal upon him, that he should deceive the nations no more, till the thousand years should be fulfilled: and after that he must be loosed a little season.

7 And when the thousand years are expired, Satan shall be loosed out of his prison,

10 And the devil that deceived them was cast into the lake of fire and

brimstone, where the beast and the false prophet are, and shall be tormented day and night for ever and ever. (KJV)

Therefore, Satan is the only personage portrayed in the Bible as going into perdition after ascending out of the bottomless pit. Although II Thessalonians 2:3 calls Antichrist the son of perdition, i.e., the son of Satan, or the son of destruction, the Antichrist never is called the man of perdition, nor does he ever ascend from out of the bottomless pit to go into perdition. Instead, the Antichrist literally is killed at the Battle of Armageddon, then immediately resurrected as part of the Second Resurrection and thrown into the eternal Lake of Fire.

Verse 9 continues: "The seven heads (of the beast) are seven mountains." It is only logical to conclude that the heads of the beast are symbolic just as the beast itself is symbolic. Mountain, in Bible prophecy, usually represents a kingdom or empire:

Daniel 2:44, 45

44 And in the days of these kings shall the God of heaven set up a kingdom, which shall never be destroyed: and the kingdom shall not be left to other people, but it shall break in pieces and consume all these kingdoms, and it shall stand for ever.

45 Forasmuch as thou sawest that the stone was cut out of the mountain without hands, and that it brake in pieces the iron, the brass, the clay, the silver, and the gold; the great God hath made known to the king what shall come to pass hereafter: and the dream is certain, and the interpretation thereof sure. (KJV)

Micah 3:12

12 Therefore shall Zion for your sake be plowed as a field, and Jerusalem shall become heaps, and the mountain of the house as the high places of the forest. (KJV)

Micah 4:1, 2

1 But in the last days it shall come to pass, that the mountain of the house of the LORD shall be established in the top of the mountains, and it shall be exalted above the hills; and people shall flow unto it.

2 And many nations shall come, and say, Come, and let us go up to the mountain of the LORD, and to the house of the God of Jacob; and he will

teach us of his ways, and we will walk in his paths: for the law shall go forth of Zion, and the word of the LORD from Jerusalem. (KJV)

Isaiah 2:1-4
1 The word that Isaiah the son of Amoz saw concerning Judah and Jerusalem.
2 And it shall come to pass in the last days, that the mountain of the LORD's house shall be established in the top of the mountains, and shall be exalted above the hills; and all nations shall flow unto it.
3 And many people shall go and say, Come ye, and let us go up to the mountain of the LORD, to the house of the God of Jacob; and he will teach us of his ways, and we will walk in his paths: for out of Zion shall go forth the law, and the word of the LORD from Jerusalem.
4 And he shall judge among the nations, and shall rebuke many people: and they shall beat their swords into plowshares, and their spears into pruninghooks: nation shall not lift up sword against nation, neither shall they learn war any more. (KJV)

Isaiah 30:29-31
29 Ye shall have a song, as in the night when a holy solemnity is kept; and gladness of heart, as when one goeth with a pipe to come into the mountain of the LORD, to the mighty One of Israel.
30 And the LORD shall cause his glorious voice to be heard, and shall shew the lighting down of his arm, with the indignation of his anger, and with the flame of a devouring fire, with scattering, and tempest, and hailstones.
31 For through the voice of the LORD shall the Assyrian be beaten down, which smote with a rod. (KJV)

Zechariah 8:3
3 Thus saith the LORD; I am returned unto Zion, and will dwell in the midst of Jerusalem: and Jerusalem shall be called a city of truth; and the mountain of the LORD of hosts the holy mountain. (KJV)

Therefore, these mountains of the beast represent world empires which oppress Israel during Bible times. This is further verified by John, himself, who said the seven mountains or heads represent "seven kings: five are fallen, and one is and the other is not yet come, and when he cometh, he must continue a short space." (Rev. 17:10). Compare this statement in verse 10 with a similar statement in verse 8: "the beast that was, and is not, and yet is." These statements correlate perfectly with the recorded history of the seven world empires! At the time John wrote Revelation, five of the seven world empires (Egypt, Assyria, Babylon, Persia, and Greece) were history, which matches the phrase "five are fallen." Rome was the existent empire at that point in time, hence the phrase "and one is." Likewise, the empire of the empire of the Antichrist was future then, even as it is now at the time these words are being written, thus matching the scriptural phrase which reads as follows: "the other is not yet come, and when he cometh, he must continue a short space."

Note verse 11: John states "the beast...is the eighth (empire), and is OF the seven (world empires)." The meaning here is two-fold. First, Satan INDIRECTLY controls the seven world empires existent at various times BEFORE the Rapture, but AFTER the Rapture he DIRECTLY controls an eighth empire which is actually a continuation of the seventh empire. Second, please note also that the beast in Revelation 17 must represent a personage who is alive during the time of all seven of the world empires identified above because the seven heads are an integral part of the beast himself! Therefore, the beast in Revelation 17 represents Satan, and the seven heads represent the seven world empires which Satan INDIRECTLY controls before the pre-tribulation Rapture!

However, in both Revelation 13 and 17, the "seven-headed beast" also symbolizes the Antichrist. As confusing as this may seem since we have just proven that the "seven-headed beast" represents Satan, we know this to be true for several reasons. For instance, in Revelation 12, the "dragon," i.e., Satan, has all seven of his heads crowned, thus indicating power and authority over all seven world empires which are existent before the Rapture. But, in Revelation 13, only the "ten horns" on the seventh head of the beast are crowned, thus indicating a personage, namely the Antichrist, who controls the seventh world empire, but not the other six which are history. Likewise, in Revelation 13, Satan is called the "dragon" whenever it is necessary to distinguish a difference between the Antichrist and Satan. Then also, we know that the "beast" in Revelation 13 is a man because both personal attributes and accomplishments of the Antichrist are ascribed to the "beast" throughout the chapter. Therefore, since the symbolism of the seven-headed beast is associated with both the Antichrist and Satan in these scriptures, we must conclude that two different personalities simultaneously occupy the same physical body (from the time of the Rapture until Armageddon).

Revelation 13:1-4

1 And I stood upon the sand of the sea, and saw a beast rise up out of the sea, having seven heads and ten horns, and upon his horns ten crowns, and upon his heads the name of blasphemy.

2 And the beast which I saw was like unto a leopard, and his feet were as the feet of a bear, and his mouth as the mouth of a lion: and the dragon gave him his power, and his seat, and great authority.

3 And I saw one of his heads as it were wounded to death; and his deadly wound was healed: and all the world wondered after the beast.

4 And they worshipped the dragon which gave power unto the beast: and they worshipped the beast, saying, Who is like unto the beast? who is able to make war with him? (KJV)

In summary, the "beast" represents both Satan and the man Antichrist, whereas the "dragon" symbolizes Satan alone. Likewise, the "seven heads" represent the seven world empires indirectly controlled by Satan, whereas the ten crowned-horns of the seventh head represent the Roman Empire countries which form the nucleus of the "empire" of Antichrist. Furthermore, just as we saw in Daniel's visions, not only are the modern-day countries of the old Roman Empire associated with the Antichrist through symbolism in this passage, but the old Grecian, Persian and Babylonian empires are, too, because in the passage above, it describes the beast as "like unto a leopard," with symbolic feet "as the feet of a bear," and a symbolic mouth "as the mouth of a lion." Then finally, we also observe that the "sea" or "water" from which the "beast" emerges is said quite clearly to represent the masses of humanity throughout the world. (Rev. 17:15).

Furthermore, since the symbolism of the seven-headed beast is associated with both Satan and the Antichrist, this coupling of personalities within one symbolic image clearly illustrates the dual nature of two separate personalities operating within one human body. This also explains why only the seventh head (Antichrist) is "wounded to death," while the other six heads are history. As confirmation, a dual personality operating within one body is even implied by several other scriptures! In each case, actions and/or attributes of BOTH Satan and the Antichrist are ascribed to the same individual:

Revelation 11:7
7 And when they shall have finished their testimony, the beast that ascendeth out of the bottomless pit shall make war against them, and shall overcome them, and kill them. (KJV)

The context indicates it is Antichrist who wars against the Two Witnesses after invading Israel. Yet, this passage identifies the beast (Antichrist) as one who will "ascend out of the bottomless pit," an obvious reference to Satan. (Rev. 20:1-3, 7-10).

Revelation 17:11
11 And the beast that was, and is not, even he is the eighth, and is of the seven, and goeth into perdition. (KJV)

Previously we proved this beast to be Satan ("goeth into perdition"); but the context (Rev. 17:12, 13) indicates it is also the Antichrist:

Revelation 17:12, 13
12 And the ten horns which thou sawest are ten kings, which have received no kingdom as yet; but receive power as kings one hour with the beast.
13 These have one mind, and shall give their power and strength unto the beast. (KJV)

Likewise, another scriptural example:

Ezekiel 28:11-16
11 Moreover the word of the LORD came unto me, saying,
12 Son of man, take up a lamentation upon the king of Tyrus, and say unto him, Thus saith the Lord GOD; Thou sealest up the sum, full of wisdom, and perfect in beauty.
13 Thou hast been in Eden the garden of God; every precious stone was thy covering, the sardius, topaz, and the diamond, the beryl, the onyx, and the jasper, the sapphire, the emerald, and the carbuncle, and gold: the workmanship of thy tabrets and of thy pipes was prepared in thee in the day that thou wast created.

14 Thou art the anointed cherub that covereth; and I have set thee so: thou wast upon the holy mountain of God; thou hast walked up and down in the midst of the stones of fire.

15 Thou wast perfect in thy ways from the day that thou wast created, till iniquity was found in thee.

16 By the multitude of thy merchandise they have filled the midst of thee with violence, and thou hast sinned: therefore I will cast thee as profane out of the mountain of God: and I will destroy thee, O covering cherub, from the midst of the stones of fire. (KJV)

Previously we proved the passage above to be an obvious reference to Satan. Yet, the next several verses allude to both Satan and Antichrist (e.g., "bring thee to ashes in the sight of all them that behold thee" and "all they that know thee among the people," etc.):

Ezekiel 28:17-19

17 Thine heart was lifted up because of thy beauty, thou hast corrupted thy wisdom by reason of thy brightness: I will cast thee to the ground, I will lay thee before kings, that they may behold thee.

18 Thou hast defiled thy sanctuaries by the multitude of thine iniquities, by the iniquity of thy traffick; therefore will I bring forth a fire from the midst of thee, it shall devour thee, and I will bring thee to ashes upon the earth in the sight of all them that behold thee.

19 All they that know thee among the people shall be astonished at thee: thou shalt be a terror, and never shalt thou be any more. (KJV)

Likewise for the following passage. First, Satan:

Isaiah 14:12-14

12 How art thou fallen from heaven, O Lucifer, son of the morning! how art thou cut down to the ground, which didst weaken the nations!

13 For thou hast said in thine heart, I will ascend into heaven, I will exalt my throne above the stars of God: I will sit also upon the mount of the congregation, in the sides of the north:

14 I will ascend above the heights of the clouds; I will be like the most High. (KJV)

Then, both Satan and Antichrist:

Isaiah 14:15-20

15 Yet thou shalt be brought down to hell, to the sides of the pit.

16 They that see thee shall narrowly look upon thee, and consider thee, saying, Is this the man that made the earth to tremble, that did shake kingdoms;

17 That made the world as a wilderness, and destroyed the cities thereof; that opened not the house of his prisoners?

18 All the kings of the nations, even all of them, lie in glory, every one in his own house.

19 But thou art cast out of thy grave like an abominable branch, and as the raiment of those that are slain, thrust through with a sword, that go down to the stones of the pit; as a carcase trodden under feet.

20 Thou shalt not be joined with them in burial, because thou hast destroyed thy land, and slain thy people: the seed of evildoers shall never be renowned. (KJV)

"Wounded to death." Many times it is speculated that the Antichrist will actually die from his deadly wound and then be resurrected back to life by Satan. Supposedly, this will happen immediately after the Rapture when Scripture tells us that Satan will possess and indwell the physical body of the Antichrist until near the end of Armageddon when he is destroyed by Christ and then resurrected into the eternal Lake Of Fire. However, to the best of my knowledge, there is no scriptural support for the idea that Satan truly has the power to raise people from the dead. When it is stated in Revelation 13 that the Antichrist is wounded to death, we should note very carefully that this statement only means that he will be inflicted with a deadly wound; never is it said that he will die at that point in time. Since the Bible is full of statements which describe the deaths of individuals very clearly and without any equivocation, it seems reasonable to suppose that if this scripture had intended to say that the Antichrist will be killed then, it would have done so plainly and unequivocally.

Furthermore, as we saw in chapter 3 of this book, Daniel 11:20-21 does not lend any support to this theory, either. Instead, an analysis of the original Hebrew words used in this scriptural passage clearly indicate a reference to the poison assassination of the Syrian ruler, Seleucus IV, who eventually was succeeded by Antiochus Epiphanes through the use of flattery and the division of spoils from the more prosperous regions of his kingdom. Likewise, since the Bible clearly portrays Christ resurrecting Lazarus back to life, it is likely that the Bible also would state very plainly that the Antichrist will be resurrected, too, if such were to be the case. But, instead, after noting that the Antichrist will be inflicted with a deadly wound, it goes on to say that the deadly wound will be healed, causing the whole world to marvel.

As for Mystery Babylon, this scarlet-clad woman represents a specific religious system which is existent during all of the seven world empires and dominated by Satan for the following scriptural reasons:

First, playing the part of a symbolic whore (as in verse 1) ALWAYS refers to religious fornication (unfaithfulness) and idolatry. (Rev. 17:1-4) (Isa. 23:17) (Isa. 57:3-7) (Jer. 3:2-9) (Ezek. 16) (Ezek. 20:30-32) (Ezek. 23:7-49) (Hos. 4:12-19) (Nah. 3:4). In this case, the whore entices the nations of the earth to commit spiritual fornication. (Rev. 17:2).

The whore represents Satan's church because she holds a golden cup, full of her UNCLEANNESS and ABOMINATIONS, with which she entices people to commit religious fornication. (Compare: Ezekiel 23:29-33).

Her name, "Mystery Babylon," identifies her with the ritual and mysteries of the ancient Babylonian cult. This particular cult was the beginning of Satan's church, and it was concerned primarily with sorceries and astrology! (Gen. 10:8-10) (Gen. 11:4) (Isa. 47:12, 13). The fact that the woman sits upon the seven heads (mountains; empires) proves that she dominated, or will dominate, each of the major world empires portrayed in the Bible as oppressors of Israel. She dominated Assyria (Nah. 3:4), Egypt (Exod. 7:11, 22) (Exod. 8:7, 18) (II Tim. 3:8), Babylon (Dan. 2:2), Persia (which held occult beliefs), Greece (where ancient temple sites dedicated to idolatry still remain), and Rome (which also was full of idolatries and occult beliefs), and the seventh world empire (empire of the Antichrist) will be no exception. It also will be dominated by idolatry, astrology, drugs, witchcraft and sorceries!!!

Her title, "Mother of harlots and abominations of the earth," can leave no doubt that she heads a poisonous combination of evil religious systems! Accordingly, all of the various false cults scattered throughout the world are represented by the symbolic "harlots," whereas the symbolic "Mother" itself represents the very specific religious system that has perpetuated the abominations of the ancient and mysterious Babylonian cult. Likewise, the word "abominations" in the Bible not only refers to the whoredoms and idolatry associated with demonology, but it also refers to sorceries and witchcraft of all kinds. (Deut. 18:9-12) (Deut. 32:16, 17) (II Kings 17:1-25) (II Kings 21:2-11) (Ezek. 16).

Mystery Babylon is said to be drunk "with the blood of the saints, and with the blood of the martyrs of Jesus." Even a brief, cursory analysis of world history will show that the pages of history are full of bloody accounts portraying Christians dying for Jesus at the hands of relentless religious persecutors!

Revelation 17 concludes by stating that "the woman which thou sawest is that great city, which reigneth over the kings of the earth." Right now that city is Rome and has been for centuries, but it has not always been so. Historically, the whore came into existence when the rebel Nimrod built a city in defiance of God and named it Babel. This was the beginning of the ancient and mysterious Babylonian rites which have dominated the major biblical world empires. When "Christianity" became the official religion of the old Roman Empire, innumerable pagan rites and beliefs which had been inherited from the ancient and mysterious Babylonian religion were incorporated and syncretized into the Roman Church in order to make "Christianity" seem more familiar and acceptable to the various tribes and groups of people living throughout the empire. (See, e.g., *The Two Babylons* by the late Rev. Alexander Hislop; and *A Woman Rides The Beast* by Dave Hunt.) Thus, the Roman Catholic Church, headquartered in Rome, has been the current manifestation of the Mystery Babylon Woman for the last several centuries of time.

However, during the very last days, Babylon once again will become the headquarters of Satan's church. (Rev. 17 and 18) (Jer. 50:4-9) (Jer. 51:4-8) (Rev. 16:19) (Isa. 14) (Isa. 13) (Isa. 47:9-13). In fact, as we saw earlier, Zechariah even describes this relocation of "Mystery Babylon" from Rome to the city of Babylon. (Zechariah 5:5-11). But, eventually, near the time of Armageddon, "Mystery Babylon" will be destroyed by the Roman Empire countries who will hate her and despise her. (Rev. 17:16).

In conclusion, a massive array of scriptural evidence leaves us no choice but to conclude that Antichrist will control a very powerful and influential religious system which will be energized and given great credence through his extraordinary accomplishments. This development, in turn, will enable him to foist a most devastating religious deception upon all of mankind! Accordingly, the only possible defense against such deadly spiritual deception is accurate biblical knowledge and tremendous intellectual honesty.

A Time Of Testing

As dramatic biblical prophecies unfold before our very eyes, it will be a time of tremendous excitement and anticipation on the part of born-again, Bible-believing Christians. Many people will expect the Return of Christ at any moment. Most likely, many preachers and commentators will interpret certain prophetic passages in the Bible or private visions and dreams to "prove" that it is time for the Lord's Return or that certain erroneous prophetic scenarios are happening. In fact, even as we enter the late part of year 2001 A.D., already we have been inundated with "special revelations" and "predictions" and a general mood of high expectations on the part of many people. Although, for the moment, I get the impression that many people have become skeptical about any more "Rapture date" predictions, that attitude could change back to unrestrained optimism very quickly under the right circumstances. So, when astounding prophecies begin to be fulfilled, at first there will be a time of terror when Russian aggression and/or war and/or terrorism threatens the world. But, as the Antichrist springs into action to save the world, the general mood of most people will quickly give way to jubilation and anticipation.

But what if the Lord does not return any time soon? What if several or more years go by and the world increasingly is enveloped by a sense of peace and security and prosperity even as the Antichrist becomes more convincing and credible with each passing day? As Jesus said: "In such an hour as ye think not the Son of man cometh." (Matt. 24:44). Likewise, as noted previously, Daniel predicted that Antichrist will destroy people (by deceiving them) through peace and prosperity. (Dan. 8:25). That is why it is very possible that such a scenario explains the following scripture:

II Peter 3:3-4

3 Knowing this first, that there shall come in the last days scoffers, walking after their own lusts,

4 And saying, Where is the promise of his coming? for since the fathers fell asleep, all things continue as they were from the beginning of

the creation. (KJV)

Of course, there always have been a few people who scoffed at the biblical doctrine concerning the Second Coming of Christ, but historically, modern churches and denominations generally have tended to ignore it. But if the scenario just described does take place, then naturally, many people would become deeply disillusioned and disappointed. But the Bible teaches that it is very important for God to test us, which is why the Return of Jesus will be delayed for a short while. Here is what the Bible says about God testing us in our Christian faith:

James 1:1-4, 12-15
1 James, a servant of God and of the Lord Jesus Christ, to the twelve tribes which are scattered abroad, greeting.
2 My brethren, count it all joy when ye fall into divers temptations;
3 Knowing this, that the trying of your faith worketh patience.
4 But let patience have her perfect work, that ye may be perfect and entire, wanting nothing.
12 Blessed is the man that endureth temptation: for when he is tried, he shall receive the crown of life, which the Lord hath promised to them that love him.
13 Let no man say when he is tempted, I am tempted of God: for God cannot be tempted with evil, neither tempteth he any man:
14 But every man is tempted, when he is drawn away of his own lust, and enticed.
15 Then when lust hath conceived, it bringeth forth sin: and sin, when it is finished, bringeth forth death. (KJV)

I Peter 1:2, 6-7
2 Elect according to the foreknowledge of God the Father, through sanctification of the Spirit, unto obedience and sprinkling of the blood of Jesus Christ: Grace unto you, and peace, be multiplied.
6 Wherein ye greatly rejoice, though now for a season, if need be, ye are in heaviness through manifold temptations:
7 That the trial of your faith, being much more precious than of gold that perisheth, though it be tried with fire, might be found unto praise and honour and glory at the appearing of Jesus Christ: (KJV) (Compare Luke 8:4-15)

II Cor. 11:23-28

23 Are they ministers of Christ? (I speak as a fool) I am more; in labours more abundant, in stripes above measure, in prisons more frequent, in deaths oft.

24 Of the Jews five times received I forty stripes save one.

25 Thrice was I beaten with rods, once was I stoned, thrice I suffered shipwreck, a night and a day I have been in the deep;

26 In journeyings often, in perils of waters, in perils of robbers, in perils by mine own countrymen, in perils by the heathen, in perils in the city, in perils in the wilderness, in perils in the sea, in perils among false brethren;

27 In weariness and painfulness, in watchings often, in hunger and thirst, in fastings often, in cold and nakedness.

28 Beside those things that are without, that which cometh upon me daily, the care of all the churches. (KJV)

II Cor. 12:5-10

5 Of such an one will I glory: yet of myself I will not glory, but in mine infirmities.

6 For though I would desire to glory, I shall not be a fool; for I will say the truth: but now I forbear, lest any man should think of me above that which he seeth me to be, or that he heareth of me.

7 And lest I should be exalted above measure through the abundance of the revelations, there was given to me a thorn in the flesh, the messenger of Satan to buffet me, lest I should be exalted above measure.

8 For this thing I besought the Lord thrice, that it might depart from me.

9 And he said unto me, My grace is sufficient for thee: for my strength is made perfect in weakness. Most gladly therefore will I rather glory in my infirmities, that the power of Christ may rest upon me.

10 Therefore I take pleasure in infirmities, in reproaches, in necessities, in persecutions, in distresses for Christ's sake: for when I am weak, then am I strong. (KJV)

Contextually, the apostle Paul is speaking of himself in the two passages quoted above from II Corinthians. The word "infirmities" is translated from the Greek word ASTHENEIA, which means "feebleness" (of mind or body), and by implication "malady" and "frailty." It is translated throughout the Bible as "disease," "infirmity," "sickness" and "weakness." This dictionary meaning also is confirmed by Paul in II Cor. 12:10: "...for when I am weak, then am I strong (through complete dependence on the Lord Jesus Christ)."

Likewise, the word "distresses" comes from the Greek word STENOCHORIA, and it means "narrowness of room," i.e., (figuratively) "calamity," and it is translated as "anguish" or "distress" throughout the Bible. The word "temptations" comes from the Greek word PEIRASMOS, and it means a putting to "proof" (by a good experiment or an evil experience), which by implication means "adversity." Finally, we should note also that James 1:13, 14 correctly translates "tempted" as "tempted" because in that passage it is talking about something completely unrelated to the subject of "testing" and "trial."

Therefore, these passages teach that the "testing" and "proving" of our faith through "disease, sickness, weakness, calamity, anguish, difficulties, adversity, and trials" is a very important part of God's plan for man. It is important because God wants to make sure of our commitment to Him, and to test our worthiness to be "kings" and "priests" and "joint-heirs with Christ" over all of the universe someday. (Dan. 7:27) (Rev. 2:26) (Rev. 21:7-10) (Rev. 22:5) (Isa. 32:1) (Isa. 56:5) (Isa. 60:8) (Romans 8:16-19). James 1:2-5 also explains that God wants to teach us important lessons in life, and help us to develop our faith to maturity. Accordingly, these scriptural considerations often take priority over the biblical promises of prosperity and healing, typifying the dilemma that often comes in an unavoidable conflict between moral principles. This is why the advocates of "health and wealth" are wrong in saying that it is always God's will for Christians to be healthy and prosperous. The need for "testing" also explains why God may "delay" the Return of Christ for a short while.

I Peter 1:2

2 Elect according to the foreknowledge of God the Father, through sanctification of the Spirit, unto obedience and sprinkling of the blood of Jesus Christ: Grace unto you, and peace, be multiplied. (KJV)

Ephesians 1:4-5

4 According as he hath chosen us in him before the foundation of the world, that we should be holy and without blame before him in love:

5 Having predestinated us unto the adoption of children by Jesus Christ to himself, according to the good pleasure of his will, (KJV)

The word "foreknowledge" is translated from the Greek word PROGNOSIS, which means "forethought." When the Bible talks about the foreknowledge or predestination of God, it is referring to the Divine predestination or pre-determination of God's plan of salvation for mankind, NOT an arbitrary decision by God which predetermines the eternal destiny (Heaven or Hell) of people before they are even born! The scriptural evidence for this is quite impressive:

1.) Numerous scriptures promise that "whosoever will" believe can be saved:

John 12:44-46
44 Jesus cried and said, He that believeth on me, believeth not on me, but on him that sent me.
45 And he that seeth me seeth him that sent me.
46 I am come a light into the world, that whosoever believeth on me should not abide in darkness. (KJV)

Matthew 7:24
24 Therefore whosoever heareth these sayings of mine, and doeth them, I will liken him unto a wise man, which built his house upon a rock: (KJV)

Matthew 11:6
6 And blessed is he, whosoever shall not be offended in me. (KJV)

Matthew 12:50
50 For whosoever shall do the will of my Father which is in heaven, the same is my brother, and sister, and mother. (KJV)

Matthew 18:3-6
3 And said, Verily I say unto you, Except ye be converted, and become as little children, ye shall not enter into the kingdom of heaven.
4 Whosoever therefore shall humble himself as this little child, the same is greatest in the kingdom of heaven.

5 And whoso shall receive one such little child in my name receiveth me.

6 But whoso shall offend one of these little ones which believe in me, it were better for him that a millstone were hanged about his neck, and that he were drowned in the depth of the sea. (KJV)

Luke 12:8, 9

8 Also I say unto you, Whosoever shall confess me before men, him shall the Son of man also confess before the angels of God:

9 But he that denieth me before men shall be denied before the angels of God. (KJV)

Luke 14:27

27 And whosoever doth not bear his cross, and come after me, cannot be my disciple. (KJV)

John 3:15-17

15 That whosoever believeth in him should not perish, but have eternal life.

16 For God so loved the world, that he gave his only begotten Son, that whosoever believeth in him should not perish, but have everlasting life.

17 For God sent not his Son into the world to condemn the world; but that the world through him might be saved. (KJV)

Compare the following scriptural passages with the above scriptures: John 4:14; Heb. 2:9; John 6:44-69; John 3:1-18; Rom. 3:25; Rev. 1:5; Heb. 9:22; I Peter 1:18-19; John 12:44-46; John 4:14; Acts 2:21; Acts 10:43; Rom. 9:30-10:1; Rom. 10:9-13; I John 4:13-15; I John 5:1-5; Rev. 22:16, 17.

2.) It is God's desire for everyone to be saved, if possible:

I Timothy 2:4

4 Who will have all men to be saved, and to come unto the knowledge of the truth. (KJV)

II Peter 3:9

9 The Lord is not slack concerning his promise, as some men count

slackness; but is longsuffering to us-ward, not willing that any should perish, but that all should come to repentance. (KJV)

3.) God is no respecter of persons, so He does NOT arbitrarily pick and choose who will go to Heaven and who will go to Hell:

Acts 10:34, 35
34 Then Peter opened his mouth, and said, Of a truth I perceive that God is no respecter of persons:
35 But in every nation he that feareth him, and worketh righteousness, is accepted with him. (KJV)

Gal. 3:27, 28
27 For as many of you as have been baptized into Christ have put on Christ.
28 There is neither Jew nor Greek, there is neither bond nor free, there is neither male nor female: for ye are all one in Christ Jesus. (KJV)

Col. 3:11
11 Where there is neither Greek nor Jew, circumcision nor uncircumcision, Barbarian, Scythian, bond nor free: but Christ is all, and in all. (KJV)

Rom. 1:16, 17
16 For I am not ashamed of the gospel of Christ: for it is the power of God unto salvation to every one that believeth; to the Jew first, and also to the Greek.
17 For therein is the righteousness of God revealed from faith to faith: as it is written, The just shall live by faith. (KJV)

4.) Some people use the following passages correctly to prove that man is evil and that no one comes to Christ for salvation except that the Father draw him first. A problem arises, though, when people try to infer that because the Father must draw men before they can come to Christ, that necessarily must imply that He only draws some people to Christ, not everyone as the Bible actually teaches.

John 6:35-40, 44
35 And Jesus said unto them, I am the bread of life: he that cometh to

me shall never hunger; and he that believeth on me shall never thirst.

36 But I said unto you, That ye also have seen me, and believe not.

37 All that the Father giveth me shall come to me; and him that cometh to me I will in no wise cast out.

38 For I came down from heaven, not to do mine own will, but the will of him that sent me.

39 And this is the Father's will which hath sent me, that of all which he hath given me I should lose nothing, but should raise it up again at the last day.

40 And this is the will of him that sent me, that every one which seeth the Son, and believeth on him, may have everlasting life: and I will raise him up at the last day.

44 No man can come to me, except the Father which hath sent me draw him: and I will raise him up at the last day. (KJV)

John 6:65

65 No one can come to Me, unless it has been granted him from the Father. (KJV)

Romans 3:10-12

10 As it is written, There is none righteous, no, not one:

11 There is none that understandeth, there is none that seeketh after God.

12 They are all gone out of the way, they are together become unprofitable; there is none that doeth good, no, not one. (KJV)

However, John 16:8, 9 states that the Holy Spirit is come to "reprove" (not just some, but all of) the "world." The Greek word for "reprove" is ELEGCHO, and it means to "confute" or "admonish." The dictionary definition of "confute" is to "prove (a person) to be in the wrong." The Greek word ELEGCHO is sometimes even translated as "convict." Therefore, although it is true that no one can be saved unless God draws him, it is also true that the Holy Spirit draws or convicts everyone in the world. It is up to each individual to accept or reject God:

John 16:7-11

7 Nevertheless I tell you the truth; It is expedient for you that I go away: for if I go not away, the Comforter will not come unto you; but if I

depart, I will send him unto you.

8 And when he is come, he will reprove the world of sin, and of righteousness, and of judgment:

9 Of sin, because they believe not on me;

10 Of righteousness, because I go to my Father, and ye see me no more;

11 Of judgment, because the prince of this world is judged. (KJV)

Jesus also said, "I pray for them: I pray not for the world, but for them which thou hast given me; for they are thine." (John 17:9) Sometimes people ask why would not Jesus pray for the whole world if He came to save the world? However, nowhere in Scripture does it say that Jesus can not pray for whomever He wishes. After all, God also has free will. If Jesus wanted to say a special prayer for born-again believers, then why not?

Bear in mind that it is always important to harmonize all relevant scriptures with each other on any given issue. Or in other words, not what one verse says about something, but what the whole Bible teaches. Accordingly, the above scripture must be interpreted in such a manner so that it harmonizes with the dozens of scriptures which clearly state in each instance that "whosoever will" choose Christ as their Lord and Saviour will be saved. It also must harmonize with several scriptures which say that one can be a true believer, but later, still backslide. Finally, the interpretation must agree with the scriptures which say that freedom is a God-given gift to people. Therefore, it is wrong to say the above passage proves that Jesus did not come to save the world, but rather, only a select few who are arbitrarily chosen by God.

John 6:35-40

35 And Jesus said unto them, I am the bread of life: he that cometh to me shall never hunger; and he that believeth on me shall never thirst.

36 But I said unto you, That ye also have seen me, and believe not.

37 All that the Father giveth me shall come to me; and him that cometh to me I will in no wise cast out.

38 For I came down from heaven, not to do mine own will, but the will of him that sent me.

39 And this is the Father's will which hath sent me, that of all which he hath given me I should lose nothing, but should raise it up again at the

last day.

40 And this is the will of him that sent me, that every one which seeth the Son, and believeth on him, may have everlasting life: and I will raise him up at the last day. (KJV)

The above passage also is used sometimes to prove that only some people are elected or predestinated because the above passage implies that not everyone is allowed an opportunity to accept or reject Christ when it says, "All that the Father giveth me shall come to me..."

However, first, please note verse 40. It states clearly that whosoever believes in Christ Jesus will have eternal life. The meaning of this verse is quite obvious, thus proving the validity of freewill and the falseness of predestination. Therefore, verse 39 can not contradict the clear and obvious meaning of verse 40.

Now, concerning verse 39. The verses which precede verse 39 say that people who are saved (actually, "being saved" in the Greek meaning) do so by accepting Christ of their own free will. Accordingly, God will give to Jesus Christ all of those individuals who freely accept Christ as Lord and Saviour, and Jesus will not lose any of them because we are given the assurance that every single one of them will be resurrected at the last day. Not even one single believer will fail to be resurrected to eternal life with God.

5.) Previously, we proved from Scripture that it is part of God's plan to test individuals. But this would be silly and completely unnecessary if the doctrinal proposition that God predetermines who is saved — and who is not — was valid.

6.) If the doctrinal teaching which advocates predestination was correct, then why would not God make everyone morally "good" so that everyone could go to Heaven? And would not it take a very cruel and malicious God to create some people morally "bad," or not to "draw" some individuals to Him while "drawing" others? Would not that be a "respecter of persons" on the part of God?

7.) Sometimes God elects or predetermines an individual for a mission or purpose or status-in-life even before he or she is born. (Mal. 1:2) (Rom. 9:11, 12). As the Bible teaches — that is His privilege to do so. But, it has nothing to do with whether or not a person will choose to serve God; that is an entirely different matter which is always left to the free will of each individual.

Jeremiah 1:5

Before I formed thee in the belly I knew thee; and before thou camest forth out of the womb I sanctified thee, and I ordained thee a prophet unto the nations. (KJV)

The phrase, "I knew thee" is translated from the Hebrew word "yada":

yada' (yaw-dah')

a primitive root; to know (properly, to ascertain by seeing); used in a great variety of senses, figuratively, literally, euphemistically and inferentially (including observation, care, recognition; and causatively, instruction, designation, etc.):

KJV — acknowledge, acquaintance (-ted with), advise, appoint, declare...

Therefore, according to *Strong's Hebrew-Greek Dictionary*, YADA can mean "to know," but it can also be defined as "appoint" or "declare," meaning that Jeremiah 1:5 could just as easily read: "Before I formed thee in the belly I appointed thee;" or "Before I formed thee in the belly I declared thee;"

8.) Biblical prophecy is not necessarily proof that everything in the future is predetermined in the sense that everything already has happened in the future, thus allowing God to "see" into the future in order to "see" what will happen. Instead, Bible prophecies are merely predictions made by an infinite God who has the power and the knowledge to ensure their complete fulfillment in one way or another. Accordingly, God can not see into the future to ascertain what freewill individuals will do because that would be a violation of the logic law of non-contradiction which is a Divine attribute since God is ultimate rationality. The logic violation would be a freewill God looking into the future to see what freewill individuals will do because, supposedly, they already would have accomplished it in the future. However, it is impossible for both free will and predestination to coexist because they are logical contradictions. You either have freedom, or you have predestination in which everything must happen according to the way it already has happened in the future; you can not have both.

For God to look into the future to see what decisions people will make in the future, logic would necessitate a predestinated, preprogrammed reality where people would be nothing more than programmed biological robots following a very detailed, programmed script. Free choices would not be an option for people to exercise. The story of Adam and Eve in the Garden of Eden would be a cruel hoax and a fairy tale because they really would not have had the choice to obey or disobey God as the Bible portrays. Likewise, the Bible would contain many other deceptions as well.

Some of those deceptions would include the stories narrated in Genesis 11:1-9 and Genesis 18:1-21 which indicate that God heard (from His angels) disturbing reports about situations on earth that prompted Him to make a special Personal visit to see for Himself if the reports really were true and accurate. If predestination was truly the reality in which we live, then those Bible stories, by logical necessity, would be false and deceptive. They would be false because if reality truly is predestinated, God would not have had to make Personal visits to see for Himself if the reports were accurate; He simply would have known already, or He could have looked into that mythical fabric of time and space where everything that ever will happen in the distant infinity of time would be there for Him to see for Himself.

Yet another deception found in the Bible, if predestination is truly our reality, would be the numerous scriptures which claim that people have the freedom either to choose or reject Christ Jesus as their personal Lord and Saviour. (Hebrews 2:9; John 6:44-69; John 3:1-18; Romans 3:25; Revelation 1:5; Hebrews 9:22; I Peter 1:18-19; John 12:44-46; Matt. 7:24-27; Matt. 11:6; Matt. 12:50; Matt. 16:25-27; Matt. 18:3-6; Luke 12:8, 9; Luke 14:27; John 3:15-21; John 4:14; Acts 2:21; Acts 10:43; Rom. 9:30-10:1; Rom. 10:9-13; I John 4:13-15; I John 5:1-5; Rev. 22:16, 17; I Tim. 2:4; II Peter 3:9; Acts 10:34, 35; Gal. 3:27, 28; Col. 3:11; Rom. 1:16, 17.) Obviously we must either have the freedom to choose or (if predestination is our reality) not have the freedom to choose; we can not have it both ways.

Likewise, yet another deception would be those scriptures which teach that people can backslide and lose their promise of eternal life with God if they fail to "abide in Christ." (I Cor. 9:24-27; Rev. 3:5-6; John 15:1-6; Rom. 11:16-24; Hebrews 6:4-6; II Thess. 2:3; I Tim. 4:1.) In a predestinated reality, people would not have to worry about failing to "abide in Christ" or having their name blotted out of the Book of Life because everything in life would be preprogrammed in advance since everything already would have happened in the future, and the earthly affairs of life would be nothing more than a fatalistic "what will be, will be."

The law of non-contradiction is one of the very few realities in life which can be viewed as an absolute certainty (as opposed to almost everything else in life that must be viewed as true or false on the basis of its degree of probability after an assessment of all pertinent evidence at hand). However, any attack against the validity of the law of non-contradiction presupposes it validity. Otherwise, you would be forced to affirm and deny its validity simultaneously since you would be adopting the position that anything could be both true and false at the same time and in the same sense. Obviously the law of non-contradiction really is an absolute certainty in life.

But, even though we, as human beings, are very frail and finite in both our abilities and understanding, it is true also that the personal, infinite, triune God of the Christian Bible has given us a rational capability to comprehend reality to a limited degree. Thus, He has revealed Himself to us in His Holy Word so that we might study His Word, and thereby gain a small, finite level of understanding concerning His infinite, rational thoughts and actions and attributes. That is why Jesus said:

Matthew 22:37-38

37 Jesus said unto him, Thou shalt love the Lord thy God with all thy heart, and with all thy soul, and with all thy mind.

38 This is the first and great commandment. (KJV)

Please note, in this passage, that the mind was emphasized equally with the heart and soul. That is because God wants us to love and appreciate Him with all of our God-given abilities to the fullest extent possible. Therefore, finite rational mind can meet with the infinite rational Mind and gain a finite, limited appreciation of the infinite rational Mind, God.

Accordingly, the law of non-contradiction is not an absolute which is independent of God, but rather, it is an attribute of God, the infinite Intelligence. So, rationality (i.e., the law of non-contradiction) is an attribute of God, and is reflected in the nature of His creation. Therefore, because we are rational beings who live in a rational universe created by a rational God, we are free to employ logic by logically concluding that any attack against rationality presupposes rationality, i.e., any attack against the validity of the law of non-contradiction presupposes its validity. That is the very nature of a rational God as reflected in His rational creation, our universe.

Likewise, people would not truly have freewill, as the Bible teaches, if it was possible for God to see into the future to see our "freewill" decisions. Obviously this is true because predestination would require every single thought and action throughout all of eternity to be preprogrammed in its entirety at the outset of creation. In fact, this would deny even God, Himself, the capacity for making freewill decisions of any kind because everything would be predetermined. Accordingly, God would be a prisoner of predestination, forced to think and act as predestined in advance because everything already would have happened in the future. Fortunately, this view of reality is not taught in God's Holy Word.

If God really could "see" into the future and "watch" what people do of their own freewill, then obviously in order for God to "see" us do something of our own "freewill," that something will have had to happen in order for Him to "see" it happen. But, if it already has "happened" somewhere in the fabric of time, then it cannot have NOT "happened" because that would necessitate a logical absurdity. Accordingly, everything would have to be predetermined or preprogrammed or predestinated, and freewill would be a monstrous fabrication taught by the Bible.

In conclusion, therefore, biblical prophecy is simply a matter of God making predictions, then ensuring their fulfillment through His infinite Knowledge and Power. This theological belief is confirmed in the following scriptural passages. Please note that in each passage, it says that God "declares" the future, and it happens; nothing is ever said about God "seeing" the future because it already has happened. That is why these passages talk about "things that are not yet done," obviously meaning that everything has not already happened even from God's unique perspective in time:

Isaiah 46:9-10

9 Remember the former things of old: for I am God, and there is none else; I am God, and there is none like me,

10 Declaring the end from the beginning, and from ancient times the

things that are not yet done, (KJV)

Isaiah 48:3
I have declared the former things from the beginning; and they went forth out of my mouth, and I shewed them; I did them suddenly, and they came to pass. (KJV)

Isaiah 48:5
I have even from the beginning declared it to thee; before it came to pass I shewed it thee... (KJV)

And, of course, God is eternal; from everlasting to everlasting:

Micah 5:2
....yet out of thee shall he come forth unto me that is to be ruler in Israel; whose goings forth have been from of old, from everlasting. (KJV)

Ps. 41:13
Blessed be the LORD God of Israel from everlasting, and to everlasting. Amen, and Amen. (KJV)

Ps. 90:2
...even from everlasting to everlasting, thou art God. (KJV)

Ps. 93:2
...thou art from everlasting. (KJV)

Finally, sometimes it might be questioned how people could have freewill if God sometimes intervenes into the affairs of people, especially when Divine intervention is necessary to ensure fulfillment of biblical prophecies. Accordingly, we must recognize that no moral principle, including freedom, is autonomous to itself. This is why Christians say that God is a God of love and mercy, but also a God of justice and judgment. Complexity, not contradiction, is involved in such instances. In other words, when moral laws and principles come into direct and unavoidable conflict with each other, and due to circumstances, it is impossible to comply with all of them, it is our moral duty and obligation to choose the highest level of good possible.

For example, if telling a lie was the only way possible to save an innocent life from death, then obviously you should do so because the higher law (preservation of innocent life) should take precedence over the lower law (truth). (See the following scriptures for real-life examples of this principle in action... Joshua 2:3, 4; Hebrews 11:31; James 2:25, 26; Exodus 1:15-21; 22:2; I Samuel 16:1-5; II Kings 6:8-23; 7:5-7; Matthew 5:19; 23:23; John 19:11; Genesis 9:6; 14; Acts 5:29; James 4:17; Hebrews 11:17. cf. Hebrews 4:15 and I John 3:4 and II Corinthians 5:21 and I Peter 1:19 with Luke 2:44-49; cf. Leviticus 5:1 with Matthew 27:12-14.) Obviously the dynamic interplay between human freewill and Divine interventionism can become quite complex, and sometimes human free will must be compromised to a certain extent so that the eternal plan of the Divine Free Will can be accomplished.

However, there are self-imposed Divine rules governing this dynamic tension which can be determined by our knowledge of God as He has revealed Himself in Scripture. For instance, God always respects an individual's right freely to decide for himself whether or not he will accept Christ as Lord and Saviour. Nor will He ever force someone against their will to commit sin or immorality of any kind. Nor will He force someone to do something they would not do anyway of their own volition. Nevertheless, as previously stated, Divine intervention into the affairs of people is the means by which God ensures the fulfillment of biblical prophecies.

9.) Sometimes it is said that scriptures such as the following prove that the names of "saved" individuals were written in the "Book of Life" before the world was even created, thus proving the predestination of individuals:

Ephesians 1:3-6

3 Blessed [be] the God and Father of our Lord Jesus Christ, who hath blessed us with all spiritual blessings in heavenly [places] in Christ:

4 According as he hath chosen us in him before the foundation of the world, that we should be holy and without blame before him in love:

5 Having predestinated us unto the adoption of children by Jesus Christ to himself, according to the good pleasure of his will,

6 To the praise of the glory of his grace, wherein he hath made us accepted in the beloved. (KJV)

Revelation 13:8
8 And all that dwell upon the earth shall worship him, whose names are not written in the book of life of the Lamb slain from the foundation of the world. (KJV)

Actually, Revelation 13:8 could be interpreted in several different ways. It could be read as, "names are not written...from the foundation of the world," thereby meaning some names were not written into the book of life at the foundation of the world. But, it could just as easily be viewed as, "...the book of life of the Lamb slain" and "...the book of life... from the foundation of the world," meaning that the book of life was created by Christ, and also that the book of life was created at the foundation of the world. Some might even interpret it in a third way as, "the Lamb slain from the foundation of the world," meaning Christ was slain before the foundation of the world. However, in order to maintain scriptural harmony and consistency, I believe that the second interpretive option is correct.

Therefore, these passages teach that God knew before the world was created that Jesus would die on the cross for our sins because He was certain that free-willed man tempted by Satan would fall into sin due to the weaknesses and vulnerabilities of a finite, created human nature. That, also, is why He created a "Book of Life" — so that people who chose to obey God could have their names recorded in it. Obviously if people truly did not have freewill, then it would have been pointless of Jesus to warn Christians to remain faithful-and-true or risk having their names blotted out of the Book of Life:

Revelation 3:5
5 He that overcometh, the same shall be clothed in white raiment; and I will not blot out his name out of the book of life, but I will confess his name before my Father, and before his angels. (KJV)

Revelation 22:19
19 And if any man shall take away from the words of the book of this prophecy, God shall take away his part out of the book of life, and out of the holy city, and from the things which are written in this book. (KJV)

10.) One last issue we should address involves the singular question on whether unqualified eternal security or conditional eternal security exists for believers in Christ Jesus. Accordingly, here are several scriptures which make it very clear that true believers can, indeed, backslide or "fall away" or apostatize from their belief in Christ due to habitual, unrepentant sin:

John 15:1-6

1 I am the true vine, and my Father is the husbandman.

2 Every branch in me that beareth not fruit he taketh away: and every branch that beareth fruit, he purgeth it, that it may bring forth more fruit.

3 Now ye are clean through the word which I have spoken unto you.

4 Abide in me, and I in you. As the branch cannot bear fruit of itself, except it abide in the vine; no more can ye, except ye abide in me.

5 I am the vine, ye are the branches: He that abideth in me, and I in him, the same bringeth forth much fruit: for without me ye can do nothing.

6 If a man abide not in me, he is cast forth as a branch, and is withered; and men gather them, and cast them into the fire, and they are burned. (KJV)

Rom. 11:16-24

16 For if the firstfruit be holy, the lump is also holy: and if the root be holy, so are the branches.

17 And if some of the branches be broken off, and thou, being a wild olive tree, wert graffed in among them, and with them partakest of the root and fatness of the olive tree;

18 Boast not against the branches. But if thou boast, thou bearest not the root, but the root thee.

19 Thou wilt say then, The branches were broken off, that I might be graffed in.

20 Well; because of unbelief they were broken off, and thou standest by faith. Be not highminded, but fear:

21 For if God spared not the natural branches, take heed lest he also spare not thee.

22 Behold therefore the goodness and severity of God: on them which fell, severity; but toward thee, goodness, if thou continue in his goodness: otherwise thou also shalt be cut off.

23 And they also, if they abide not still in unbelief, shall be graffed in:

for God is able to graff them in again.

24 For if thou wert cut out of the olive tree which is wild by nature, and wert graffed contrary to nature into a good olive tree: how much more shall these, which be the natural branches, be graffed into their own olive tree? (KJV)

An honest reading and assessment of the above two symbolic passages clearly demonstrates that any person may be added or grafted into the family of God through Christ Jesus, but that they also can be cut out or taken away after having been grafted in. Furthermore, verse 23 in the second passage above even continues by saying that "God is able to graff them in again" after having been grafted out previously! So, in other words, God can graft someone in, cut them out later, and graft them back in once AGAIN! Obviously it is possible, then, to backslide from our faith in Christ, but it also is possible for us to become saved once again if we repent of our sins and renew our faith in Christ. In like manner, the collective implication of the following scriptural passages is that names may or may not be entered into the Book Of Life, but that if they are entered, they also can be deleted:

Phil. 4:3

3 And I intreat thee also, true yokefellow, help those women which laboured with me in the gospel, with Clement also, and with other my fellowlabourers, whose names are in the book of life. (KJV)

Revelation 17:8

8 The beast that thou sawest was, and is not; and shall ascend out of the bottomless pit, and go into perdition: and they that dwell on the earth shall wonder, whose names were not written in the book of life... (KJV)

Revelation 20:15

15 And whosoever was not found written in the book of life was cast into the lake of fire. (KJV)

Revelation 21:27

27 And there shall in no wise enter into it any thing that defileth, neither whatsoever worketh abomination, or maketh a lie: but they which are written in the Lamb's book of life. (KJV)

Revelation 22:19

19 And if any man shall take away from the words of the book of this prophecy, God shall take away his part out of the book of life, and out of the holy city, and from the things which are written in this book. (KJV)

Revelation 3:5

5 He that overcometh, the same shall be clothed in white raiment; and I will not blot out his name out of the book of life, but I will confess his name before my Father, and before his angels. (KJV)

The key point in the passages above centers around our spiritual attitude toward God. Accordingly, we must be honest and sincere and repentant about the sins we commit in the flesh because true Christians should not persist in habitual, unrepentant sin or in an obvious depraved and sinful lifestyle. Instead, there should be evident in our lives a constant, continual attempt to become more "Christ-like" and holy every day with the help and guidance of the Holy Spirit because Jesus said that if we love Him, we will obey His commandments. Thus, whenever we sin as the Bible says we will, we should appropriate forgiveness through Christ Jesus Who always stands ready to forgive us so long as we repent sincerely as we continue our honest, imperfect efforts at steady obedience to Christ. Theologians, of course, call this ongoing process Progressive Sanctification. So, if we truly believe in Christ Jesus, we will obey His commandments as we are led by the Spirit of God:

Romans 8:12-14

12 Therefore, brethren, we are debtors, not to the flesh, to live after the flesh.

13 For if ye live after the flesh, ye shall die: but if ye through the Spirit do mortify the deeds of the body, ye shall live.

14 For as many as are led by the Spirit of God, they are the sons of God. (KJV)

I John 1:6-10

6 If we say that we have fellowship with him, and walk in darkness, we lie, and do not the truth:

7 But if we walk in the light, as he is in the light, we have fellowship one with another, and the blood of Jesus Christ his Son cleanseth us from

all sin.

8 If we say that we have no sin, we deceive ourselves, and the truth is not in us.

9 If we confess our sins, he is faithful and just to forgive us our sins, and to cleanse us from all unrighteousness.

10 If we say that we have not sinned, we make him a liar, and his word is not in us. (KJV)

James 2:26

26 For as the body without the spirit is dead, so faith without works is dead also. (KJV)

Matthew 7:21-23

21 Not every one that saith unto me, Lord, Lord, shall enter into the kingdom of heaven; but he that doeth the will of my Father which is in heaven.

22 Many will say to me in that day, Lord, Lord, have we not prophesied in thy name? and in thy name have cast out devils? and in thy name done many wonderful works?

23 And then will I profess unto them, I never knew you: depart from me, ye that work iniquity. (KJV)

Luke 6:45-46

45 A good man out of the good treasure of his heart bringeth forth that which is good; and an evil man out of the evil treasure of his heart bringeth forth that which is evil: for of the abundance of the heart his mouth speaketh.

46 And why call ye me, Lord, Lord, and do not the things which I say? (KJV)

But, sooner or later there can come a point in time — after God has chastised us in an unsuccessful attempt at persuading us to quit our persistent, unrepentant sin — where God will expunge or blot our name from the Book of Life, AFTER it has been entered, because of our unrepentant attitude and stubborn refusal to appropriate forgiveness through Christ Jesus. Therefore, even though "overcomers" have their names recorded in the Book of Life, it is possible for them to have their names blotted out later. That is why, for instance, God said in one of the symbolic tree-branch passages above that "toward thee, goodness, if thou continue in his goodness: otherwise thou also shalt be cut off."

The scriptural definition of an "overcomer" is as follows:

I John 5:1-5

1 Whosoever believeth that Jesus is the Christ is born of God: and every one that loveth him that begat loveth him also that is begotten of him.

2 By this we know that we love the children of God, when we love God, and keep his commandments.

3 For this is the love of God, that we keep his commandments: and his commandments are not grievous.

4 For whatsoever is born of God overcometh the world: and this is the victory that overcometh the world, even our faith.

5 Who is he that overcometh the world, but he that believeth that Jesus is the Son of God? (KJV)

I John 2:12-17

12 I write unto you, little children, because your sins are forgiven you for his name's sake.

13 I write unto you, fathers, because ye have known him that is from the beginning. I write unto you, young men, because ye have overcome the wicked one. I write unto you, little children, because ye have known the Father.

14 I have written unto you, fathers, because ye have known him that is from the beginning. I have written unto you, young men, because ye are strong, and the word of God abideth in you, and ye have overcome the wicked one.

15 Love not the world, neither the things that are in the world. If any man love the world, the love of the Father is not in him.

16 For all that is in the world, the lust of the flesh, and the lust of the eyes, and the pride of life, is not of the Father, but is of the world.

17 And the world passeth away, and the lust thereof: but he that doeth the will of God abideth for ever. (KJV)

Hebrews 6:4-6

4 For it is impossible for those who were once enlightened, and have tasted of the heavenly gift, and were made partakers of the Holy Ghost,

5 And have tasted the good word of God, and the powers of the world to come,

6 If they shall fall away, to renew them again unto repentance; seeing they crucify to themselves the Son of God afresh, and put him to an open shame. (KJV)

So, it is possible for a Christian believer to "fall away" from the faith because here in this passage we are warned that a believer who once has been enlightened by the Holy Spirit to salvation, and has understood the Word of God comprehensively, and has experienced the power of God in their life, and even has received the gift of the Holy Ghost or Holy Spirit Baptism, will find it impossible to fall away or apostatize later and then find repentance again through Christ. This passage is paralleled in Matthew 12:31 where Jesus said: "All manner of sin and blasphemy shall be forgiven unto men: but the blasphemy against the Holy Ghost shall not be forgiven unto men." (KJV) So, a total denunciation of God made by a believer with full knowledge and understanding of spiritual things, including blasphemy of the Holy Ghost, leaves that person in a most precarious position, indeed.

Hebrews 6:7-9

7 For the earth which drinketh in the rain that cometh oft upon it, and bringeth forth herbs meet for them by whom it is dressed, receiveth blessing from God:

8 But that which beareth thorns and briers is rejected, and is nigh unto cursing; whose end is to be burned.

9 But, beloved, we are persuaded better things of you, and things that accompany salvation, though we thus speak. (KJV)

The remainder of our passage in Hebrews 6:4-9 simply reaffirms earlier scriptures above which teach that symbolic trees branches bringing forth good fruit as visible evidence of sincere faith in Christ will be rewarded by God just as symbolic tree branches bringing forth bad fruit, indicating a lack of sincere belief in Christ, will be punished by God. In this instance, however, the example used involves symbolic herbs and thorns in the earth rather than symbolic tree branches with fruit. Then finally, of course, verse 9 concludes with Paul giving assurances to his immediate audience that he is certain or persuaded that they all belong to the (good) herb category, and not the (bad) thorns-and-briers category.

Luke 8:13
13 They on the rock are they, which, when they hear, receive the word with joy; and these have no root, which for a while believe, and in time of temptation fall away. (KJV)

Luke 15:24
24 For this my son was dead, and is alive again; he was lost, and is found. And they began to be merry. (KJV)

II Thess. 2:3
Let no man deceive you by any means: for that day shall not come, except there come a falling away first, and that man of sin be revealed. (KJV)

I Timothy 4:1
1 Now the Spirit speaketh expressly, that in the latter times some shall depart from the faith, giving heed to seducing spirits, and doctrines of devils; (KJV)

The preceding passages obviously teach that an individual can "backslide" or "fall away" or apostatize, thereby losing his salvation in Christ. Therefore, these scriptures completely invalidate both "predestination" and the "once saved, always saved" theological theories. That is why the apostle Paul said:

I Cor. 9:24-27
24 Know ye not that they which run in a race run all, but one receiveth the prize? So run, that ye may obtain.
25 And every man that striveth for the mastery is temperate in all things. Now they do it to obtain a corruptible crown; but we an incorruptible.
26 I therefore so run, not as uncertainly; so fight I, not as one that beateth the air:
27 But I keep under my body, and bring it into subjection: lest that by any means, when I have preached to others, I myself should be a castaway. (KJV)

Here is how *Strong's Hebrew-Greek Dictionary* defines the English word "castaway" in verse 27 above:

96 adokimos (ad-ok'-ee-mos);
from 1 (as a negative particle) and 1384; unapproved, i.e. rejected; by implication, worthless (literally or morally):
KJV— castaway, rejected, reprobate.

Therefore, Paul is saying in this passage that he fights against any evil desires and temptations and inappropriate appetites of the flesh so that after helping many other souls to find salvation through Christ Jesus, he does not fall into habitual or unrepentant sin himself and thereby lose his own personal salvation by becoming a castaway or reject or reprobate. Please note that Paul is not (correctly) saying here that his earthly deeds might possibly run the risk of rejection at the Judgment Seat of Christ due to wrong motives on his part (II Cor. 5:10), but that he himself might be rejected because of habitual or unrepentant sin in his life. On that basis, then, it is possible for a person to fall into habitual or unrepentant sin and thereby risk becoming a castaway. That is why it will be possible for many Christians to backslide or apostatize during the Final Great Apostasy which will occur immediately before the Rapture takes place.

Conquer The World For Christ?

II Peter 3:3-7
3 Knowing this first, that there shall come in the last days scoffers, walking after their own lusts,
4 And saying, Where is the promise of his coming? for since the fathers fell asleep, all things continue as they were from the beginning of the creation.
5 For this they willingly are ignorant of, that by the word of God the heavens were of old, and the earth standing out of the water and in the water:
6 Whereby the world that then was, being overflowed with water, perished:
7 But the heavens and the earth, which are now, by the same word are kept in store, reserved unto fire against the day of judgment and perdition

of ungodly men. (KJV)

There seem to be two distinct possibilities for the final, complete fulfillment of this biblical prophecy. One possible scenario would be that as things quiet down after the initial appearance of the Antichrist, and the world increasingly is lulled to sleep, spiritually, by world peace and prosperity and religious deception, many Christians will become persuaded that Christ will not Return any time soon because nothing will have happened. Because things will not have happened the way they always believed they would happen, serious doubts will erode their faith in biblical Christianity, generally, and the biblical doctrine of the Second Coming, in particular.

However, one other possibility regarding the identity of the "scoffers" portrayed here in this passage could be a certain growing movement within the ranks of Christianity, generally known as "Dominion" and "Reconstruction" believers, who appear to be quite militant and vociferous in their denial of a literal Second Coming of Christ any time soon. Accordingly, we should note that the word "lusts" in this passage comes from the Greek word EPITHUMIA, meaning "a longing" or desire (especially for something forbidden). But, this definition does not necessarily mean sexual immorality; it actually could mean a number of different things, including an over-emphasis on wealth and materialism or an unbiblical desire for power by "conquering" or "Christianizing" the world "for Christ" — things which I believe generally are consistent with the theology of Reconstructionists and Dominionists.

Yet another piece of scriptural evidence which also seems to suggest that "Dominionists" and "Reconstructionists" are referenced in this scripture is the fact that these "scoffers" apparently believe in God because they believe in creationism, not evolution ("things continue from the beginning of the CREATION").

Likewise, as demonstrated previously, the word "world" in the Greek is KOSMOS, and it means "orderly arrangement" and by implication "the world, including its inhabitants, literally or figuratively." It is translated as such in countless numbers of scriptural passages. So, it should be noted that Noah's Flood did not completely destroy the "world," including all the people, birds, fish and animals, as stated in verse 6, but that everything on the earth was destroyed completely without a trace when Satan's pre-Adamite world was destroyed by water (Jer. 4:23-26).

Furthermore, this view is supported by verse 7 which states that we are living on a new earth, ("the heavens and the earth, which are now"). Even further evidence is provided by verse 5: "by the word of God the heavens were of old, and the earth standing out of the water and in the water," meaning that all of the earth was not under water when it was created by God. Obviously this proves that Genesis 1 should not be interpreted to mean God first created the earth so that it was completely under water, and then, later, made the "dry" land to appear during the "third" day. Thus, the theological belief involving a pre-Adamite creation and destruction is substantiated once more by Scripture.

To summarize: these "scoffers" are people who believe in "the creation," but are "willingly ignorant" of knowledge about "the flood," i.e., the pre-Adamite flood which completely destroyed the pre-Adamite "world." Likewise, to the best of my knowledge, this description seems to match at least most of the people who view themselves as "Reconstructionist" or "Dominionist" believers. Therefore, since these people also ridicule the imminent Return of Christ Jesus, the evidence would seem to qualify them as the fulfillment of this prophecy, or at least a significant preliminary fulfillment.

Chronological Sequence Of Events
1) Incredible Rise Of The "Little Horn" Antichrist
2) Military Crisis In Israel; Little Horn Waxes Exceeding Great
3) Astounding Military Conquests Of The Antichrist
4) Extraordinary Peace And Prosperity Inspired By Antichrist
5) Religious Deception And The Final Great Apostasy
6) The Pre-Tribulation Rapture
7) The True Nature Of Antichrist Is Revealed
8) The Great Tribulation Spans Three And One-Half Years
9) Tribulation Saints Who Are Killed By Antichrist Are Resurrected
10) The Sixth Seal Is Opened
11) Seventh Seal Ushers In The Day Of The Lord, A Day Of Wrath
12) The Day Of The Lord Will Last For Seven Years
13) Day Of The Lord Coincides In Time With Daniel's 70th Week
14) Rebuilt Temple Desecrated Halfway Through Daniel's 70th Week
15) The Battle Of Armageddon; Also Called The Day Of The Lord

V. The Rapture

In Matthew 24 and Luke 21, Jesus said there would be a period of peace and prosperity and normal, everyday living on the earth immediately before His Coming in the same manner that normal, everyday living was prevalent throughout the world until Noah's Flood suddenly and unexpectedly struck all of the earth. However, in order to understand this passage properly, we must realize that the "coming of Christ" is a two-stage process accompanied by a complex series of events which precede His literal touching upon the soil of planet Earth. Based on scriptural passages we will examine later, this series of events will begin initially with the Rapture of Christian believers from the earth so that they can "escape" the apocalyptic judgments which accompany His Return. Then the Rapture will be followed by a period of testing, generally known as the Great Tribulation, which will last for three and one-half years during which time some of the people remaining on the earth will choose to become Christians. This time of testing, in turn, will be followed by a seven-year period of Divine judgments which will be unleashed upon the earth before climaxing with the events of Armageddon and the literal descent of Jesus to the earth. Therefore, the coming of Christ should be considered a two-step process which begins with the Rapture and culminates in the Second Coming of Christ only after a complex series of judgments and tribulations are completed first.

Likewise, it is important also to understand that both the Second Coming and the seven years of Divine Judgment which immediately precede the Second Coming are described throughout prophetic scriptures as "that day" and "Day Of The Lord." That is why it is so important we allow the immediate context, in conjunction with other parallel passages, help us to determine the specific event or events intended within any given scriptural passage in view. Accordingly, it is my hope and prayer that semantics will not play too large a role in hindering our efforts to understand these prophetic passages in their proper light.

Matthew 24:36-42

36 But of that day and hour knoweth no man, no, not the angels of heaven, but my Father only.

37 But as the days of Noe were, so shall also the coming of the Son of man be.

38 For as in the days that were before the flood they were eating and drinking, marrying and giving in marriage, until the day that Noe entered into the ark,

39 And knew not until the flood came, and took them all away; so shall also the coming of the Son of man be.

40 Then shall two be in the field; the one shall be taken, and the other left.

41 Two women shall be grinding at the mill; the one shall be taken, and the other left.

42 Watch therefore: for ye know not what hour your Lord doth come. (KJV)

Luke 21:28, 34-36

28 And when these things begin to come to pass, then look up, and lift up your heads; for your redemption draweth nigh.

34 And take heed to yourselves, lest at any time your hearts be overcharged with surfeiting, and drunkenness, and cares of this life, and so that day come upon you unawares.

35 For as a snare shall it come on all them that dwell on the face of the whole earth.

36 Watch ye therefore, and pray always, that ye may be accounted worthy to escape (Greek EKPHEUGO, which means to “flee out” of danger) all these things that shall come to pass, and to stand before the Son of man. (KJV)

Luke 17:22-37

22 And he said unto the disciples, The days will come, when ye shall desire to see one of the days of the Son of man, and ye shall not see it.

23 And they shall say to you, See here; or, see there: go not after them, nor follow them.

24 For as the lightning, that lighteneth out of the one part under heaven, shineth unto the other part under heaven; so shall also the Son of man be in his day.

25 But first must he suffer many things, and be rejected of this generation.

26 And as it was in the days of Noe, so shall it be also in the days of the Son of man.

27 They did eat, they drank, they married wives, they were given in

marriage, until the day that Noe entered into the ark, and the flood came, and destroyed them all.

28 Likewise also as it was in the days of Lot; they did eat, they drank, they bought, they sold, they planted, they builded;

29 But the same day that Lot went out of Sodom it rained fire and brimstone from heaven, and destroyed them all.

30 Even thus shall it be in the day when the Son of man is revealed.

31 In that day, he which shall be upon the housetop, and his stuff in the house, let him not come down to take it away: and he that is in the field, let him likewise not return back.

32 Remember Lot's wife.

33 Whosoever shall seek to save his life shall lose it; and whosoever shall lose his life shall preserve it.

34 I tell you, in that night there shall be two men in one bed; the one shall be taken, and the other shall be left.

35 Two women shall be grinding together; the one shall be taken, and the other left.

36 Two men shall be in the field; the one shall be taken, and the other left.

37 And they answered and said unto him, Where, Lord? And he said unto them, Wheresoever the body (Christ; Rev. 5:6) is, thither will the eagles (saints; Isa. 40:31) be gathered together (i.e., Raptured). (KJV)

When Jesus was asked by His disciples to tell them the signs or events which would signal the "end" was near and that God's literal Kingdom on earth was about to be established, Jesus described the incredible, chaotic conditions which would prevail throughout the world before His Return. (Matthew 24; Mark 13; Luke 21.) However, following His summation of these apocalyptic events, Jesus immediately reassured His disciples that believers would be taken to Heaven when these things first began to happen, thereby allowing them to escape the terrible tribulations and judgments He had just described. This contextual consideration is important to note because it illustrates a very common communication technique utilized by people, and explains why the Rapture in Matthew 24 is not mentioned in its "proper" chronological sequence. A failure to understand this matter explains why some critics have questioned whether the pre-tribulation Rapture is even pictured in this passage of scripture.

Matthew 24:39 compares Noah's Flood to the Coming of Christ by stating that both events involve a sudden and unexpected catastrophic judgment which strikes non-believers. In this instance, the Greek word translated as "took," in the phrase "and took them all away," comes from the Greek word AIRO, which means "to take" or "lay hold of." Therefore, this scripture simply means that just as unbelievers were taken away to judgment by the flood waters of Noah's flood immediately after Noah and his family entered their ark of safety, so likewise will catastrophic judgment and destruction devastate all of the unbelieving world immediately after Christians are Raptured to Heaven.

However, in the next verse, when it is stated "then shall two be in the field; the one shall be taken," the Greek word translated here as "taken" is derived from an entirely different Greek word, namely PARALAMBANO, meaning to "take or receive, in a gracious or impartial manner or attitude." (*Vine Dictionary*). Likewise, *Strong's Dictionary* defines it as "to receive near, i.e., associate with oneself (in any familiar or intimate act or relation)." Interestingly, it is used by Christ only six times in reference to end-time prophetic events — twice in the Olivet Discourse (Matt. 24:40-41); three times in a parallel passage of scripture (Luke 17:34-36); and once in John 14:3, which reads:

John 14:3

2 In my Father's house are many mansions: if it were not so, I would have told you. I go to prepare a place for you.

3 And if I go and prepare a place for you, I will come again, and receive you unto myself; that where I am, there ye may be also. (KJV)

So, when it is stated that Christ will "receive" us or "take" us to Himself, the Greek dictionary definition for this word indicates that He does so in a kind and loving manner because the dictionary meaning absolutely precludes the possibility of death and destruction as some would have us believe. So, obviously none of these scriptural passages refer to judgment and destruction, but rather, to a kind and loving rescue of Christians. Thus, Matthew 24:40-42 teaches that some people (believers) will be taken away in a gracious and intimate manner at the coming of Christ, while others (unbelievers) will be left behind on the earth (to face the judgments which follow).

As further corroboration, the parallel passage in Luke 21:34-36 warns against excessive concern regarding the "cares of this life" because that is when "that day (will) come upon you unawares." However, it also promises that immediately before the judgments commence, some individuals will be "taken" (to Heaven) because they will be "accounted worthy to escape (flee out of) all these things," whereas everyone else will be left behind as in a "snare" to face those judgments. That is why we are admonished to "pray always, that ye may be accounted worthy to escape all these things that shall come to pass, and to stand before the Son of man" (Luke 21:34-36).

As an incidental aside, in the scriptural passage Luke 17:34, the Greek word for "bed" is KLINE, and a more accurate translation of the word would be "couch (used for sleeping, sickness, sitting or eating)." Accordingly, this passage does not contradict other scriptural passages which condemn the sin of homosexuality.

Luke 17:37
37 And they answered and said unto him, Where, Lord? And he said unto them, Wheresoever the body (Christ; Rev. 5:6) is, thither will the eagles (saints) be gathered together (i.e., Raptured). (KJV)

Matthew 24:28
28 For wheresoever the carcase is, there will the eagles be gathered together. (KJV)

The word "carcase" in the Greek is PTOMA, and it can be translated as "dead body, corpse, carcase." Accordingly, in the above two passages, the words "body, dead body and carcase" are all references to Christ, the "Lamb as it had been slain" (Rev. 5:6). Likewise, the word "eagle" in both of the above scriptural passages is defined by *Strong's Hebrew-Greek Dictionary* as follows:

105 aetos (ah-et-os');
from the same as 109; an eagle (from its wind-like flight):
KJV-- eagle.

So, there is no justification for saying that the word "eagle" in Matthew 24:28 can also be translated as the word "vulture," as some commentaries try to do in a vain effort to explain a difficult passage of scripture. Even more so since the above Greek word translated as "eagle" is used in yet another prophetic passage of scripture:

Revelation 8:13
....and heard an angel flying through the midst of heaven, saying with a loud voice, Woe, woe, woe, to the inhabiters of the earth.... (KJV)

The word for "angel" in this passage is actually a mistranslation; it should have been translated as the English word "eagle" because it is based on the same Greek word, AETOS, which we saw previously in Matthew 24:28 and Luke 17:37. In fact, many translations even acknowledge this obvious point by translating it as such. So, both the context for this scripture and other parallel passages all indicate that this "eagle" is, in reality, a reference to Christian saints in each instance. That explains the following passage in Isaiah:

Isaiah 40:31
31 But they that wait upon the LORD shall renew their strength; they shall mount up with wings as eagles; they shall run, and not be weary; and they shall walk, and not faint. (KJV)

Therefore, in Revelation 8:13, we see eagle Christians warning the earth about the last three Trumpet-Vial plagues poised to strike the earth which will be even more severe in their destructive impact than the preceding plagues were. Then, in Luke 17:37, we are told that eagle Christians will be Raptured and gathered together wherever Christ, the "Lamb as it had been slain," may be. Then finally, in Matthew 24:28, Jesus tells us that just prior to His Second Coming, eagle Christians will be gathered around "the dead body," which as we saw earlier, is Christ, the "Lamb as it had been slain" (Rev. 5:6). So, in all of these prophetic passages, the word "eagle" is used as a direct reference to Christian believers.

As mentioned previously, to understand the Olivet Discourse properly, the coming of Christ must be viewed as a single process which begins with the Rapture and ends with the Second Coming of Christ only after a period of testing and judgment is concluded. Thus, a Rapture explains how believers who are "accounted worthy to escape all these things" are given the promised means of "escape" from the destruction which will strike the world without warning "like a thief in the night." But, because the Rapture begins a complex process of events which culminate in the literal Return of Christ, it is possible to say that any of the events in this sequence of events, including either the Rapture or the Second Coming, strikes the world without warning "like a thief in the night." However, technically speaking, once the Rapture does take place and Divine judgments commence their destruction, the Second Coming of Christ will not strike the world without warning "like a thief in the night" because it will be anticipated by all the nations of the world. This should not surprise us too much since people will be able to calculate the number of days still remaining in Daniel's 70th Week in order to determine when they will end, and that knowledge will be confirmed by many extraordinary signs in the heavens heralding the imminent Return of Christ to the earth:

Luke 21:25-27
25 And there shall be signs in the sun, and in the moon, and in the stars; and upon the earth distress of nations, with perplexity; the sea and the waves roaring;
26 Men's hearts failing them for fear, and for looking after those things which are coming on the earth: for the powers of heaven shall be shaken.
27 And then shall they see the Son of man coming in a cloud with power and great glory. (KJV)

Matthew 24:27, 29, 30
27 For as the lightning cometh out of the east, and shineth even unto the west; so shall also the coming of the Son of man be.
29 Immediately after the tribulation of those days shall the sun be darkened, and the moon shall not give her light, and the stars shall fall from heaven, and the powers of the heavens shall be shaken:
30 And then shall appear the sign of the Son of man in heaven: and then shall all the tribes of the earth mourn, and they shall see the Son of man coming in the clouds of heaven with power and great glory. (KJV)

Matthew 24:42-44
42 Watch therefore: for ye know not what hour your Lord doth come.
43 But know this, that if the goodman of the house had known in what watch the thief would come, he would have watched, and would not have

suffered his house to be broken up.

44 Therefore be ye also ready: for in such an hour as ye think not the Son of man cometh. (KJV)

This "thief in the night" illustration is further elaborated upon by the apostle Paul:

I Thess. 5:1-10

1 But of the times and the seasons, brethren, ye have no need that I write unto you.

2 For yourselves know perfectly that the day of the Lord so cometh as a thief in the night.

3 For when they shall say, Peace and safety; then sudden destruction cometh upon them, as travail upon a woman with child; and they shall not escape.

4 But ye, brethren, are not in darkness, that that day should overtake you as a thief.

5 Ye are all the children of light, and the children of the day: we are not of the night, nor of darkness.

6 Therefore let us not sleep, as do others; but let us watch and be sober.

7 For they that sleep sleep in the night; and they that be drunken are drunken in the night.

8 But let us, who are of the day, be sober, putting on the breastplate of faith and love; and for an helmet, the hope of salvation.

9 For God hath not appointed us to wrath, but to obtain salvation by our Lord Jesus Christ,

10 Who died for us, that, whether we wake or sleep, we should live together with him. (KJV)

"Day of the Lord" is defined by a careful reading of scriptures to be the "great day of God's wrath" upon the world soon AFTER the Rapture has occurred. It will last for a period of seven years during which time the seven Trumpet-Vial Plagues of fire will demolish much of the world before culminating in the Second Coming of Christ at the Battle of Armageddon. (Rev. 6:12-17) (Rev. 8:1, 2, 5-13) (Rev. 9:1-19) (Rev. 11:13-15) (Joel 2:1-11) (Joel 2:28-31) (Isa. 24:17-23) (Isa. 13:6-13) (Zech. 14:1-3) (II Peter 3:10-12) (Zeph. 1:14-18) (Amos 5:18-20) (Isa.

2:10-21). Since the Rapture will happen suddenly and unexpectedly without warning, so likewise will the "Day of the Lord" come "as a thief in the night" without warning precisely as this passage states.

"Peace and safety; then sudden destruction..." As noted in a previous chapter, the Antichrist will inspire a period of world peace and prosperity by which he will destroy (deceive) many. (Dan. 8:25). We also noted previously that this period of world peace and prosperity will be terminated by sudden destruction immediately after the Rapture when the apocalyptic judgments of Revelation are unleashed upon the earth. Therefore, because the period of "peace and safety" in the above passage is followed immediately by "sudden destruction," it obviously correlates with the scenario associated with the Antichrist.

This view is even confirmed in the very same sentence: "Peace and safety; then sudden destruction cometh upon them, as travail upon a woman with child." Since Revelation 12 uses this very same symbolic "woman in travail" to portray the Rapture, this proves beyond any reasonable doubt that the events described in this passage should be associated within the context of the Rapture. Therefore, in essence, this passage is saying that peace and safety will be ended abruptly when the Rapture begins a process of judgment and destruction.

Paul continues by saying that since we (as Christians) are "the children of light" and "not of the night, nor of darkness," we should "not sleep as others" but should "watch and be sober." The word "watch" comes from the Greek word GREGOREUO, and it means to "keep awake" (literally or figuratively) and is sometimes translated as "vigilant." In verse 4, Paul states that because we "are not in darkness," that day (i.e., "Day of the Lord") should not overtake us as a thief.

However, in verse 3, Paul says that the children of darkness will not "escape" the "sudden destruction" which will strike the world. The word used here in the Greek for the word "escape" is EKPHEUGO — the same word we saw in Luke 21 — and, again, it means to "flee out" of danger. Accordingly, the message of this passage is a very blunt warning that non-believers will not be able to flee from the coming destruction which will occur during the Great and Terrible Day Of The Lord.

But, in contrast, God has not appointed Christians to "wrath," but to "salvation by our Lord Jesus Christ." (verse 9). The word "wrath" in this passage comes from the Greek word ORGE, and it means violent "passion" or justifiable "abhorrence," which by implication means "punishment." According to the Bible, this violent punishment will be manifested primarily through the seven Trumpet-Vial plagues which occur during the Day Of The Lord. Likewise, the word used here for "salvation" in the Greek is SOTERIA, and it means "rescue" or "safety" in a physical or moral sense, and is translated throughout the Bible as "deliver, health, salvation, save and saving." Therefore, this passage is saying that God has not destined believers to wrath during the Great and Terrible Day Of The Lord, but instead, has appointed them to a physical rescue to safety, i.e., the Rapture.

This "escape" or "rescue" from the "wrath" of God is confirmed by Jesus in the following passage:

Luke 21:28, 34-36

28 And when these things begin to come to pass, then look up, and lift up your heads; for your redemption draweth nigh.

34 And take heed to yourselves, lest at any time your hearts be overcharged with surfeiting, and drunkenness, and cares of this life, and so that day come upon you unawares.

35 For as a snare shall it come on all them that dwell on the face of the whole earth.

36 Watch ye therefore, and pray always, that ye may be accounted worthy to escape all these things that shall come to pass, and to stand before the Son of man. (KJV)

In verse 28, the word "redemption" in the Greek is APOLUTROSIS, meaning the act of "ransom" in full, i.e., figuratively "riddance" or specifically Christian "salvation"; it is translated as "deliverance" or "redemption" in the Bible. Concerning this concept of "ransom in full," there is a three-fold process involved:

1) SOUL - "Christ has redeemed us from the curse of the law." (Gal. 3:13).

2) BODY - "Waiting for the adoption, to wit, the redemption of our body." (Rom. 8:23).

3) THE EARTH - "The redemption of the purchased possession." (Eph. 1:14).

In other words, "redemption" will include the restoration of everything man lost in the Garden of Eden. The redemption of the soul is achieved through an individual's acceptance of Christ as personal Lord and Saviour. The redemption of the body will become a reality at the time of the Rapture (or subsequent resurrection or translation) when believers are translated or resurrected to Heaven with new, immortal spirit bodies. As for the redemption of the earth, it will be accomplished after the "seven-sealed" book in Heaven is opened during a sequence of events which conclude with the Return of Christ to evict Satan from the earth.

"Take heed...lest...your hearts be overcharged with surfeiting..." The Greek word for "overcharged" is BARUNO, meaning to "burden," figuratively-speaking. The Greek for "surfeiting" is KRAIPALE, which means "headache" from drunkenness, i.e., by implication a "debauch," and by analogy a "glut." So, the message of this verse is a warning not to burden your heart with debauchery and gluttony and drunkenness and cares of this life — a definite reference to the extraordinary peace and prosperity which the Antichrist will create to help him to deceive and destroy people. (Dan. 8:25).

"So that day come upon you unawares." All of the prophets of God used expressions such as "that day" to indicate the Day of the Lord, a day of darkness and gloominess and judgment. That meaning is consistent with the context of this passage. Concerning the word "unawares," the Greek dictionary defines it as meaning "non-apparent" and "unexpected," i.e., adverbially "suddenly." Thus, to an unbelieving world, everything will seem fine and dandy because there will be no apparent indication that disaster is about to strike — precisely as in the days before Noah's flood. Not surprisingly, therefore, when the Antichrist performs his incredible miracles and creates an economic paradise throughout the world, it will not be very easy to convince people he actually is quite evil and deceptive, and that God's devastating judgments upon the earth are imminent.

"For as a snare shall it come." The Greek word for "snare" is PAGIS, and it is defined as "a trap to ensnare suddenly and unexpectedly." So, again, there is this reference to a sudden and unanticipated destruction "as in the days of Noah." But Jesus also admonished us to "watch" and "pray" so that we (as Christians) will "escape" all of these things. This word "escape" is the same one used by Paul in I Thess. 5:1-10 to warn that "children of darkness" would not escape or evade the day of God's wrath and judgment. But, here in this passage, Jesus teaches that Christians can avoid the chaos and destruction coming upon the world. It will be possible for them to "escape," i.e., "to flee out of" disaster and "to get safely away from danger," according to the Greek dictionary.

This "escape from destruction" is also confirmed in Revelation 3:10:

Revelation 3:10

10 Because thou hast kept the word of my patience, I also will keep thee from the hour of temptation, which shall come upon all the world, to try them that dwell upon the earth. (KJV)

The word "temptation" is translated more accurately as "trial" in *Young's Literal Translation Of The Bible.* Since the word "trial" is immediately preceded by the article ("the") in the original writings, the Greek most definitely should be translated as "the trial." This, in turn, denotes this trial as very significant because it is the Great Tribulation testing which will occur immediately after the Rapture when all of the world will be tested for three and one-half years. At that time, some people will accept Christ as their Lord and Saviour and become "tribulation saints" while many others will swear allegiance to the Antichrist, instead, by taking the "mark of the beast."

However, because many ordinary, unsaved people who survive Armageddon will be allowed to enter the Millennial Kingdom of Christ as subjects under the rulership of Christ and the saints, these people will be individuals who will abstain from taking the mark of the beast even though they will not convert to Christianity, either (until later, during the Millennium, when most of them will convert to Christianity in response to the salvation message as it is proclaimed throughout the world from Jerusalem: Zech. 14:16; Matt. 25:31-46; Rev. 20:3, 8; Rev. 21:3, 24, 26; Dan. 7:27; Micah 4:1-5; Isa. 2:2-4; I Cor. 15:24-28).

But, God has promised that He will "keep" those Christians who keep the word of the patience, i.e., endurance. The word used here for "keep" is translated from the Greek TEREO, and it means to guard from loss or injury. Therefore, since many of the Christians who will be living on the earth during the Great Tribulation will be killed by the Antichrist, they obviously will not be the ones who will be guarded from loss or injury. By logical necessity, then, this passage must mean, instead, that the Christians who are guaranteed "safekeeping" from the Great Tribulation are Christians who will be Raptured out of the world before the Great Tribulation begins. Although it is true that Tribulation Christians (including 144,000 Christian Jews) who manage to survive the Great Tribulation will not be harmed by the Antichrist during the subsequent seven years of Divine Judgments because they will be "sealed" with God's protection (Rev. 7:1-8), this passage does not apply to them, either. At that point in time, we are talking about a period of Divine judgment during the Day of the Lord after the Great Tribulation is over, not a period of testing during the Great Tribulation as specified in this passage.

Furthermore, according to *Thayer's Greek-English Lexicon Of The New Testament*, the meaning of the verb "will keep" (TEREO or TERESO), whenever it is used in conjunction with the preposition "from" (EN), is defined as being "to cause one to persevere or stand firm in a thing." But, whenever the verb "will keep" is used with another form of the preposition "from" (EK), it is defined as "by guarding to cause one to escape in safety out of." Since EK is the preposition used here in this instance, this means that Christians are promised an escape or removal from the location of "the trial" or Great Tribulation, not a preservation through it. Therefore, this passage in Revelation 3:10 most definitely guarantees Christians a Rapture escape from the Great Tribulation.

Just how will this Rapture escape take place?

I Thess. 4:13-17

13 But I would not have you to be ignorant, brethren, concerning them which are asleep, that ye sorrow not, even as others which have no hope.

14 For if we believe that Jesus died and rose again, even so them also which sleep in Jesus will God bring with him.

15 For this we say unto you by the word of the Lord, that we which are alive and remain unto the coming of the Lord shall not prevent them which are asleep.

16 For the Lord himself shall descend from heaven with a shout, with the voice of the archangel, and with the trump of God: and the dead in Christ shall rise first:

17 Then we which are alive and remain shall be caught up together with them in the clouds, to meet the Lord in the air: and so shall we ever be with the Lord. (KJV)

I Cor. 15:49-54

49 And as we have borne the image of the earthy, we shall also bear the image of the heavenly.

50 Now this I say, brethren, that flesh and blood cannot inherit the kingdom of God; neither doth corruption inherit incorruption.

51 Behold, I shew you a mystery; We shall not all sleep, but we shall all be changed,

52 In a moment, in the twinkling of an eye, at the last trump: for the trumpet shall sound, and the dead shall be raised incorruptible, and we shall be changed.

53 For this corruptible must put on incorruption, and this mortal must put on immortality.

54 So when this corruptible shall have put on incorruption, and this mortal shall have put on immortality, then shall be brought to pass the saying that is written, Death is swallowed up in victory. (KJV)

Some people teach that the "last trump," mentioned here in I Cor. 15:51, 52, must sound after all of the other trumpets in Revelation have been blown, thus making it synonymous with the 7th Trumpet in Revelation or the Great Trumpet portrayed in Matthew 24:31. However, according to the Greek dictionary, the Greek word which is translated "last" should be translated as "end-times" or "last things." Therefore, an "end-time trump" or a "last things trump," to which Christians will respond, is the correct interpretation for the phrase "last trump." Hence there is no need necessarily for this scripture to mean that this trumpet must blow after all other trumpets of any type have blown; instead, it means that the sounding of this trumpet ushers in the beginning of the "last things" which God has ordained to be, starting with the Rapture.

Likewise, some have objected that a silent, surprise Rapture is not compatible with shouting and trumpet-blowing, but that objection is easily refuted by John 5:25 which states that only righteous people will hear the voice of the Lord at the time of the Rapture. In a similar vein, others have questioned whether or not there can be several raptures involving saints who escape the Great Tribulation (Rev. 4:1) (Rev. 12:1-5); plus, martyred tribulation saints who are resurrected immediately after the Great Tribulation (Rev. 7:9-17) (Rev. 15:1-8); plus, the two witnesses who are resurrected to Heaven just before the Return of Christ (Rev. 11:3-12); plus, the translation or gathering of the "elect" just prior to the Second Coming of Christ which will include both the 144,000 Christian Jews and the surviving tribulation saints who are not killed by the Antichrist (Matt. 24:31) (Mark 13:27). However, the concept of several raptures is in complete harmony with I Cor. 15:20-23 which teaches there will be different groups of saints in Heaven with "every man in his own order (Greek TAGMA, defined as a company or body of individuals)." Therefore, quite obviously the evidence indicates that the "last trump" pictured in I Cor. 15:51-52 is not the same trumpet as the 7th Trumpet of the 7th Seal in Revelation or the Great Trumpet mentioned in Matthew 24:31.

Likewise, Daniel's second vision establishes the time element associated with the Rapture:

Daniel 7:8-11

8 I considered the horns, and, behold, there came up among them another little horn, before whom there were three of the first horns plucked up by the roots: and, behold, in this horn were eyes like the eyes of man, and a mouth speaking great things.

9 I beheld till the thrones were cast down, and the Ancient of days did sit, whose garment was white as snow, and the hair of his head like the pure wool: his throne was like the fiery flame, and his wheels as burning fire.

10 A fiery stream issued and came forth from before him: thousand thousands ministered unto him, and ten thousand times ten thousand stood before him: the judgment was set, and the books were opened.

11 I beheld then because of the voice of the great words which the horn spake: I beheld even till the beast was slain, and his body destroyed, and given to the burning flame. (KJV)

"Thrones were cast down." This phrase in verse 9 could also be translated as "set down" or "put in place." Likewise, the heavenly scene described in verses 9 and 10 is pictured in much greater detail in Revelation 4 and 5 where the judgment throne of God is set up and surrounded by the thrones of the "24 elders."

It is instructive to note that Daniel's narrative describing endtime earthly events is interrupted by verses 9 and 10 which portray events in Heaven immediately after Christians have been "Raptured" or "caught-up" to Heaven. Therefore, verses 8 and 11 establish a precise time-frame which tells us when the Rapture will take place relative to events on earth. More specifically, verse 8 portrays a series of earthly events which conclude with the little horn Antichrist "speaking great things." The next two verses, i.e., verses 9 and 10, then describe various events which take place in Heaven immediately after the Rapture. Then, verse 11 picks up where it left off in verse 8 by resuming its narration of the exact same earthly activity (i.e., "the voice of the great words which the horn spake"). Without question, this interruption in the continuity of the narrative establishes the fact that Antichrist will begin his ascendancy to power before the Rapture occurs. The context of this passage also indicates that the Rapture will occur before persecutions are initiated against the tribulation saints, thus further confirming that the Rapture is pre-tribulation in nature.

John 14:1-3:

1 Let not your heart be troubled: ye believe in God, believe also in me.

2 In my Father's house are many mansions: if it were not so, I would have told you. I go to prepare a place for you.

3 And if I go and prepare a place for you, I will come again, and receive you unto myself; that where I am, there ye may be also. (KJV)

In this passage, Jesus promised to go to Heaven and "prepare" a "mansion" for all believers so that they might be with the Lord wherever He is. Since Jesus will be in Heaven during the "Great Tribulation" and the "Day of the Lord," but on earth at the time of Armageddon and His Millennial Reign, it becomes apparent that there must be a "Rapture" or "escape" BEFORE God's judgments descend upon the earth if the saints are to inherit and occupy "mansions" in Heaven at the time of His Coming. So, by logical necessity, there must be a separate and distinct "gathering of the saints in the air" which will precede the Second Coming of Christ soon enough to give sufficient time for the saints to inherit and occupy their mansions in Heaven before returning to the earth with Christ at His Second Coming. Likewise, we also must allow sufficient time between the Rapture and the Second Coming to permit the Judgment Seat of Christ and the Marriage Of The Lamb to occur. Obviously a pre-tribulation Rapture meets all of these scriptural requirements.

Parenthetically, we should note that the word "Rapture," although not actually found in the English versions of the Bible, is the English derivative of the Latin word "rapturo" which was used in the old Latin versions of the Bible. Hence its modern-day popularity as a convenient way to express a complex biblical doctrine. It is based upon the Greek word HARPAZO in I Thess. 4:17, and it means "to carry off; grasp hastily; snatch up." Although the Greek word HARPAZO was translated into the Latin word "rapturo" in the Latin versions, the translators of the English versions chose, instead, to translate this Greek word into the English words "caught up." Nevertheless, from all of this we get our English word "Rapture," meaning the "act of transporting." Accordingly, when Jesus returns to "Rapture" the saints to Heaven, those who will have died before that moment, during the New Testament era, will come with Him to have their spirits reunited with a resurrected immortal body (I Thess. 4:13-15) (II Cor. 5:8) (Phil. 1:21-24) (Heb. 12:22-23) (Rev. 6:9-11). (Old Testament believers were resurrected immediately after Christ was resurrected; Luke 16:19-31; Matt. 27:52-53; Eph. 4:8-10; Heb. 2:14-15.) Then, we which are still alive also will be transformed instantaneously into a new and immortal body before we all go to Heaven so that "wherever He is, there may we be also."

Other scriptural passages expressing the truth of a Rapture are:

I Thess. 5:23

23 And the very God of peace sanctify you wholly; and I pray God your whole spirit and soul and body be preserved blameless unto the coming of our Lord Jesus Christ. (KJV)

Col. 3:4

4 When Christ, who is our life, shall appear, then shall ye also appear with him in glory. (KJV)

I Tim. 6:14

14 That thou keep this commandment without spot, unrebukeable, until the appearing of our Lord Jesus Christ: (KJV)

II Thess. 2:1

1 Now we beseech you, brethren, by the coming of our Lord Jesus Christ, and by our gathering together unto him. (KJV)

I Thess. 2:19

19 For what is our hope, or joy, or crown of rejoicing? Are not even ye in the presence of our Lord Jesus Christ at his coming? (KJV)

Titus 2:13

13 Looking for that blessed hope, and the glorious appearing of the great God and our Saviour Jesus Christ; (KJV)

II Thess. 1:10

10 When he shall come to be glorified in his saints, and to be admired in all them that believe (because our testimony among you was believed) in that day. (KJV)

I Cor. 15:23

23 But every man in his own order: Christ the firstfruits; afterward they that are Christ's at his coming. (KJV)

Heb. 9:28

28 So Christ was once offered to bear the sins of many; and unto them that look for him shall he appear the second time without sin unto salvation. (KJV)

James 5:7-8

7 Be patient therefore, brethren, unto the coming of the Lord. Behold, the husbandman waiteth for the precious fruit of the earth, and hath long patience for it, until he receive the early and latter rain.

8 Be ye also patient; stablish your hearts: for the coming of the Lord draweth nigh. (KJV)

I John 2:28

28 And now, little children, abide in him; that, when he shall appear, we may have confidence, and not be ashamed before him at his coming. (KJV)

Revelation 4:1

1 After this I looked, and, behold, a door was opened in heaven: and the first voice which I heard was as it were of a trumpet talking with me; which said, Come up hither, and I will shew thee things which must be hereafter (i.e., after the seven church ages). (KJV)

This scripture portrays the saints of God ascending to Heaven at the sound of the trumpet in a manner reminiscent of the trumpet mentioned in I Thessalonians 4:13-17. This is because John the Revelator acts as a "type" representing believers, a role that he often performs throughout Revelation. Furthermore, as conclusive proof that this passage describes the Rapture of the saints, please note that they are in Heaven immediately afterwards:

Revelation 4:4, 10; 5:8-10
4 And round about the throne were four and twenty seats: and upon the seats I saw four and twenty elders sitting, clothed in white raiment; and they had on their heads crowns of gold.
10 The four and twenty elders fall down before him that sat on the throne, and worship him that liveth for ever and ever, and cast their crowns before the throne, saying,
8 And when he had taken the book, the four beasts and four and twenty elders fell down before the Lamb, having every one of them harps, and golden vials full of odours, which are the prayers of saints.
9 And they sung a new song, saying, Thou art worthy to take the book, and to open the seals thereof: for thou wast slain, and hast redeemed us to God by thy blood out of every kindred, and tongue, and people, and nation;
10 And hast made us unto our God kings and priests: and we shall reign on the earth. (KJV)

In the phrase, "For Thou wast slain, and hast redeemed us to God by Thy blood," the word "us" is derived from the Greek word HEMAS, which means "us," and not the Greek word AUTOS, which means "them." Although some of the newer translations translate the word "us" as the word "them," there is no apparent justification for doing so except for theological bias. Not wanting to believe in a future reign of Christ on earth with the saints is not sufficient reason for changing the text of the Bible. Only the Codex Alexandrinus manuscript omits the word "us"; all of the other ancient manuscripts have it included. Translations such as the *King James Version* and *Young's Literal Translation Of The Bible* are correct when they render the word as "us" instead of "them." Therefore, the twenty-four elders and the four beasts portrayed in this passage of scripture must represent Christian believers because only saintly believers are redeemed; angels are not. Now compare the following:

Revelation 1:5, 6
.....Unto him that loved us, and washed us from our sins in his blood,

And hath made us kings and priests unto God and his Father; to him be glory and dominion for ever and ever.... (KJV)

Please note the similarities between the above two accounts relative to the doxology and the attributes of the creatures who are praising God. A careful reading of the book of Revelation will show that many of the characteristics attributed to Christ and the saints in chapter one are repeated periodically throughout the remainder of Revelation. In fact, sometimes it is the only way possible to identify the "angel" or "creature" in view within a given passage of scripture. On that basis, because it is quite clear in Revelation 1:5-6 that Christians are praising and worshipping God, this most likely is the case in Revelation 5:8-10, also. Likewise, since there are no translations which read "them" instead of "us" in Revelation 1:5-6, we probably should read these disputed passages in Revelation 4 and 5 the same way — no matter how many modern translations say otherwise. Therefore, the "twenty-four elders" and the "four beasts" both must represent saints because only saints are redeemed.

If the "four beasts" and/or the "twenty-four elders" are not saints, then where are the saints? Since we can establish from Scripture that the saints "will judge the world" and "execute upon them the judgment written" (Rev. 5:9-10; Dan. 7:21-22, 27; I Cor. 6:2-3; Rev. 1:5-6; Ps. 149:5-9), they should be in prominent display. But, if the "four beasts" are not groups of saints, then why are they clearly involved so extensively in the execution of judgments upon the earth? (Rev. 6). Moreover, since the scriptural evidence very convincingly indicates that the elders do represent the saints, and since their number is 24, we also must conclude that they represent believers from both the Old and New Testament ages — typified by the 12 patriarchs and the twelve apostles. In a similar manner, as a parallel reference support for this point, the 12 gates and the 12 foundation stones of the New Jerusalem likewise are named for the 12 tribes from Old Testament times and the 12 apostles from New Testament times.

It is for certain that the "twenty-four elders" represent saints because the angel who shows John the Revelation vision also is identified as an "elder" and as a saint:

Revelation 1:1

1 The Revelation of Jesus Christ, which God gave unto him, to shew unto his servants things which must shortly come to pass; and he sent and

signified it by his angel unto his servant John: (KJV)

Revelation 5:5-7

5 And one of the elders saith unto me, Weep not: behold, the Lion of the tribe of Juda, the Root of David, hath prevailed to open the book, and to loose the seven seals thereof.

6 And I beheld, and, lo, in the midst of the throne and of the four beasts, and in the midst of the elders, stood a Lamb as it had been slain, having seven horns and seven eyes, which are the seven Spirits of God sent forth into all the earth.

7 And he came and took the book out of the right hand of him that sat upon the throne. (KJV)

Revelation 7:13-15

13 And one of the elders answered, saying unto me, What are these which are arrayed in white robes? and whence came they?

14 And I said unto him, Sir, thou knowest. And he said to me, These are they which came out of great tribulation, and have washed their robes, and made them white in the blood of the Lamb.

15 Therefore are they before the throne of God, and serve him day and night in his temple: and he that sitteth on the throne shall dwell among them. (KJV)

Revelation 19:9-10

9 And he saith unto me, Write, Blessed are they which are called unto the marriage supper of the Lamb. And he saith unto me, These are the true sayings of God.

10 And I fell at his feet to worship him. And he said unto me, See thou do it not: I am thy fellowservant, and of thy brethren that have the testimony of Jesus: worship God: for the testimony of Jesus is the spirit of prophecy. (KJV)

Revelation 22:8-9

8 And I John saw these things, and heard them. And when I had heard and seen, I fell down to worship before the feet of the angel which shewed me these things.

9 Then saith he unto me, See thou do it not: for I am thy fellowservant, and of thy brethren the prophets, and of them which keep the sayings of this book: worship God. (KJV)

Evidently, John was so overwhelmed by the Revelation shown to him that twice he began to worship the "angel" who was showing it to him.

"I am thy fellowservant, and of thy brethren." This angel, who identifies himself as a saint, is also identified as one of the angels who pours out the seven vials of plagues upon the earth. (Rev. 17:1). Obviously this proves the validity of our interpretation concerning the identity of the angels throughout most of Revelation; it is the saints who will execute judgment upon the earth when it is being "redeemed." This also confirms that the saints must be Raptured to Heaven before the process of redemption begins; Bible students call this truth the "Pre-tribulation Rapture."

Revelation 22:16

16 I Jesus have sent mine angel to testify unto you these things in the churches. I am the root and the offspring of David, and the bright and morning star. (KJV)

As further confirmation that the twenty-four elders represent Christians, please note that the elders sit on thrones and wear crowns (Rev. 4:4, 10); only people, not angels, are promised such rewards if they "overcome":

Revelation 2:10

10 Fear none of those things which thou shalt suffer: behold, the devil shall cast some of you into prison, that ye may be tried; and ye shall have tribulation ten days: be thou faithful unto death, and I will give thee a crown of life. (KJV)

Revelation 1:5-6

5 And from Jesus Christ, who is the faithful witness, and the first begotten of the dead, and the prince of the kings of the earth. Unto him that loved us, and washed us from our sins in his own blood,

6 And hath made us kings and priests unto God and his Father; to him be glory and dominion for ever and ever. Amen. (KJV)

Revelation 3:20-21

20 Behold, I stand at the door, and knock: if any man hear my voice, and open the door, I will come in to him, and will sup with him, and he

with me.

21 To him that overcometh will I grant to sit with me in my throne, even as I also overcame, and am set down with my Father in his throne. (KJV)

Revelation 20:4-6

4 And I saw thrones, and they sat upon them, and judgment was given unto them: and I saw the souls of them that were beheaded for the witness of Jesus, and for the word of God, and which had not worshipped the beast, neither his image, neither had received his mark upon their foreheads, or in their hands; and they lived and reigned with Christ a thousand years.

5 But the rest of the dead lived not again until the thousand years were finished. This is the first resurrection.

6 Blessed and holy is he that hath part in the first resurrection: on such the second death hath no power, but they shall be priests of God and of Christ, and shall reign with him a thousand years. (KJV)

2 Timothy 4:8

8 Henceforth there is laid up for me a crown of righteousness, which the Lord, the righteous judge, shall give me at that day: and not to me only, but unto all them also that love his appearing. (KJV)

Matthew 19:27-29

27 Then answered Peter and said unto him, Behold, we have forsaken all, and followed thee; what shall we have therefore?

28 And Jesus said unto them, Verily I say unto you, That ye which have followed me, in the regeneration when the Son of man shall sit in the throne of his glory, ye also shall sit upon twelve thrones, judging the twelve tribes of Israel.

29 And every one that hath forsaken houses, or brethren, or sisters, or father, or mother, or wife, or children, or lands, for my name's sake, shall receive an hundredfold, and shall inherit everlasting life. (KJV)

1 Cor. 9:25-27

25 And every man that striveth for the mastery is temperate in all things. Now they do it to obtain a corruptible crown; but we an incorruptible.

26 I therefore so run, not as uncertainly; so fight I, not as one that beateth the air:

27 But I keep under my body, and bring it into subjection: lest that by any means, when I have preached to others, I myself should be a castaway. (KJV)

As an aside to the primary subject currently under analysis, we might note that *Strong's Hebrew-Greek Dictionary* defines the English word "castaway" in verse 27 immediately above in the following manner:

96 adokimos (ad-ok'-ee-mos);
from 1 (as a negative particle) and 1384; unapproved, i.e. rejected; by implication, worthless (literally or morally):
KJV— castaway, rejected, reprobate.

Therefore, Paul is saying in this passage that he fights against any evil desires and temptations and inappropriate appetites of the flesh so that after helping many other souls to find salvation through Christ Jesus, he does not fall into habitual or unrepentant sin himself and thereby lose his own personal salvation by becoming a castaway or reject or reprobate. Please note that Paul is not correctly saying here that his earthly deeds might possibly run the risk of rejection at the Judgment Seat of Christ due to wrong motives on his part (II Cor. 5:10), but that he himself might be rejected because of habitual or unrepentant sin in his life. On that basis, then, it is possible for a person to fall into habitual or unrepentant sin and thereby risk becoming a castaway. That is why it will be possible for many Christians to backslide or apostatize during the Final Great Apostasy which will occur immediately before the Rapture takes place.

After the saints are Raptured into Heaven and the bema judgment of Christ is complete, they will be organized into various groups for maximum efficiency, each with a specific function to perform. In Revelation they are known as angels, horsemen, twenty-four elders, and four beasts. Although these heavenly creatures might seem very strange and unusual to us, please bear in mind that just as in chapter one of Revelation, similes (not symbols) are used to describe heavenly things. For example, Revelation 5 portrays Christ as both a "Lamb" and a "Lion," not in the literal or symbolic sense, but as a way of describing His personal attributes or characteristics which are shared in common with the creature or animal in view.

In like manner, the "four beasts" are said to have certain personal characteristics similar to those possessed by a lion, calf, eagle and a man. Furthermore, because a more accurate translation of the term "four beasts" in Revelation 5:8 and elsewhere would be "four living ones" or "four living creatures," we actually have a direct connection to a description of Christ Himself in Revelation 1:18 where He is described there also as "he who is living." Hence we have a precedent for calling Christians "living ones" after they are given the gift of immortality by God. Here is how *Young's Literal Translation* renders these two key passages:

Revelation 1:18
18 And he who is living, and I did become dead, and, lo, I am living to the ages of the ages. Amen! and I have the keys of the hades and of the death. (Young's Literal Translation)

Revelation 5:8
8 And when he took the scroll, the four living creatures and the twenty-four elders fell before the Lamb, having each one harps and golden vials full of perfumes, which are the prayers of the saints, (Young's Literal Translation)

It is important to note also that the four beasts are four groups of saints for two more reasons. Since four is the number used by the Bible whenever it is necessary to show that God is dealing with the whole world (e.g., four directions, four seasons, four winds, four world empires in Daniel's visions, four Gospel accounts, four cherubim in Ezekiel, etc.), it is quite sensical to infer that the four beasts must be associated with important heavenly activities which involve the whole world in one way or another. Subsequent descriptions of their heavenly activities disclose, in fact, that they are heavily involved with the redemption of the world itself. Since this is something that only saints, not angels, could do, these beasts must be groups of saints. Likewise, the four beasts could easily represent large groups of Christian believers, also, because they are "full of eyes," thus confirming the possibility of their humanity.

Additional corroboration for a pre-tribulation Rapture may be ascertained through careful consideration of the chart *Harmony Of The Parallel Accounts* which is located at the end of the next chapter. The proof becomes manifest by virtue of the direct, continuous correlation which can be seen between the two sets of apocalyptic events which are narrated in the parallel accounts of Revelation 4-11 and Revelation 12-16. The difference in their accounts is due primarily to the fact that Revelation 4-11 describes events and circumstances from the vantage point of an observer in Heaven, whereas Revelation 12-16 describes the same series of events and circumstances from the vantage point of an observer on the earth. But, without question, there is a demonstrable and unmistakable correlation between the two sets of events. Since this chart portrays the Rapture as the very first event described in Revelation 4-11, this automatically provides indisputable proof that the Rapture, indeed, occurs before any of the apocalyptic events described in Revelation begin.

Scriptural passages which are consistent with a pre-tribulation Rapture because Christian believers are said to be with Christ at His Second Coming to the earth include the following scriptures:

I Thess. 3:13

13 To the end he may stablish your hearts unblameable in holiness before God, even our Father, at the coming of our Lord Jesus Christ with all his saints. (KJV)

Jude 14, 15

14 And Enoch also, the seventh from Adam, prophesied of these, saying, Behold, the Lord cometh with ten thousands of his saints,

15 To execute judgment upon all, and to convince all that are ungodly among them of all their ungodly deeds which they have ungodly committed, and of all their hard speeches which ungodly sinners have spoken against him. (KJV)

Col. 3:4

4 When Christ, who is our life, shall appear, then shall ye also appear with him in glory. (KJV)

Scriptures which indicate that judgment will begin for people still alive on the earth immediately after Armageddon include the following:

Matthew 25:31-46

31 When the Son of man shall come in his glory, and all the holy

angels with him, then shall he sit upon the throne of his glory:

32 And before him shall be gathered all nations: and he shall separate them one from another, as a shepherd divideth his sheep from the goats.... (KJV)

Matthew 13:36-50

40 ....As therefore the tares are gathered and burned in the fire; so shall it be in the end of this world.

41 The Son of man shall send forth his angels, and they shall gather out of his kingdom all things that offend, and them which do iniquity;

42 And shall cast them into a furnace of fire: there shall be wailing and gnashing of teeth....

49 So shall it be at the end of the world: the angels shall come forth, and sever the wicked from among the just,

50 And shall cast them into the furnace of fire: there shall be wailing and gnashing of teeth. (KJV)

II Tim. 4:1

1 I charge thee therefore before God, and the Lord Jesus Christ, who shall judge the quick (i.e., "living") and the dead at his appearing (i.e., "manifestation" or Second Coming) and his kingdom (which is fully established only after the Millennial Reign Of Christ). (KJV)

In other words, the Lord Jesus Christ will judge the people still living on the earth immediately after His Second Coming at the Battle of Armageddon, and He also will judge the dead at the Great White Throne Judgment immediately after the Millennium when His Kingdom will be made manifest throughout the earth.

Scriptures which indicate that each believer's works or earthly deeds will be tested immediately after the Rapture to determine their inner character and nature and motivation include the following passages:

Luke 14:14

14 And thou shalt be blessed; for they cannot recompense thee: for thou shalt be recompensed at the resurrection of the just. (KJV)

I Cor. 3:8-15

8 Now he that planteth and he that watereth are one: and every man

shall receive his own reward according to his own labour.

9 For we are labourers together with God: ye are God's husbandry, ye are God's building.

10 According to the grace of God which is given unto me, as a wise masterbuilder, I have laid the foundation, and another buildeth thereon. But let every man take heed how he buildeth thereupon.

11 For other foundation can no man lay than that is laid, which is Jesus Christ.

12 Now if any man build upon this foundation gold, silver, precious stones, wood, hay, stubble;

13 Every man's work shall be made manifest: for the day shall declare it, because it shall be revealed by fire; and the fire shall try every man's work of what sort it is.

14 If any man's work abide which he hath built thereupon, he shall receive a reward.

15 If any man's work shall be burned, he shall suffer loss: but he himself shall be saved; yet so as by fire. (KJV)

II Tim. 4:8

8 Henceforth there is laid up for me a crown of righteousness, which the Lord, the righteous judge, shall give me at that day: and not to me only, but unto all them also that love his appearing. (KJV)

I Peter 5:4

4 And when the chief Shepherd shall appear, ye shall receive a crown of glory that fadeth not away. (KJV)

I Peter 1:7

7 That the trial of your faith, being much more precious than of gold that perisheth, though it be tried with fire, might be found unto praise and honour and glory at the appearing of Jesus Christ: (KJV)

Rom. 14:10-12

10 But why dost thou judge thy brother? or why dost thou set at nought thy brother? for we shall all stand before the judgment seat of Christ.

11 For it is written, As I live, saith the Lord, every knee shall bow to me, and every tongue shall confess to God.

12 So then every one of us shall give account of himself to God. (KJV)

II Cor. 5:10

10 For we must all appear before the judgment seat of Christ; that every one may receive the things done in his body, according to that he hath done, whether it be good or bad. (KJV)

First, it should be noted that in Romans 14:10-12, the phrase "judgment seat of Christ" actually should be translated as "judgment seat of God" because the English word "Christ" is translated from the Greek word THEOS in this instance, defined by Strong in the following manner:

2316 theos (theh'-os);

of uncertain affinity; a deity, especially (with 3588) the supreme Divinity; figuratively, a magistrate; by Hebraism, very:

KJV— X exceeding, God, god [-ly, -ward].

However, John 5:22 states that "the Father judgeth no man, but hath committed all judgment unto the Son." When we also consider that Christ Jesus is God, we must conclude that there is no conflict between this passage and the other scriptures which say that Christ will judge believers at His Appearing.

In both Romans 14:10-12 and II Corinthians 5:10, the Greek word which is translated as "judgment seat" is BEMA, defined by *Strong's Hebrew-Greek Dictionary* as follows:

968 bema (bay'-ma);

from the base of 939; a step, i.e. foot-breath; by implication, a rostrum, i.e. a tribunal:

KJV— judgment-seat, set [foot] on, throne.

It is in direct contrast to another Greek word, CRITERION, which also is translated as "judgment seat" in other New Testament passages. According to *Thayer's Greek-English Lexicon Of The New Testament*, CRITERION means "the instrument or means of trying or judging anything; the rule by which one judges" or "the place where judgment is given; the tribunal of a judge; a bench of judges."

Thus, the Greek word BEMA used for judgment seat in the above scriptures carries the connotation of honor and reward rather than justice and judgment, thereby confirming the very plain and obvious meaning of I Cor. 3:9-15 which clearly states that Christians will have the quality and character of their earthly deeds or works judged by Christ to determine the degree of righteousness attained by each believer. This becomes even more evident with II Cor. 5:10 when that verse is placed in the context of the verses surrounding it because only believers could have "an house not made with hands, eternal in the heavens" or experience "mortality (that) might be swallowed up of life" or have the confidence that "whilst we are at home in the body, we are absent from the Lord."

It also should be emphasized that this "judgment of the saints" has nothing to do with a judicial judgment to determine whether or not an individual is a believer because the salvation which the believer receives through Christ Jesus delivers him from all judgment. (John 5:24) (Rom. 8:1) (I John 4:17). To say otherwise would deny the efficacy of the death of Christ Jesus and nullify God's promise that "their sins and iniquities will I remember no more" (Heb. 10:17). Instead, it merely determines the extent of each person's reward based on their motives for doing the things they did during their lifetime.

"Things done in his body, according to that he hath done, whether it be good or bad." The Greek word translated as "bad" in this phrase is based on the Greek word PHAULOS rather than KAKOS or PONERAS which are the usual Greek words employed for the word "bad" whenever moral or ethical evil is the intended meaning. In this instance, however, according to Richard C. Trench in *New Testament Synonyms*, the Greek word PHAULOS is used to indicate "...evil under another aspect, not so much...malignity, but...good-for-nothingness.... worthlessness..."

So, the purpose of the bema judgment is not to determine the moral goodness or evil of our earthly deeds, but whether each deed is acceptable or worthless to the Kingdom and Glory of God. That is why I Cor. 3:13 says that "Every man's work shall be made manifest: for the day shall declare it, because it shall be revealed by fire; and the fire shall try every man's work of what sort it is." However, the works which do survive the test of fire are the deeds for which believers are rewarded:

I Cor. 3:14-15

14 If any man's work abide which he hath built thereupon, he shall

receive a reward.

15 If any man's work shall be burned, he shall suffer loss: but he himself shall be saved; yet so as by fire. (KJV)

More specifically, the "works" or earthly deeds of believers which will be judged at the "judgment seat of Christ" will include the following things:

1. Doctrines and the degree of intellectual honesty exhibited by a person when deciding their doctrinal beliefs (Rom. 2:14-16; Rom. 14)
2. Conduct and behavior and attitude toward other people (Matt. 18; Rom. 14)
3. Carnal traits (Col. 3; Rom. 1-2; Rom. 8:1-13; Rom. 14:1-23)
4. Every word that is spoken (Matt. 12:32-37; Rom. 14)
5. Things that affect others, such as slander, quarrels, idle words, foolishness (folly), dishonesty, broken promises, wrong dealings, etc. (Rom. 1:29-32; I Cor. 6:9-11; Gal. 5:19-21; Col. 3; Eph. 4:1-32; Eph. 5:1-33; Rom. 12:1-21; Rom. 14:1-23)
6. Personal things such as lost or neglected opportunities, talents wasted, loose living, lack of spirituality, etc. (Rom. 2:14-16; Heb. 2:1-4; Gal. 5:1-26; Gal. 6:1-10; Col. 3)
7. Spiritual things such as a refusal to walk in the light to one degree or another, disobedience, rejection, failure to cooperate and yield to the Spirit, degree of intellectual honesty, spiritual attitude, etc. (I Cor. 12; Rom. 12; Eph. 4:1-32; Eph. 5:1-33)

In the New Testament, there are five major types of crowns which constitute the primary areas of judgment for which rewards are given at the bema judgment:

I Cor. 9:25

25 And every man that striveth for the mastery is temperate in all things. Now they do it to obtain a corruptible crown; but we an incorruptible. (KJV)

I Thess. 2:19

19 For what is our hope, or joy, or crown of rejoicing? Are not even ye in the presence of our Lord Jesus Christ at his coming? (KJV)

James 1:12

12 Blessed is the man that endureth temptation: for when he is tried,

he shall receive the crown of life, which the Lord hath promised to them that love him. (KJV)

II Tim. 4:8

8 Henceforth there is laid up for me a crown of righteousness, which the Lord, the righteous judge, shall give me at that day: and not to me only, but unto all them also that love his appearing. (KJV)

I Peter 5:2-4

2 Feed the flock of God which is among you, taking the oversight thereof, not by constraint, but willingly; not for filthy lucre, but of a ready mind;

3 Neither as being lords over God's heritage, but being ensamples to the flock.

4 And when the chief Shepherd shall appear, ye shall receive a crown of glory that fadeth not away. (KJV)

An indication of the nature of the crowns or rewards which are given at the bema judgment is suggested by the Greek word STEPHANOO which is used for "crown" in these passages. *Strong's Hebrew-Greek Dictionary* defines it as an "honorary wreath" which I Corinthians 9:25 and II Timothy 2:5 describe as a victory wreath. It is in stark contrast to another Greek word DIADEMA which is employed whenever a kingly or imperial crown is the intended meaning. Hence the word which is used for the crowns given to saints at the bema judgment is associated with the honor and dignity bestowed on an overcomer or conqueror. Although we will reign as priests and kings with Christ over all the universe, the kingly crown DIADEMA belongs to Christ Jesus alone. Our crowns will be the crowns which are reserved for victors and overcomers through Christ.

The bema judgment of Christ will occur immediately after the Rapture because Luke 14:14 says that believers will be recompensed at the resurrection of the just. Since the Rapture, by definition, involves the translation and resurrection of believers (I Thess. 4:13-17), recompense or rewards must be given at that time. Likewise, several other scriptures above also associate some type of judgment or recompense between the Rapture and the revelation or manifestation or appearance of Christ to the earth.

Additionally, when Christ returns with all the believers at His Second

Coming, they already will have been rewarded according to Revelation 19:8. This is evident from the statement that the saints are "arrayed in fine linen, clean and white: for the fine linen is the righteousness of saints," thus indicating that the imparted righteousness received from Christ by each believer has already undergone examination in order to establish the basis for each person's reward. Revelation 4 and 5 further confirm that believers are judged immediately after the Rapture because even in those passages, they are wearing crowns of rewards and sitting on thrones; are called "living ones" because they have been immortalized; are dressed in the white garments of righteousness; and have authority as kings and priests over all the earth and universe. In light of all these reasons, there can be no question that the bema judgment of Christ begins immediately after the Rapture.

The following scripture at first glance seems to conflict with the above scriptural passages when apparently it indicates that believers will be given their rewards immediately after the Second Coming of Christ:

Revelation 11:15, 18
15 And the seventh angel sounded; and there were great voices in heaven, saying, The kingdoms of this world are become the kingdoms of our Lord, and of his Christ; and he shall reign for ever and ever.
18 And the nations were angry, and thy wrath is come (i.e., Armageddon), and the time of the dead, that they should be judged (i.e., Great White Throne Judgment), and that thou shouldest give reward unto thy servants the prophets, and to the saints, and them that fear thy name, small and great (i.e., believers are rewarded for their works); and shouldest destroy them which destroy the earth (i.e., Armageddon). (KJV)

However, perhaps immediately after the Rapture, believers initially are only given rewards involving crowns and positions of authority based upon their level of personal righteousness as determined in the bema judgment of Christ. But, then later, after Christ has returned to the earth at His Second Coming, additional rewards are granted to believers when more time is available since the pressing need to redeem the earth no longer will exist. Or, as an alternative explanation, since the tribulation saints who are not executed by the Antichrist are the "elect" portrayed in Matthew 24:31 who will be gathered by the angels just prior to the Second Coming of Christ, perhaps they, instead, are the saints who are given their rewards at that time.

Accordingly, the question now is: What are the qualifications for going in the Rapture? Luke 21:36 says to "pray always, that ye may be accounted worthy to escape." Jesus said that if you are an "overcomer," you will "eat of the tree of life, which is in the midst of the paradise of God" (Rev. 2:7); and that you will "not be hurt of the second death" (Rev. 2:11); and that you will "eat of the hidden manna" and that you will receive a "white stone" with a "new name written" in it (Rev. 2:17); and that you will receive "power over the nations" (Rev. 2:26); and that you "shall be clothed in white raiment" and will not have your name blotted out of the book of life (Rev. 3:5); and that you will be a "pillar" in the temple of God (Rev. 3:12); and, finally, that you will sit with Jesus "in the throne" (Rev. 3:21). Later in the Revelation, Jesus also said that overcomers will "inherit all things" (Rev. 21:7).

The definition of an "overcomer" is as follows:

I John 5:1-5

1 Whosoever believeth that Jesus is the Christ is born of God: and every one that loveth him that begat loveth him also that is begotten of him.

2 By this we know that we love the children of God, when we love God, and keep his commandments.

3 For this is the love of God, that we keep his commandments: and his commandments are not grievous.

4 For whatsoever is born of God overcometh the world: and this is the victory that overcometh the world, even our faith.

5 Who is he that overcometh the world, but he that believeth that Jesus is the Son of God? (KJV)

I John 2:13-17

13 I write unto you, fathers, because ye have known him that is from the beginning. I write unto you, young men, because ye have overcome the wicked one. I write unto you, little children, because ye have known the Father.

14 I have written unto you, fathers, because ye have known him that is from the beginning. I have written unto you, young men, because ye are strong, and the word of God abideth in you, and ye have overcome the wicked one.

15 Love not the world, neither the things that are in the world. If any

man love the world, the love of the Father is not in him.

16 For all that is in the world, the lust of the flesh, and the lust of the eyes, and the pride of life, is not of the Father, but is of the world.

17 And the world passeth away, and the lust thereof: but he that doeth the will of God abideth for ever. (KJV)

Eph. 2:5-10

5 Even when we were dead in sins, hath quickened us together with Christ, (by grace ye are saved;)

6 And hath raised us up together, and made us sit together in heavenly places in Christ Jesus:

7 That in the ages to come he might shew the exceeding riches of his grace in his kindness toward us through Christ Jesus.

8 For by grace are ye saved through faith; and that not of yourselves: it is the gift of God:

9 Not of works, lest any man should boast.

10 For we are his workmanship, created in Christ Jesus unto good works, which God hath before ordained that we should walk in them. (KJV)

Titus 3:4-8

4 But after that the kindness and love of God our Saviour toward man appeared,

5 Not by works of righteousness which we have done, but according to his mercy he saved us, by the washing of regeneration, and renewing of the Holy Ghost;

6 Which he shed on us abundantly through Jesus Christ our Saviour;

7 That being justified by his grace, we should be made heirs according to the hope of eternal life.

8 This is a faithful saying, and these things I will that thou affirm constantly, that they which have believed in God might be careful to maintain good works. These things are good and profitable unto men. (KJV)

John 3:16-21

16 For God so loved the world, that he gave his only begotten Son, that whosoever believeth in him should not perish, but have everlasting life.

17 For God sent not his Son into the world to condemn the world; but that the world through him might be saved.

18 He that believeth on him is not condemned: but he that believeth not is condemned already, because he hath not believed in the name of the only begotten Son of God.

19 And this is the condemnation, that light is come into the world, and men loved darkness rather than light, because their deeds were evil.

20 For every one that doeth evil hateth the light, neither cometh to the light, lest his deeds should be reproved.

21 But he that doeth truth cometh to the light, that his deeds may be made manifest, that they are wrought in God. (KJV)

Matthew 25:1-13

1 Then shall the kingdom of heaven be likened unto ten virgins, which took their lamps, and went forth to meet the bridegroom.

2 And five of them were wise, and five were foolish.

3 They that were foolish took their lamps, and took no oil with them:

4 But the wise took oil in their vessels with their lamps.

5 While the bridegroom tarried, they all slumbered and slept.

6 And at midnight there was a cry made, Behold, the bridegroom cometh; go ye out to meet him.

7 Then all those virgins arose, and trimmed their lamps.

8 And the foolish said unto the wise, Give us of your oil; for our lamps are gone out.

9 But the wise answered, saying, Not so; lest there be not enough for us and you: but go ye rather to them that sell, and buy for yourselves.

10 And while they went to buy, the bridegroom came; and they that were ready went in with him to the marriage: and the door was shut.

11 Afterward came also the other virgins, saying, Lord, Lord, open to us.

12 But he answered and said, Verily I say unto you, I know you not.

13 Watch therefore, for ye know neither the day nor the hour wherein the Son of man cometh. (KJV)

A parable is used primarily as a story to illustrate an important, basic truth. Often, as in the case here, cultural customs and circumstances are used only as the backdrop to the story so as to make it more interesting and understandable to the audience. The singular truth expressed in this parable, therefore, is the reality that we always should be "ready" to go because no one knows when the Lord will Return for His saints. Although we always should exercise great care and caution when finding a counterpart in reality to the various elements contained within the story, the answers do seem fairly obvious in this case.

The five wise virgins with oil in their lamps represent true, born-again Christians who have the Holy Spirit dwelling in their hearts because they are in a proper relationship with God through Christ Jesus, their Lord and Saviour. However, the five foolish virgins represent unsaved individuals who are not "overcomers" of the world through Christ Jesus as Scripture admonishes us to be. (I John 5:1-5; I John 2:13-17; Eph. 2:5-10; Titus 3:4-8; John 3:16-21.) Therefore, they are not ready when the bridegroom (Christ) suddenly appears to claim His bride (the church). This is the same truth expressed in the verses immediately preceding this passage:

Matthew 24:36-51

36 But of that day and hour knoweth no man, no, not the angels of heaven, but my Father only.

37 But as the days of Noe were, so shall also the coming of the Son of man be.

38 For as in the days that were before the flood they were eating and drinking, marrying and giving in marriage, until the day that Noe entered into the ark,

39 And knew not until the flood came, and took them all away; so shall also the coming of the Son of man be.

40 Then shall two be in the field; the one shall be taken, and the other left.

41 Two women shall be grinding at the mill; the one shall be taken, and the other left.

42 Watch therefore: for ye know not what hour your Lord doth come.

43 But know this, that if the goodman of the house had known in what watch the thief would come, he would have watched, and would not have suffered his house to be broken up.

44 Therefore be ye also ready: for in such an hour as ye think not the Son of man cometh.

45 Who then is a faithful and wise servant, whom his lord hath made ruler over his household, to give them meat in due season?

46 Blessed is that servant, whom his lord when he cometh shall find so

doing.

47 Verily I say unto you, That he shall make him ruler over all his goods.

48 But and if that evil servant shall say in his heart, My lord delayeth his coming;

49 And shall begin to smite his fellowservants, and to eat and drink with the drunken;

50 The lord of that servant shall come in a day when he looketh not for him, and in an hour that he is not aware of,

51 And shall cut him asunder, and appoint him his portion with the hypocrites: there shall be weeping and gnashing of teeth. (KJV)

Moving on to a different aspect of God's Judgment Day, the following passage portrays two different resurrections:

John 5:25-29

25 Verily, verily, I say unto you, The hour is coming, and now is, when the dead shall hear the voice of the Son of God: and they that hear shall live.

26 For as the Father hath life in himself; so hath he given to the Son to have life in himself;

27 And hath given him authority to execute judgment also, because he is the Son of man.

28 Marvel not at this: for the hour is coming, in the which all that are in the graves shall hear his voice,

29 And shall come forth; they that have done good, unto the resurrection of life; and they that have done evil, unto the resurrection of damnation. (KJV)

In the first resurrection pictured (verse 25), all who hear the voice of God will live; this occurs at the time of the Rapture (and the later, subsequent resurrection or translation of the Great Tribulation Saints). Then, in a later, subsequent resurrection (verses 28 and 29), there comes a time when everyone (who is still in the grave after the Millennial Reign of Christ) will hear the voice of Jesus Christ, our God and Saviour. Some of these people will be judged as having done "good" and will receive eternal life; others will be judged as having done "evil" and will be punished with eternal death and torment. This is the Great White Throne Judgment.

Likewise, Daniel narrates a similar, parallel passage:

Daniel 12:1-4

1 And at that time shall Michael stand up, the great prince which standeth for the children of thy people: and there shall be a time of trouble, such as never was since there was a nation even to that same time: and at that time thy people shall be delivered, every one that shall be found written in the book.

2 And many of them that sleep in the dust of the earth shall awake, some to everlasting life, and some to shame and everlasting contempt.

3 And they that be wise shall shine as the brightness of the firmament; and they that turn many to righteousness as the stars for ever and ever.

4 But thou, O Daniel, shut up the words, and seal the book, even to the time of the end: many shall run to and fro, and knowledge shall be increased. (KJV)

Once again, a first resurrection (verse 1) is portrayed wherein all whose names are written in the Book Of Life are delivered or resurrected or translated during a terrible time of trouble. Then, at a later time (verse 2) during the Great White Throne Judgment, those who are still in their graves will awake, some to everlasting life, the others to eternal damnation and tormenting fire.

The passage in II Thess. 2:1-3 reads as follows:

II Thess. 2:1-3

1 Now we beseech you, brethren, by the coming of our Lord Jesus Christ, and by our gathering together unto him,

2 That ye be not soon shaken in mind, or be troubled, neither by spirit, nor by word, nor by letter as from us, as that the day of Christ is at hand.

3 Let no man deceive you by any means: for that day (Day of the Lord) shall not come, except there come a falling away first, and that man of sin be revealed, the son of perdition. (KJV)

The phrase "day of Christ" is more-accurately interpreted by other translations such as *Young's Literal Translation* as "Day of the Lord." Likewise, *Strong's Hebrew-Greek Dictionary* will show that the English word translated here as "Christ" is not from the Greek word, CHRISTOS — which normally is used whenever the word "Christ" is intended — but from the word KURIOS. Strong defines KURIOS as follows:

> 2962 kurios (koo'-ree-os);
> from kuros (supremacy); supreme in authority, i.e. (as noun) controller; by implication, Mr. (as a respectful title):
> KJV— God, Lord, master, Sir.

So, based on references such as *Strong's Hebrew-Greek Dictionary*, the proper rendering for the phrase "day of Christ" is actually "day of the Lord," thereby allowing this passage to be consistent with the prophetic teachings found elsewhere throughout biblical scriptures. Therefore, this period of time should not be confused with the Rapture of the saints to meet the Lord in the air (i.e., "our gathering together unto him," mentioned in verse one) because the "Day of the Lord" is a period of Divine wrath and judgment upon the earth which begins immediately after the Great Tribulation and the Sixth Seal have taken place.

The preceding scriptural passage presents an interesting picture. Apparently, there were people during the days of the apostles who were teaching that some Christians had missed the Rapture ("our gathering together unto him") which for obvious reasons had many people quite concerned and agitated about facing the judgments and tribulation associated with the Day of the Lord. Therefore, Paul felt it necessary to reaffirm his earlier eschatological teaching regarding the doctrine of the Rapture by reassuring them that the terrible Day Of The Lord, with all of its horrendous judgments, would not happen until the Final Great Apostasy took place and the man of sin (i.e., Antichrist) was revealed to the whole world. So, in light of this passage, we must conclude that from the very beginning of Christianity, there always have been those who have promoted false theories about when the Rapture will happen despite the scriptural evidence at hand.

Sometimes people will disparage the Rapture doctrine because it supposedly was first promulgated by a person of questionable background or character during the early 1800's. But, quite frankly, it really does not matter because the pre-tribulation Rapture was the prevalent doctrine taught during New Testament times as seen in the above passage. Unfortunately, a few centuries after Christ, many biblical teachings, including the doctrine of the Rapture, became lost or distorted. But if, and when, the Rapture doctrine was "rediscovered" after the Dark Ages, it was not any less valid than the "faith without works" doctrine was when earlier it was "rediscovered" by Martin Luther. Obviously just because a biblical doctrine is alleged to be recent in "discovery" does not affect its validity if it truly is located in the Bible. Accordingly, I think it is very important, no actually, vital and essential, to base our theology on biblical Scripture alone, and nothing else.

Yet another passage which often is misunderstood involves the following scripture which portrays the separation of "evil" people from "good" people who still are alive on earth immediately after the Battle of Armageddon is concluded. Although sometimes people will conclude erroneously that this scripture teaches that Christians will be taken or Raptured at this point in time, in actuality, the good "sheep" pictured in this passage should be distinguished in identity from the Raptured Christians (saints) who return with Christ at His Second Coming to the earth:

Matthew 25:31-46

31 When the Son of man shall come in his glory, and all the holy angels with him, then shall he sit upon the throne of his glory:

32 And before him shall be gathered all nations: and he shall separate them one from another, as a shepherd divideth his sheep from the goats:

33 And he shall set the sheep on his right hand, but the goats on the left.

34 Then shall the King say unto them on his right hand, Come, ye blessed of my Father, inherit the kingdom prepared for you from the foundation of the world:

35 For I was an hungred, and ye gave me meat: I was thirsty, and ye gave me drink: I was a stranger, and ye took me in:

36 Naked, and ye clothed me: I was sick, and ye visited me: I was in prison, and ye came unto me.

37 Then shall the righteous answer him, saying, Lord, when saw we thee an hungred, and fed thee? or thirsty, and gave thee drink?

38 When saw we thee a stranger, and took thee in? or naked, and clothed thee?

39 Or when saw we thee sick, or in prison, and came unto thee?

40 And the King shall answer and say unto them, Verily I say unto you, Inasmuch as ye have done it unto one of the least of these my brethren, ye have done it unto me.

41 Then shall he say also unto them on the left hand, Depart from me, ye cursed, into everlasting fire, prepared for the devil and his angels:

42 For I was an hungred, and ye gave me no meat: I was thirsty, and ye gave me no drink:

43 I was a stranger, and ye took me not in: naked, and ye clothed me not: sick, and in prison, and ye visited me not.

44 Then shall they also answer him, saying, Lord, when saw we thee an hungred, or athirst, or a stranger, or naked, or sick, or in prison, and did not minister unto thee?

45 Then shall he answer them, saying, Verily I say unto you, Inasmuch as ye did it not to one of the least of these, ye did it not to me.

46 And these shall go away into everlasting punishment: but the righteous into life eternal. (KJV)

In other words, this passage describes a period of judgment for "unsaved" or "unconverted" people still alive on the earth immediately after the Battle of Armageddon. Please note that Jesus did NOT indicate this narrative was a parable by beginning with a qualifying phrase such as: "is like unto," or "like," or "such as," etc. Instead, He very clearly said, "when the Son of Man shall come in his glory..." Therefore, the evidence quite obviously mandates we take Jesus at His Word, literally, and apply this passage literally to the time of His Second Coming.

On that basis, then, the purpose of this judgment will be to determine which "unsaved" individuals surviving after Armageddon will be deemed worthy to remain alive on the earth during the Millennial Reign of Christ. Therefore, each person will be judged strictly on his own individual merits since this would be the only fair method in judging. (The word for "nations" used in Matthew 25:31-46 is ETHNOS, which also means races, peoples, families, and individuals.) People will be classified as either "sheep" or "goat," depending upon their actions during the time-period between the Rapture and Armageddon. Those people who help Jews or Christians during their time of tribulation if presented with an opportunity to do so, and who also never accept the "mark of the beast," will be classified as sheep. The others will be classified as goats and thrown into hell immediately.

Compare this parallel passage of scripture which also describes the separation of "good" people from "evil" people who still remain on the earth immediately after the Battle of Armageddon:

Matthew 13:36-43, 47-50

36 Then Jesus sent the multitude away, and went into the house: and his disciples came unto him, saying, Declare unto us the parable of the tares of the field.

37 He answered and said unto them, He that soweth the good seed is the Son of man;

38 The field is the world; the good seed are the children of the kingdom; but the tares are the children of the wicked one;

39 The enemy that sowed them is the devil; the harvest is the end of the world; and the reapers are the angels.

40 As therefore the tares are gathered and burned in the fire; so shall it be in the end of this world.

41 The Son of man shall send forth his angels, and they shall gather out of his kingdom all things that offend, and them which do iniquity;

42 And shall cast them into a furnace of fire: there shall be wailing and gnashing of teeth.

43 Then shall the righteous shine forth as the sun in the kingdom of their Father. Who hath ears to hear, let him hear.

47 Again, the kingdom of heaven is like unto a net, that was cast into the sea, and gathered of every kind:

48 Which, when it was full, they drew to shore, and sat down, and gathered the good into vessels, but cast the bad away.

49 So shall it be at the end of the world: the angels shall come forth, and sever the wicked from among the just,

50 And shall cast them into the furnace of fire: there shall.be wailing and gnashing of teeth. (KJV)

Some people have thought perhaps this scripture teaches that the saints will be Raptured at the time of the Second Coming of Christ (i.e., a "post-tribulation" Rapture). But, as we saw earlier, the scriptural evidence overwhelmingly proves a pre-tribulation Rapture; an honest appraisal of all the evidence allows no other conclusion. The problem in understanding this passage comes from our limited view of the full scope and extent of God's Kingdom. We must realize that there will be more than just Christians living in it; there also will be Jews living in the nation of Israel, and there also will be non-Jewish people living in all of the Gentile nations throughout the world. Accordingly, this scripture parallels the passage above in Matthew 25:31-46 which describes the judgment of the sheep and goats immediately after Christ Returns at the Battle of Armageddon. It has nothing to do with the Raptured saints who return with Christ at His Second Coming. But, verse 28 in the following passage does picture the Raptured saints being gathered around Christ in Heaven immediately before His Return to the earth to fight at the Battle of Armageddon:

Matthew 24:21-28

21 For then shall be great tribulation, such as was not since the beginning of the world to this time, no, nor ever shall be.

22 And except those days should be shortened, there should no flesh be saved: but for the elect's sake those days shall be shortened.

23 Then if any man shall say unto you, Lo, here is Christ, or there; believe it not.

24 For there shall arise false Christs, and false prophets, and shall shew great signs and wonders; insomuch that, if it were possible, they shall deceive the very elect.

25 Behold, I have told you before.

26 Wherefore if they shall say unto you, Behold, he is in the desert; go not forth: behold, he is in the secret chambers; believe it not.

27 For as the lightning cometh out of the east, and shineth even unto the west; so shall also the coming of the Son of man be.

28 For wheresoever the carcase is, there will the eagles be gathered together. (KJV)

The word "carcase" in the Greek is PTOMA, and it can be translated as "dead body, corpse, carcase." However, the word "eagle" is translated correctly, as confirmed by the following scriptural passage:

Isaiah 40:31

31 But they that wait upon the LORD shall renew their strength; they shall mount up with wings as eagles; they shall run, and not be weary; and they shall walk, and not faint. (KJV)

Therefore, Jesus is saying that just prior to His Second Coming, eagles (i.e., Christians) will be gathered around "the dead body" (i.e., Christ, the "Lamb as it had been slain" — Rev. 5:6). He then elaborates further on this "gathering" of eagle saints from throughout the earth and the universe:

Matthew 24:29-31

29 Immediately after the tribulation of those days shall the sun be darkened, and the moon shall not give her light, and the stars shall fall from heaven, and the powers of the heavens shall be shaken:

30 And then shall appear the sign of the Son of man in heaven: and then shall all the tribes of the earth mourn, and they shall see the Son of man coming in the clouds of heaven with power and great glory.

31 And he shall send his angels with a great sound of a trumpet, and they shall gather together his elect from the four winds, from one end of heaven to the other. (KJV)

Mark 13:24-27

24 But in those days, after that tribulation, the sun shall be darkened, and the moon shall not give her light,

25 And the stars of heaven shall fall, and the powers that are in heaven shall be shaken.

26 And then shall they see the Son of man coming in the clouds with great power and glory.

27 And then shall he send his angels, and shall gather together his elect from the four winds, from the uttermost part of the earth to the uttermost part of heaven. (KJV)

The identity of the "elect" who are translated or gathered by the angels "from the uttermost part of the earth to the uttermost part of heaven" just before the Second Coming is quite simple to determine. They are both tribulation saints, including the 144,000 Jews, who will have been given God's seal of protection after escaping execution by the Antichrist during the Great Christian Tribulation (Mark 13:27) (Luke 21:16), and Raptured saints who will be busy exploring the mysteries and wonders of God's great universe after the Rapture (Isa. 40:31). Therefore, the above scriptural passages in the Olivet Discourse by no means necessitate a Second Coming Rapture.

Matthew 16:27-17:9

27 For the Son of man shall come in the glory of his Father with his angels; and then he shall reward every man according to his works.

28 Verily I say unto you, There be some standing here, which shall not taste of death, till they see the Son of man coming in his kingdom.

1 And after six days Jesus taketh Peter, James, and John his brother, and bringeth them up into an high mountain apart,

2 And was transfigured before them: and his face did shine as the sun, and his raiment was white as the light.

3 And, behold, there appeared unto them Moses and Elias talking with him.

4 Then answered Peter, and said unto Jesus, Lord, it is good for us to be here: if thou wilt, let us make here three tabernacles; one for thee, and one for Moses, and one for Elias.

5 While he yet spake, behold, a bright cloud overshadowed them: and behold a voice out of the cloud, which said, This is my beloved Son, in whom I am well pleased; hear ye him.

6 And when the disciples heard it, they fell on their face, and were sore afraid.

7 And Jesus came and touched them, and said, Arise, and be not afraid.

8 And when they had lifted up their eyes, they saw no man, save Jesus only.

9 And as they came down from the mountain, Jesus charged them, saying, Tell the vision to no man, until the Son of man be risen again from the dead. (KJV)

Verse 27 in the passage above is a reference to the Judgment of Sheep and Goats, as portrayed in Matthew 25, when Jesus Returns to the earth with His Saints, and judges which people surviving Armageddon will be allowed to remain on the earth to repopulate the world, and which ones will be sent to eternal punishment immediately. Then in verse 28, using the phrase "Verily I say unto you" for added emphasis on something extraordinary He was about to pronounce, Jesus promised that some of the individuals standing there with Him would be privileged to see Him in His glorified Divine state sometime before they died (although there was no promise that they also would see everything else He had just predicted in the previous verse of scripture). Then sure enough, as promised, a few days later, subsequent verses in this passage describe how some of the disciples actually saw Him in a vision, briefly, displayed in all of His Divine glory during His marvelous supernatural transfiguration.

Matthew 10:23

23 But when they persecute you in this city, flee ye into another: for

verily I say unto you, Ye shall not have gone over the cities of Israel, till the Son of man be come. (KJV)

The phrase “have gone over” in the above passage is translated from the Greek word TELEO, which is defined by *Strong's Hebrew-Greek Dictionary* as meaning “to end, ie. complete, execute, conclude, discharge (a debt)” and is translated in the KJV as “accomplish, make an end, expire, fill up, finish, go over, pay, perform.”

So, essentially, this passage is saying that the cities of Israel will not be “gone over” or completely evangelized before the Second Coming of Christ. This is literally true because all of the cities of Israel were not fully evangelized by the early church due to the severe persecution which they endured, and also because the city of Jerusalem was destroyed soon thereafter in 70 A.D. (Acts 8:1-4; Acts 9:1-4; Acts 11:19-21; Acts 12:1). Nor have they been fully evangelized since then, nor will they ever be completely evangelized until the Millennium (Isa. 2:1-4; Isa. 11:9; Rom. 11:25-29; Zech. 12:10 through Zech. 13:1).

Trumpet Comparisons		
Last Trump **I Cor. 15:51-52**	**7th Trumpet** **Revelation 11:15-19**	**Great Trumpet** **Matthew 24:30-31**
Lord descends from Heaven when the Last Trump is blown.	Lord descends after the 7th Trumpet is blown.	Great Trump is blown at Second Coming.
Blown with a shout, with the voice of the arch-angel.	Blown with the voice of the 7th angel.	Numerous angels with the great sound of a trumpet.
Called the trumpet of God.	Called the trumpet of the 7th angel.	Called a trumpet.
Purpose: Rapture of the saints.	Purpose: Usher in the events of the 7th Plague.	Purpose: Gather all saints throughout the heavens and the earth, including tribulation saints who evade execution.
Blown before the Seven-Sealed Book is opened.	Blown just prior to the 7th Plague of the 7th Seal.	Blown after the 7th Seal is over.

VI. World Chaos And Judgment

Outline Of Revelation

Revelation is a very organized book. Chapter one deals with Christ and His qualifications to be the Redeemer. Chapters two and three have a four-fold application: (1) a message to seven local church congregations in the days that John was given the Revelation; (2) a message to all believers during all of the history of Christianity; (3) the seven basic types of churches prevalent throughout church history; and (4) the seven basic church eras in the history of Christianity, and the major spiritual characteristics which dominate each one. Chapters 4-11 deal with events between the Rapture and Armageddon, using Heaven as a reference point. Likewise, chapters 12-16 cover the same events, but from an earthly perspective. Chapters 17 and 18 deal with Satan's system during the last days: a religious part and an economic part. Chapters 19 and 20 deal with the Millennial Reign of Christ on earth, and Chapters 21 and 22 view eternal conditions on earth.

Christ, The Revelator

Revelation 1:1-20

1 The Revelation of Jesus Christ, which God gave unto him, to shew unto his servants things which must shortly come to pass; and he sent and signified it by his angel unto his servant John:

2 Who bare record of the word of God, and of the testimony of Jesus Christ, and of all things that he saw.

3 Blessed is he that readeth, and they that hear the words of this prophecy, and keep those things which are written therein: for the time is at hand.

4 John to the seven churches which are in Asia: Grace be unto you, and peace, from him which is, and which was, and which is to come; and from the seven Spirits which are before his throne;

5 And from Jesus Christ, who is the faithful witness, and the first begotten of the dead, and the prince of the kings of the earth. Unto him that loved us, and washed us from our sins in his own blood,

6 And hath made us kings and priests unto God and his Father; to him be glory and dominion for ever and ever. Amen.

7 Behold, he cometh with clouds; and every eye shall see him, and they also which pierced him: and all kindreds of the earth shall wail because of him. Even so, Amen.

8 I am Alpha and Omega, the beginning and the ending, saith the Lord, which is, and which was, and which is to come, the Almighty.

9 I John, who also am your brother, and companion in tribulation, and in the kingdom and patience of Jesus Christ, was in the isle that is called Patmos, for the word of God, and for the testimony of Jesus Christ.

10 I was in the Spirit on the Lord's day, and heard behind me a great voice, as of a trumpet,

11 Saying, I am Alpha and Omega, the first and the last: and, What thou seest, write in a book, and send it unto the seven churches which are in Asia; unto Ephesus, and unto Smyrna, and unto Pergamos, and unto Thyatira, and unto Sardis, and unto Philadelphia, and unto Laodicea.

12 And I turned to see the voice that spake with me. And being turned, I saw seven golden candlesticks;

13 And in the midst of the seven candlesticks one like unto the Son of man, clothed with a garment down to the foot, and girt about the paps with a golden girdle.

14 His head and his hairs were white like wool, as white as snow; and his eyes were as a flame of fire;

15 And his feet like unto fine brass, as if they burned in a furnace; and his voice as the sound of many waters.

16 And he had in his right hand seven stars: and out of his mouth went a sharp twoedged sword: and his countenance was as the sun shineth in his strength.

17 And when I saw him, I fell at his feet as dead. And he laid his right hand upon me, saying unto me, Fear not; I am the first and the last:

18 I am he that liveth, and was dead; and, behold, I am alive for evermore, Amen; and have the keys of hell and of death.

19 Write the things which thou hast seen, and the things which are, and the things which shall be hereafter;

20 The mystery of the seven stars which thou sawest in my right hand, and the seven golden candlesticks. The seven stars are the angels of the seven churches: and the seven candlesticks which thou sawest are the seven churches. (KJV)

Christ is portrayed in this chapter as Prophet, Judge, King and Priest. Prophet in the sense that He is called the Faithful Witness. Judge because He has "eyes...as a flame of fire," illustrating His perfect perception of reality; and "feet like unto fine brass," denoting His power to enforce judgment. (cf. Rev. 2:18). A King because He has a "voice as the sound of many waters" and a "sharp two edged sword" out of His "mouth," thereby demonstrating the power of His Word. Priest because He wears priestly attire (cf. Exod. 28:4) and has "washed us from our sins in his own blood." In these descriptions, please notice that "heavenly things" are described literally by the use of similes, i.e., comparisons to things familiar to people; there is very little symbolism involved, and when it is, it is explained (e.g., the "sevens stars" and the "seven golden candlesticks").

"The seven Spirits." Isaiah 11:1-3 gives us insight into this matter:

Isaiah 11:1-3

1 And there shall come forth a rod out of the stem of Jesse, and a Branch shall grow out of his roots:

2 And the spirit of the LORD shall rest upon him, the spirit of wisdom and understanding, the spirit of counsel and might, the spirit of knowledge and of the fear of the LORD;

3 And shall make him of quick understanding in the fear of the LORD: and he shall not judge after the sight of his eyes, neither reprove after the hearing of his ears: (KJV)

"Seven." Seven is the number used in the Bible to denote "completeness" (not "perfection").

The Seven Churches Surveyed

Revelation 2:1-7

1 Unto the angel of the church of Ephesus write; These things saith he that holdeth the seven stars in his right hand, who walketh in the midst of the seven golden candlesticks;

2 I know thy works, and thy labour, and thy patience, and how thou canst not bear them which are evil: and thou hast tried them which say they are apostles, and are not, and hast found them liars:

3 And hast borne, and hast patience, and for my name's sake hast laboured, and hast not fainted.

4 Nevertheless I have somewhat against thee, because thou hast left thy first love.

5 Remember therefore from whence thou art fallen, and repent, and do the first works; or else I will come unto thee quickly, and will remove thy candlestick out of his place, except thou repent.

6 But this thou hast, that thou hatest the deeds of the Nicolaitans, which I also hate.

7 He that hath an ear, let him hear what the Spirit saith unto the churches; To him that overcometh will I give to eat of the tree of life, which is in the midst of the paradise of God. (KJV)

Ephesian church. 33-100 A.D. Characterized as faithful in service, but guilty of "leaving their first (i.e., most intense) love."

Revelation 2:8-11

8 And unto the angel of the church in Smyrna write; These things saith the first and the last, which was dead, and is alive;

9 I know thy works, and tribulation, and poverty, (but thou art rich) and I know the blasphemy of them which say they are Jews, and are not, but are the synagogue of Satan.

10 Fear none of those things which thou shalt suffer: behold, the devil shall cast some of you into prison, that ye may be tried; and ye shall have tribulation ten days: be thou faithful unto death, and I will give thee a crown of life.

11 He that hath an ear, let him hear what the Spirit saith unto the churches; He that overcometh shall not be hurt of the second death. (KJV)

Smyrnan church. 100-312 A.D. The expression, "tribulation ten days," is a reference to the terrible persecutions that took place during the reign of ten different Caesars. She is characterized as faithful during persecution; and materially poor, but spiritually rich.

Revelation 2:12-17

12 And to the angel of the church in Pergamos write; These things saith he which hath the sharp sword with two edges;

13 I know thy works, and where thou dwellest, even where Satan's

seat is: and thou holdest fast my name, and hast not denied my faith, even in those days wherein Antipas was my faithful martyr, who was slain among you, where Satan dwelleth.

14 But I have a few things against thee, because thou hast there them that hold the doctrine of Balaam, who taught Balac to cast a stumblingblock before the children of Israel, to eat things sacrificed unto idols, and to commit fornication.

15 So hast thou also them that hold the doctrine of the Nicolaitans, which thing I hate.

16 Repent; or else I will come unto thee quickly, and will fight against them with the sword of my mouth.

17 He that hath an ear, let him hear what the Spirit saith unto the churches; To him that overcometh will I give to eat of the hidden manna, and will give him a white stone, and in the stone a new name written, which no man knoweth saving he that receiveth it. (KJV)

Church of Pergamos. 312-590 A.D. This marks the beginning of a merger between "church" and "state." "Where Satan's seat is" alludes to the fact that, at this point in time, the ritual and mysteries and doctrines of "Mystery Babylon" increasingly became assimilated into the "church." The "Nicolaitans" comes from two Greek words: NICO, meaning "conquer"; and LAITANES, meaning "laity." Therefore, "Nicolaitans" means "conquerors of the laity," thus picturing the beginning of ecclesiastical control and domination of the clergy over laity. The "white stone" depicts a new and righteous beginning for eternity.

Revelation 2:18-29

18 And unto the angel of the church in Thyatira write; These things saith the Son of God, who hath his eyes like unto a flame of fire, and his feet are like fine brass;

19 I know thy works, and charity, and service, and faith, and thy patience, and thy works; and the last to be more than the first.

20 Notwithstanding I have a few things against thee, because thou sufferest that woman Jezebel, which calleth herself a prophetess, to teach and to seduce my servants to commit fornication, and to eat things sacrificed unto idols.

21 And I gave her space to repent of her fornication; and she repented not.

22 Behold, I will cast her into a bed, and them that commit adultery with her into great tribulation, except they repent of their deeds.

23 And I will kill her children with death; and all the churches shall know that I am he which searcheth the reins and hearts: and I will give unto every one of you according to your works.

24 But unto you I say, and unto the rest in Thyatira, as many as have not this doctrine, and which have not known the depths of Satan, as they speak; I will put upon you none other burden.

25 But that which ye have already hold fast till I come.

26 And he that overcometh, and keepeth my works unto the end, to him will I give power over the nations:

27 And he shall rule them with a rod of iron; as the vessels of a potter shall they be broken to shivers: even as I received of my Father.

28 And I will give him the morning star.

29 He that hath an ear, let him hear what the Spirit saith unto the churches. (KJV)

Church of Thyatira. 590-1517 A.D. Was tremendously influenced and corrupted by Jezebel, a wicked woman symbolizing the Roman Church, which seduced Christians to embrace "fornication" (spiritual unfaithfulness) by syncretizing Christian beliefs with the pagan beliefs and rituals of the ancient Babylonian religion. Verse 22 indicates that it will go through the Great Tribulation which takes place after the Rapture.

Revelation 3:1-6

1 And unto the angel of the church in Sardis write; These things saith he that hath the seven Spirits of God, and the seven stars; I know thy works, that thou hast a name that thou livest, and art dead.

2 Be watchful, and strengthen the things which remain, that are ready to die: for I have not found thy works perfect before God.

3 Remember therefore how thou hast received and heard, and hold fast, and repent. If therefore thou shalt not watch, I will come on thee as a thief, and thou shalt not know what hour I will come upon thee.

4 Thou hast a few names even in Sardis which have not defiled their garments; and they shall walk with me in white: for they are worthy.

5 He that overcometh, the same shall be clothed in white raiment; and I will not blot out his name out of the book of life, but I will confess his name before my Father, and before his angels.

6 He that hath an ear, let him hear what the Spirit saith unto the churches. (KJV)

Church of Sardis. 1517-1750 A.D. The Reformation Era.

Revelation 3:7-13

7 And to the angel of the church in Philadelphia write; These things saith he that is holy, he that is true, he that hath the key of David, he that openeth, and no man shutteth; and shutteth, and no man openeth;

8 I know thy works: behold, I have set before thee an open door, and no man can shut it: for thou hast a little strength, and hast kept my word, and hast not denied my name.

9 Behold, I will make them of the synagogue of Satan, which say they are Jews, and are not, but do lie; behold, I will make them to come and worship before thy feet, and to know that I have loved thee.

10 Because thou hast kept the word of my patience, I also will keep thee from the hour of temptation, which shall come upon all the world, to try them that dwell upon the earth.

11 Behold, I come quickly: hold that fast which thou hast, that no man take thy crown.

12 Him that overcometh will I make a pillar in the temple of my God, and he shall go no more out: and I will write upon him the name of my God, and the name of the city of my God, which is new Jerusalem, which cometh down out of heaven from my God: and I will write upon him my new name.

13 He that hath an ear, let him hear what the Spirit saith unto the churches. (KJV)

Church of Philadelphia. 1750 A.D. The Rapture. A tremendous missionary and revival era. Characterized as faithful to God's Word.

Revelation 3:14-22

14 And unto the angel of the church of the Laodiceans write; These things saith the Amen, the faithful and true witness, the beginning of the creation of God;

15 I know thy works, that thou art neither cold nor hot: I would thou wert cold or hot.

16 So then because thou art lukewarm, and neither cold nor hot, I will

spue thee out of my mouth.

17 Because thou sayest, I am rich, and increased with goods, and have need of nothing; and knowest not that thou art wretched, and miserable, and poor, and blind, and naked:

18 I counsel thee to buy of me gold tried in the fire, that thou mayest be rich; and white raiment, that thou mayest be clothed, and that the shame of thy nakedness do not appear; and anoint thine eyes with eyesalve, that thou mayest see.

19 As many as I love, I rebuke and chasten: be zealous therefore, and repent.

20 Behold, I stand at the door, and knock: if any man hear my voice, and open the door, I will come in to him, and will sup with him, and he with me.

21 To him that overcometh will I grant to sit with me in my throne, even as I also overcame, and am set down with my Father in his throne.

22 He that hath an ear, let him hear what the Spirit saith unto the churches. (KJV)

Church of Laodicea. 1900 A.D. The Great Tribulation. Characterized by wealth, "lukewarmness," spiritual poorness and heresy. Represents the spirit of "modernism" and "religious liberalism" that masks unbelief through the use of religious terminology and ritual.

Rapture To Heaven

Revelation 4

1 After this I looked, and, behold, a door was opened in heaven: and the first voice which I heard was as it were of a trumpet talking with me; which said, Come up hither, and I will shew thee things which must be hereafter.

2 And immediately I was in the spirit: and, behold, a throne was set in heaven, and one sat on the throne.

3 And he that sat was to look upon like a jasper and a sardine stone: and there was a rainbow round about the throne, in sight like unto an emerald.

4 And round about the throne were four and twenty seats: and upon the seats I saw four and twenty elders sitting, clothed in white raiment; and

they had on their heads crowns of gold.

5 And out of the throne proceeded lightnings and thunderings and voices: and there were seven lamps of fire burning before the throne, which are the seven Spirits of God.

6 And before the throne there was a sea of glass like unto crystal: and in the midst of the throne, and round about the throne, were four beasts full of eyes before and behind.

7 And the first beast was like a lion, and the second beast like a calf, and the third beast had a face as a man, and the fourth beast was like a flying eagle.

8 And the four beasts had each of them six wings about him; and they were full of eyes within: and they rest not day and night, saying, Holy, holy, holy, Lord God Almighty, which was, and is, and is to come.

9 And when those beasts give glory and honour and thanks to him that sat on the throne, who liveth for ever and ever,

10 The four and twenty elders fall down before him that sat on the throne, and worship him that liveth for ever and ever, and cast their crowns before the throne, saying,

11 Thou art worthy, O Lord, to receive glory and honour and power: for thou hast created all things, and for thy pleasure they are and were created. (KJV)

Revelation 5

1 And I saw in the right hand of him that sat on the throne a book written within and on the backside, sealed with seven seals.

2 And I saw a strong angel proclaiming with a loud voice, Who is worthy to open the book, and to loose the seals thereof?

3 And no man in heaven, nor in earth, neither under the earth, was able to open the book, neither to look thereon.

4 And I wept much, because no man was found worthy to open and to read the book, neither to look thereon.

5 And one of the elders saith unto me, Weep not: behold, the Lion of the tribe of Juda, the Root of David, hath prevailed to open the book, and to loose the seven seals thereof.

6 And I beheld, and, lo, in the midst of the throne and of the four beasts, and in the midst of the elders, stood a Lamb as it had been slain, having seven horns and seven eyes, which are the seven Spirits of God sent forth into all the earth.

7 And he came and took the book out of the right hand of him that sat upon the throne.

8 And when he had taken the book, the four beasts and four and twenty elders fell down before the Lamb, having every one of them harps, and golden vials full of odours, which are the prayers of saints.

9 And they sung a new song, saying, Thou art worthy to take the book, and to open the seals thereof: for thou wast slain, and hast redeemed us to God by thy blood out of every kindred, and tongue, and people, and nation;

10 And hast made us unto our God kings and priests: and we shall reign on the earth.

11 And I beheld, and I heard the voice of many angels round about the throne and the beasts and the elders: and the number of them was ten thousand times ten thousand, and thousands of thousands;

12 Saying with a loud voice, Worthy is the Lamb that was slain to receive power, and riches, and wisdom, and strength, and honour, and glory, and blessing.

13 And every creature which is in heaven, and on the earth, and under the earth, and such as are in the sea, and all that are in them, heard I saying, Blessing, and honour, and glory, and power, be unto him that sitteth upon the throne, and unto the Lamb for ever and ever.

14 And the four beasts said, Amen. And the four and twenty elders fell down and worshipped him that liveth for ever and ever. (KJV)

The above two chapters describe a visible, majestic, all-powerful Divine personage seated amidst the heavenly splendor and glory of His Divine Throne, attended and worshipped by exotic heavenly creatures, some of whom have lesser thrones surrounding the Divine Throne. Now compare these two chapters with the abbreviated parallel description of the same thing which is offered in the following passage:

Daniel 7:9, 10

9 I beheld till the thrones were cast down, and the Ancient of days did sit, whose garment was white as snow, and the hair of his head like the pure wool: his throne was like the fiery flame, and his wheels as burning fire.

10 A fiery stream issued and came forth from before him: thousand thousands ministered unto him, and ten thousand times ten thousand stood

before him: the judgment was set, and the books were opened. (KJV)

A careful analysis of Revelation will show that it is concerned primarily with the redemption of earth and its inhabitants. Therefore, since the saints are seen throughout the book of Revelation, it is not surprising to find them extensively involved in the implementation of God's program of redemption for the earth. That honor and privilege is consistent with the fact that we will be joint-rulers with Christ over all of the universe, forever, as the following scriptures attest:

Revelation 5:9, 10
9 And they sung a new song, saying, Thou art worthy to take the book, and to open the seals thereof: for thou wast slain, and hast redeemed us to God by thy blood out of every kindred, and tongue, and people, and nation;
10 And hast made us unto our God kings and priests: and we shall reign on the earth. (KJV)

Daniel 7:21, 22, 27
21 I beheld, and the same horn made war with the saints, and prevailed against them;
22 Until the Ancient of days came, and judgment was given to the saints of the most High; and the time came that the saints possessed the kingdom.
27 And the kingdom and dominion, and the greatness of the kingdom under the whole heaven, shall be given to the people of the saints of the most High, whose kingdom is an everlasting kingdom, and all dominions shall serve and obey him. (KJV)

I Cor. 6:2, 3
2 Do ye not know that the saints shall judge the world? and if the world shall be judged by you, are ye unworthy to judge the smallest matters?
3 Know ye not that we shall judge angels? how much more things that pertain to this life? (KJV)

Revelation 1:5, 6
5 And from Jesus Christ, who is the faithful witness, and the first

begotten of the dead, and the prince of the kings of the earth. Unto him that loved us, and washed us from our sins in his own blood,

6 And hath made us kings and priests unto God and his Father; to him be glory and dominion for ever and ever. Amen. (KJV)

Ps. 149:5-9

5 Let the saints be joyful in glory: let them sing aloud upon their beds.

6 Let the high praises of God be in their mouth, and a twoedged sword in their hand;

7 To execute vengeance upon the heathen, and punishments upon the people;

8 To bind their kings with chains, and their nobles with fetters of iron;

9 To execute upon them the judgment written: this honour have all his saints. Praise ye the LORD. (KJV)

After the saints (Christian believers) are Raptured into Heaven, they will be organized into groups for maximum efficiency, each with a specific function to perform. In Revelation they are known as angels, horsemen, elders and beasts. Although these exotic heavenly creatures might seem very strange and unusual to us, please bear in mind that just as in chapter one of Revelation, similes (not symbols) are used to describe heavenly things. For example, Revelation 5 portrays Christ as both a "Lamb" and a "Lion," not in the literal or symbolical sense, but as a way of describing His personal attributes or characteristics which are shared in common with the creature or animal in view.

In like manner, the "four beasts" are said to possess personal characteristics similar in some respects to those possessed by a lion, and a calf, and an eagle and a man. Since a more accurate translation of the words "four beasts" would be "four living ones" or "four living creatures," we even have a direct and obvious reference to a description of Christ Himself in Revelation 1:18. Thus, we have a precedent for calling Christians "living ones" after they are given the gift of immortality by God. We also should note that the four beasts are actually four groups of saints not only because four is the number used by the Bible whenever it is necessary to show that God is dealing with the whole world (e.g., four directions, four seasons, four winds, four world empires in Daniel's visions, four Gospel accounts, four cherubim in Ezekiel, etc.), but also because the four beasts are "full" of "eyes," thereby confirming their humanity.

"Angels." It should be noted that the word "angel" comes from the Greek word AGGELOS, meaning "messenger," and the identity of the messenger is determined by the context. For example:

Revelation 22:8, 9

8 And I John saw these things, and heard them. And when I had heard and seen, I fell down to worship before the feet of the angel which shewed me these things.

9 Then saith he unto me, See thou do it not: for I am thy fellowservant, and of thy brethren the prophets, and of them which keep the sayings of this book: worship God. (KJV)

"Twenty-Four Elders." These twenty-four elders represent saints for the following reasons:

Many modern translations interpret the word "us" in Revelation 5:8-10 as "them," thereby causing this passage to imply that the elders and the beasts are something other than human. But, although many of the newer translations translate the word "us" as "them," there is no apparent justification for doing so except for theological bias. Not wanting to believe in a future reign of Christ on earth with the saints is not sufficient reason for changing the text of the Bible. Only the Codex Alexandrinus manuscript omits the word "us"; all of the other ancient manuscripts have it included. Translations such as the *King James Version* and *Young's Literal Translation Of The Bible* are correct when they render the word as "us" instead of "them." Therefore, the twenty-four elders and the four beasts portrayed in this passage of scripture must represent Christian believers because only saintly believers are redeemed; angels are not.

Now compare the following:

Revelation 1:5, 6

....Unto him that loved us, and washed us from our sins in his blood, And hath made us kings and priests unto God and his Father; to him be glory and dominion for ever and ever.... (KJV)

Please note the similarities between the above two accounts relative to the doxology and the attributes of the creatures who are praising God. A careful reading of the book of Revelation will show that many of the characteristics attributed to Christ and the saints in chapter one are repeated periodically throughout the remainder of Revelation. In fact, sometimes it is the only way possible to identify the "angel" or "creature" in view within a given passage of scripture. On that basis, because it is quite clear in Revelation 1:5-6 that Christians are praising and worshipping God, this most likely is the case in Revelation 5:8-10, also. Likewise, since there are no translations which read "them" instead of "us" in Revelation 1:5-6, we probably should read these disputed passages in Revelation 4 and 5 the same way — no matter how many modern translations say otherwise. Therefore, the "twenty-four elders" and the "four beasts" both must represent saints because only saints are redeemed.

If the "four beasts" and/or the "twenty-four elders" are not saints, then where are the saints? Since we can establish from Scripture that the saints "will judge the world" and "execute upon them the judgment written" (Rev. 5:9-10; Dan. 7:21-22, 27; I Cor. 6:2-3; Rev. 1:5-6; Ps. 149:5-9), they should be in prominent display. But, if the "four beasts" are not groups of saints, then why are they clearly involved so extensively in the execution of judgments upon the earth? (Rev. 6). Moreover, since the scriptural evidence very convincingly indicates that the elders do represent the saints, and since their number is 24, we also must conclude that they represent believers from both the Old and New Testament ages — typified by the 12 patriarchs and the twelve apostles. In a similar manner, as a parallel reference support for this point, the 12 gates and the 12 foundation stones of the New Jerusalem likewise are named for the 12 tribes from Old Testament times and the 12 apostles from New Testament times.

It is for certain that the "twenty-four elders" represent saints because the angel who shows John the Revelation vision also is identified as an "elder" and as a saint:

Revelation 1:1

1 The Revelation of Jesus Christ, which God gave unto him, to shew unto his servants things which must shortly come to pass; and he sent and signified it by his angel unto his servant John: (KJV)

Revelation 5:5-7

5 And one of the elders saith unto me, Weep not: behold, the Lion of the tribe of Juda, the Root of David, hath prevailed to open the book, and to loose the seven seals thereof.

6 And I beheld, and, lo, in the midst of the throne and of the four beasts, and in the midst of the elders, stood a Lamb as it had been slain, having seven horns and seven eyes, which are the seven Spirits of God sent forth into all the earth.

7 And he came and took the book out of the right hand of him that sat upon the throne. (KJV)

Revelation 7:13-15

13 And one of the elders answered, saying unto me, What are these which are arrayed in white robes? and whence came they?

14 And I said unto him, Sir, thou knowest. And he said to me, These are they which came out of great tribulation, and have washed their robes, and made them white in the blood of the Lamb.

15 Therefore are they before the throne of God, and serve him day and night in his temple: and he that sitteth on the throne shall dwell among them. (KJV)

Revelation 19:9-10

9 And he saith unto me, Write, Blessed are they which are called unto the marriage supper of the Lamb. And he saith unto me, These are the true sayings of God.

10 And I fell at his feet to worship him. And he said unto me, See thou do it not: I am thy fellowservant, and of thy brethren that have the testimony of Jesus: worship God: for the testimony of Jesus is the spirit of prophecy. (KJV)

Revelation 22:8-9

8 And I John saw these things, and heard them. And when I had heard and seen, I fell down to worship before the feet of the angel which shewed me these things.

9 Then saith he unto me, See thou do it not: for I am thy fellowservant, and of thy brethren the prophets, and of them which keep the sayings of this book: worship God. (KJV)

Evidently, John was so overwhelmed by the Revelation shown to him that twice he began to worship the "angel" who was showing it to him.

"I am thy fellowservant, and of thy brethren." This angel, who identifies himself as a saint, is also identified as one of the angels who pours out the seven vials of plagues upon the earth. (Rev. 17:1). Obviously this proves the validity of our interpretation concerning the identity of the angels throughout most of Revelation; it is the saints who will execute judgment upon the earth when it is being "redeemed." This also confirms that the saints must be Raptured to Heaven before the process of redemption begins; Bible students call this truth the "Pre-tribulation Rapture."

Revelation 22:16
16 I Jesus have sent mine angel to testify unto you these things in the churches. I am the root and the offspring of David, and the bright and morning star. (KJV)

As further confirmation that the twenty-four elders represent Christians, please note that the elders sit on thrones and wear crowns (Rev. 4:4, 10); only people, not angels, are promised such rewards if they "overcome":

Revelation 2:10
10 Fear none of those things which thou shalt suffer: behold, the devil shall cast some of you into prison, that ye may be tried; and ye shall have tribulation ten days: be thou faithful unto death, and I will give thee a crown of life. (KJV)

Revelation 1:5-6
5 And from Jesus Christ, who is the faithful witness, and the first begotten of the dead, and the prince of the kings of the earth. Unto him that loved us, and washed us from our sins in his own blood,
6 And hath made us kings and priests unto God and his Father; to him be glory and dominion for ever and ever. Amen. (KJV)

Revelation 3:20-21
20 Behold, I stand at the door, and knock: if any man hear my voice, and open the door, I will come in to him, and will sup with him, and he with me.
21 To him that overcometh will I grant to sit with me in my throne, even as I also overcame, and am set down with my Father in his throne. (KJV)

Revelation 20:4-6

4 And I saw thrones, and they sat upon them, and judgment was given unto them: and I saw the souls of them that were beheaded for the witness of Jesus, and for the word of God, and which had not worshipped the beast, neither his image, neither had received his mark upon their foreheads, or in their hands; and they lived and reigned with Christ a thousand years.

5 But the rest of the dead lived not again until the thousand years were finished. This is the first resurrection.

6 Blessed and holy is he that hath part in the first resurrection: on such the second death hath no power, but they shall be priests of God and of Christ, and shall reign with him a thousand years. (KJV)

2 Timothy 4:8

8 Henceforth there is laid up for me a crown of righteousness, which the Lord, the righteous judge, shall give me at that day: and not to me only, but unto all them also that love his appearing. (KJV)

Matthew 19:27-29

27 Then answered Peter and said unto him, Behold, we have forsaken all, and followed thee; what shall we have therefore?

28 And Jesus said unto them, Verily I say unto you, That ye which have followed me, in the regeneration when the Son of man shall sit in the throne of his glory, ye also shall sit upon twelve thrones, judging the twelve tribes of Israel.

29 And every one that hath forsaken houses, or brethren, or sisters, or father, or mother, or wife, or children, or lands, for my name's sake, shall receive an hundredfold, and shall inherit everlasting life. (KJV)

1 Cor. 9:25

25 And every man that striveth for the mastery is temperate in all things. Now they do it to obtain a corruptible crown; but we an incorruptible. (KJV)

"Lightnings and thunderings and voices." Several times throughout the book of Revelation, we read about these powerful and mysterious phenomena. Interestingly, they always seem to accompany God's judgment and wrath as an outward, visible indicator of God's righteous anger toward sin and evil.

"Rainbow round about the throne." God promised Noah He would never "destroy" ALL "flesh" again. This covenant is valid for "PERPETUAL generations," and the rainbow, shown to Noah as a sign, is near God's throne during the events of Revelation, signifying God will NOT forget His promise during the forthcoming period of incredibly horrendous judgments upon the earth. (Gen. 9:11-17) (Rev. 4:3).

Generally speaking, Revelation 4 and 5 deal with events in Heaven immediately after the Rapture where we see the saints gathered around the throne of God as they are organized for the vital task of executing the program of redemption which is about to begin. We also observe that in the hand of God lies a small book sealed with seven seals which apparently contains the "legal" commission to execute God's redemptive objective for the world, while the seals collectively represent the legal procedures which must be followed in order to realize God's redemptive objective. Not surprisingly, a biblical precedent for this "legal" procedure was established in ancient Israel. (Lev. 25:23-28) (Jer. 32:6-15). Christ is the only creature deemed "worthy" of breaking the seals of the book because He is the only perfect, sinless human Who could die as the ultimate, innocent sacrifice in payment for the sins of all people, thereby nullifying Satan's claim on the earth.

Breaking The First Seal

Revelation 6:1-2

1 And I saw when the Lamb opened one of the seals, and I heard, as it were the noise of thunder, one of the four beasts saying, Come and see.

2 And I saw, and behold a white horse: and he that sat on him had a bow; and a crown was given unto him: and he went forth conquering, and to conquer. (KJV)

Controversy and speculation always have shrouded the true identity of the white horseman who appears as a result of the First Seal being opened. Often it is said that he represents Antichrist, but that theory, although very popular, is not likely to be true because, as we demonstrated earlier, similes, not symbols, are used in Revelation when describing heavenly things. Accordingly, there is a substantial body of scriptural evidence weighing quite heavily against the notion that the white horseman does, in fact, represent Antichrist:

1. Actually, no one can point to any clear-cut scriptures in the Bible which say Antichrist will pretend to be the Messiah of the Jews! Instead, the Scriptures make it quite clear that Israel will be one of the first countries attacked by the Antichrist during his initial ascendancy to power, thereby precluding any possibility of deception in the sense that he will pretend to be the Jewish Messiah. (Dan. 8:8, 9). He will pretend to be a god of the universe, however, as we saw in earlier chapters of this book.

Daniel 8:9
And out of one of them came forth a little horn (Antichrist), which waxed exceeding great, toward the south, and toward the east, and toward the pleasant land (Palestine; Israel). (KJV)

The context of this verse shows the "little horn" Antichrist originating from one of the four divisions of the Grecian Empire which emerged following the death of Alexander the Great. Almost immediately, the little horn, representing both a tiny, new country and the personage of Antichrist, waxes "exceeding great" very quickly as it conquers in a southern and eastern direction. Please note that the "pleasant land" Israel is mentioned specifically as one of the first countries attacked by the Antichrist in his initial rise to power, thereby precluding any reasonable possibility that he might pretend to be the promised Messiah to the Jews. The fact that the scriptural evidence also clearly indicates that the Antichrist will originate from the country of Lebanon decreases that possibility even further.

Later, in this same passage of scripture, Daniel elaborates on the above prophecy in verse 9:

Daniel 8:23-24
And in the latter time of their kingdom, when the transgressors are come to the full, a king of fierce countenance and understanding dark sentences, shall stand up. And his power shall be mighty, but not by his own power: and he shall destroy wonderfully.... (KJV)

It is when the communists "come to the full" that "a king of fierce countenance.... shall stand up." This fierce-looking man is the Antichrist, and he will appear unexpectedly as the apparent answer to the hopes and prayers of people throughout the world when it will appear as if we are facing imminent destruction. Nothing will seem too difficult for this man to achieve! Although the "church-world" and "religious leaders" will seem dazed and confused while fumbling around for plausible explanations, the Antichrist will have the answers! During an extraordinary period of crisis and fear and confusion, he will mesmerize the whole world with his incredible accomplishments and enchanting oratory.

"And he shall destroy wonderfully." (Daniel 8:24). When you consider the multitude of fantastic weapons now available to modern man, it certainly makes sense that the Antichrist — from a small country with a small army — would require supernatural power to achieve what the Bible predicts he will do. This is more apparent in *Young's Literal Translation*: "And wonderful things he destroyeth." Further clarification is provided in an analysis of the word "destroy." In this case, the Hebrew word translated as "destroy" is SHACHATH, meaning "to ruin." Obviously it will be a most remarkable performance.

Other than from Satan, where could a man obtain this fantastic power and ability? That is what Daniel was saying in the phrases, "understanding dark sentences" and "his power shall be mighty, but not by his own power." Such amazing power and super-intelligence will be satanic-inspired — as the apostle Paul likewise explains in the following scriptural passage: "Even him, whose coming (ascendancy to power and prominence) is after the working of Satan with all power and signs and lying wonders." (II Thess. 2:9).

This also is confirmed in Revelation 13:4 where, immediately after the Rapture when the true nature of Antichrist has been "revealed" or uncovered to the whole world, we are told everyone realizes that Antichrist derives his extraordinary power and war-making ability from the dragon, Satan:

Revelation 13:4

4 And they worshipped the dragon which gave power unto the beast: and they worshipped the beast, saying, Who is like unto the beast? who is able to make war with him? (KJV)

Daniel 7:25 gives us additional insight: "And he (Antichrist) shall speak great words against the most High...and think to change times and laws..." In other words, Antichrist will boldly defy God while advocating his own standard of morals and values for all of society. No decent standard or sensible norm will be safe from attack or immune to criticism. Accordingly, from the very outset, there never will be any pretense on his part at being very sympathetic to the Jews in Israel or to Christians in general, nor will he ever pretend to be the Jewish Messiah as some people suppose — especially since Israel is one of the very first countries which he attacks when he first rises to power. (Dan. 8:9). Instead, he begins soon after his initial appearance to criticize and defy traditional Christian beliefs and values and morality, and then by the time the Rapture occurs, reaches the point where he is even quite willing to kill anyone who proclaims their faith in Christ. Later, he even has the audacity to violate the sanctity of the sacred Holy of Holies room in the rebuilt Jewish Temple while he is boldly proclaiming himself to be the god of gods.

II John 1:7
7 For many deceivers are entered into the world, who confess not that Jesus Christ is come in the flesh. This is a deceiver and an antichrist. (KJV)

I John 4:3
3 And every spirit that confesseth not that Jesus Christ is come in the flesh is not of God: and this is that spirit of antichrist, whereof ye have heard that it should come; and even now already is it in the world. (KJV)

I John 2:18, 22
18 Little children, it is the last time: and as ye have heard that antichrist shall come, even now are there many antichrists; whereby we know that it is the last time.
22 Who is a liar but he that denieth that Jesus is the Christ? He is antichrist, that denieth the Father and the Son. (KJV)

In these passages, not only are we told that a specific, unique personage called "antichrist" will appear some day, but that since the inception of Christianity, there always have been people who have denied that the historic Jesus Christ is God manifested in the flesh, or as noted in I John 2:22, that both God the Father and God the Son are the true God in

Heaven. These people, too, are "little" antichrists in a manner of speaking. So, while we are warned against the heresy these people teach, we also are given further insight as to exactly what the Antichrist will advocate, and how the Bible itself actually defines the word "antichrist."

Since *Merriam-Webster's Collegiate Dictionary* defines the prefix "anti" as meaning "one that is opposed," this means that the Antichrist will be opposed (to the true God in Heaven). As we noted in the paragraph above while commenting on I John 2:22, the Bible says that Antichrist will deny the true God in Heaven, i.e., the personal, infinite, triune God of Christianity. This is completely consistent with Daniel when he says in Daniel 7:25 that the Antichrist "shall speak great words against the most High," and in Daniel 11:36-37 where he states that the Antichrist will "magnify himself above every god, and shall speak marvellous things against the God of gods... nor regard any god: for he shall magnify himself above all." This, then, is how we should define the word "antichrist" because that is how the Bible defines it.

That is why it is wrong to think that the Antichrist will ever pretend to be the Jewish Messiah — even when he first appears as a savior who rescues the world from apparent imminent destruction. Instead, the Antichrist will deny both God the Father and God the Son while proclaiming himself to be a god above all. Therefore, it is not a coincidence that the popular New Age Movement teaches we can achieve godhood and extraordinary powers of the mind through "higher consciousness" techniques or "cosmic Christ consciousness." Accordingly, the historical evidence proving the true identity of Jesus is ignored by these people and their followers, and He is relegated to the status of just another ordinary psychic seer.

Sometimes it is said John 5:43 proves that the Antichrist will pretend to be the Jewish Messiah:

John 5:43

43 I am come in my Father's name, and ye receive me not: if another shall come in his own name, him ye will receive. (KJV)

However, Jesus simply was saying that many of the people listening in His audience were so hardheaded and unreceptive that they would not receive Him despite the impressive Godly evidence of His ministry. Yet, on the other hand, they were so foolish that they would actually believe some ordinary man and accept him as their Messiah without any sign of Godly inspiration as proof of his identity. Which is precisely what they did some years later, causing many Jews to suffer at the hands of the Romans.

Furthermore, please note that Jesus did not say "when" another man comes along in his own name, thus implying the absolute necessity for this event to happen. Instead, He said "if" this happens, clearly implying that it might or might not happen — as an acknowledgement to the reality of freewill in men and their inherent, God-given right to freedom. But, since this word "if" carries the element of doubt and uncertainty with it, this passage can not possibly be a reference to the Antichrist because numerous Old Testament prophecies had already been given by God saying absolutely that Antichrist would appear at the endtimes. This definition concerning the word "if" is confirmed by *Strong's Hebrew-Greek Dictionary*:

1437 ean (eh-an');
from 1487 and 302; a conditional particle; in case that, provided, etc.; often used in connection with other particles to denote indefiniteness or uncertainty:
KJV— before, but, except, (and) if, (if) so, (what-, whither-) soever, though, when (-soever), whether (or), to whom, [who-] so (-ever).

Sometimes the following passage also is used to bolster the belief that Antichrist will pretend to be the Jewish Messiah:

Daniel 11:35-39
35 ....even to the time of the end: because it is yet for a time appointed.
36 And the king shall do according to his will; and he shall exalt himself, and magnify himself above every god, and shall speak marvellous things against the God of gods, and shall prosper till the indignation be accomplished: for that that is determined shall be done.
37 Neither shall he regard the God of his fathers, nor the desire of women, nor regard any god: for he shall magnify himself above all.
38 But in his estate shall he honour the God of forces: and a god whom his fathers knew not shall he honour with gold, and silver, and with precious stones, and pleasant things.
39 Thus shall he do in the most strong holds with a strange god, whom

he shall acknowledge and increase with glory: and he shall cause them to rule over many, and shall divide the land for gain. (KJV)

"And the king shall do according to his will." Daniel describes Antichrist as "exceeding great" (Dan. 8:9), while Alexander the Great is described simply as "very great" (Dan. 8:8). Therefore, it is reasonable to infer that the miraculous military feats accomplished by the Antichrist will appear extraordinary even when compared to the amazing military conquests waged by Alexander the Great. Other scriptures also testify to the incredible military conquests which the Antichrist will achieve in fulfillment of this implied comparison. Accordingly, since Alexander the Great conquered his enemies with lightning speed, so likewise will the Antichrist. Nothing will be able to stop him or thwart his will. As John noted: "Who is able to make war with him?"

"And the king shall do according to his will." From the very beginning, the Antichrist will defy God by doing whatever he pleases. Daniel also says that he will "exalt" and "magnify" himself — statements which are reminiscent of the self-deification delusion that snared Adam and Eve in the Garden of Eden. He even will "magnify himself above every god," and be so bold as to "speak marvellous things against the God of gods." Obviously these statements seem to imply that the Antichrist, indeed, will advocate "god-hood" for everyone — just as the New Agers teach.

"Shall prosper till the indignation be accomplished." The Hebrew word for "indignation" is ZAAM, meaning "rage; fury, especially, God's displeasure at sin." Therefore, this passage simply is saying that the Antichrist will "prosper" in his plans to deceive people before the Rapture by inspiring world peace and prosperity, and then later, after the Rapture, continue to "prosper" by initiating war against Christian believers for three and one-half years. But then, after that, the Day of God's Wrath begins and the Antichrist no longer "prospers" in his plans because God's "indignation" is unleashed in the form of the Trumpet-Vial plagues, culminating in His Return at the Battle of Armageddon.

"Neither shall he regard the God of his fathers." Reference to the personal, infinite, triune God of the Christian Bible is not necessarily intended here in this passage because the letter "G" is not capitalized in the word "God" in the Hebrew. Here is how *Strong's Hebrew-Greek Dictionary* defines the word "God":

430 'elohiym (el-o-heem');

plural of 433; gods in the ordinary sense; but specifically used (in the plural thus, especially with the article) of the supreme God; occasionally applied by way of deference to magistrates; and sometimes as a superlative:

KJV— angels, X exceeding, God (gods)- dess, -ly), X (very) great, judges, X mighty.

So, the word "God" actually can be translated as "gods in the ordinary sense" or it can be rendered as "the supreme God." However, we should note, too, that the article "the" was added arbitrarily by the KJV translators because they jumped to the same conclusion that everyone else did — so the presence of the article "the" does not lend any support to the theory that this word must refer to the true God of the Bible. Accordingly, I believe it is erroneous to assume this phrase necessarily refers to the Jewish fathers of the Antichrist in an attempt to prove the Antichrist will pretend to be the Jewish Messiah. Besides, it could just as easily refer to the Islamic supreme god, Allah, if the Antichrist is a Moslem or Druze Moslem. Instead, it means precisely what it actually says, i.e., he ignores his ancestors' religion by simply declining to honor or worship the god whom his ancestors worshipped, whomever that may be. Corroboration on this point is provided in this very same passage when it continues by saying that neither will he "regard any god: for he shall magnify himself above all" before the Rapture, but that after the Rapture, he will publicly honor the "god of forces" who is none other than Satan himself (Rev. 13:4).

"He shall honour the god of forces." New Age thinking and Eastern mysticism probably will ascribe such power to the "universal spirit" or the "cosmic consciousness." But, those who are wise will understand that it is Satan who is the source of such abilities, not some "universal power" achieved through "higher consciousness" or a "sudden leap in evolution." However, immediately after the Rapture, everyone in the world will understand that Satan is the real reason for the incredible power and abilities of Antichrist. (Rev. 13:2, 4) (Dan. 11:39) (Hab. 1:11). Perhaps this is what II Thess. 2:3-12 means when it states that the Antichrist is "revealed" (APOKALUPTO; disclosed, uncovered, revealed) immediately after the Rapture when the Holy Spirit is "taken out of the way" (but not out of the world) as a mortally-wounded Antichrist is indwelt and possessed by Satan himself. This does not mean, though, that people will believe that Satan is evil. Instead, they most likely will think — as many people believe already — that Satan is Lucifer and that he is the morally good guy. Especially since he will have been responsible for creating world peace and prosperity through his human surrogate of instrumentality, Antichrist, while God will be held responsible for taking it away with His judgments upon the earth. That is why Revelation says several times that AFTER the Great Tribulation — during the Great and Terrible Day Of The Lord — people on earth will curse God while refusing to repent of their sins.

"Shall honor the god of forces." According to *Strong's Hebrew-Greek Dictionary* and Rev. Alexander Hislop, author of the classic, *The Two Babylons*, a more accurate translation of the word "forces" is "fortifications." Therefore, this phrase may be an allusion to the great rebel Nimrod, who (as documented by Hislop; pp. 30-55) can be termed "the god of fortifications." Apparently, the Antichrist will be a modern-day version of Nimrod, who was viewed in his days as an extraordinary benefactor because he taught people how to protect themselves from the wild animals by building walls around their cities, and because he was a mighty hunter of these same wild animals who were threatening to overrun the earth. But, after giving people the benefits and blessings of safety and security, he used his prestige to persuade people to rebel against God, thus beginning the great Babylonian apostasy.

2. Please note that the colors associated with the four horsemen — white, red, black, and pale — apply to the horses, not the riders. The colors represent the nature of the objectives to be accomplished, not the moral character of the individual riders. Therefore, the "white horseman" does not symbolize a "counterfeit Christ" — but if he did, then the remaining three horsemen would have to be designated as entities even more evil and destructive than the Antichrist.

3. Obviously the white horseman can not be the Antichrist because the scene of activity portrayed in this passage is in Heaven, whereas Antichrist is never in Heaven.

4. The horsemen are in Heaven and are sent forth on their missions by the four living ones (saints, as previously proven) who also are in Heaven. Furthermore, the living ones even talk to the horsemen. Accordingly, logic would necessitate the very strong implication that the horsemen likewise represent groups of saints in the same manner that the "living

ones" represent groups of saints.

5. It is completely inconsistent to say that the white horseman represents a man, and then claim that the remaining three horsemen are merely impersonal things such as war and famine and death. Logical consistency obviously demands personal identities for all four of the horsemen if we assign a personal identity to one of them such as the White Horseman.

6. White always represents righteousness in the Bible. (e.g., Christ has white hair; the saints have white robes; the Great Judgment Throne is white; etc..)

7. The "bow" represents God's Word:

Hab. 3:8-9

8 Was the LORD displeased against the rivers? was thine anger against the rivers? was thy wrath against the sea, that thou didst ride upon thine horses and thy chariots of salvation?

9 Thy bow was made quite naked, according to the oaths of the tribes, even thy word. Selah. Thou didst cleave the earth with rivers. (KJV)

8. The passage in Habakkuk 3:8-13 vividly portrays the Lord going forth throughout the earth on horses of salvation accompanied by saints, possessing the bow ("thy word") for the purpose of salvation during a terrible period of wrath and trouble:

Hab. 3:8-13

8 Was the Lord displeased against the rivers? was thine anger against the rivers? was thy wrath against the sea, that THOU DIDST RIDE UPON THINE HORSES AND THY CHARIOTS OF SALVATION?

9 THY BOW was made quite naked, according to the oaths of the tribes, EVEN THY WORD. Selah. Thou didst cleave the earth with rivers.

10 The mountains saw thee, and they trembled: the overflowing of the water passed by: the deep uttered his voice, and lifted up his hands on high.

11 THE SUN AND MOON STOOD STILL IN THEIR HABITATION: at the light of thine arrows they went, and at the shining of thy glittering spear.

12 Thou didst march through the land in indignation, thou didst thresh

the heathen in anger.

13 THOU WENTEST FORTH FOR THE SALVATION OF THY PEOPLE, EVEN FOR SALVATION WITH THINE ANOINTED.... (KJV)

This is precisely the scene described in Revelation! The white horseman obviously represents a group of saints going forth throughout the earth for the purpose of salvation. (The color of the horse signifies the precise nature of the mission for each horseman.) The parallel-account of Revelation also portrays the exact same situation: angels (saints) flying in the sky preaching the gospel to people on earth.

Revelation 14:6, 7

6 And I saw another angel fly in the midst of heaven, having the everlasting gospel to preach unto them that dwell on the earth, and to every nation, and kindred, and tongue, and people,

7 Saying with a loud voice, Fear God, and give glory to him; for the hour of his judgment is come: and worship him that made heaven, and earth, and the sea, and the fountains of waters. (KJV)

Matthew 24:7-14

7 For nation shall rise against nation, and kingdom against kingdom: and there shall be famines, and pestilences, and earthquakes, in divers places.

8 All these are the beginning of sorrows.

9 Then shall they deliver you up to be afflicted, and shall kill you: and ye shall be hated of all nations for my name's sake.

10 And then shall many be offended, and shall betray one another, and shall hate one another.

11 And many false prophets shall rise, and shall deceive many.

12 And because iniquity shall abound, the love of many shall wax cold.

13 But he that shall endure unto the end, the same shall be saved.

14 And this gospel of the kingdom shall be preached in all the world for a witness unto all nations; and then shall the end come. (KJV)

Mark 13:8-13

8 For nation shall rise against nation, and kingdom against kingdom:

and there shall be earthquakes in divers places, and there shall be famines and troubles: these are the beginnings of sorrows.

9 But take heed to yourselves: for they shall deliver you up to councils; and in the synagogues ye shall be beaten: and ye shall be brought before rulers and kings for my sake, for a testimony against them.

10 And the gospel must first be published among all nations.

11 But when they shall lead you, and deliver you up, take no thought beforehand what ye shall speak, neither do ye premeditate: but whatsoever shall be given you in that hour, that speak ye: for it is not ye that speak, but the Holy Ghost.

12 Now the brother shall betray the brother to death, and the father the son; and children shall rise up against their parents, and shall cause them to be put to death.

13 And ye shall be hated of all men for my name's sake: but he that shall endure unto the end, the same shall be saved. (KJV)

"Then shall the end come." The word "end" means the end of the "Dispensation of Grace" — not the Battle of Armageddon or the annihilation of earth. As we will prove later, for three and one-half years after the Rapture, people will continue to have an opportunity to accept Christ as their personal Saviour; people who will do so generally are termed "tribulation saints."

Compare also the following scriptures with Matthew 24:7-14 and Mark 13:8-13:

Luke 21:10-19

10 Then said he unto them, Nation shall rise against nation, and kingdom against kingdom:

11 And great earthquakes shall be in divers places, and famines, and pestilences; and fearful sights and great signs shall there be from heaven.

12 But before all these, they shall lay their hands on you, and persecute you, delivering you up to the synagogues, and into prisons, being brought before kings and rulers for my name's sake.

13 And it shall turn to you for a testimony.

14 Settle it therefore in your hearts, not to meditate before what ye shall answer:

15 For I will give you a mouth and wisdom, which all your adversaries shall not be able to gainsay nor resist.

16 And ye shall be betrayed both by parents, and brethren, and kinsfolks, and friends; and some of you shall they cause to be put to death.

17 And ye shall be hated of all men for my name's sake.

18 But there shall not an hair of your head perish.

19 In your patience possess ye your souls. (KJV)

Please note that verse 16 above states that only some of the tribulation saints will be killed by the Antichrist; those who are not killed and who also "endure unto the end" (i.e., keep their faith) likewise shall be saved.

Joel 2:28-32

28 And it shall come to pass afterward, that I will pour out my spirit upon all flesh; and your sons and your daughters shall prophesy, your old men shall dream dreams, your young men shall see visions:

29 And also upon the servants and upon the handmaids in those days will I pour out my spirit.

30 And I will shew wonders in the heavens and in the earth, blood, and fire, and pillars of smoke.

31 The sun shall be turned into darkness, and the moon into blood, before the great and the terrible day of the LORD come.

32 And it shall come to pass, that whosoever shall call on the name of the LORD shall be delivered: for in mount Zion and in Jerusalem shall be deliverance, as the LORD hath said, and in the remnant whom the LORD shall call. (KJV)

Acts 2:16-21

16 But this is that which was spoken by the prophet Joel;

17 And it shall come to pass in the last days, saith God, I will pour out of my Spirit upon all flesh: and your sons and your daughters shall prophesy, and your young men shall see visions, and your old men shall dream dreams:

18 And on my servants and on my handmaidens I will pour out in those days of my Spirit; and they shall prophesy:

19 And I will shew wonders in heaven above, and signs in the earth beneath; blood, and fire, and vapour of smoke:

20 The sun shall be turned into darkness, and the moon into blood, before that great and notable day of the Lord come:

21 And it shall come to pass, that whosoever shall call on the name of

the Lord shall be saved. (KJV)

9. The symbolism of Antichrist and the beast is associated with TEN crowns. (Rev. 13:1) (Rev. 17). The white horseman, however, wears only ONE crown, a crown of righteousness and rejoicing and glory and life. (I Thess. 2:19) (II Timothy 4:8) (James 1:12) (I Peter 5:4) (Rev. 2:10) (Rev. 3:11).

10. "He went forth, CONQUERING and to CONQUER." The Greek word translated here as the English word "conquer" is NIKAO, and it means "to have the victory." It is used in only one other New Testament passage, namely Romans 8:37, which reads: "We are more than CONQUERORS through him that loved us."

11. Passages scattered throughout the book of Revelation, when viewed collectively, clearly state that sometimes "angels" in Revelation are actually Christian saints performing a given task which will have been assigned to them by God as part of the overall effort in carrying forth God's program of redemption for the world. For instance, the passages in Revelation 19:9-10 and Revelation 22:8-9 read:

Revelation 19:9-10

9 And he saith unto me, Write, Blessed are they which are called unto the marriage supper of the Lamb. And he saith unto me, These are the true sayings of God.

10 And I fell at his feet to worship him. And he said unto me, See thou do it not: I am thy fellowservant, and of thy brethren that have the testimony of Jesus: worship God: for the testimony of Jesus is the spirit of prophecy...

Revelation 22:8-9

8 And I John saw these things, and heard them. And when I had heard and seen, I fell down to worship before the feet of the angel which shewed me these things.

9 Then saith he unto me, See thou do it not: for I am thy fellowservant, and of thy brethren the prophets, and of them which keep the sayings of this book: worship God. (KJV)

"I am thy fellowservant, and of thy brethren that have the testimony of Jesus." The angel, who speaks these words, thereby identifying himself as a saint, is also identified as one of the angels who pours out the seven vials of plagues upon the earth. (Rev. 17:1). Therefore, this proves once again our interpretation concerning the identity of the angels throughout most of the scriptures in Revelation. Obviously it is the saints who will execute judgment upon the earth when it is being "redeemed."

Accordingly, the "four horsemen" are four groups of saints for many of the same reasons we analyzed earlier when proving that the "four beasts" and the "twenty-four elders" likewise are groups of saints. Since we can establish from Scripture that the saints "will judge the world" and "execute upon them the judgment written" (Rev. 5:9, 10; Dan. 7:21, 22, 27; I Cor. 6:2, 3; Rev. 1:5, 6; Ps. 149:5-9), they obviously should be in prominent display throughout Revelation. Therefore, if the "four horsemen" are not four groups of saints, then why are they so clearly involved in world evangelism and execution of judgments upon the earth during the events narrated in Revelation?

12. It is quite apparent that the white horseman will not make his prophetic appearance until AFTER the Rapture has occurred. Accordingly, if we were to adopt the proposition, hypothetically, that the white horseman portrays the Antichrist staging his initial ascendancy to power and dominance over the world, then we would be forced to ignore a wealth of biblical scriptures which describe pre-Rapture exploits and accomplishments of the Antichrist.

Three More Horsemen

Revelation 6:3-8

3 And when he had opened the second seal, I heard the second beast say, Come and see.

4 And there went out another horse that was red: and power was given to him that sat thereon to take peace from the earth, and that they should kill one another: and there was given unto him a great sword.

5 And when he had opened the third seal, I heard the third beast say, Come and see. And I beheld, and lo a black horse; and he that sat on him had a pair of balances in his hand.

6 And I heard a voice in the midst of the four beasts say, A measure of wheat for a penny, and three measures of barley for a penny; and see thou hurt not the oil and the wine.

7 And when he had opened the fourth seal, I heard the voice of the

fourth beast say, Come and see.

8 And I looked, and behold a pale horse: and his name that sat on him was Death, and Hell followed with him. And power was given unto them over the fourth part of the earth, to kill with sword, and with hunger, and with death, and with the beasts of the earth. (KJV)

Three more seals of the "book" are opened in rapid sequence, resulting in the appearance of three additional horsemen who immediately ride forth throughout the earth to create a devastating scenario of global fighting and famine and horrible, stenching death for a major segment of the earth's population. However, we should note that most of their efforts seem to be directed primarily at only the fourth part of the earth which roughly corresponds to the geographical area which once comprised the former Babylonian, Persian, Grecian, and Roman empires, nucleus of the endtime empire of Antichrist. (Rev. 13:1, 2).

That observation, in turn, leads us to conclude that the empire of the Antichrist will be targeted deliberately in order to hinder the deadly persecution against new Christian converts which the Antichrist will begin soon after the Rapture. Keep in mind that even though the Antichrist will seem invincible and will exercise power over "ALL kindreds, and tongues, and nations" (Rev. 13:4-8), the fact remains that most of his activities will center primarily in Bible lands due to the impossibility of exercising complete control over all of the earth in such a short time. That explains why special attention is given to a specific "fourth part of the earth" by the three apocalyptic horsemen.

Compare the following with verse 8 in the passage above:

Amos 5:16-20

16 Therefore the LORD, the God of hosts, the Lord, saith thus; Wailing shall be in all streets; and they shall say in all the highways, Alas! alas! and they shall call the husbandman to mourning, and such as are skilful of lamentation to wailing.

17 And in all vineyards shall be wailing: for I will pass through thee, saith the LORD.

18 Woe unto you that desire the day of the LORD! to what end is it for you? the day of the LORD is darkness, and not light.

19 As if a man did flee from a lion, and a bear met him; or went into the house, and leaned his hand on the wall, and a serpent bit him.

20 Shall not the day of the LORD be darkness, and not light? even very dark, and no brightness in it? (KJV)

The Fifth Seal

Revelation 6:9-11

9 And when he had opened the fifth seal, I saw under the altar the souls of them that were slain for the word of God, and for the testimony which they held:

10 And they cried with a loud voice, saying, How long, O Lord, holy and true, dost thou not judge and avenge our blood on them that dwell on the earth?

11 And white robes were given unto every one of them; and it was said unto them, that they should rest yet for a little season, until their fellowservants also and their brethren, that should be killed as they were, should be fulfilled. (KJV)

This particular seal does not directly affect the earth itself. It simply shows the deadly results of the violent persecutions waged against the new Christian believers who "were slain for the word of God, and for the testimony which they held" during the Great Tribulation. These martyred tribulation saints are pictured in Heaven as impatiently awaiting their resurrection "under the altar" until all of the tribulation saints destined to die during the Great Tribulation, do so.

The Sixth Seal

Revelation 6:12-17

12 And I beheld when he had opened the sixth seal, and, lo, there was a great earthquake; and the sun became black as sackcloth of hair, and the moon became as blood;

13 And the stars of heaven fell unto the earth, even as a fig tree casteth her untimely figs, when she is shaken of a mighty wind.

14 And the heaven departed as a scroll when it is rolled together; and every mountain and island were moved out of their places.

15 And the kings of the earth, and the great men, and the rich men, and

the chief captains, and the mighty men, and every bondman, and every free man, hid themselves in the dens and in the rocks of the mountains;

16 And said to the mountains and rocks, Fall on us, and hide us from the face of him that sitteth on the throne, and from the wrath of the Lamb:

17 For the great day of his wrath is come; and who shall be able to stand? (KJV)

The sixth seal, when opened, unleashes an absolutely incredible and horrible earthquake which completely devastates and pulverizes the earth by shaking and moving every single mountain and island on the earth! Meanwhile, simultaneously as this happens, the moon becomes like blood while the sun seems to transform itself to the color of black. Even the surrounding atmosphere of the earth undergoes an incredible twisting and rolling effect at that time which will not be very dissimilar, perhaps, to a super nuclear explosion — although we should note that this passage makes it very clear that this plague will not be the result of a man-made explosion because it is stated that it will be the direct result of the sixth seal when it is opened! Accordingly, please note, too, that people on earth fully realize and acknowledge the fact that this devastating plague is a judgment sent directly from God Himself, not something they unleash upon themselves! (Rev. 6:15-17).

This seal marks the end of the Dispensation of Grace! Please observe that not even one single person is converted to salvation after this point in time. In fact, it is mentioned very explicitly several times throughout the book of Revelation that, after the Great Tribulation is concluded, not even one person ever repents of his sins despite the incredible and destructive severity of the plagues which comprise the seventh seal! Contextually, the prophetic stage is now set for the dark and gloomy and terrible "Day of the Lord" — a day of wrath and judgment — to begin!

Joel 2:28-31

28 And it shall come to pass afterward, that I will pour out my spirit upon all flesh; and your sons and your daughters shall prophesy, your old men shall dream dreams, your young men shall see visions:

29 And also upon the servants and upon the handmaids in those days will I pour out my spirit.

30 And I will shew wonders in the heavens and in the earth, blood, and fire, and pillars of smoke.

31 The sun shall be turned into darkness, and the moon into blood, before the great and the terrible day of the LORD come. (KJV)

Acts 2:16-21

16 But this is that which was spoken by the prophet Joel;

17 And it shall come to pass in the last days, saith God, I will pour out of my Spirit upon all flesh: and your sons and your daughters shall prophesy, and your young men shall see visions, and your old men shall dream dreams:

18 And on my servants and on my handmaidens I will pour out in those days of my Spirit; and they shall prophesy:

19 And I will shew wonders in heaven above, and signs in the earth beneath; blood, and fire, and vapour of smoke:

20 The sun shall be turned into darkness, and the moon into blood, before that great and notable day of the Lord come:

21 And it shall come to pass, that whosoever shall call on the name of the Lord shall be saved. (KJV)

The 144,000 Jews

Revelation 7:1-8

1 And after these things I saw four angels standing on the four corners of the earth, holding the four winds of the earth, that the wind should not blow on the earth, nor on the sea, nor on any tree.

2 And I saw another angel ascending from the east, having the seal of the living God: and he cried with a loud voice to the four angels, to whom it was given to hurt the earth and the sea,

3 Saying, Hurt not the earth, neither the sea, nor the trees, till we have sealed the servants of our God in their foreheads.

4 And I heard the number of them which were sealed: and there were sealed an hundred and forty and four thousand of all the tribes of the children of Israel.

5 Of the tribe of Juda were sealed twelve thousand. Of the tribe of Reuben were sealed twelve thousand. Of the tribe of Gad were sealed twelve thousand.

6 Of the tribe of Aser were sealed twelve thousand. Of the tribe of Nephthalim were sealed twelve thousand. Of the tribe of Manasses were sealed twelve thousand.

7 Of the tribe of Simeon were sealed twelve thousand. Of the tribe of Levi were sealed twelve thousand. Of the tribe of Issachar were sealed twelve thousand.

8 Of the tribe of Zabulon were sealed twelve thousand. Of the tribe of Joseph were sealed twelve thousand. Of the tribe of Benjamin were sealed twelve thousand. (KJV)

Immediately after the Rapture, the true nature of the Antichrist is "revealed" or "disclosed" to the world after he miraculously recovers from a deadly wound, thereby causing everyone to realize that his extraordinary power and abilities are from Satan, not from any alleged evolutionary mental powers of the mind. Then, after his evil nature and identity are exposed, he begins to execute Christians for three and one-half years of Great Tribulation. After the Great Tribulation is concluded, the Sixth Seal is opened, followed by God's protective sealing of tribulation saints who manage to escape execution by the Antichrist.

Thus, the "four angels" are commanded not to harm the earth and the sea until the process of protective sealing is completed. The Jewish tribulation saints — symbolized as the 144,000 Jews — are mentioned specifically in the passage above in Revelation 7 to illustrate the reality that the Dispensation of Grace will have just ended at that point in time so that the Dispensation of Law (Daniel's 70th Week) can resume without mixing dispensations. Revelation 7 then concludes its narration by portraying the martyred tribulation saints resurrected into Heaven before the Seventh Seal begins.

Therefore, Jews who become Christians AFTER the Rapture are not killed by the Antichrist as many other Christians throughout the world are. Keep in mind that the Antichrist will be negotiating a seven year treaty (Daniel's 70th Week) with Israel at that point in time, and he certainly would not be killing Jews at the very same time he was conducting important negotiations with them. Additionally, Satan will understand then that national Israel gained the protection of God during the Second Crisis when they turned back to God collectively as a nation. So, he will want to tempt Israel into sin by persuading Israel to sign a treaty with him whereby, in essence, he assumes the role of God as protector of Israel and her land in Palestine BEFORE he dares to attack Israel. For that reason, the 144,000 Jews will be safe so long as they remain within the country of Israel, outside the sphere of influence for the Antichrist.

Often it is said these 144,000 Jews evangelize the world during the Great Tribulation, but that is not very likely! These Jews are converted to salvation at the very same time all other tribulation saints are saved. If they were to venture outside of Palestine in an attempt to evangelize the world, they would be killed immediately by the Antichrist. Furthermore, the 144,000 Jews never are seen in Revelation until now in this passage when both the Great Tribulation and the Dispensation of Grace have just ended, so this gives us further reason to believe they will not preach the Gospel message to the world during the Great Tribulation.

Accordingly, it will be Raptured Christians, seen as the White Horseman in Revelation 6, and portrayed as an angel in Revelation 14, who will preach the gospel to the whole world! Obviously immortalized Christians who are capable of flying or elevating above the earth throughout the skies will be completely immune to any interference or attack by the Antichrist on the earth below. Something which, I am sure, will further enrage the Antichrist as he stands by, helplessly, watching and listening to them. Thus, God's only purpose in "sealing" the surviving tribulation saints, including the 144,000 Jews, will be as stated in this scripture: to provide them protection from the seven Trumpet-Vial plagues during the Great and Terrible Day of the Lord.

It is interesting to note that Dr. Joseph A. Seiss teaches in his *Lectures On The Apocalypse* that:

All Jewish names are significant, and the meaning of those which here are given is not hard to trace. Juda means "confession" or "praise" of God; Reuben, "viewing the Son"; Gad, "a company"; Aser, "blessed"; Nepthalim, a "wrestler" or "striving with"; Manasses, "forgetfulness"; Simeon, "hearing and obeying"; Levi, "joining" or "cleaving" to; Issachar, "reward" or "what is given by way of reward"; Zebulun, a "home" or "dwelling-place"; Joseph, "added" or "an addition"; Benjamin, "a son of the right hand, a son of old age". Now put these several things together in their order, and we have described to us: Confessors or praisers of God, looking upon the Son, a band of blessed ones, wrestling with forgetfulness, hearing and obeying the word, cleaving unto the reward of a shelter and home, an addition, sons of the day of God's right hand, begotten in the extremity of the age.

This is most extraordinary and not likely to be coincidental, especially since the sequential order of the names and even some of the names are changed from the way they are normally listed in other passages of the Bible. This also explains why the names of "Levi" and "Joseph" were substituted for the names of "Dan" and "Ephraim" — so that the intended meaning of the passage could be achieved.

"Dan" means "judging or exercise of judicial prerogatives," but these 144,000 Jews never are said to be judges. Likewise, "Ephraim" means "increase, growth by multiplication," but obviously this would not apply either because the 144,000 are a fixed number.

"Ephraim" is actually the same tribe as "Joseph"; "Dan" is the only tribe not mentioned in this listing. It is very possible that the omission of "Dan" indicates that the names are only a geographical designation, not a tribal one. This could be symbolic of the unity of the 12 Jewish tribes. (See Ezekiel 48.) Likewise, since people's free will always determines who will accept Christ as Saviour and who will not, it is very probable that the number "144,000" also should be taken symbolically, and not literally.

Sometimes it is said that the United States and Britain represent the alleged 10 "lost" tribes of Israel, and that although the tribes of Judah and Benjamin currently live in the land of Israel, they are not really heirs to the promises made by God to the ancient people of Israel. But such claims are easily refuted because members of all twelve tribes of Israel were partially regathered in the land of Israel during both Old and New Testament times, and many of the Jews living abroad in other countries were easily identifiable as belonging to all twelve tribes of Israel. (Ezra 7:7; Ezra 7:13; Ezra 7:28; Ezra 6:16; Ezra 6:21; Ezra 9:1; Ezra 10:1; Ezra 10:5; Nehemiah 7:7, 66; Nehemiah 9:1; Nehemiah 12:47; Luke 1:80; Matthew 15:24; Luke 7:9; John 1:31; John 1:47; John 3:10; John 12:13; Acts 2:22; Acts 2:36; Acts 3:12; Acts 4:8; Acts 4:10; Acts 5:21; Acts 5:35; Acts 9:15; Acts 13:16; Acts 13:24; Acts 21:28; James 1:1; Romans 11:2-5).

Tribulation Saints Resurrected

The passage below, in the remaining part of chapter 7, gives a very powerful and detailed picture of the martyred tribulation saints in Heaven, thus proving that the Dispensation of Grace has been concluded. As one of the Raptured Christian Elders told John the Revelator as he stood in amazement, looking at this vast new multitude of believers who will have just joined the ranks of believers already in Heaven from the time of the Rapture: "These are they which came out of great tribulation, and have washed their robes, and made them white in the blood of the Lamb." Hence, for that reason, we should not assume these tribulation saints are second-class citizens in Heaven for any reason; they are now just one other group of believers in Heaven who, jointly, will inherit all things through Christ Jesus. That point is emphasized in Revelation 20 when the Millennial Reign of Christ commences and it states, specifically, in that passage, that these tribulation saints will reign with Christ during His Millennial Reign on the earth, and that they are part of the First Resurrection, too.

Revelation 7:9-17

9 After this I beheld, and, lo, a great multitude, which no man could number, of all nations, and kindreds, and people, and tongues, stood before the throne, and before the Lamb, clothed with white robes, and palms in their hands;

10 And cried with a loud voice, saying, Salvation to our God which sitteth upon the throne, and unto the Lamb.

11 And all the angels stood round about the throne, and about the elders and the four beasts, and fell before the throne on their faces, and worshipped God,

12 Saying, Amen: Blessing, and glory, and wisdom, and thanksgiving, and honour, and power, and might, be unto our God for ever and ever. Amen.

13 And one of the elders answered, saying unto me, What are these which are arrayed in white robes? and whence came they?

14 And I said unto him, Sir, thou knowest. And he said to me, These are they which came out of great tribulation, and have washed their robes, and made them white in the blood of the Lamb.

15 Therefore are they before the throne of God, and serve him day and night in his temple: and he that sitteth on the throne shall dwell among them.

16 They shall hunger no more, neither thirst any more; neither shall the sun light on them, nor any heat.

17 For the Lamb which is in the midst of the throne shall feed them, and shall lead them unto living fountains of waters: and God shall wipe

away all tears from their eyes. (KJV)

The Seven Plagues Of The Seventh Seal

Revelation 8:1-6

1 And when he had opened the seventh seal, there was silence in heaven about the space of half an hour.

2 And I saw the seven angels which stood before God; and to them were given seven trumpets.

3 And another angel came and stood at the altar, having a golden censer; and there was given unto him much incense, that he should offer it with the prayers of all saints upon the golden altar which was before the throne.

4 And the smoke of the incense, which came with the prayers of the saints, ascended up before God out of the angel's hand.

5 And the angel took the censer, and filled it with fire of the altar, and cast it into the earth: and there were voices, and thunderings, and lightnings, and an earthquake.

6 And the seven angels which had the seven trumpets prepared themselves to sound. (KJV)

The Seventh Seal will last for a period of seven years, during which time the seven great Trumpet-Vial Plagues destroy much of the earth. This period of time also is called the Day Of The Lord or The Great Day Of His Wrath And Anger. It corresponds in time to the seven years of Daniel's 70th Week — both of which commence only AFTER the Great Tribulation is over. Obviously it is appropriate for God's Day Of Wrath to coincide in time with the resumption of Law (Daniel's 70th Week) because God's Wrath is the only possible consequence under the Law without Christ. So, after the Rapture, we have the Great Tribulation for three and one-half years, and then and only then, do we have the seven years which comprise — simultaneously — both the great and terrible Day Of The Lord and Daniel's 70th Week.

Each of the seven plagues will contain the element of fire in order to help purge the earth of all its sin and sinful results! Likewise, it is important to note also that the trumpets and vials actually portray the exact same series of plagues. Obviously a trumpet located in Heaven and directed toward the earth while being blown would, to an observer on earth, have the appearance of a vial pouring down upon the earth. That is why in each instance, any given vial and its corresponding trumpet both are directed against the same precise target. Common sense logic tells us that such extraordinary and continuous correlation between two sets of sequential events is not very likely to be only a coincidence!

Later we will prove conclusively that chapters 4-11 are parallel in time to chapters 12-16; this will confirm that the plagues of the seven trumpets correspond to the seven plagues of the vials. They sound different simply because they are described from two different viewpoints, similar to the manner in which honest witnesses can give comprehensive testimonial accounts of the same accident in which some details may vary or be omitted from one account to another, especially if their vantage view is considerably different for one reason or another.

The opening of the Seventh Seal is an extraordinary, monumental event, deserving of a hushed period of silence as the awesome implications and consequences of this last Great Seal are contemplated. The Dispensation of Grace will have been concluded — so no one on the earth can be saved any longer. Likewise, the Tribulation Saints slain by Antichrist will have been resurrected into Heaven at this point in time, while the surviving Tribulation Saints, including the 144,000 Jews, will have been sealed for protection from the catastrophic plagues poised to be released upon the earth. Thus begins the Great Day of the Lord, the Great Day of His Wrath — a seven year period of Divine Judgment for the earth. (Rev. 6:12-17) (Rev. 8:1, 2, 5-13) (Rev. 9:1-19) (Rev. 11:13-15) (Joel 2:1-11; 2:28-31) (Isa. 24:17-23) (Isa. 13:6-13) (Zech. 14:1-3) (II Peter 3:10-12) (Zeph. 1:14-18) (Amos 5:18-20) (Isa. 2:10-21).

The First Plague

Revelation 8:7

7 The first angel sounded, and there followed hail and fire mingled with blood, and they were cast upon the earth: and the third part of trees was burnt up, and all green grass was burnt up. (KJV)

Revelation 16:1-2

1 And I heard a great voice out of the temple saying to the seven

angels, Go your ways, and pour out the vials of the wrath of God upon the earth.

2 And the first went, and poured out his vial upon the earth; and there fell a noisome and grievous sore upon the men which had the mark of the beast, and upon them which worshipped his image. (KJV)

This first plague consists of hail and fire which burns up all the green grass and one-third of all the trees throughout the world. Quite naturally, people also are affected by this fiery plague of fire and hail, resulting in "NOISOME and grievous sore(s) upon the men which had the mark of the beast." Thus, just as we have demonstrated with this description, it is very easy to harmonize the individual descriptions of the respective Trumpet and Vial plagues into one consistent whole, thereby illustrating the viability of our insistence that Revelation 4-11 and Revelation 12-16 are parallel accounts narrating the same set of sequential events.

The Second Plague

Revelation 16:3

3 And the second angel poured out his vial upon the sea; and it became as the blood of a dead man: and every living soul died in the sea. (KJV)

Revelation 8:8-9

8 And the second angel sounded, and as it were a great mountain burning with fire was cast into the sea: and the third part of the sea became blood;

9 And the third part of the creatures which were in the sea, and had life, died; and the third part of the ships were destroyed. (KJV)

The second great plague is unleashed in the form of an incredible "great mountain burning with fire" which falls into the sea. The consequences resulting from this extraordinary plague are that one-third of all the sea life, and every single person seeking refuge in the seas from the horrific first plague, all die. One third of the ships in these waters likewise are destroyed. Accordingly, the final result of all these enormous numbers in the death-count toll and destruction of property is a very bloody sea throughout one-third of the world.

We should note, too, that just as we saw earlier with the second, third and fourth horsemen, most of the death and destruction which is rained down upon the earth from Heaven during this plague seems to be targeted primarily at only one-third or one-fourth part of the earth. Since either percentage number mentioned in these scriptures would correspond roughly to the approximate size of the nucleus of Antichrist's earthly empire, it would appear that the heart of his earthly domain always seems to bear the brunt of the plagues and destruction unleashed upon the earth by the saints in Heaven above.

The Third Plague

Revelation 8:10-11

10 And the third angel sounded, and there fell a great star from heaven, burning as it were a lamp, and it fell upon the third part of the rivers, and upon the fountains of waters;

11 And the name of the star is called Wormwood: and the third part of the waters became wormwood; and many men died of the waters, because they were made bitter. (KJV)

Revelation 16:4-7

4 And the third angel poured out his vial upon the rivers and fountains of waters; and they became blood.

5 And I heard the angel of the waters say, Thou art righteous, O Lord, which art, and wast, and shalt be, because thou hast judged thus.

6 For they have shed the blood of saints and prophets, and thou hast given them blood to drink; for they are worthy.

7 And I heard another out of the altar say, Even so, Lord God Almighty, true and righteous are thy judgments. (KJV)

In the third great Trumpet-Vial plague, one-third of the earth's rivers and drinking-water are poisoned and turned to blood by a gigantic meteorite, killing many more people in the process. Yet again, we note that there is this special targeting of one-third part of the earth, roughly corresponding to the approximate size of the nucleus of Antichrist's earthly empire where Antichrist will concentrate his personal activities.

This special targeting of attention obviously makes a great deal of sense because Antichrist is the enemy with whom they are concerned primarily. There also is the desire to punish the Antichrist, and many of the people living in the heart of his empire, who collectively will be responsible for the mass executions of many Christian believers during the Great Tribulation. This is made quite evident in the impassioned statements of the third angel.

The Fourth Plague

Revelation 16:8-9

8 And the fourth angel poured out his vial upon the sun; and power was given unto him to scorch men with fire.

9 And men were scorched with great heat, and blasphemed the name of God, which hath power over these plagues: and they repented not to give him glory. (KJV)

Revelation 8:12-13

12 And the fourth angel sounded, and the third part of the sun was smitten, and the third part of the moon, and the third part of the stars; so as the third part of them was darkened, and the day shone not for a third part of it, and the night likewise.

13 And I beheld, and heard an angel flying through the midst of heaven, saying with a loud voice, Woe, woe, woe, to the inhabiters of the earth by reason of the other voices of the trumpet of the three angels, which are yet to sound! (KJV)

During the fourth Trumpet-Vial plague, the sun is blackened for one-third of a day, and then it suddenly shines with such intensity that it actually scorches men, prompting them to curse God because of the plagues He is raining down on them without mercy. Likewise for the moon and the stars which discontinue shining for a third part of the night, each night. The fourth plague is followed by an angel flying in the heavenlies and warning the people on the earth that they are about to be plagued by the terrible three woes — absolutely incredible, destructive and terrifying plagues which will dwarf the effects of the previous four devastating plagues.

"And they repented not." This is an extraordinary statement! Despite the severity of the plagues, and knowing that those plagues are from God, people do not repent of their sins! In recent years, the New Age Movement, perhaps, has given us some insight as to how this incredible mindset could develop. One of the falsehoods which the New Agers propagate is the lie that Satan, i.e., Lucifer, is really a "good guy"; it is just that he is "misunderstood." On that basis, it becomes easier to imagine how people could develop the extraordinary "mind-set" predicted in the Bible. For when God takes away the peace and prosperity of the world which will have been established by the Antichrist (and Satan), it will be very easy to see how people could "reason" that Lucifer is "good" because he will have created "paradise" on earth, whereas God is "evil" because He will be responsible for its termination due to the plagues He sends on the earth. That perspective gives us more insight regarding the actual extent and effectiveness of the deception that Antichrist will perpetrate on the world! Obviously his program of religious deception will achieve very impressive results.

Revelation 8:13
...and heard an angel flying through the midst of heaven, saying with a loud voice, Woe, woe, woe, to the inhabiters of the earth... (KJV)

The word for "angel" in this passage is actually a mistranslation in the KJV. It should have been translated as the English word "eagle" because it is based on the same Greek word, AETOS, which is also used in Matthew 24:28 and Luke 17:37 where it is translated as the English word "eagle" even in the KJV. In fact, many translations even acknowledge this obvious point by translating it as such.

Luke 17:37
37 And they answered and said unto him, Where, Lord? And he said unto them, Wheresoever the body (Christ; Rev. 5:6) is, thither will the eagles (saints) be gathered together (i.e., Raptured). (KJV)

Matthew 24:28
28 For wheresoever the carcase is, there will the eagles be gathered together. (KJV)

The word "carcase" in the Greek is PTOMA, and it can be translated as "dead body, corpse, carcase." Accordingly, in the above two passages, the words "body, dead body and carcase" are all references to Christ, the "Lamb as it had been slain" (Rev. 5:6). Likewise, the word "eagle" in both of the above scriptural passages is defined by *Strong's Hebrew-Greek Dictionary* as follows:

105 aetos (ah-et-os');
from the same as 109; an eagle (from its wind-like flight):
KJV-- eagle.

So, there is no justification for saying that the word "eagle" in Matthew 24:28 can also be translated as the word "vulture," as some commentaries try to do in a vain effort to explain a difficult passage of scripture. Even more so since the above Greek word translated as "eagle" is used in Revelation 8:13 as we noted earlier. These scriptures also help to explain the following passage in Isaiah:

Isaiah 40:31
31 But they that wait upon the LORD shall renew their strength; they shall mount up with wings as eagles; they shall run, and not be weary; and they shall walk, and not faint. (KJV)

Therefore, in Revelation 8:13, we see eagle Christians warning the earth about the last three Trumpet-Vial plagues poised to strike the earth which will be even more severe in their destructive impact than the preceding plagues were. Then, in Luke 17:37, we are told that eagle Christians will be Raptured and gathered together wherever Christ, the "Lamb as it had been slain," may be. Then finally, in Matthew 24:28, Jesus tells us that just prior to His Second Coming, eagle Christians will be gathered around "the dead body," which as we saw earlier, is Christ, the "Lamb as it had been slain" (Rev. 5:6). So, in all of these prophetic passages, the word "eagle" is used as a direct reference to Christian believers.

Matthew 24:21-28
21 For then shall be great tribulation, such as was not since the beginning of the world to this time, no, nor ever shall be.
22 And except those days should be shortened, there should no flesh

be saved: but for the elect's sake those days shall be shortened.

23 Then if any man shall say unto you, Lo, here is Christ, or there; believe it not.

24 For there shall arise false Christs, and false prophets, and shall shew great signs and wonders; insomuch that, if it were possible, they shall deceive the very elect.

25 Behold, I have told you before.

26 Wherefore if they shall say unto you, Behold, he is in the desert; go not forth: behold, he is in the secret chambers; believe it not.

27 For as the lightning cometh out of the east, and shineth even unto the west; so shall also the coming of the Son of man be.

28 For wheresoever the carcase is, there will the eagles be gathered together. (KJV)

The Fifth Plague

This plague involves a horde of mysterious and supernatural "locusts." They are definitely intelligent because they are instructed to hurt ONLY people, and even then to totally exclude those with God's seal of protection. Apparently they are disembodied spirits from the creation which Satan ruled over, eons before the creation of Adam and Eve. (II Peter 3:5-9) (Isa. 14:12-14) (Isa. 45:18) (Gen. 1:28) (Jer. 4:23-26) (Ezek. 28:11-17) (Gen. 1:2). These hideous "locusts" torment people for a period of five months, and the pain they inflict will be so severe that people actually will attempt suicide, but death will be impossible due to direct Divine intervention.

Revelation 9:1-12

1 And the fifth angel sounded, and I saw a star fall from heaven unto the earth: and to him was given the key of the bottomless pit.

2 And he opened the bottomless pit; and there arose a smoke out of the pit, as the smoke of a great furnace; and the sun and the air were darkened by reason of the smoke of the pit.

3 And there came out of the smoke locusts upon the earth: and unto them was given power, as the scorpions of the earth have power.

4 And it was commanded them that they should not hurt the grass of the earth, neither any green thing, neither any tree; but only those men

which have not the seal of God in their foreheads.

5 And to them it was given that they should not kill them, but that they should be tormented five months: and their torment was as the torment of a scorpion, when he striketh a man.

6 And in those days shall men seek death, and shall not find it; and shall desire to die, and death shall flee from them.

7 And the shapes of the locusts were like unto horses prepared unto battle; and on their heads were as it were crowns like gold, and their faces were as the faces of men.

8 And they had hair as the hair of women, and their teeth were as the teeth of lions.

9 And they had breastplates, as it were breastplates of iron; and the sound of their wings was as the sound of chariots of many horses running to battle.

10 And they had tails like unto scorpions, and there were stings in their tails: and their power was to hurt men five months.

11 And they had a king over them, which is the angel of the bottomless pit, whose name in the Hebrew tongue is Abaddon, but in the Greek tongue hath his name Apollyon.

12 One woe is past; and, behold, there come two woes more hereafter. (KJV)

Revelation 16:10-11

10 And the fifth angel poured out his vial upon the seat of the beast; and his kingdom was full of darkness; and they gnawed their tongues for pain,

11 And blasphemed the God of heaven because of their pains and their sores, and repented not of their deeds. (KJV)

"And I saw a star fall from Heaven unto the earth." The Greek word for "fall" is "PIPTO, probably akin to PETOMAI (which means [to] fly) through the idea of alighting; to fall (literally or figuratively)." Therefore, it could mean that Satan (figuratively, a "fallen" angel) will be given the key to the bottomless pit since the word for "star" can be taken literally or figuratively. But on the other hand, it could mean that a "heavenly angel" flies or descends or falls to the earth to open the bottomless pit; this rendering is supported by a literal translation of this same word in the two other passages in Revelation that use it: "The four and twenty elders fall down before him that sat on the throne....." (Rev. 4:10). "And said to the mountains and rocks, Fall on us, and hide us...." (Rev. 6:16).

"The seat of the beast." (Rev. 16:10). The Greek word for "seat" is THRONOS, meaning "a stately seat ("throne"); by implication power or (concretely) a potentate." Therefore, this passage teaches that the fifth plague will be targeted primarily at the "nucleus" of the Antichrist's empire, i.e., the areas that once comprised the Babylonian, Persian, Grecian, and Roman empires.

Concerning the king or angel of the bottomless pit (abyss), Dr. Seiss notes that: "This king has a descriptive name. It is given in Hebrew and in Greek, showing that this administration has to do with Jews and Gentiles. Christ is named Jesus because He is the Saviour. This king is named Abaddon in Hebrew and Apollyon in Greek, because he is a destroyer — the opposite of saviour."

The Sixth Plague

Revelation 16:12-16

12 And the sixth angel poured out his vial upon the great river Euphrates; and the water thereof was dried up, that the way of the kings of the east might be prepared.

13 And I saw three unclean spirits like frogs come out of the mouth of the dragon, and out of the mouth of the beast, and out of the mouth of the false prophet.

14 For they are the spirits of devils, working miracles, which go forth unto the kings of the earth and of the whole world, to gather them to the battle of that great day of God Almighty.

15 Behold, I come as a thief. Blessed is he that watcheth, and keepeth his garments, lest he walk naked, and they see his shame.

16 And he gathered them together into a place called in the Hebrew tongue Armageddon. (KJV)

Revelation 9:13-21

13 And the sixth angel sounded, and I heard a voice from the four horns of the golden altar which is before God,

14 Saying to the sixth angel which had the trumpet, Loose the four angels which are bound in the great river Euphrates.

15 And the four angels were loosed, which were prepared for an hour,

and a day, and a month, and a year, for to slay the third part of men.

16 And the number of the army of the horsemen were two hundred thousand thousand: and I heard the number of them.

17 And thus I saw the horses in the vision, and them that sat on them, having breastplates of fire, and of jacinth, and brimstone: and the heads of the horses were as the heads of lions; and out of their mouths issued fire and smoke and brimstone.

18 By these three was the third part of men killed, by the fire, and by the smoke, and by the brimstone, which issued out of their mouths.

19 For their power is in their mouth, and in their tails: for their tails were like unto serpents, and had heads, and with them they do hurt.

20 And the rest of the men which were not killed by these plagues yet repented not of the works of their hands, that they should not worship devils, and idols of gold, and silver, and brass, and stone, and of wood: which neither can see, nor hear, nor walk:

21 Neither repented they of their murders, nor of their sorceries, nor of their fornication, nor of their thefts. (KJV)

The Euphrates river dries-up completely so "that the way of the kings of the east might be prepared." But something else is also involved: "Saying to the sixth angel which had the trumpet, Loose the four angels which are bound in the great Euphrates river. And the four angels were loosed, which were prepared for an hour, and a day, and a month, and a year, for to slay the third part of men. And the number of the army of horsemen (angels) were two hundred thousand thousand..." (Rev. 9:14-16).

Four is the number used whenever the world is in view. These four angels should be considered as four groups of angels just as the four horsemen were considered as four groups of saints. This makes sense when you read that these "four angels" actually slay a third of all the people on the earth! As further evidence, the passage implies that the "angels" and the "horsemen" are one and the same. Additionally, these angels represent a special, distinct class of the angels who rebelled with Satan during the Pre-Adamite creation. Their distinction:

Gen. 6:1-4

1 And it came to pass, when men began to multiply on the face of the earth, and daughters were born unto them,

2 That the sons of God saw the daughters of men that they were fair; and they took them wives of all which they chose.

3 And the LORD said, My spirit shall not always strive with man, for that he also is flesh: yet his days shall be an hundred and twenty years.

4 There were giants in the earth in those days; and also after that, when the sons of God came in unto the daughters of men, and they bare children to them, the same became mighty men which were of old, men of renown. (KJV)

The mere fact it is even stated that these "sons of God" thought women were fair and beautiful, or that, together with women, they were capable of producing children, clearly should prove something extraordinary and exceptional is portrayed here in this passage. Certainly, it would not be noteworthy to observe that ordinary men thought women were beautiful, and that together, they were capable of having children. This alone should indicate that the "sons of God" were not human! Furthermore, the very expression ("sons of God") even denotes a special meaning, especially since women are called "daughters of men." Therefore, since several other Old Testament passages (Job 1:6, 7) (Job 2:1, 2) (Job 38:4-7) (Dan. 3:25, 28) called angels "sons of God," why not apply the same definition here also?

It is said that giant offspring resulted from this very unusual biological mating. Numerous scriptures describe these same giants as being anywhere from twelve to eighteen feet tall. (I Sam. 17:4) (Deut. 3:11) (Num. 13:33) (Deut. 1:28) (Deut. 2:10-21) (Deut. 9:2) (Josh. 11:21, 22) (Josh. 14:12-14) (Josh. 12:4) (Josh. 13:12) (Deut. 3:13). Obviously human beings could not possibly produce such giant offspring! Furthermore, *Young's Literal Translation* translates the word "giants" as "fallen ones." Moffatt's translation renders it as "Nephilim giants." (Nephilim means "fallen ones." YOUNG.) *Strong's Hebrew-Greek Dictionary* says that the Hebrew is NePHIYL, meaning a "feller," i.e., a "bully" or "tyrant," and is based on the word NAPHAL, a primary root, meaning to "fall," literally or figuratively. The evidence, therefore, seems very clear that these giants were (morally) "fallen giants."

Evidently, Satan's purpose in breeding giants, both before and after the flood, was to contaminate the human race to the point where eventually there would not have been any pure-bred human beings remaining on the earth. If that had ever happened, then Christ never could have become "human," and therefore, never would have died on the cross for our sins. If Satan had been successful with this strategy, he possibly could have remained "prince of the world" indefinitely. Nevertheless, by the time Noah's flood occurred, a substantial percentage of the earth's population was tainted by angelic blood. However, not only was Noah a "righteous" man, he also was a "perfect" or pure-bred man because the Hebrew word used here of "perfection" is TAMIYM, meaning PHYSICAL perfection. It is used an additional 46 times throughout the Bible, and in every instance, refers to sacrificial animals which were required to be of pure-bred stock! Accordingly, this helps to explain why God destroyed even children in Noah's flood.

Some people have speculated that these "sons of God" refer to the so-called godly line of Seth (a son of Adam and Eve), and that the "daughters of men" refer to the so-called godless line of Cain (another son of Adam and Eve). But, the truth is NONE of them were godly or they would not have perished in the flood! Besides, it is difficult to believe that only the men of Seth's line and the women of Cain's line found each other physically attractive while their gender counterparts, in both Cain's line and Seth's line, did not. Even if one could possibly believe this scenario, it still was impossible! Seth had only one son (Enos) of marriageable age 325 years after creation, and Genesis 6:1, 2 states that the "sons of God" took "daughters of men" at the very BEGINNING of creation when daughters first were born. Likewise, Cain's line was completely destroyed in the flood. (Gen. 6:18) (Gen. 7:7) (Gen. 8:18) (Gen. 9:1) (I Peter 3:20). But since giants were born after the flood as well as before, how could women of Cain's line have children after the flood when they were non-existent?

Some people use Matthew 22:30 to prove that angels are sexless. But this passage only teaches that there are no marriages in Heaven; it does not preclude the possibility that morally-fallen angels can acquire a sexual capability. Furthermore, angels have been seen on numerous occasions throughout the Bible, and in each case they appeared to be male in gender. Therefore, in conclusion, these "sons of God" must be angelic in nature.

The fate of these special "fallen" angels:

II Peter 2:4, 5

For if God spared not the angels that sinned, but cast them down to hell... to be reserved unto judgment... but saved Noah... (KJV)

Jude 6, 7

And the angels which kept not their first estate, but left their own habitation, he hath reserved in everlasting chains under darkness unto the judgment...(their sin?) Even as Sodom and Gomorrah... going after strange flesh... (KJV)

"Fallen" angels who did not commit the sex sin are still in the heavenlies with Satan UNTIL the time of the Rapture! (Rev. 12).

I Peter 3:19, 20

Jesus "went and preached unto the spirits in prison; which sometime were disobedient, when once the longsuffering of God waited in the days of Noah." (KJV)

These spirits are angels! (Ps. 104:4) (Heb. 1:13, 14). Men have a spirit, but never are they called "spirits" anywhere in the Bible. As further evidence, if one were to assume these spirits were men, then that would be synonymous with saying God is a respecter of persons, showing partiality to those who lived during the time of Noah. Obviously such thinking would destroy the very moral foundation and basis of God in His dealings with living beings!

These angels destroy one-third of all the people on earth (Rev. 9:18-21), and the destruction they accomplish is quite catastrophic in nature:

Joel 1:15-20

15 Alas for the day! for the day of the LORD is at hand, and as a destruction from the Almighty shall it come.

16 Is not the meat cut off before our eyes, yea, joy and gladness from the house of our God?

17 The seed is rotten under their clods, the garners are laid desolate, the barns are broken down; for the corn is withered.

18 How do the beasts groan! the herds of cattle are perplexed, because they have no pasture; yea, the flocks of sheep are made desolate.

19 O LORD, to thee will I cry: for the fire hath devoured the pastures of the wilderness, and the flame hath burned all the trees of the field.

20 The beasts of the field cry also unto thee: for the rivers of waters are dried up, and the fire hath devoured the pastures of the wilderness. (KJV)

Joel 2:1-11

1 Blow ye the trumpet in Zion, and sound an alarm in my holy mountain: let all the inhabitants of the land tremble: for the day of the LORD cometh, for it is nigh at hand;

2 A day of darkness and of gloominess, a day of clouds and of thick darkness, as the morning spread upon the mountains: a great people and a strong; there hath not been ever the like, neither shall be any more after it, even to the years of many generations.

3 A fire devoureth before them; and behind them a flame burneth: the land is as the garden of Eden before them, and behind them a desolate wilderness; yea, and nothing shall escape them.

4 The appearance of them is as the appearance of horses; and as horsemen, so shall they run.

5 Like the noise of chariots on the tops of mountains shall they leap, like the noise of a flame of fire that devoureth the stubble, as a strong people set in battle array.

6 Before their face the people shall be much pained: all faces shall gather blackness.

7 They shall run like mighty men; they shall climb the wall like men of war; and they shall march every one on his ways, and they shall not break their ranks:

8 Neither shall one thrust another; they shall walk every one in his path: and when they fall upon the sword, they shall not be wounded.

9 They shall run to and fro in the city; they shall run upon the wall, they shall climb up upon the houses; they shall enter in at the windows like a thief.

10 The earth shall quake before them; the heavens shall tremble: the sun and the moon shall be dark, and the stars shall withdraw their shining:

11 And the LORD shall utter his voice before his army: for his camp is very great: for he is strong that executeth his word: for the day of the LORD is great and very terrible; and who can abide it? (KJV)

As for the identity of the "kings of the east" who are mentioned in one of the passages describing the sixth plague, it is very possible that they are, in fact, vast hordes of Asian soldiers — precisely as conventional prophecy wisdom teaches. On the other hand, they might be the group of former commonwealth nations, including the United States of America, who apparently are mentioned in Ezekiel 38 as protesting the initial invasion of Israel by the Antichrist a few years before Armageddon begins. However, regardless of whichever group of nations it turns out to be, they will be a separate and distinct group of ordinary people with no direct connection to the 200,000,000 angelic horsemen of the sixth plague.

Legal Possession Of The Earth

Revelation 10:1-11

1 And I saw another mighty angel come down from heaven, clothed with a cloud: and a rainbow was upon his head, and his face was as it were the sun, and his feet as pillars of fire:

2 And he had in his hand a little book open: and he set his right foot upon the sea, and his left foot on the earth,

3 And cried with a loud voice, as when a lion roareth: and when he had cried, seven thunders uttered their voices.

4 And when the seven thunders had uttered their voices, I was about to write: and I heard a voice from heaven saying unto me, Seal up those things which the seven thunders uttered, and write them not.

5 And the angel which I saw stand upon the sea and upon the earth lifted up his hand to heaven,

6 And sware by him that liveth for ever and ever, who created heaven, and the things that therein are, and the earth, and the things that therein are, and the sea, and the things which are therein, that there should be time no longer:

7 But in the days of the voice of the seventh angel, when he shall begin to sound, the mystery of God should be finished, as he hath declared to his servants the prophets.

8 And the voice which I heard from heaven spake unto me again, and said, Go and take the little book which is open in the hand of the angel which standeth upon the sea and upon the earth.

9 And I went unto the angel, and said unto him, Give me the little book. And he said unto me, Take it, and eat it up; and it shall make thy belly bitter, but it shall be in thy mouth sweet as honey.

10 And I took the little book out of the angel's hand, and ate it up; and it was in my mouth sweet as honey: and as soon as I had eaten it, my belly was bitter.

11 And he said unto me, Thou must prophesy again before many

peoples, and nations, and tongues, and kings. (KJV)

We know that the "mighty angel" in verse 1 is Christ by the description: "clothed with a cloud"; "rainbow was upon his head" (signifying God's promise never to destroy the world again); face as "the sun"; feet as "pillars of fire"; voice that sounds like when "a lion roareth." Since this chapter also portrays John (representing the saints) and the "mighty angel" taking "legal" possession of planet earth, it is sensible to assume that the "mighty angel" is Christ because only Christ would have the power and the "legal right" to accomplish this task.

"The seven thunders." John was told not to record what the seven thunders said because apparently this is God's military secret for that point in time. Evidently, then, God is not allowing Satan to know everything in advance in order to minimize Satan's futile attempts at thwarting His plans for the future. Since the first rule in military strategy is to keep your enemy guessing, and since God is Infinite Wisdom, and since He will be engaged in the final stages of purging all evil from His universe, even God has His military secrets for the endtimes! This is one of them!

"The little book." This is the "title deed" to planet earth. In this instance, John acts as a "type," representing all of the saints, collectively, when he accepts possession of it by eating it in a symbolic gesture. Apparently this is what the apostle Paul referred to in the following scriptural passage:

Eph. 1:11-14

11 In whom also we have obtained an inheritance, being predestinated according to the purpose of him who worketh all things after the counsel of his own will:

12 That we should be to the praise of his glory, who first trusted in Christ.

13 In whom ye also trusted, after that ye heard the word of truth, the gospel of your salvation: in whom also after that ye believed, ye were sealed with that holy Spirit of promise,

14 Which is the earnest of our inheritance until the redemption of the purchased possession, unto the praise of his glory. (KJV)

When John first ate the "book," it tasted "sweet," symbolizing the joy and happiness of the saints at inheriting the earth. But, as it became "bitter" in his belly, the symbolism then reflected the stark nature of the unpleasant task facing the saints in their efforts to purge the earth of the results of sin and evil. However, no matter how unpleasant this task might be, it is an essential mission that has to be accomplished.

Latter Half Of Daniel's 70th Week

Revelation 11:1, 2

1 And there was given me a reed like unto a rod: and the angel stood, saying, Rise, and measure the temple of God, and the altar, and them that worship therein.

2 But the court which is without the temple leave out, and measure it not; for it is given unto the Gentiles: and the holy city shall they tread under foot forty and two months. (KJV)

"Reed like unto a rod." A "reed" is an instrument of measure, generally six long cubits in ancient Israel. (Ezek. 40:5; 41:8). A "long cubit" was about 20½ inches, thus making this reed about 123 inches or 10.25 feet in length. Likewise, the "rod" became a symbol of authority and power in Bible times. (Jer. 48:17) (Exod. 4:2, 17, 20; 7:9-20) (Exod. 8:16, 17) (Exod. 9:23) (Exod. 10:13; 14:6; 17:5-7) (Num. 20) (Exod. 17:9-13; 21:20) (Ps. 89:32; 125:3) (Prov. 13:24; 22:15; 29:15) (Micah 5:1) (Ps. 2:9) (I Cor. 4:21) (Heb. 9:1-28) (Rev. 2:27). In this passage, we see John once again acting in his capacity as a "type" representing all the saints throughout the ages, and exercising his power and authority to measure the temple of God and the alter in anticipation of actual physical possession. Since it is only natural to survey and inventory property that one is about to redeem, this is what John does symbolically.

"The holy city (i.e., Jerusalem) shall they tread under foot forty and two months." Compare the following scriptures:

Daniel 9:27

27 And he shall confirm the covenant with many for one week: and in the midst of the week he shall cause the sacrifice and the oblation to cease, and for the overspreading of abominations he shall make it desolate, even until the consummation, and that determined shall be poured upon the desolate. (KJV)

Luke 21:20-24

20 And when ye shall see Jerusalem compassed with armies, then know that the desolation thereof is nigh.

21 Then let them which are in Judaea flee to the mountains; and let them which are in the midst of it depart out; and let not them that are in the countries enter thereinto.

22 For these be the days of vengeance, that all things which are written may be fulfilled.

23 But woe unto them that are with child, and to them that give suck, in those days! for there shall be great distress in the land, and wrath upon this people.

24 And they shall fall by the edge of the sword, and shall be led away captive into all nations: and Jerusalem shall be trodden down of the Gentiles, until the times of the Gentiles be fulfilled. (KJV)

Zechariah 11:15-17

15 And the LORD said unto me, Take unto thee yet the instruments of a foolish shepherd.

16 For, lo, I will raise up a shepherd in the land, which shall not visit those that be cut off, neither shall seek the young one, nor heal that that is broken, nor feed that that standeth still: but he shall eat the flesh of the fat, and tear their claws in pieces.

17 Woe to the idol shepherd that leaveth the flock! the sword shall be upon his arm, and upon his right eye: his arm shall be clean dried up, and his right eye shall be utterly darkened. (KJV)

Zechariah 13:8-9

8 And it shall come to pass, that in all the land, saith the LORD, two parts therein shall be cut off and die; but the third shall be left therein.

9 And I will bring the third part through the fire, and will refine them as silver is refined, and will try them as gold is tried: they shall call on my name, and I will hear them: I will say, It is my people: and they shall say, The LORD is my God. (KJV)

Matthew 24:15-20

15 When ye therefore shall see the abomination of desolation, spoken of by Daniel the prophet, stand in the holy place, (whoso readeth, let him understand:)

16 Then let them which be in Judaea flee into the mountains:
17 Let him which is on the housetop not come down to take any thing out of his house:
18 Neither let him which is in the field return back to take his clothes.
19 And woe unto them that are with child, and to them that give suck in those days!
20 But pray ye that your flight be not in the winter, neither on the sabbath day: (KJV)

Jeremiah 30:5-7
5 For thus saith the LORD; We have heard a voice of trembling, of fear, and not of peace.
6 Ask ye now, and see whether a man doth travail with child? wherefore do I see every man with his hands on his loins, as a woman in travail, and all faces are turned into paleness?
7 Alas! for that day is great, so that none is like it: it is even the time of Jacob's trouble; but he shall be saved out of it. (KJV)

After having witnessed the power of God (through the miraculous recovery of national Israel during the Second Crisis), the Antichrist will not dare bother Israel again until he first tempts them into sin. That, in turn, is something he eventually will accomplish by enticing Israel to sign a special seven year treaty with him (i.e., Daniel's 70th Week) in which he guarantees Israel its historic land in Palestine. Signing this treaty will be a sin for Israel because it will signal the usurpation of God as the protector and guarantor of their promised land. This treaty, as mentioned previously, will not take effect until AFTER the Great Tribulation is over.

However, midway through the seven years of Daniel's 70th Week, the Antichrist will violate his seven year treaty with Israel when he begins desecrating the rebuilt temple in Jerusalem for three and one-half years while he is persecuting the Jews. This horrific time of tribulation and desecration and persecution is known as "Jacob's Trouble" (Jer. 30:5-7) and the "Times Of The Gentiles" (Luke 21:24). It is during this Jewish persecution that the ministry and testimony of the Two Witnesses will emerge in order to hinder the activities of the Antichrist in Israel.

Likewise, Jesus called this same period of time the greatest tribulation in human history because it will begin during the Day Of The Lord when the worst of the seven great Trumpet-Vial plagues are destroying the earth's surface. The Scriptures also prophesy that two-thirds of the Israelis will be "cut off" (i.e., killed), and that most of the others will be sent into captivity. However, the Bible also states that the survivors will be "tried" and "refined" as pure gold, and when they finally "call" upon the Lord God, they will become His people again forever. (Compare Romans 11:21-32). During this three and one-half year period of time, the Antichrist also will desecrate the Jewish Temple by sitting in it and declaring himself to be a god. However, as noted previously, the Antichrist will not pretend to be the true, Christian God of the Bible, but rather, a god of the universe:

II Thess. 2:4
4 Who opposeth and exalteth himself above all that is called God, or that is worshipped; so that he as God sitteth in the temple of God, shewing himself that he is God. (KJV)

Daniel 8:11-14
11 Yea, he magnified himself even to the prince of the host, and by him the daily sacrifice was taken away, and the place of his sanctuary was cast down.
12 And an host was given him against the daily sacrifice by reason of transgression, and it cast down the truth to the ground; and it practised, and prospered.
13 Then I heard one saint speaking, and another saint said unto that certain saint which spake, How long shall be the vision concerning the daily sacrifice, and the transgression of desolation, to give both the sanctuary and the host to be trodden under foot?
14 And he said unto me, Unto two thousand and three hundred days; then shall the sanctuary be cleansed. (KJV)

Daniel 8:26
26 And the vision of the evening and the morning which was told is true: wherefore shut thou up the vision; for it shall be for many days. (KJV)

Although this prophecy states that the Sanctuary (rebuilt temple in Jerusalem) will be desecrated for a period of "2300 days," a more accurate translation would read "2300 evening-mornings." This is because the Hebrew word translated as "days" in this passage is actually two words: BOQER, meaning "dawn" or "morning"; and `EREB, meaning “dusk” or “evening.” Accordingly, this passage should read “2300 evening-mornings” — which is how many translations do interpret it. However, since Jewish religious law requires this type of sacrifice each morning and each evening of every day, this passage actually states that 2300 such sacrifices will be abolished, and 2300 such sacrifices obviously represent a total of 1150 literal days.

“And the place of his sanctuary was cast down.” The Hebrew word for “place” is MAKOWN, meaning a “fixture,” i.e., a “basis; generally a place, especially as an abode.” The Hebrew word for “sanctuary” in this particular passage is MIQDASH or MIQQeDASH, meaning a “consecrated thing or place, especially a palace, sanctuary or asylum.” And the Hebrew word for “cast down” is SHALAK, meaning to “throw out, down or away (literally or figuratively).” Therefore, this passage probably states that the Antichrist will “throw down” or demolish the most holy part of the temple, i.e., the “Holy of Holies,” the sacred inner sanctum of a three-sectioned temple.

Revelation 11:3-4

3 And I will give power unto my two witnesses, and they shall prophesy a thousand two hundred and threescore days, clothed in sackcloth.

4 These are the two olive trees, and the two candlesticks standing before the God of the earth. (KJV)

Zechariah 4:11-14

11 Then answered I, and said unto him, What are these two olive trees upon the right side of the candlestick and upon the left side thereof?

12 And I answered again, and said unto him, What be these two olive branches which through the two golden pipes empty the golden oil out of themselves?

13 And he answered me and said, Knowest thou not what these be? And I said, No, my lord.

14 Then said he, These are the two anointed ones, that stand by the LORD of the whole earth. (KJV)

The scriptures in Malachi 3:1-3 and 4:5-6 state with clarity and certainty that Elijah will be sent to the earth as one of the Two Witnesses. However, Luke 1:17 identifies John the Baptist as someone who came “in the spirit and power of Elias (Elijah)," while Jesus said that John the Baptist could have fulfilled the prophecy about Elijah if Israel had accepted Him as Messiah. (Matt. 11:12-14; 17:10-13). Thus, there could have been a "spiritual" interpretation and fulfillment for this prophecy in Malachi. But, once Israel exercised her collective free will and rejected Jesus as Messiah, a completely literal fulfillment for Malachi's prophecy became necessary once the Revelation was given to John the Revelator years later. Otherwise, Revelation 11:3-4 could not have identified the Two Witnesses as the "two anointed ones" pictured in Zechariah 4:11-14 who "stand by the LORD of the whole earth." This fact, by itself, makes it very likely that Elijah and Enoch will be the Two Witnesses because the Bible states that everyone must die and then face judgment, and Elijah and Enoch are unique in that they never died, but were translated to Heaven before the prophecies in Revelation and Zechariah were revealed! Although the miracles performed by the Two Witnesses will resemble the miracles performed by Elijah and Moses during their ministries, and it was Elijah and Moses who appeared with Christ during His supernatural "transfiguration" (Mark 9:1-8), the fact remains that the "two anointed ones" must be mortal men who were standing beside God in Heaven thousands of years ago. Additionally, there is no reason to believe that Moses and Elijah are the only individuals through whom a Sovereign, Infinite God could perform these kinds of miracles. Therefore, the Two Witnesses probably will be Elijah and Enoch, not Elijah and Moses.

Revelation 11:5-12

5 And if any man will hurt them, fire proceedeth out of their mouth, and devoureth their enemies: and if any man will hurt them, he must in this manner be killed.

6 These have power to shut heaven, that it rain not in the days of their prophecy: and have power over waters to turn them to blood, and to smite the earth with all plagues, as often as they will.

7 And when they shall have finished their testimony, the beast that ascendeth out of the bottomless pit shall make war against them, and shall overcome them, and kill them.

8 And their dead bodies shall lie in the street of the great city, which spiritually is called Sodom and Egypt, where also our Lord was crucified.

9 And they of the people and kindreds and tongues and nations shall see their dead bodies three days and an half, and shall not suffer their dead

bodies to be put in graves.

10 And they that dwell upon the earth shall rejoice over them, and make merry, and shall send gifts one to another; because these two prophets tormented them that dwelt on the earth.

11 And after three days and an half the Spirit of life from God entered into them, and they stood upon their feet; and great fear fell upon them which saw them.

12 And they heard a great voice from heaven saying unto them, Come up hither. And they ascended up to heaven in a cloud; and their enemies beheld them. (KJV)

"Their testimony." This passage does not say what the testimony of the Two Witnesses will be, but a parallel passage of scripture does. Not only is it a prophecy to the Jews foretelling the imminent appearance of their long-awaited Messiah, but it also is an appeal to moral and spiritual purity:

Revelation 16:15

15 Behold, I come as a thief. Blessed is he that watcheth, and keepeth his garments, lest he walk naked, and they see his shame. (KJV)

"The Two Witnesses." These two prophets of God miraculously hinder the activities of the Antichrist for a period of three and one-half years until he finally succeeds in killing them after their ministry is completed. The Two Witnesses then re-enact the death, resurrection and ascension of Christ as a way of preparing the minds of the Jews, spiritually and psychologically, to accept Christ as their Messiah at His Second Coming.

"Television and modern communications." It is stated that people from all "kindreds and tongues and nations shall see their dead bodies three days and an half." Obviously television with world-wide satellite coverage would be required for the fulfillment of this scripture. The fact that people from all over the world rejoice and send gifts to one another during these 3½ days likewise necessitates the modern-day inventions of television communications and satellite technology.

Revelation 11:13, 14

13 And the same hour was there a great earthquake, and the tenth part

of the city fell, and in the earthquake were slain of men seven thousand: and the remnant were affrighted, and gave glory to the God of heaven.

14 The second woe is past; and, behold, the third woe cometh quickly. (KJV)

The Seventh Plague

Revelation 11:15-19

15 And the seventh angel sounded; and there were great voices in heaven, saying, The kingdoms of this world are become the kingdoms of our Lord, and of his Christ; and he shall reign for ever and ever.

16 And the four and twenty elders, which sat before God on their seats, fell upon their faces, and worshipped God,

17 Saying, We give thee thanks, O Lord God Almighty, which art, and wast, and art to come; because thou hast taken to thee thy great power, and hast reigned.

18 And the nations were angry, and thy wrath is come, and the time of the dead, that they should be judged, and that thou shouldest give reward unto thy servants the prophets, and to the saints, and them that fear thy name, small and great; and shouldest destroy them which destroy the earth.

19 And the temple of God was opened in heaven, and there was seen in his temple the ark of his testament: and there were lightnings, and voices, and thunderings, and an earthquake, and great hail. (KJV)

Revelation 16:17-21

17 And the seventh angel poured out his vial into the air; and there came a great voice out of the temple of heaven, from the throne, saying, It is done.

18 And there were voices, and thunders, and lightnings; and there was a great earthquake, such as was not since men were upon the earth, so mighty an earthquake, and so great.

19 And the great city was divided into three parts, and the cities of the nations fell: and great Babylon came in remembrance before God, to give unto her the cup of the wine of the fierceness of his wrath.

20 And every island fled away, and the mountains were not found.

21 And there fell upon men a great hail out of heaven, every stone

about the weight of a talent: and men blasphemed God because of the plague of the hail; for the plague thereof was exceeding great. (KJV)

"A great earthquake." The greatest earthquake in history takes place during this catastrophic plague, the last of the horrific "three woes." It is so devastating and cataclysmic in its destructive force that it completely obliterates all of the cities and mountains and islands throughout the whole world. Furthermore, this incredible global earthquake will even be accompanied by gigantic pieces of hail, each weighing approximately 100 pounds, and originating from both polar ice caps. (Job 38:22, 23).

"Lightnings, and voices, and thunderings." Several times throughout the book of Revelation, we read about these powerful and mysterious phenomena. Most interestingly, they always seem to accompany God's judgment and wrath as an outward, visible indicator of God's righteous anger toward sin and evil.

Matthew 24:27-31

27 For as the lightning cometh out of the east, and shineth even unto the west; so shall also the coming of the Son of man be.

28 For wheresoever the carcase is, there will the eagles be gathered together.

29 Immediately after the tribulation of those days shall the sun be darkened, and the moon shall not give her light, and the stars shall fall from heaven, and the powers of the heavens shall be shaken:

30 And then shall appear the sign of the Son of man in heaven: and then shall all the tribes of the earth mourn, and they shall see the Son of man coming in the clouds of heaven with power and great glory.

31 And he shall send his angels with a great sound of a trumpet, and they shall gather together his elect from the four winds, from one end of heaven to the other. (KJV)

Luke 21:25-27

25 And there shall be signs in the sun, and in the moon, and in the stars; and upon the earth distress of nations, with perplexity; the sea and the waves roaring;

26 Men's hearts failing them for fear, and for looking after those things which are coming on the earth: for the powers of heaven shall be shaken.

27 And then shall they see the Son of man coming in a cloud with power and great glory. (KJV)

Just prior to the Return of Christ with His saints, the "angels" will gather or translate certain "elect" people who will be living on the earth immediately before Armageddon begins. These special "elect" individuals will be none other than the Tribulation Saints, including the 144,000 Jews, who will have been given God's seal of protection after escaping execution by the Antichrist during the Great Christian Tribulation. They also, of course, will be a part of the saintly group of believers who return with Christ at His Second Coming. Then, at that point, after years of incredible plagues and pestilence and famine and war, the seventh Trumpet-Vial plague is released upon the earth just before the Battle of Armageddon commences and Christ Returns to the earth with His saints to establish God's Kingdom on earth for eternity. Tremendous signs and wonders will abound everywhere as the world, literally, is shaken and seemingly torn apart while many people's hearts will fail them as extraordinary levels of stark, utter fear grabs them completely in its grip!

Proof Of The Parallel Accounts

The last few verses of chapter 11 most definitely conclude with the events of Armageddon and the Second Coming of Christ:

"...Kingdoms of this world are become the Kingdoms of our Lord."
"...He shall reign for ever and ever."
"...Nations were angry and Thy wrath is come."
"...Give reward unto thy servants."
"...Destroy them which destroy the earth."

Compare: "That there should be TIME NO LONGER: but in the days of the voice of the seventh angel, when he shall begin to sound, the mystery of God should be FINISHED." (Rev. 10:6, 7). A more accurate rendering of this passage would say something to the effect that the fulfillment of the "mystery of God" will not be delayed any longer. (The Greek word for "time" is CHRONOS, and it means a space of "time"; by implication, "delay.") Accordingly, this passage clearly states that the seventh plague ushers in a new and different era for mankind; an era when everyone understands exactly what God has planned for both the earth and the universe as God begins to establish His Kingdom throughout the earth.

Therefore, chapters 4-11 in Revelation clearly end with a description of Armageddon and the Return of Christ after narrating the Rapture and subsequent events which occur from the time of the Rapture to the Battle of Armageddon. However, chapters 12-16 in Revelation also describe these very same events, thus verifying the testimonial prophecy contained within the first parallel account. So, both accounts in Revelation commence with a description of the Rapture, then correlate a long series of events together, and then finally conclude with a description of Armageddon and the Return of Christ. This remarkable harmony which exists between the two parallel accounts in Revelation is vividly demonstrated by the chart located at the end of this chapter, entitled *Harmony Of The Parallel Accounts*. Furthermore, we also should note that an offering of dual testimony is completely harmonious with the Bible because several scriptural passages say that testimony should be confirmed by two or more witnesses. Therefore, the scriptural evidence clearly confirms the validity of the parallel accounts.

The Time Element In Revelation

Please refer to the chart located within this same section. A careful survey of the events narrated in chapters 4-11 will show there are approximately ten and one-half years between the Rapture and Armageddon. We can make this determination because all of the major events are NUMBERED in their sequence of occurrence; there are seven seals which are opened, one after the other, and then during the seventh seal, there are seven horrific plagues which are released upon the earth, one at a time. There are even scriptures stating exact time-lengths for some of the more important events. Additionally, there are five scriptures which say that people converted to salvation after the Rapture will be martyred during a three and one-half year period of time and then resurrected into Heaven at the conclusion of that same time-period. Next follows a period of time during which several plagues are unleashed upon the earth; one of these plagues will endure for a period of five months while one of the other plagues will continue for over 13 months. Then finally, we encounter another three and one-half year period of time, according to several scriptures, during which the rebuilt temple in Jerusalem is subjected to desecration.

In conclusion, we have a period of three and one-half years, and then an unknown period of time, and then finally another period of three and one-half years. But, if we also permit the unknown period of time to represent three and one-half years, we allow complete scriptural harmony. First, we allow enough time for everything to happen because the seven plagues of fire are unleashed upon the earth, one at a time, and one plague is not permitted to happen until the previous one either has endured for a specified amount of time or has accomplished all of the destruction it is capable of doing! This is at least true of the sixth and seventh plagues because the three and one-half year period of desecration involving the rebuilt temple occurs BETWEEN the time of these two plagues. We also permit the tribulation saints to become saved and resurrected into Heaven BEFORE beginning the Dispensation of Law with the advent of Daniel's 70th Week. Thus, we are not forced to mix the dispensations of grace and law. Furthermore, the Olivet Discourse in Matthew 24 and Luke 21 is structured in such a manner so as to support this conclusion. First, we observe the Dispensation of Grace during which time people can be saved through a tumultuous period of wars, plagues, famines, earthquakes and persecutions:

Matthew 24:7-14

7 For nation shall rise against nation, and kingdom against kingdom: and there shall be famines, and pestilences, and earthquakes, in divers places.

8 All these are the beginning of sorrows.

9 Then shall they deliver you up to be afflicted, and shall kill you: and ye shall be hated of all nations for my name's sake.

10 And then shall many be offended, and shall betray one another, and shall hate one another.

11 And many false prophets shall rise, and shall deceive many.

12 And because iniquity shall abound, the love of many shall wax cold.

13 But he that shall endure unto the end, the same shall be saved.

14 And this gospel of the kingdom shall be preached in all the world for a witness unto all nations; and then shall the end come. (KJV)

Then (perhaps even several years later) after the "end" (of the Dispensation of Grace), we read that the Jewish persecution and tribulation which will occur during the latter-half of Daniel's 70th Week (Dispensation of Law) commences:

Matthew 24:15-20

15 When ye therefore shall see the abomination of desolation, spoken of by Daniel the prophet, stand in the holy place, (whoso readeth, let him understand:)

16 Then let them which be in Judaea flee into the mountains:

17 Let him which is on the housetop not come down to take any thing out of his house:

18 Neither let him which is in the field return back to take his clothes.

19 And woe unto them that are with child, and to them that give suck in those days!

20 But pray ye that your flight be not in the winter, neither on the sabbath day: (KJV)

As further proof that Daniel's 70th Week begins when the seven plagues commence, please note Revelation 15:

Revelation 15:1-8

1 And I saw another sign in heaven, great and marvellous, seven angels having the seven last plagues; for in them is filled up the wrath of God.

2 And I saw as it were a sea of glass mingled with fire: and them that had gotten the victory over the beast, and over his image, and over his mark, and over the number of his name, stand on the sea of glass, having the harps of God.

3 And they sing the song of Moses the servant of God, and the song of the Lamb, saying, Great and marvellous are thy works, Lord God Almighty; just and true are thy ways, thou King of saints.

4 Who shall not fear thee, O Lord, and glorify thy name? for thou only art holy: for all nations shall come and worship before thee; for thy judgments are made manifest.

5 And after that I looked, and, behold, the temple of the tabernacle of the testimony in heaven was opened:

6 And the seven angels came out of the temple, having the seven plagues, clothed in pure and white linen, and having their breasts girded with golden girdles.

7 And one of the four beasts gave unto the seven angels seven golden vials full of the wrath of God, who liveth for ever and ever.

8 And the temple was filled with smoke from the glory of God, and from his power; and no man was able to enter into the temple, till the seven plagues of the seven angels were fulfilled. (KJV)

This scriptural passage emphasizes the symbolic relevance and importance of the holy temple in Heaven during the period of time that the seven plagues of Divine wrath and judgment are unleashed upon the earth! In fact, it is even stated that the glory of God causes a smoke-like phenomenon to fill the holy temple during this time which makes it impossible for any person to enter the temple. Thus, it is vividly demonstrated that God, once again, after 2000 years, is dealing with the Jews on the basis of their ancient covenant relationship, known theologically as the Dispensation of Law.

Finally, we note, also, that Daniel 12 likewise makes a very specific reference to three different and distinct time-periods which will occur during the time of the end, thus further confirming our belief that there are three different periods of three and one-half years. (note Daniel 12:7, 11, 12). So, although conventional prophecy wisdom teaches that there are only 7 years between the Rapture and Armageddon, the fact remains that no matter how many people may believe that theory, it still remains an arbitrary assumption which can not be proven. Just because Daniel's 70th Week is in the time-period between the Rapture and Armageddon is no reason necessarily to believe that there are ONLY seven years between the Rapture and Armageddon!

Three Time Zones Between The Rapture And Armageddon	
Events	**3½ Years Duration**
Rapture (Rev. 4) Six Seals (Rev. 6) Jews Sealed (Rev. 7) Tribulation Saints Resurrected (Rev. 7)	Rev. 12:6 Rev. 12:14 Rev. 13:5 Dan. 7:25 Dan. 12:7
First Six Plagues of the Seventh Seal (Rev. 8-10)	Dan. 9:27 Dan. 12:12
Desecration Of The Temple (Rev. 11) Two Witnesses (Rev. 11) Armageddon (Rev. 11) Second Coming (Rev. 11)	Rev. 11:2 Rev. 11:3 Dan. 9:27 Dan. 12:11

We should note that the passage in Daniel 12:12 allows 75 days (1335 days minus the 1260 days which comprise the first half of Daniel's 70th Week) for the protective sealing of the 144,000 Jews which takes place immediately before the Day Of The Lord and Daniel's 70th Week begin. Likewise, the passage in Daniel 12:11 makes allowance for an additional 30 days to transpire after Daniel's 70th Week concludes in order to give time for the 7th Trumpet-Vial plague to be released. Thus, all time-periods given in scripture are completely harmonious with each other.

The Seven Plagues Are From God

Sometimes it is alleged that the seven plagues are the results of a nuclear conflict because their description often resembles a description of nuclear warfare. However, although a convincing case can sometimes be made, the fact remains that the scriptures very clearly and emphatically say repeatedly, many times, that the plagues are from God, and that the people on the earth know it (which explains why they curse God for sending the plagues on them), but still they will not repent. (Rev. 6:12-17) (Rev. 16:9) (Rev. 16:11) (Rev. 16:17-21). It is even stated in the Revelation that the first four plagues represent the specific and direct efforts of the "four angels, to whom it was given to hurt the earth and the sea." (Rev. 7:1-3). Accordingly, these scriptures make it quite clear and obvious that the seven plagues will originate from God Himself, through the agency of the saints carrying out His program of earthly redemption, and not from any nuclear warfare taking place on the earth between nations of people.

Apparently there is no radioactive residue present after Armageddon because the Jews begin burial of the dead soon afterwards. (Ezek. 38 and 39). Several scriptures even describe the weapons of war which actually are utilized during Armageddon as being made of wood. Obviously the impact of nuclear weapons, if they are used at all, is very limited. This is not too surprising when you consider that the seven plagues are designed to purge the earth of the results of sin, and weapons (and factories making such items) are not likely to be ignored. Another reason for little, if any, nuclear activity during the plagues is that weapons of war will be relatively scarce just before Armageddon because money which normally would have been allocated to weapons will have been used, instead, to help create a world of peace and prosperity before the Rapture.

The Manchild Rapture

Revelation 12:1-17

1 And there appeared a great wonder in heaven; a woman clothed with the sun, and the moon under her feet, and upon her head a crown of twelve stars:

2 And she being with child cried, travailing in birth, and pained to be delivered.

3 And there appeared another wonder in heaven; and behold a great red dragon, having seven heads and ten horns, and seven crowns upon his heads.

4 And his tail drew the third part of the stars of heaven, and did cast them to the earth: and the dragon stood before the woman which was ready to be delivered, for to devour her child as soon as it was born.

5 And she brought forth a man child, who was to rule all nations with a

rod of iron: and her child was caught up unto God, and to his throne.

6 And the woman fled into the wilderness, where she hath a place prepared of God, that they should feed her there a thousand two hundred and threescore days.

7 And there was war in heaven: Michael and his angels fought against the dragon; and the dragon fought and his angels,

8 And prevailed not; neither was their place found any more in heaven.

9 And the great dragon was cast out, that old serpent, called the Devil, and Satan, which deceiveth the whole world: he was cast out into the earth, and his angels were cast out with him.

10 And I heard a loud voice saying in heaven, Now is come salvation, and strength, and the kingdom of our God, and the power of his Christ: for the accuser of our brethren is cast down, which accused them before our God day and night.

11 And they overcame him by the blood of the Lamb, and by the word of their testimony; and they loved not their lives unto the death.

12 Therefore rejoice, ye heavens, and ye that dwell in them. Woe to the inhabiters of the earth and of the sea! for the devil is come down unto you, having great wrath, because he knoweth that he hath but a short time.

13 And when the dragon saw that he was cast unto the earth, he persecuted the woman which brought forth the man child.

14 And to the woman were given two wings of a great eagle, that she might fly into the wilderness, into her place, where she is nourished for a time, and times, and half a time, from the face of the serpent.

15 And the serpent cast out of his mouth water as a flood after the woman, that he might cause her to be carried away of the flood.

16 And the earth helped the woman, and the earth opened her mouth, and swallowed up the flood which the dragon cast out of his mouth.

17 And the dragon was wroth with the woman, and went to make war with the remnant of her seed, which keep the commandments of God, and have the testimony of Jesus Christ. (KJV)

Chapter 12 entails a considerable amount of symbolism in which we observe a sun-clad woman standing on the moon while wearing a crown of twelve stars upon her head, and pregnant with a "man-child." The correct interpretation? Please keep in mind that the book of Revelation is concerned primarily with the post-Rapture "church" — there is no history involved here after the first three chapters (only the "hereafter"), and the

Jews are mentioned only if they directly affect the church! This is important because many erroneous interpretations and conclusions have been drawn while violating this point we are making about Revelation. Revelation is for and about the church! (Rev. 1:1) (Rev. 1:11) (Rev. 2:7) (Rev. 2:11) (Rev. 2:17) (Rev. 2:29) (Rev. 3:6) (Rev. 3:13) (Rev. 3:22) (Rev. 22:16).

This second parallel account of apocalyptic events in Revelation begins with a narration of the Rapture in the same manner that Revelation 4-11 does. Since a woman, in prophecy, usually symbolizes some type of church (Eph. 5:24-33) (II Cor. 11:2), the sun-clad woman represents the visible, "professing" church of Christ just as the scarlet-clad woman represents Satan's church in Revelation 17. Likewise, because there are numerous "born-again" Christians within the church BEFORE the Rapture, it is said to be clothed with sunlight, the garment of righteousness and evidence of the indwelling Holy Spirit. ("Ye are the light of the world.") That is why the Christian church has complete power over the kingdom of darkness, symbolically pictured as the sun-clad woman standing on top of the moon, the empress of darkness. However, as an alternative explanation, the moon could symbolize the Old Testament Covenant, instead, because the Old Testament Covenant reflected the (sun)light radiating from the true source of eternal life, i.e., the New Covenant embodied in Christ Jesus. Then finally, the crown of twelve stars represents the New Testament church because it is the church existent at the time of the Rapture (Rev. 12:1).

"And she being with child cried, travailing in birth, and pained to be delivered." The sun-clad woman is portrayed in this passage of scripture as enduring great pain and anguish before her delivery of the manchild. Since we obviously are dealing with symbolic spiritual things in this scripture, it is apparent that this travailing in birth must symbolize the spiritual tribulation or final great apostasy which the church will experience just before the Rapture.

However, let me hasten to emphasize that this is not the Great Tribulation. The Great Tribulation happens only after the Rapture of the true church, and it is characterized by precisely three and one-half years of mass executions of (newly-converted) Christians who will not take the mark of the beast. Before the Rapture, the Bible states repeatedly that the Antichrist will destroy (deceive) people only through miracles and peace and prosperity, not physical torture. Therefore, persecution of Christians before the Rapture will be spiritual and deceptive in nature, whereas after the Rapture, it will be physical and brutal in nature even though just as much deception will continue in a different form.

Sometimes it is taught that a spiritual "latter rain" during the endtimes will spark a great revival among people. (Joel 2:23, 24) (Jer. 5:24) (Hosea 6:3) (Zech. 10:1) (James 5:7). Although this is true, it will not happen before the Rapture; that period is marked only by deception and apostasy! It is only after the Rapture, during the Great Tribulation, that mass numbers of people will become saved through Christ Jesus at a time when people will dream special dreams and see visions and prophesy:

Revelation 6:12-17

12 And I beheld when he had opened the sixth seal, and, lo, there was a great earthquake; and the sun became black as sackcloth of hair, and the moon became as blood;

13 And the stars of heaven fell unto the earth, even as a fig tree casteth her untimely figs, when she is shaken of a mighty wind.

14 And the heaven departed as a scroll when it is rolled together; and every mountain and island were moved out of their places.

15 And the kings of the earth, and the great men, and the rich men, and the chief captains, and the mighty men, and every bondman, and every free man, hid themselves in the dens and in the rocks of the mountains;

16 And said to the mountains and rocks, Fall on us, and hide us from the face of him that sitteth on the throne, and from the wrath of the Lamb:

17 For the great day of his wrath is come; and who shall be able to stand? (KJV)

This seal marks the end of the Dispensation of Grace! Please observe that not one single person is converted to salvation after this point in time. In fact, it is mentioned very explicitly several times throughout the book of Revelation that, after the Great Tribulation is concluded, not even one person will repent of their sins despite the incredible severity of the plagues comprising the seventh seal! Contextually, the prophetic stage is now set for the dark and gloomy and terrible "Day of the Lord" — a day of wrath and judgment — to begin!

Joel 2:28-31

28 And it shall come to pass afterward, that I will pour out my spirit

upon all flesh; and your sons and your daughters shall prophesy, your old men shall dream dreams, your young men shall see visions:

29 And also upon the servants and upon the handmaids in those days will I pour out my spirit.

30 And I will shew wonders in the heavens and in the earth, blood, and fire, and pillars of smoke.

31 The sun shall be turned into darkness, and the moon into blood, before the great and the terrible day of the LORD come. (KJV)

Acts 2:16-21

16 But this is that which was spoken by the prophet Joel;

17 And it shall come to pass in the last days, saith God, I will pour out of my Spirit upon all flesh: and your sons and your daughters shall prophesy, and your young men shall see visions, and your old men shall dream dreams:

18 And on my servants and on my handmaidens I will pour out in those days of my Spirit; and they shall prophesy:

19 And I will shew wonders in heaven above, and signs in the earth beneath; blood, and fire, and vapour of smoke:

20 The sun shall be turned into darkness, and the moon into blood, before that great and notable day of the Lord come:

21 And it shall come to pass, that whosoever shall call on the name of the Lord shall be saved. (KJV)

"And she brought forth a man child, who was to rule all nations with a rod of iron." According to *Strong's Greek Dictionary*, the English word "man" comes from the root Greek word "arrhen" or "arsen" and is translated in the *King James Version* as "male" or "man." Likewise, the word "child" is derived from the Greek word "huios," and again, according to *Strong's Greek Dictionary* is "apparently a primary word; a son (sometimes of animals), used very widely of immediate, remote or figuratively, kinship... and translated by KJV as child, foal, son."

Generally, when two nouns are written side by side as in this case, they are written in the same gender so as to maintain harmony and consistency. However, in this particular verse, the actual literal form of the Greek word "arsen" is in the neuter gender, not masculine; if the masculine gender had been intended, then the masculine variation of the root word "arsen" would have been employed, i.e., "arsena." So, in other words, we have the neuter "arsen" linked beside the masculine "huios." As further proof that the Greek text intended for the word "man" to be in the neuter gender in this instance, the word "man" in verse 13 further down in this same passage reverts back to its masculine form, "arsena."

Therefore, we must conclude God wanted to reveal that the manchild is a son (born in a mere moment) with the spiritual strength and maturity and wisdom of an adult man, fully capable of doing his (their) assigned tasks while God finalizes His redemption of the earth and the universe in the apocalyptic events about to unfold. Yet, the usual masculinity of the word "man" was deliberately downplayed and de-emphasized in verse 5 by using its neuter form. Accordingly, the manchild is not a man or even a group of men and women, but rather, a large group of individuals who are all members of one body, the true church of God, who are perfected by God to be like Christ. (Eph. 4:13).

Sometimes people will quote the following passage as proof that the manchild represents Jesus (born out of the nation or woman, Israel):

Isaiah 66:7
7 Before she travailed, she brought forth; before her pain came, she was delivered of a man child. (KJV)

Although scholars generally agree this passage refers to Jesus being born from Israel, please note one huge discrepancy between this passage and Revelation 12:5. In this passage, the manchild (Jesus) is born first, then — and only then — does the woman (Israel) travail with pain (which is Israel's destruction by the Romans in 70 A.D. for rejecting Jesus as their Messiah). In stark contrast, the sunclad woman in Revelation 12 first travails with pain to be delivered (the final great apostasy which takes place immediately before the Rapture), and then only after the travailing, does she finally give birth to the manchild (the Raptured church). Obviously, the manchild pictured here in this Revelation about the future does not represent an historical fulfillment; it is the Rapture!

The "manchild" represents Christians who are "CAUGHT-UP" (I Thess. 4:16, 17) (Rev. 12:5) at the time of the Rapture. He (saints) will rule with a "rod of iron," as noted in the following passages:

Revelation 12:5
5 And she brought forth a man child, who was to rule all nations with a

rod of iron: and her child was caught up unto God, and to his throne. (KJV)

Revelation 2:26-28

26 And he that overcometh, and keepeth my works unto the end, to him will I give power over the nations:

27 And he shall rule them with a rod of iron; as the vessels of a potter shall they be broken to shivers: even as I received of my Father.

28 And I will give him the morning star. (KJV)

1 Cor. 6:2

2 Do ye not know that the saints shall judge the world? and if the world shall be judged by you, are ye unworthy to judge the smallest matters? (KJV)

Ps. 149:5-9

5 Let the saints be joyful in glory: let them sing aloud upon their beds.

6 Let the high praises of God be in their mouth, and a twoedged sword in their hand;

7 To execute vengeance upon the heathen, and punishments upon the people;

8 To bind their kings with chains, and their nobles with fetters of iron;

9 To execute upon them the judgment written: this honour have all his saints. Praise ye the LORD. (KJV)

Daniel 7:21-22

21 I beheld, and the same horn made war with the saints, and prevailed against them;

22 Until the Ancient of days came, and judgment was given to the saints of the most High; and the time came that the saints possessed the kingdom. (KJV)

It should be noted that a woman travailing in birth is utilized in yet another New Testament passage, and there it also refers to the Rapture:

I Thess. 5:1-10

1 But of the times and the seasons, brethren, ye have no need that I write unto you.

2 For yourselves know perfectly that the day of the Lord so cometh as a thief in the night.

3 For when they shall say, Peace and safety; then sudden destruction cometh upon them, as travail upon a woman with child; and they shall not escape.

4 But ye, brethren, are not in darkness, that that day should overtake you as a thief.

5 Ye are all the children of light, and the children of the day: we are not of the night, nor of darkness.

6 Therefore let us not sleep, as do others; but let us watch and be sober.

7 For they that sleep sleep in the night; and they that be drunken are drunken in the night.

8 But let us, who are of the day, be sober, putting on the breastplate of faith and love; and for an helmet, the hope of salvation.

9 For God hath not appointed us to wrath, but to obtain salvation by our Lord Jesus Christ,

10 Who died for us, that, whether we wake or sleep, we should live together with him. (KJV)

I Thess. 4:15-17

15 For this we say unto you by the word of the Lord, that we which are alive and remain unto the coming of the Lord shall not prevent them which are asleep.

16 For the Lord himself shall descend from heaven with a shout, with the voice of the archangel, and with the trump of God: and the dead in Christ shall rise first:

17 Then we which are alive and remain shall be caught up together with them in the clouds, to meet the Lord in the air: and so shall we ever be with the Lord. (KJV)

"War In Heaven." The "voice of the archangel" is a reference to Michael, the archangel. He and his angels will appear with the Lord at the time of the Rapture, the timing of which is a secret so that Satan and his minions can not interfere with events. The sudden, "surprise" Rapture of the "manchild" saints will trigger an extraordinary war in the heavenlies as Satan attempts to destroy Christian believers as they are translated or resurrected into Heaven. But, the archangel Michael and his angels will wage war against Satan and his angels in an awesome, supernatural battle of epic proportions. This final conflict in Heaven not only will provide safe passage for believers as they are transported into Heaven, but Satan and his angels will be cast out and banished from the heavens forever.

Daniel 8:9-10
9 And out of one of them came forth a little horn, which waxed exceeding great, toward the south, and toward the east, and toward the pleasant land.
10 And it waxed great, even to the host of heaven; and it cast down some of the host and of the stars to the ground, and stamped upon them. (KJV)

Daniel 12:1
1 And at that time shall Michael stand up, the great prince which standeth for the children of thy people: and there shall be a time of trouble, such as never was since there was a nation even to that same time: and at that time thy people shall be delivered, every one that shall be found written in the book. (KJV)

Hag. 2:6-7
6 For thus saith the LORD of hosts; Yet once, it is a little while, and I will shake the heavens, and the earth, and the sea, and the dry land;
7 And I will shake all nations, and the desire of all nations shall come: and I will fill this house with glory, saith the LORD of hosts. (KJV)

Heb. 12:26-27
26 Whose voice then shook the earth: but now he hath promised, saying, Yet once more I shake not the earth only, but also heaven.
27 And this word, Yet once more, signifieth the removing of those things that are shaken, as of things that are made, that those things which cannot be shaken may remain. (KJV)

Just as soon as Christians are Raptured, the condition of the church becomes one of desperation, symbolized by a "wilderness" experience. (ALL subject-matter is symbolic so as to be consistent in the method of interpretation.) The dragon (Satan; Rev. 12:9) then persecutes the "remnant of her seed" (tribulation saints). We also are told that Satan sends out a devastating flood of persecution for a period of three and one-half years. (Rev. 12:6) (Rev. 12:15-17).

"A great red dragon, having seven heads and ten horns, and seven crowns upon his heads." The seven-headed dragon presented in the above scriptural passage represents Satan, as confirmed in verse 9. This symbolic dragon is somewhat analogous to the symbolic seven-headed beast which is portrayed in both Revelation 13 and 17 — with several important differences. Whereas the seven-headed dragon represents Satan exclusively, the seven-headed beast is used to symbolize both Satan and Antichrist, a matter we will discuss more fully, later. In both symbolic images, however, the seven heads represent the seven major world empires which oppress Israel at one time or another down throughout history. Likewise, whereas the seven-headed dragon is wearing crowns on all seven of its heads, in Revelation 13, the seven-headed beast is wearing crowns only on the ten horns of the seventh head. By comparison, the seven-headed beast in Revelation 17 is not wearing any crowns at all on its seven heads and ten horns.

Revelation 17:12 indicates that the ten horns are crowned on the seven-headed beast in Revelation 13 because both the beast Antichrist and the ten-horn kings have power and authority at that point in time, whereas the seven-headed beast and the ten horns in Revelation 17 were not yet empowered at the time of John's Revelation. That is why, in Revelation 17, John said that the seven mountains or heads of the beast represent "seven kings: five are fallen, and one is and the other is not yet come, and when he cometh, he must continue a short space." (Rev. 17:10). Similarly in Revelation 17:8, "the beast that was, and is not, and yet is." Quite obviously these statements correlate perfectly with the recorded history of the seven biblical world empires! At the time John wrote Revelation, five of the seven world empires (Egypt, Assyria, Babylon, Persia, and Greece) were history, which matches the phrase "five are fallen." Rome was the existent empire at the time of his revelation, hence the phrase "and one is." Likewise, the empire of the Antichrist was future then, even as it is now at the time these words are being written, thereby matching the scriptural phrase which reads as follows: "the other is not yet come, and when he cometh, he must continue a short space."

As we have demonstrated during our analysis of Revelation, chapters 4-11 in Revelation narrate a sequential series of post-Rapture events which are parallel in time to the events portrayed in Revelation 12-16. Both accounts begin with the pre-tribulation Rapture, then correlate with each other through a long series of apocalyptic events which, in each case, culminate in the Battle of Armageddon and the Return of Christ. Furthermore, it is important to note that all of the events portrayed in Revelation 4-11 and 12-16 happen in a very specific time-frame relative to all of the other events which occur. Many of them even are numbered in their sequence of occurrence within the first parallel account. Accordingly, since all seven heads of the dragon are crowned, thereby indicating power and authority, before the manchild Christians are Raptured to Heaven, all seven biblical world empires must exist at one time or another before the Rapture. Since the seventh empire is the empire of Antichrist, it obviously has to be in existence before the Rapture can occur. Which means, of course, that the Antichrist will appear before the pre-tribulation Rapture to inspire the final great apostasy!

The Seven-Headed Beast

Revelation 13:1-4

1 And I stood upon the sand of the sea, and saw a beast rise up out of the sea, having seven heads and ten horns, and upon his horns ten crowns, and upon his heads the name of blasphemy.

2 And the beast which I saw was like unto a leopard, and his feet were as the feet of a bear, and his mouth as the mouth of a lion: and the dragon gave him his power, and his seat, and great authority.

3 And I saw one of his heads as it were wounded to death; and his deadly wound was healed: and all the world wondered after the beast.

4 And they worshipped the dragon which gave power unto the beast: and they worshipped the beast, saying, Who is like unto the beast? who is able to make war with him? (KJV)

As we saw in an earlier chapter of this book, there are several clues which help us to identify the "beast" portrayed in both Revelation 13 and 17. Therefore, first, please note verse 8 in Revelation 17, which reads as follows: "The beast that...shall ascend out of the bottomless pit and go into perdition." Obviously there is ONLY one individual mentioned anywhere in the Bible who meets all of these requirements, and that person is none other than Satan:

Revelation 20:1-3, 7, 10

1 And I saw an angel come down from heaven, having the key of the bottomless pit and a great chain in his hand.

2 And he laid hold on the dragon, that old serpent, which is the Devil, and Satan, and bound him a thousand years,

3 And cast him into the bottomless pit, and shut him up, and set a seal upon him, that he should deceive the nations no more, till the thousand years should be fulfilled: and after that he must be loosed a little season.

7 And when the thousand years are expired, Satan shall be loosed out of his prison,

10 And the devil that deceived them was cast into the lake of fire and brimstone, where the beast and the false prophet are, and shall be tormented day and night for ever and ever. (KJV)

Satan is the only personage portrayed in the Bible as going into perdition after ascending out of the bottomless pit. Although II Thessalonians 2:3 calls Antichrist the son of perdition, i.e., the son of Satan, or the son of destruction, the Antichrist never is called the man of perdition, nor does he ever ascend from out of the bottomless pit to go into perdition. Instead, the Antichrist literally is killed at the Battle of Armageddon, then immediately resurrected as part of the Second Resurrection and thrown into the eternal Lake of Fire.

Verse 9 continues: "The seven heads (of the beast) are seven mountains." It is only logical to conclude that the heads of the beast are symbolic just as the beast itself is symbolic. Mountain, in Bible prophecy, usually represents a kingdom or empire:

Daniel 2:44, 45

44 And in the days of these kings shall the God of heaven set up a kingdom, which shall never be destroyed: and the kingdom shall not be left to other people, but it shall break in pieces and consume all these kingdoms, and it shall stand for ever.

45 Forasmuch as thou sawest that the stone was cut out of the mountain without hands, and that it brake in pieces the iron, the brass, the clay, the silver, and the gold; the great God hath made known to the king what shall come to pass hereafter: and the dream is certain, and the interpretation thereof sure. (KJV)

Micah 3:12

12 Therefore shall Zion for your sake be plowed as a field, and Jerusalem shall become heaps, and the mountain of the house as the high places of the forest. (KJV)

Micah 4:1, 2

1 But in the last days it shall come to pass, that the mountain of the house of the LORD shall be established in the top of the mountains, and it shall be exalted above the hills; and people shall flow unto it.

2 And many nations shall come, and say, Come, and let us go up to the mountain of the LORD, and to the house of the God of Jacob; and he will teach us of his ways, and we will walk in his paths: for the law shall go forth of Zion, and the word of the LORD from Jerusalem. (KJV)

Isaiah 2:1-4

1 The word that Isaiah the son of Amoz saw concerning Judah and Jerusalem.

2 And it shall come to pass in the last days, that the mountain of the LORD's house shall be established in the top of the mountains, and shall be exalted above the hills; and all nations shall flow unto it.

3 And many people shall go and say, Come ye, and let us go up to the mountain of the LORD, to the house of the God of Jacob; and he will teach us of his ways, and we will walk in his paths: for out of Zion shall go forth the law, and the word of the LORD from Jerusalem.

4 And he shall judge among the nations, and shall rebuke many people: and they shall beat their swords into plowshares, and their spears into pruninghooks: nation shall not lift up sword against nation, neither shall they learn war any more. (KJV)

Isaiah 30:29-31

29 Ye shall have a song, as in the night when a holy solemnity is kept; and gladness of heart, as when one goeth with a pipe to come into the mountain of the LORD, to the mighty One of Israel.

30 And the LORD shall cause his glorious voice to be heard, and shall shew the lighting down of his arm, with the indignation of his anger, and with the flame of a devouring fire, with scattering, and tempest, and hailstones.

31 For through the voice of the LORD shall the Assyrian be beaten

down, which smote with a rod. (KJV)

Zechariah 8:3
3 Thus saith the LORD; I am returned unto Zion, and will dwell in the midst of Jerusalem: and Jerusalem shall be called a city of truth; and the mountain of the LORD of hosts the holy mountain. (KJV)

Therefore, these mountains of the beast represent world empires which oppress Israel during Bible times. This is further verified by John, himself, who said the seven mountains or heads represent "seven kings: five are fallen, and one is and the other is not yet come, and when he cometh, he must continue a short space." (Rev. 17:10). Compare this statement in verse 10 with a similar statement in verse 8: "the beast that was, and is not, and yet is." These statements correlate perfectly with the recorded history of the seven world empires! At the time John wrote Revelation, five of the seven world empires (Egypt, Assyria, Babylon, Persia, and Greece) were history, which matches the phrase "five are fallen." Rome was the existent empire at that point in time, hence the phrase "and one is." Likewise, the empire of the Antichrist was future then, even as it is now at the time these words are being written, thus matching the scriptural phrase which reads as follows: "the other is not yet come, and when he cometh, he must continue a short space."

Note verse 11: John states "the beast...is the eighth (empire), and is OF the seven (world empires)." The meaning here is two-fold. First, Satan INDIRECTLY controls the seven world empires existent at various times BEFORE the Rapture, but AFTER the Rapture he DIRECTLY controls an eighth empire which is actually a continuation of the seventh empire. Second, please note also that the beast in Revelation 17 must represent a personage who is alive during the time of all seven of the world empires identified above because the seven heads are an integral part of the beast himself! Therefore, the beast in Revelation 17 represents Satan, and the seven heads represent the seven world empires which Satan INDIRECTLY controls before the pre-tribulation Rapture!

However, in both Revelation 13 and 17, the "seven-headed beast" also symbolizes the Antichrist. As confusing as this may seem since we have just proven that the "seven-headed beast" represents Satan, we know this to be true for several reasons. For instance, in Revelation 12, the "dragon," i.e., Satan, has all seven of his heads crowned, thus indicating power and authority over all seven world empires which are existent before the Rapture. But, in Revelation 13, only the "ten horns" on the seventh head of the beast are crowned, thus indicating a personage, namely the Antichrist, who controls the seventh world empire, but not the other six which are history. Likewise, in Revelation 13, Satan is called the "dragon" whenever it is necessary to distinguish a difference between the Antichrist and Satan. Then also, we know that the "beast" in Revelation 13 is a man because both personal attributes and accomplishments of the Antichrist are ascribed to the "beast" throughout the chapter. Therefore, since the symbolism of the seven-headed beast is associated with both the Antichrist and Satan in these scriptures, we must conclude that two different personalities simultaneously occupy the same physical body (from the time of the Rapture until Armageddon).

Revelation 13:1-4

1 And I stood upon the sand of the sea, and saw a beast rise up out of the sea, having seven heads and ten horns, and upon his horns ten crowns, and upon his heads the name of blasphemy.

2 And the beast which I saw was like unto a leopard, and his feet were as the feet of a bear, and his mouth as the mouth of a lion: and the dragon gave him his power, and his seat, and great authority.

3 And I saw one of his heads as it were wounded to death; and his deadly wound was healed: and all the world wondered after the beast.

4 And they worshipped the dragon which gave power unto the beast: and they worshipped the beast, saying, Who is like unto the beast? who is able to make war with him? (KJV)

In summary, the "beast" represents both Satan and the man Antichrist, whereas the "dragon" symbolizes Satan alone. Likewise, the "seven heads" represent the seven world empires indirectly controlled by Satan, whereas the ten crowned-horns of the seventh head represent the Roman Empire countries which form the nucleus of the "empire" of Antichrist. Furthermore, just as we saw in Daniel's visions, not only are the modern-day countries of the old Roman Empire associated with the Antichrist through symbolism in this passage, but the old Grecian, Persian and Babylonian empires are, too, because in the passage above, it describes the beast as "like unto a leopard," with symbolic feet "as the feet of a bear," and a symbolic mouth "as the mouth of a lion." Then finally, we also observe that the "sea" or "water" from which the "beast" emerges is said quite clearly to represent the masses of humanity throughout the world. (Rev. 17:15).

Furthermore, since the symbolism of the seven-headed beast is associated with both Satan and the Antichrist, this coupling of personalities within one symbolic image clearly illustrates the dual nature of two separate personalities operating within one human body. This also explains why only the seventh head (Antichrist) is "wounded to death," while the other six heads are history. As confirmation, a dual personality operating within one body is even implied by several other scriptures! In each case, actions and/or attributes of BOTH Satan and Antichrist are ascribed to the same individual:

Revelation 11:7
7 And when they shall have finished their testimony, the beast that ascendeth out of the bottomless pit shall make war against them, and shall overcome them, and kill them. (KJV)

The context indicates it is Antichrist who wars against the Two Witnesses after invading Israel. Yet, this passage identifies the beast (Antichrist) as one who will "ascend out of the bottomless pit," an obvious reference to Satan. (Rev. 20:1-3, 7-10).

Revelation 17:11
11 And the beast that was, and is not, even he is the eighth, and is of the seven, and goeth into perdition. (KJV)

Previously we proved this beast to be Satan ("goeth into perdition"), but the context (Rev. 17:12, 13) indicates it is also the Antichrist:

Revelation 17:12, 13
12 And the ten horns which thou sawest are ten kings, which have received no kingdom as yet; but receive power as kings one hour with the beast.
13 These have one mind, and shall give their power and strength unto the beast. (KJV)

Now compare likewise with Ezekiel 28:11-16:

Ezekiel 28:11-16

11 Moreover the word of the LORD came unto me, saying,

12 Son of man, take up a lamentation upon the king of Tyrus, and say unto him, Thus saith the Lord GOD; Thou sealest up the sum, full of wisdom, and perfect in beauty.

13 Thou hast been in Eden the garden of God; every precious stone was thy covering, the sardius, topaz, and the diamond, the beryl, the onyx, and the jasper, the sapphire, the emerald, and the carbuncle, and gold: the workmanship of thy tabrets and of thy pipes was prepared in thee in the day that thou wast created.

14 Thou art the anointed cherub that covereth; and I have set thee so: thou wast upon the holy mountain of God; thou hast walked up and down in the midst of the stones of fire.

15 Thou wast perfect in thy ways from the day that thou wast created, till iniquity was found in thee.

16 By the multitude of thy merchandise they have filled the midst of thee with violence, and thou hast sinned: therefore I will cast thee as profane out of the mountain of God: and I will destroy thee, O covering cherub, from the midst of the stones of fire. (KJV)

Previously we proved the passage above to be an obvious reference to Satan. Yet, the next several verses allude to both Satan and Antichrist (e.g., "bring thee to ashes in the sight of all them that behold thee," etc.):

Ezekiel 28:17-19

17 Thine heart was lifted up because of thy beauty, thou hast corrupted thy wisdom by reason of thy brightness: I will cast thee to the ground, I will lay thee before kings, that they may behold thee.

18 Thou hast defiled thy sanctuaries by the multitude of thine iniquities, by the iniquity of thy traffick; therefore will I bring forth a fire from the midst of thee, it shall devour thee, and I will bring thee to ashes upon the earth in the sight of all them that behold thee.

19 All they that know thee among the people shall be astonished at thee: thou shalt be a terror, and never shalt thou be any more. (KJV)

Likewise for the following passage in Isaiah 14:12-20. First, Satan:

12 How art thou fallen from heaven, O Lucifer, son of the morning!

how art thou cut down to the ground, which didst weaken the nations!

13 For thou hast said in thine heart, I will ascend into heaven, I will exalt my throne above the stars of God: I will sit also upon the mount of the congregation, in the sides of the north:

14 I will ascend above the heights of the clouds; I will be like the most High. (KJV)

Then, both Satan and Antichrist:

Isaiah 14:15-20

15 Yet thou shalt be brought down to hell, to the sides of the pit.

16 They that see thee shall narrowly look upon thee, and consider thee, saying, Is this the man that made the earth to tremble, that did shake kingdoms;

17 That made the world as a wilderness, and destroyed the cities thereof; that opened not the house of his prisoners?

18 All the kings of the nations, even all of them, lie in glory, every one in his own house.

19 But thou art cast out of thy grave like an abominable branch, and as the raiment of those that are slain, thrust through with a sword, that go down to the stones of the pit; as a carcase trodden under feet.

20 Thou shalt not be joined with them in burial, because thou hast destroyed thy land, and slain thy people: the seed of evildoers shall never be renowned. (KJV)

"Wounded to death." Many times it is speculated that the Antichrist will actually die from his deadly wound and then be resurrected back to life by Satan. Supposedly, this will happen immediately after the Rapture when Scripture tells us that Satan will possess and indwell the physical body of the Antichrist until near the end of Armageddon when he is destroyed by Christ and then resurrected into the eternal Lake Of Fire. However, to the best of my knowledge, there is no scriptural support for the idea that Satan truly has the power to raise people from the dead. When it is stated in Revelation 13 that the Antichrist is wounded to death, we should note very carefully that this statement only means that he will be inflicted with a deadly wound; never is it said that he will die at that point in time. Since the Bible is full of statements which describe the deaths of individuals very clearly and without any equivocation, it seems reasonable to suppose that if this scripture had intended to say that the Antichrist will be killed then, it would have done so plainly and unequivocally.

Furthermore, as we saw in chapter 3 of this book, Daniel 11:20-21 does not lend any support to this theory, either. Instead, an analysis of the original Hebrew words used in this scriptural passage clearly indicate a reference to the poison assassination of the Syrian ruler, Seleucus IV, who eventually was succeeded by Antiochus Epiphanes through the use of flattery and the division of spoils from the more prosperous regions of his kingdom. Likewise, since the Bible clearly portrays Christ resurrecting Lazarus back to life, it is likely that the Bible also would state very plainly that the Antichrist will be resurrected, too, if such were to be the case. But, instead, after noting that the Antichrist will be inflicted with a deadly wound, it goes on to say that the deadly wound will be healed, causing the whole world to marvel.

The obvious question is why Satan would even be interested in sharing a frail human body with the man Antichrist? The answer probably is found in a passage we just read, namely Isaiah 14:12-14. The truth is, Satan for eons of time has desired to "be like the Most High" and receive worship; controlling the body of a world leader would be an obvious way to realize said objective. Furthermore, after he and his angels are banished from the heavenlies and literally cast down to the earth, he will not have very many options still available to him anyway.

Revelation 13:5-18

5 And there was given unto him a mouth speaking great things and blasphemies; and power was given unto him to continue forty and two months.

6 And he opened his mouth in blasphemy against God, to blaspheme his name, and his tabernacle, and them that dwell in heaven.

7 And it was given unto him to make war with the saints, and to overcome them: and power was given him over all kindreds, and tongues, and nations.

8 And all that dwell upon the earth shall worship him, whose names are not written in the book of life of the Lamb slain from the foundation of the world.

9 If any man have an ear, let him hear.

10 He that leadeth into captivity shall go into captivity: he that killeth with the sword must be killed with the sword. Here is the patience and the

faith of the saints.

11 And I beheld another beast coming up out of the earth; and he had two horns like a lamb, and he spake as a dragon.

12 And he exerciseth all the power of the first beast before him, and causeth the earth and them which dwell therein to worship the first beast, whose deadly wound was healed.

13 And he doeth great wonders, so that he maketh fire come down from heaven on the earth in the sight of men,

14 And deceiveth them that dwell on the earth by the means of those miracles which he had power to do in the sight of the beast; saying to them that dwell on the earth, that they should make an image to the beast, which had the wound by a sword, and did live.

15 And he had power to give life unto the image of the beast, that the image of the beast should both speak, and cause that as many as would not worship the image of the beast should be killed.

16 And he causeth all, both small and great, rich and poor, free and bond, to receive a mark in their right hand, or in their foreheads:

17 And that no man might buy or sell, save he that had the mark, or the name of the beast, or the number of his name.

18 Here is wisdom. Let him that hath understanding count the number of the beast: for it is the number of a man; and his number is Six hundred threescore and six. (KJV)

Here it is stated that the Antichrist will persecute new Christian converts for a period of three and one-half years, and that he will be successful in killing many of them even though many others will avoid execution by fleeing or hiding from his jurisdiction. (Rev. 13:5-10) (Luke 21:16). Meanwhile, the "False Prophet" will begin performing a variety of extraordinary miracles which will be as impressive as the ones previously effected by the Antichrist. In fact, these miracles will be so impressive that apparently they will astound and deceive even technologically-sophisticated people throughout the world. Concurrently, he also will bring to "life" (perhaps through the use of supernatural power) an image of the Antichrist which everyone will be forced to worship under an absolute penalty of death. Likewise, everyone will also be forced to swear allegiance and loyalty to the Antichrist by accepting a special mark on their forehead or right hand that displays either the name or the number (666) of the beast (Antichrist). Then, anyone who will not accept this mark, but still manages to evade execution (beheading; Rev. 20:4), will find it impossible legally to buy or sell. So, if current trends in technology continue unabated, and economic transactions at that point in time are controlled through computers in a society that is "cashless" due to the use of "credit" or "electronic" money, then dissidents will find it very difficult to survive.

"Count the number of the beast: for it is the number of a man; and his number is Six hundred threescore and six..." The most favorite pastime activity for many students of Bible prophecy centers around finding the many different ways in which numbers can be assigned to letters of the alphabet in different languages and then ascertaining how the names of prominent people can be manipulated to add up to 666 in one language or another. However, I believe it is a waste of time trying to discover the identity of the Antichrist by playing such number games — games in which it may be fun to indulge, but which tarnish the image and credibility of Bible prophecy after people, especially unbelievers, tire of hearing about the endless parade of possibilities, including the pope, Ronald Reagan, Henry Kissinger, Prince Charles, Bill Clinton, etc., etc..

So, what does the infamous six trilogy really mean? Based on my best information and scriptural understanding, I believe the primary meaning of the number sequence, 666, is symbolic in nature. Just as the number seven represents or symbolizes completeness in the Bible, so likewise does the number six symbolize man. For instance, throughout biblical scriptures, from Genesis to the prophetic book of Revelation, the number seven occurs quite frequently in a context denoting completeness, and in Revelation, examples of this can be seen in the seven churches, seven spirits, seven stars, seven seals, seven vials, seven trumpets. In a similar vein, the number six, in Scripture, represents man. In prophetic passages we can see this illustrated by the following examples:

Revelation 4:8

8 And the four beasts had each of them six wings about him; and they were full of eyes within: and they rest not day and night, saying, Holy, holy, holy, Lord God Almighty, which was, and is, and is to come. (KJV)

Previously we demonstrated with abundant scriptural proof that the "four beasts" in view here in this passage are groups of saints who are in Heaven immediately after the Rapture. The reason that each beast or group of saints has six wings about them resides in the nature of the identity of these beasts, namely their humanity. Thus, the number six is used as part of a simile in a prophetic passage once again to represent man. This is further demonstrated in Ezekiel's description of the new, eternal Temple of God which will be built in Jerusalem during the Millennial Reign of Christ Jesus on the earth:

Ezekiel 40:5
5 And behold a wall on the outside of the house round about, and in the man's hand a measuring reed of six cubits long by the cubit and an hand breadth: so he measured the breadth of the building, one reed; and the height, one reed. (KJV)

Ezekiel 40:12
12 The space also before the little chambers was one cubit on this side, and the space was one cubit on that side: and the little chambers were six cubits on this side, and six cubits on that side. (KJV)

Ezekiel 41:1
1 Afterward he brought me to the temple, and measured the posts, six cubits broad on the one side, and six cubits broad on the other side, which was the breadth of the tabernacle. (KJV)

Ezekiel 41:3
3 Then went he inward, and measured the post of the door, two cubits; and the door, six cubits; and the breadth of the door, seven cubits. (KJV)

Ezekiel 41:5
5 After he measured the wall of the house, six cubits; and the breadth of every side chamber, four cubits, round about the house on every side. (KJV)

Ezekiel 41:8
8 I saw also the height of the house round about: the foundations of the side chambers were a full reed of six great cubits. (KJV)

Ezekiel 46:1
1 Thus saith the Lord GOD; The gate of the inner court that looketh

toward the east shall be shut the six working days; but on the sabbath it shall be opened, and in the day of the new moon it shall be opened. (KJV)

Ezekiel 46:4
4 And the burnt offering that the prince shall offer unto the LORD in the sabbath day shall be six lambs without blemish, and a ram without blemish. (KJV)

Ezekiel 46:6
6 And in the day of the new moon it shall be a young bullock without blemish, and six lambs, and a ram: they shall be without blemish. (KJV)

All of the above passages in Ezekiel deal with some aspect of the new temple or the sacrifices which will be offered there to symbolize and commemorate the finished, substitutionary work of Christ on the cross which enabled redemption from sin for all of mankind. Likewise, a cursory glance at these scriptures will show that the number six is associated with the temple repeatedly throughout the descriptions as a way of symbolizing man and his dependency on Divine providence and grace. Thus, we must conclude that the number six is used in the Bible as a way of symbolizing man.

Therefore, just as the number six represents man, so likewise do the triple digits of six, i.e., 666, represent people's rebellion against God in its ultimate expression as the evil counterfeit trinity comprised of Satan, Antichrist and the False Prophet. Sometimes it is thought that the number 666 symbolizes other things such as the UPC (Universal Product Code) computer bar symbols stamped on the products we buy which always include the numbers "666" in their coding. However, the actual meaning intended by Scripture is symbolic in nature in the same way that the number six, representing man, will find its symbolic meaning expressed in the dimensions for God's new, eternal temple which will be built in Jerusalem during the Millennium. Although the number 666 may be associated with things such as UPC codes, this is simply another way for the symbolic message inherently carried by the numbers 666 to find their symbolic expression or manifestation in modern life. "Here is wisdom. Let him that hath understanding count the number of the beast."

Concerning the "mark" referenced in Revelation 13, it is translated from the Greek word CHARAGMA, and is defined by *Strong's Hebrew-*

Greek Dictionary in the following manner:

5480 charagma (khar'-ag-mah);
from the same as 5482; a scratch or etching, i.e. stamp (as a badge of servitude), or sculptured figure (statue):
KJV— graven, mark.

Many recent news reports describe in some detail the many marvels of modern technology relative to microchip implants in human beings. These microchips are at least 200 times smaller in size than a strand of human hair, and can be implanted or injected into the human body with the use of a hypodermic needle. They have an almost unlimited number of uses in modern society, including the ability to provide positive personal identification of people and animals which can be tracked via satellite technology. Although these microchips are, in reality, powerful, self-contained computers that are powered by temperature changes in the human body and can be reprogrammed via satellite to perform additional functions, they are being sold to an unsuspecting general public only as a means of locating lost or missing children; nothing is ever said about the tremendous potential for controlling people through such microchip technology. Obviously because these microchips have the ability to store large amounts of information on individuals which can be updated at any time via satellite, it would be very easy for a government to implement electronic control over people in all of their social and economic activities by utilizing such devices.

Accordingly, computer microchips could prove ultimately to be the fulfillment of Revelation 13 when it speaks of the "mark," i.e., a scratch or etching designed to be a mark or badge of servitude which people will be forced to accept as a sign of allegiance and loyalty to the Antichrist. That is why this mark will include the numbers 666. The mark will be a symbolic way of expressing allegiance to the symbolic message inherently carried by the numbers 666. However, one point I want to emphasize is this: God will not "trick" people into accepting the mark of the beast. When the mark of the beast is actually implemented throughout society, there will be no doubt in anyone's mind as to what is going on. Therefore, Christians need not worry about utilizing modern electronic conveniences for fear of unknowingly accepting the mark of the beast (although they may wish to limit their usage of such conveniences for the sake of privacy and personal freedom). When the mark of the beast is actually instituted as a legal requirement, everyone will know precisely what is happening and what the eternal consequences will be if one accepts it. (Rev. 14:6-11).

Matthew 24:7-14

7 For nation shall rise against nation, and kingdom against kingdom: and there shall be famines, and pestilences, and earthquakes, in divers places.

8 All these are the beginning of sorrows.

9 Then shall they deliver you up to be afflicted, and shall kill you: and ye shall be hated of all nations for my name's sake.

10 And then shall many be offended, and shall betray one another, and shall hate one another.

11 And many false prophets shall rise, and shall deceive many.

12 And because iniquity shall abound, the love of many shall wax cold.

13 But he that shall endure unto the end, the same shall be saved.

14 And this gospel of the kingdom shall be preached in all the world for a witness unto all nations; and then shall the end come. (KJV)

Mark 13:8-13

8 For nation shall rise against nation, and kingdom against kingdom: and there shall be earthquakes in divers places, and there shall be famines and troubles: these are the beginnings of sorrows.

9 But take heed to yourselves: for they shall deliver you up to councils; and in the synagogues ye shall be beaten: and ye shall be brought before rulers and kings for my sake, for a testimony against them.

10 And the gospel must first be published among all nations.

11 But when they shall lead you, and deliver you up, take no thought beforehand what ye shall speak, neither do ye premeditate: but whatsoever shall be given you in that hour, that speak ye: for it is not ye that speak, but the Holy Ghost.

12 Now the brother shall betray the brother to death, and the father the son; and children shall rise up against their parents, and shall cause them to be put to death.

13 And ye shall be hated of all men for my name's sake: but he that shall endure unto the end, the same shall be saved. (KJV)

Revelation 13:11-12

11 And I beheld another beast coming up out of the earth; and he had two horns like a lamb, and he spake as a dragon.

12 And he exerciseth all the power of the first beast before him, and causeth the earth and them which dwell therein to worship the first beast, whose deadly wound was healed. (KJV)

This second "beast" also is a man because personal pronouns are used to refer to him just as they are used when referring to the Antichrist. However, this False Prophet seemingly differs from the first beast, Antichrist, in the fact that he originates or springs up from the "earth" rather than from the "sea." That is why some people have speculated that perhaps he will ascend from the netherworld or the world of the dead, departed spirits. But, just as the words "water" and "sea" can symbolize the masses of humanity in biblical prophecy, so likewise can the word "earth" symbolize the masses of humanity as a comparison of scriptures in Daniel 7 will prove:

Daniel 7:3

3 And four great beasts came up from the sea, diverse one from another. (KJV)

Daniel 7:17

17 These great beasts, which are four, are four kings, which shall arise out of the earth. (KJV)

"Two horns like a lamb." These two horns apparently symbolize or represent two major world religious powers (rather than political-military kingdoms) which he dominates and controls since they are characterized as being "like a lamb." They seem to correlate with the "two women" in the passage we saw earlier in Zechariah which portrays the "wicked woman" (Satan's Church) flying to the "land of Shinar" which is, of course, Babylon, in order to establish its new religious headquarters ("to build it an house"):

Zechariah 5:5-11

5 Then the angel that talked with me went forth, and said unto me, Lift up now thine eyes, and see what is this that goeth forth.

6 And I said, What is it? And he said, This is an ephah that goeth forth. He said moreover, This is their resemblance through all the earth.

7 And, behold, there was lifted up a talent of lead: and this is a woman that sitteth in the midst of the ephah.

8 And he said, This is wickedness. And he cast it into the midst of the ephah; and he cast the weight of lead upon the mouth thereof.

9 Then lifted I up mine eyes, and looked, and, behold, there came out two women, and the wind was in their wings; for they had wings like the wings of a stork: and they lifted up the ephah between the earth and the heaven.

10 Then said I to the angel that talked with me, Whither do these bear the ephah?

11 And he said unto me, To build it an house in the land of Shinar: and it shall be established, and set there upon her own base. (KJV)

"Ephah." A measure of about one bushel and three pints.

"Talent of Lead." More than 122 lbs., which was an extreme amount of weight for a lid covering the top of an ephah basket. Despite the weight of the lid, that still did not hold the "woman of wickedness" down, thus illustrating the power of evil.

"Two Women." It is possible that the "two women" who carry the "wicked woman" to Babylon represent two major world religions, perhaps Islam and "professing" Christianity consisting of Roman Catholicism and mainline Protestant denominations. The "wings" possibly refer to the mode of travel employed, namely air-travel by modern airplanes.

"Then shall the end come." The word "end" means the end of the "Dispensation of Grace" — not the Battle of Armageddon or the total annihilation of the earth. This means for three and one-half years after the Rapture, people still will have an opportunity to accept Christ as their personal Lord and Saviour, but after that, no one will be saved because God's period of grace and salvation will have been lifted from the earth.

Luke 21:10-19

10 Then said he unto them, Nation shall rise against nation, and kingdom against kingdom:

11 And great earthquakes shall be in divers places, and famines, and pestilences; and fearful sights and great signs shall there be from heaven.

12 But before all these, they shall lay their hands on you, and

persecute you, delivering you up to the synagogues, and into prisons, being brought before kings and rulers for my name's sake.

13 And it shall turn to you for a testimony.

14 Settle it therefore in your hearts, not to meditate before what ye shall answer:

15 For I will give you a mouth and wisdom, which all your adversaries shall not be able to gainsay nor resist.

16 And ye shall be betrayed both by parents, and brethren, and kinsfolks, and friends; and some of you shall they cause to be put to death.

17 And ye shall be hated of all men for my name's sake.

18 But there shall not an hair of your head perish.

19 In your patience possess ye your souls. (KJV)

Please note that verse 16 above states that only some of the tribulation saints will be killed by the Antichrist; those who are not killed and who also "endure unto the end" (i.e., keep their faith until the end) shall likewise be saved. (See the chart entitled *Harmony Of The Olivet Discourse With Revelation And Other Scriptures*.) These tribulation saints who evade execution by the Antichrist and who also "endure unto the end" are the "elect" who are translated at the Second Coming of Christ. (Matt. 24:31) (Mark 13:27).

144,000 Jews Again

Revelation 14:1-5

1 And I looked, and, lo, a Lamb stood on the mount Sion, and with him an hundred forty and four thousand, having his Father's name written in their foreheads.

2 And I heard a voice from heaven, as the voice of many waters, and as the voice of a great thunder: and I heard the voice of harpers harping with their harps:

3 And they sung as it were a new song before the throne, and before the four beasts, and the elders: and no man could learn that song but the hundred and forty and four thousand, which were redeemed from the earth.

4 These are they which were not defiled with women; for they are virgins. These are they which follow the Lamb whithersoever he goeth.

These were redeemed from among men, being the firstfruits unto God and to the Lamb.

5 And in their mouth was found no guile: for they are without fault before the throne of God. (KJV)

These are the same Jews who are converted to salvation during the Great Christian Tribulation. They are pictured here in this passage as they sing "a new song" to the accompaniment of music from Heaven. The fact that they are "virgins" gives us a clear indication of the very low moral values which will prevail throughout society, generally, during this period of time. Although this does not necessarily mean they are not married since that would not be a case of defilement, it might indicate that to be known as a person who abstains from sexual immorality will be a distinguishing characteristic of a Christian in a non-believing society full of rampant sexual immorality. Just as Christ represents the "first fruits" of Christian believers in general, these particular Jews represent the "first fruits" of REDEEMED Israel (Zech. 12:10-14) (Isa. 4:3) (Isa. 10:20-22) (Isa. 30:15) (Jer. 33:16) (Ezek. 39:25-29).

Completion Of The Parallel Account

The remainder of chapter 14 portrays "angels" (i.e., "messengers," in this instance, saints) flying in the sky above the earth preaching the gospel message while predicting prophetic events to the people below on earth. Some of the angels (groups of saints since only saints can judge and evangelize the world) specifically warn people upon the earth that they will face eternal punishment and damnation if they swear allegiance to the Antichrist by taking his "mark." For that reason, multitudes of people who are not Christians will avoid taking the mark of the beast, which is why they will be permitted to remain on the earth after Armageddon. (Zech. 14:16) (Matt. 25:31-46) (Rev. 20:3, 8; 21:3, 24, 26). Therefore, it should be noted that this teaching does not necessarily conflict with the following passages:

II Thess. 2:9-12

9 Even him, whose coming is after the working of Satan with all power and signs and lying wonders,

10 And with all deceivableness of unrighteousness in them that perish; because they received not the love of the truth, that they might be saved.

11 And for this cause God shall send them strong delusion, that they should believe a lie:

12 That they all might be damned who believed not the truth, but had pleasure in unrighteousness. (KJV)

Revelation 13:7-9

7 And it was given unto him to make war with the saints, and to overcome them: and power was given him over all kindreds, and tongues, and nations.

8 And all that dwell upon the earth shall worship him, whose names are not written in the book of life of the Lamb slain from the foundation of the world.

9 If any man have an ear, let him hear. (KJV)

Sometimes people say these two passages teach that after the Rapture there will be only two groups of people: those individuals who will accept Christ as their personal Saviour during the Great Christian Tribulation, and those who will not. However, this is not what the Bible teaches. There actually is a third group of people who do not become Christians, but neither do they swear allegiance to the Antichrist by accepting his "mark." It is these people who will be allowed to remain alive on the earth as human subjects under the rulership of Christ and the saints.

To believe otherwise is to make the message of the angel warning against acceptance of the "mark" both pointless and deceptive. It also would contradict the aforementioned passages which state, e.g., that "everyone that is left of all the nations which came against Jerusalem shall even go up from year to year to worship the king, the Lord of hosts..." Apparently, these people will love "truth" to a certain degree, or at least to a degree sufficient to keep them from being deceived into taking the mark of the beast. In that respect, religious beliefs are somewhat analogous to other aspects of life such as political beliefs; just as there are people scattered all over the political spectrum of thought, so likewise are people, then and now, scattered all over the religious spectrum of thought. It seems as if everyone ascertains and accepts "truth" to varying degrees of totality. This is how we can understand why many people will believe enough truth to avoid taking the mark of the beast, but not enough truth to become a true Christian believer in Christ Jesus. Nevertheless, any person who does not worship the Antichrist or accept his "mark" of allegiance, will have their name written in the "book of life" — not as a Christian saint, but as an ordinary human subject living on the earth within the Kingdom of God.

Revelation 14:6-20

6 And I saw another angel fly in the midst of heaven, having the everlasting gospel to preach unto them that dwell on the earth, and to every nation, and kindred, and tongue, and people,

7 Saying with a loud voice, Fear God, and give glory to him; for the hour of his judgment is come: and worship him that made heaven, and earth, and the sea, and the fountains of waters.

8 And there followed another angel, saying, Babylon is fallen, is fallen, that great city, because she made all nations drink of the wine of the wrath of her fornication.

9 And the third angel followed them, saying with a loud voice, If any man worship the beast and his image, and receive his mark in his forehead, or in his hand,

10 The same shall drink of the wine of the wrath of God, which is poured out without mixture into the cup of his indignation; and he shall be tormented with fire and brimstone in the presence of the holy angels, and in the presence of the Lamb:

11 And the smoke of their torment ascendeth up for ever and ever: and they have no rest day nor night, who worship the beast and his image, and whosoever receiveth the mark of his name.

12 Here is the patience of the saints: here are they that keep the commandments of God, and the faith of Jesus.

13 And I heard a voice from heaven saying unto me, Write, Blessed are the dead which die in the Lord from henceforth: Yea, saith the Spirit, that they may rest from their labours; and their works do follow them.

14 And I looked, and behold a white cloud, and upon the cloud one sat like unto the Son of man, having on his head a golden crown, and in his hand a sharp sickle.

15 And another angel came out of the temple, crying with a loud voice to him that sat on the cloud, Thrust in thy sickle, and reap: for the time is come for thee to reap; for the harvest of the earth is ripe.

16 And he that sat on the cloud thrust in his sickle on the earth; and the

earth was reaped.

17 And another angel came out of the temple which is in heaven, he also having a sharp sickle.

18 And another angel came out from the altar, which had power over fire; and cried with a loud cry to him that had the sharp sickle, saying, Thrust in thy sharp sickle, and gather the clusters of the vine of the earth; for her grapes are fully ripe.

19 And the angel thrust in his sickle into the earth, and gathered the vine of the earth, and cast it into the great winepress of the wrath of God.

20 And the winepress was trodden without the city, and blood came out of the winepress, even unto the horse bridles, by the space of a thousand and six hundred furlongs. (KJV)

Chapter 15 provides another glimpse of the martyred tribulation saints who are resurrected into Heaven BEFORE the seven Trumpet-Vial plagues are unleashed upon the earth! Likewise, the temple of God in Heaven is filled with smoke from the glory and power of God during the time in which the seven plagues are released upon the earth, thus symbolizing the truth that God is dealing with Israel again on the basis of their covenant relationship (Daniel's 70th Week) at that point in time:

Revelation 15:1-8

1 And I saw another sign in heaven, great and marvellous, seven angels having the seven last plagues; for in them is filled up the wrath of God.

2 And I saw as it were a sea of glass mingled with fire: and them that had gotten the victory over the beast, and over his image, and over his mark, and over the number of his name, stand on the sea of glass, having the harps of God.

3 And they sing the song of Moses the servant of God, and the song of the Lamb, saying, Great and marvellous are thy works, Lord God Almighty; just and true are thy ways, thou King of saints.

4 Who shall not fear thee, O Lord, and glorify thy name? for thou only art holy: for all nations shall come and worship before thee; for thy judgments are made manifest.

5 And after that I looked, and, behold, the temple of the tabernacle of the testimony in heaven was opened:

6 And the seven angels came out of the temple, having the seven plagues, clothed in pure and white linen, and having their breasts girded

with golden girdles.

7 And one of the four beasts gave unto the seven angels seven golden vials full of the wrath of God, who liveth for ever and ever.

8 And the temple was filled with smoke from the glory of God, and from his power; and no man was able to enter into the temple, till the seven plagues of the seven angels were fulfilled. (KJV)

Harmony Of The Parallel Accounts In The Book Of Revelation		
Chapters 4-11 parallel Chapters 12-16		
Events	**Passage**	**Passage**
Rapture	4:1-3	12:1-5
Saints In Heaven	4:4-11 5:1-14	
Satan Opposes Rapture		12:3-4
War In Heaven		12:7-8
Satan Cast To Earth		12:9-12
Four Horsemen/Gospel Preached	6:1-8	14:6-20
Persecution Of Saints		12:13-13:18
Earthquakes	6:12-17	12:15-16
After 6th Seal, Day Of Lord Begins	6:12-17	
144,000 Jews On Earth	7:1-8	14:1-5
Tribulation Saints Resurrected	7:9-17	15:1-8
1st Trumpet-Vial (Earth)	8:7	16:1-2
2nd Trumpet-Vial (Sea)	8:8-9	16:3
3rd Trumpet-Vial (Rivers)	8:10-11	16:4-7
4th Trumpet-Vial (Sun)	8:12-13	16:8-9
5th Trumpet-Vial (Seat Of Beast)	9:1-12	16:10-11
6th Trumpet-Vial (Euphrates)	9:13-21	16:12
Christ Takes Legal Possession	10:1-11	
Satan Musters Armies		16:13-16
Desecration Of Rebuilt Temple	11:1-2	
Two Witnesses	11:1-3	16:15
7th Trumpet-Vial (Second Coming)	11:15-19	16:16-21

Harmony Of The Olivet Discourse With Revelation And Other Scriptures					
Subject	***Matt. 24***	***Mark 13***	***Luke 21***	***Revelation***	***Others***
False Messiahs	4-5	5-6	8		
Wars And Commotions	6	7	9		
Rapture	37-44	34-37	28, 34-36	4:1-4; 12:1-12	I Thess. 4:16, 17
Tribulation	8, 37-39	8	28, 36	12:12	Dan. 12:1
Peace Taken	7	8	10	6:4	
Famines	7	8	11	6:5-6	
Pestilences	7	8	11	6:8	Amos 5:16-20
Earthquakes	7	8	11	6:12-17; 13:1-18	
Tribulation Saints	9-13	9-13	12-19	6:9-11; 7:9-17; 12:15-17; 13	Dan. 7:25
Gospel Preached	14	10		6:1-2; 14:6-20	Hab. 3:8-13
Some Trib. Saints Killed			12-16		
Age Of Grace Ended	13-14	13	19	6:12-17	
Jewish Persecution	15-27	14-23	20-24	11:1-2; 16:13-16	Jer. 30:7 Zech. 14:2
Saints In Heaven	28			5:1-14	Dan. 7:9-10 Ps. 149:5-9
Return Of Christ	29-31	24-27	25-27	19:11-16	Zech. 14:4-5
Saints Return With Christ	31	27		19:14	Jude 14 Zech. 14:5
Trib. Saints Translated	31	27			

VII. Armageddon

Prelude To The Battle

In Revelation 16:12-16 we are told that after the sixth plague is unleashed upon the earth, three "unclean spirits of devils" go forth throughout the world performing miracles so as to entice all of the nations to invade and plunder Israel. After a period of time they are successful, resulting in the Battle of Armageddon:

Revelation 16:12-16

12 And the sixth angel poured out his vial upon the great river Euphrates; and the water thereof was dried up, that the way of the kings of the east might be prepared.

13 And I saw three unclean spirits like frogs come out of the mouth of the dragon, and out of the mouth of the beast, and out of the mouth of the false prophet.

14 For they are the spirits of devils, working miracles, which go forth unto the kings of the earth and of the whole world, to gather them to the battle of that great day of God Almighty.

15 Behold, I come as a thief. Blessed is he that watcheth, and keepeth his garments, lest he walk naked, and they see his shame.

16 And he gathered them together into a place called in the Hebrew tongue Armageddon. (KJV)

The prophet Ezekiel describes this very same scene in greater detail in Ezekiel 38 where we observe Gog (i.e., Antichrist) invading the land of Israel, three and one-half years before the Battle of Armageddon commences:

Ezekiel 38:1-7

1 And the word of the LORD came unto me, saying,

2 Son of man, set thy face against Gog, the land of Magog, the chief prince of Meshech and Tubal, and prophesy against him,

3 And say, Thus saith the Lord GOD; Behold, I am against thee, O Gog, the chief prince of Meshech and Tubal:

4 And I will turn thee back, and put hooks into thy jaws, and I will

bring thee forth, and all thine army, horses and horsemen, all of them clothed with all sorts of armour, even a great company with bucklers and shields, all of them handling swords:

5 Persia, Ethiopia, and Libya with them; all of them with shield and helmet:

6 Gomer, and all his bands; the house of Togarmah of the north quarters, and all his bands: and many people with thee.

7 Be thou prepared, and prepare for thyself, thou, and all thy company that are assembled unto thee, and be thou a guard unto them. (KJV)

It is evident from even a cursory glance at the wording of the text that the terms "Gog" and "Magog" are not synonymous with each other because Gog is a person (e.g., "chief prince of..." and "prophesy against him"), whereas Magog is designated as a "land." Likewise, please note verse 17: "Thus saith the Lord God; Art thou he of whom I have spoken in old time by my servants the prophets of Israel, which prophesied in those days many years that I would bring thee against them (i.e., Israel; verse 18)." This passage clearly identifies "Gog" as the same individual spoken of by the "prophets of Israel" who often prophesied he would invade Israel in the "last days"! Obviously there was only one such individual, and that person was none other than the Antichrist.

Here is how *Strong's Hebrew-Greek Dictionary* defines the terms "Gog" and "Magog":

1136 Gog (gogue);
of Hebrew origin [1463]; Gog, a symb. name for some future Antichrist:
KJV— Gog.

3098 Magog (mag-ogue');
of Hebrew origin [4031]; Magog, a foreign nation, i.e. (figuratively) an Antichristian party:
KJV— Magog.

Clearly, once again, precisely as we observed in Ezekiel 38 itself, there is a most distinct difference between the two terms, Gog and Magog, in the dictionary! One expression (Gog) is a symbolic name for a future antichrist (Satan), whereas the other term (Magog) is a name reserved for any foreign nation or group of people. Furthermore, this is how these two terms are used in yet another prophetic passage that describes a similar situation, although contextually it takes place 1000 years after Armageddon occurs. Accordingly, in Revelation 20, we observe that the expression "Gog and Magog" is used to represent both Satan AND all of humanity who join Satan in his final rebellion. So, in that distant future scenario, "Gog" represents Satan, and "Magog" represents rebellious people from foreign (to Israel) nations around the world.

As we saw earlier, Gog represents both Satan and Antichrist because they will share the same physical human body after the Rapture until the Battle of Armageddon. Scriptural proof on this matter was offered in earlier chapters of this book. Therefore, when all of the scriptural evidence is considered carefully, there can be no doubt that Gog, in Ezekiel 38, represents Antichrist fighting at the Battle of Armageddon.

Some translations read "Prince of Rosh" rather than "chief prince" in an attempt to imply that we should interpret this expression as meaning the "prince of Russia." This is absolutely erroneous because ROSH appears 456 times within the Old Testament and NEVER is it used as a proper noun! ROSH is a Hebrew word meaning chief, while Russia is a Finnish word meaning rowers (of a boat). There simply is no comparison or connection between these two words which originate from two different languages. Even the first or chief day of the Jewish calendar year is called ROSH HASHANA, thereby further proving our point.

"And thou (Gog) shalt come from thy place out of the north parts...and will cause thee to come up from the north parts..." (Ezek. 38:15; 39:2). Sometimes it is said these two passages prove that "Gog and Magog" are from Russia because Russia lies far to the north of Israel. But aside from the fact we already have shown that "Gog" must represent the Antichrist, other scriptural passages in the Bible also use the word "north" to designate any invader who approaches Israel from that direction even if their country lies elsewhere in another direction. (Ezekiel 26:7) (Jeremiah 4:6-7) (Jeremiah 10:22) (Jeremiah 25:9).

As further verification, the countries listed by Ezekiel as allied with Gog are the very same countries which comprise the empire of Antichrist:

1. According to commonly-accepted scholarship, MESHECH, TUBAL, and MAGOG represent countries of northern Europe and Asia, including the various peoples of Russia. (Gen. 10). Please note that Gog (Antichrist) controls the land of Magog (Russia) and that Gog is "chief

prince" of Meshech and Tubal (also Russian territory). The fact that Gog controls all of Russia simply indicates that Russia will have been defeated or otherwise made a part of Gog's empire before that point in time which is pictured in Ezekiel 38.

2. PERSIA, ETHIOPIA, and LIBYA. Persia represents modern Iran. Ethiopia was translated from the Hebrew word CUSH, which is somewhat misleading because the descendants of Cush (a grandson of Noah) populated all of black Africa, not just Ethiopia. (Gen. 10). By the same token, Libya was translated from the Hebrew word PUT (another grandson of Noah), whose descendants populated the various Arab countries of northern Africa, including Libya. (Gen. 10).

3. GOMER and TOGARMAH represent the countries of Europe according to scholars. (Gen. 10). The phrase "and many people with thee" represents countries outside the "nucleus" of Antichrist's empire of nations.

Since both Russia and Antichrist could NOT control the same empire at the very same time, we must conclude that Russia is either conquered by the Antichrist or it becomes voluntarily submissive to the Antichrist BEFORE the Rapture because Antichrist "controls" ALL of the world (including Russia) immediately AFTER the pre-tribulation Rapture:

Revelation 13:4, 7-8

4 And they worshipped the dragon which gave power unto the beast: and they worshipped the beast, saying, Who is like unto the beast? who is able to make war with him?

7 And it was given unto him (Antichrist) to make war with the saints, and to overcome them: and power was given him over ALL kindreds, and tongues, and nations.

8 And ALL that dwell upon the earth shall worship him.... (KJV)

If you carefully and honestly compare the description of Ezekiel's battle with other scriptures describing Armageddon, it becomes quite obvious that Ezekiel's battle is the Battle of Armageddon! (Compare: Ezekiel 38:1-23; Ezekiel 39:1-20, 29; Revelation 19:11-21; Revelation 14:14-20; Zechariah 14:1-16; Zechariah 12:1-6, 9-11; Joel 3:1-17.) Please note when you read these scriptures later in this chapter that many major similarities can be found repeatedly throughout these passages:

1. Soldiers of Antichrist are struck with madness and fight each other.

2. Fire and brimstone rained down from Heaven; flesh of the soldiers literally consumed away.
3. Birds and animals "invited" to feast on the multitudes slain.
4. Great "shaking" of the earth; extraordinary earthquakes.
5. Winepress symbolism portraying massive slaughter.

Obviously there are many common points of similarity found in the various battle descriptions of Armageddon, even when you include Ezekiel 38 and 39 in the comparison. There simply can be no question remaining as to the identity of Ezekiel's battle. The battle in Ezekiel sounds so similar in so many different ways to passages describing Armageddon that we must conclude Ezekiel 38, in actuality, also portrays the Battle of Armageddon.

Furthermore, Ezekiel even concludes the events described in Ezekiel 38 and 39 by stating that God NEVER will hide His face from Israel again after the battle he describes is concluded. But, this would not be a true statement if Gog really did represent Russia, thereby forcing the Battle of Armageddon to be fought at some later date. Accordingly, with that clarification in mind, please observe what God promises, very clearly and specifically, to Israel AFTER the battle in Ezekiel 38 and 39 is over:

Ezekiel 39:21-29

21 And I will set my glory among the heathen, and all the heathen shall see my judgment that I have executed, and my hand that I have laid upon them.

22 So the house of Israel shall know that I am the LORD their God from that day and forward.

23 And the heathen shall know that the house of Israel went into captivity for their iniquity: because they trespassed against me, therefore hid I my face from them, and gave them into the hand of their enemies: so fell they all by the sword.

24 According to their uncleanness and according to their transgressions have I done unto them, and hid my face from them.

25 Therefore thus saith the Lord GOD; Now will I bring again the captivity of Jacob, and have mercy upon the whole house of Israel, and will be jealous for my holy name;

26 After that they have borne their shame, and all their trespasses whereby they have trespassed against me, when they dwelt safely in their

land, and none made them afraid.

27 When I have brought them again from the people, and gathered them out of their enemies' lands, and am sanctified in them in the sight of many nations;

28 Then shall they know that I am the LORD their God, which caused them to be led into captivity among the heathen: but I have gathered them unto their own land, and have left none of them any more there.

29 Neither will I hide my face any more from them: for I have poured out my spirit upon the house of Israel, saith the Lord GOD. (KJV)

"Be thou a guard unto them." The word "guard" comes from the Hebrew MISHMAR, and it means a "guard" (the man, the post, or the prison); figuratively, a "deposit"; also a "usage" (abstractly), or an "example" (concretely). One of the dictionary definitions for the word "deposit" is "to set down; place; put." Likewise, a definition for "usage" is "the manner of using or treating a person or thing; treatment; also, the act of using." Finally, for "example" a two-fold possibility: "something deserving imitation" or "an instance or object of punishment, reprimand, etc., designed to warn or deter others." Therefore, it is very possible that God is saying Antichrist will be used as an example to the world so that they will "know" the Lord God. This view is supported by verse 16, which reads, in part: "and I (God) will bring thee (Gog; Antichrist) against my land, that the heathen (nations) may know me, when I shall be sanctified in thee, O Gog, before their eyes." (Ezek. 38:16).

"After many days thou (Gog) shalt be visited: IN THE LATTER YEARS thou shalt come into the LAND THAT IS BROUGHT BACK FROM THE SWORD, AND IS GATHERED OUT OF MANY PEOPLE, against the mountains of Israel, WHICH HAVE BEEN ALWAYS WASTE: but it is brought forth out of the nations, and they shall dwell safely all of them." (Ezekiel 38:8).

"Thou shalt be visited." *Young's Literal Translation* renders this as "thou art appointed." *Strong's Hebrew-Greek Dictionary* states that "visited" in the Hebrew means "to visit (with friendly or hostile intent); by analogy, to oversee, muster, charge, care for, miss, deposit." The biblical use of the word frequently involves a meaning of "coming into prominence and power." Therefore, Antichrist is appointed by God "in the latter years" to fulfill His purpose: to bring the nation Israel to repentance and salvation in the Lord.

"Land that is brought back from the sword, and is gathered out of many people." As noted before, this phrase proves conclusively that a "Second Crisis" will occur before the events narrated in Ezekiel 38.

"Mountains of Israel, which have been always waste." Here is an important and exciting indication of the time element involved! For centuries, Palestine was a barren desert land; it has only been within the last few decades that it has begun to "blossom like a rose" due to the partial return of the Jews. Since this prosperity has already started, that means everything has to happen relatively soon, or it would not be possible to say that the land of Israel has "always been waste."

"And dwelt safely have all of them," is the translation that *Young's Literal Translation* gives the last phrase of verse 8. After the Israelis regain their land during the Second Crisis, they will live in peace and security for a number of years — even after the Rapture when the rest of the world is filled with death and violence and famine and plagues.

Ezekiel 38:8-12

8 After many days thou shalt be visited: in the latter years thou shalt come into the land that is brought back from the sword, and is gathered out of many people, against the mountains of Israel, which have been always waste: but it is brought forth out of the nations, and they shall dwell safely all of them.

9 Thou shalt ascend and come like a storm, thou shalt be like a cloud to cover the land, thou, and all thy bands, and many people with thee.

10 Thus saith the Lord GOD; It shall also come to pass, that at the same time shall things come into thy mind, and thou shalt think an evil thought:

11 And thou shalt say, I will go up to the land of unwalled villages; I will go to them that are at rest, that dwell safely, all of them dwelling without walls, and having neither bars nor gates,

12 To take a spoil, and to take a prey; to turn thine hand upon the desolate places that are now inhabited, and upon the people that are gathered out of the nations, which have gotten cattle and goods, that dwell in the midst of the land. (KJV)

"Thou shalt ascend." Obviously another reference to modern warfare and technology, specifically aircraft.

"And thou shalt say, I will go up to the land of UNWALLED villages;

I will go up to THEM THAT ARE AT REST, THAT DWELL SAFELY, all of them dwelling without walls and having neither bars nor gates." (Ezekiel 38:11). Again, a reference to the peace and security the land of Israel will enjoy for years until the initial invasion of the Antichrist. This passage proves beyond any doubt that the first 17 verses of Ezekiel 38 deal with the moment Antichrist violates his seven year treaty with Israel, three and one-half years before Armageddon. This act of treachery by the Antichrist ushers in the time of Jacob's Trouble, a period of intense suffering and death.

However, if the first part of Ezekiel 38 did apply to the Battle of Armageddon, then it would not be possible to make the statements in this verse (verse 11) concerning the peace and security of the Jews which will exist at the time of Gog's invasion of Israel. Accordingly, verse 4 of this passage in Ezekiel 38 does not mean God will react instantaneously to the invasion of Antichrist; in fact, it will be three and one-half years — after all of the nations are gathered against Jerusalem — before He will take action.

Ezekiel 38:13-17

13 Sheba, and Dedan, and the merchants of Tarshish, with all the young lions thereof, shall say unto thee, Art thou come to take a spoil? hast thou gathered thy company to take a prey? to carry away silver and gold, to take away cattle and goods, to take a great spoil?

14 Therefore, son of man, prophesy and say unto Gog, Thus saith the Lord GOD; In that day when my people of Israel dwelleth safely, shalt thou not know it?

15 And thou shalt come from thy place out of the north parts, thou, and many people with thee, all of them riding upon horses, a great company, and a mighty army:

16 And thou shalt come up against my people of Israel, as a cloud to cover the land; it shall be in the latter days, and I will bring thee against my land, that the heathen may know me, when I shall be sanctified in thee, O Gog, before their eyes.

17 Thus saith the Lord GOD; Art thou he of whom I have spoken in old time by my servants the prophets of Israel, which prophesied in those days many years that I would bring thee against them? (KJV)

For reasons not mentioned in this passage, there is a certain group of nations, somewhat independent of Antichrist, who apparently protest this planned invasion of Israel. Very possibly they are the "kings of the east" who also send armies into Palestine at the time of Armageddon. They are "of the east" not necessarily because they are located east of Palestine, but because that is the direction from which they will approach. For instance, King Nebuchadnezzar was termed the king from the north because the Babylonians entered Palestine from that direction in their invasion, even though Babylon is not north of Palestine. (Ezek. 26:7).

This "independent" group of nations is mentioned in Ezekiel 38:13. "Sheba" and "Dedan" represent countries in Africa and Arabia; "Tarshish" is Gibralter. (Gen. 10). Gibralter has never been a country, but it was the farthest known port in the world at the time of Ezekiel and so it probably refers to a distant but then unknown land eventually boasting world-wide influence. Such a country was Great Britain, "the merchants of Tarshish." The "young lions thereof" then would represent the United States, Canada, Australia and other former commonwealth members.

Concerning the identity of the "kings of the east," it is very possible that they are, in fact, vast hordes of Asian soldiers — as conventional wisdom teaches — and not the above group of nations. However, regardless of whichever group of nations it turns out to be, they will have no connection with the 200,000,000 angelic horsemen of the sixth plague, nor is there any question regarding which group of nations will protest the invasion of Israel.

The story in Ezekiel 38 is that the Jews have been dwelling SAFELY in Palestine for several years. The Second Crisis is history, and they supposedly are under the protection of Antichrist due to their seven year treaty with him. Furthermore, while the rest of the world has been suffering very severely from the Trumpet-Vial plagues, Israel has been enjoying a period of continued prosperity. Consequently, the pretext "to take a spoil" will be the reason given to the nations of the earth to entice them into invading Palestine. The real reason, however, will be that Satan will have just seen Christ take "legal possession" of the earth (Rev. 10) and he will panic, realizing that time is running out very quickly. Therefore, Satan makes one last desperate attempt to retain control of planet Earth. Inspired by extreme hatred and frustration, he immediately initiates a very severe persecution against the Jews in Israel, including the desecration of their rebuilt temple:

Daniel 9:27

27 And he shall confirm the covenant with many for one week: and in the midst of the week he shall cause the sacrifice and the oblation to cease, and for the overspreading of abominations he shall make it desolate, even until the consummation, and that determined shall be poured upon the desolate. (KJV)

"Shall cause the sacrifice and the oblation to cease." The Hebrew word for "oblation" is MINCHAH, meaning to "apportion," i.e., "bestow"; a "donation"; specifically, a sacrificial "offering" (usually bloodless and voluntary); also translated as "gift, (meat) offering, present, sacrifice." The word "sacrifice" comes from the Hebrew word ZEBACH, meaning a "slaughter," i.e., the "flesh" of an animal; by implication, a "sacrifice." So, what this scripture predicts is (the establishment of and, subsequently,) the abolishment of the two major types of sacrifices: the vegetable or bloodless, and the animal or bloody kind.

Likewise, the Hebrew word for "overspreading" is KANAPH, meaning an "edge" or "extremity"; and when the word is applied to a building, it means a "pinnacle"; it means a "wing" when applied to a bird or an army. Also, one of the dictionary definitions of the word "pinnacle" is "the highest point or place." Moreover, the Hebrew word for "abominations" is SHIQQUWTS or SHIQQUTS, meaning "disgusting," i.e., "filthy," especially "idolatrous" or (concretely) an "idol." Furthermore, the word "for" comes from the Hebrew word KIY which is "a primary particle (the full form of the prepositional prefix) indicating causal relations of all kinds, antecedent or consequent; (by implication) very widely used as a relative conjunction or adverb; often largely modified by other particles annexed." In this particular passage of Daniel, *Young's Literal Translation* renders this word as "by." We should note also that, according to *Strong's Hebrew-Greek Dictionary*, there is no Hebrew equivalent for the word "of" in the phrase: "overspreading of abominations"; apparently, it was added by the translators in an attempt to clarify the meaning intended for this passage (a fairly common practice).

In conclusion, the preceding evidence cited here or elsewhere makes it very possible to translate Daniel 9:27 as follows: "He will confirm a covenant with many for seven years, and in the middle of the seven years he will put an end to the animal and vegetable sacrifices. And by the pinnacle (i.e., the highest point or place of a rebuilt Jewish Temple) he will set up an abomination that causes desolation (i.e., sit in the temple claiming to be god; II Thess. 2:4), until the end that is decreed is poured out on him."

Luke 21:20-24

20 And when ye shall see Jerusalem compassed with armies, then know that the desolation thereof is nigh.

21 Then let them which are in Judaea flee to the mountains; and let them which are in the midst of it depart out; and let not them that are in the countries enter thereinto.

22 For these be the days of vengeance, that all things which are written may be fulfilled.

23 But woe unto them that are with child, and to them that give suck, in those days! for there shall be great distress in the land, and wrath upon this people.

24 And they shall fall by the edge of the sword, and shall be led away captive into all nations: and Jerusalem shall be trodden down of the Gentiles, until the times of the Gentiles be fulfilled. (KJV)

Matthew 24:15-26

15 When ye therefore shall see the abomination of desolation, spoken of by Daniel the prophet, stand in the holy place, (whoso readeth, let him understand:)

16 Then let them which be in Judaea flee into the mountains:

17 Let him which is on the housetop not come down to take any thing out of his house:

18 Neither let him which is in the field return back to take his clothes.

19 And woe unto them that are with child, and to them that give suck in those days!

20 But pray ye that your flight be not in the winter, neither on the sabbath day:

21 For then shall be great tribulation, such as was not since the beginning of the world to this time, no, nor ever shall be.

22 And except those days should be shortened, there should no flesh be saved: but for the elect's sake those days shall be shortened.

23 Then if any man shall say unto you, Lo, here is Christ, or there; believe it not.

24 For there shall arise false Christs, and false prophets, and shall

shew great signs and wonders; insomuch that, if it were possible, they shall deceive the very elect.

25 Behold, I have told you before.

26 Wherefore if they shall say unto you, Behold, he is in the desert; go not forth: behold, he is in the secret chambers; believe it not. (KJV)

It is interesting to observe that Jesus advises the Jews to "flee into the mountains" when they see the armies of the Antichrist approaching Jerusalem. Likewise, because it will be a time of great distress and wrath upon the Jewish people, He advises them to flee at the first sign of danger, not stopping to do anything else. There is a parallel passage that also addresses this issue. It is a plea from God to the inhabitants of Moab (i.e., western-central Jordan) to give shelter and aid to the Jewish "outcasts" who manage to flee from the wrath of the Antichrist (called the "spoiler," "extortioner" and "oppressor" in this passage):

Isaiah 16:1-5

1 Send ye the lamb to the ruler of the land from Sela to the wilderness, unto the mount of the daughter of Zion.

2 For it shall be, that, as a wandering bird cast out of the nest, so the daughters of Moab shall be at the fords of Arnon.

3 Take counsel, execute judgment; make thy shadow as the night in the midst of the noonday; hide the outcasts; bewray not him that wandereth.

4 Let mine outcasts dwell with thee, Moab; be thou a covert to them from the face of the spoiler: for the extortioner is at an end, the spoiler ceaseth, the oppressors are consumed out of the land.

5 And in mercy shall the throne be established: and he shall sit upon it in truth in the tabernacle of David, judging, and seeking judgment, and hasting righteousness. (KJV)

"Pray ye that your flight be not...on the sabbath day." This is another indication that the land of Israel will observe the ancient Mosaic laws during the "time of the end." Jesus gave this advice because the Laws of Moses prohibited work and very extensive travel during the Sabbath day.

Jeremiah 30:5-7

5 For thus saith the LORD; We have heard a voice of trembling, of fear, and not of peace.

6 Ask ye now, and see whether a man doth travail with child? wherefore do I see every man with his hands on his loins, as a woman in travail, and all faces are turned into paleness?

7 Alas! for that day is great, so that none is like it: it is even the time of Jacob's trouble; but he shall be saved out of it. (KJV)

Zechariah 13:8-9

8 And it shall come to pass, that in all the land, saith the LORD, two parts therein shall be cut off and die; but the third shall be left therein.

9 And I will bring the third part through the fire, and will refine them as silver is refined, and will try them as gold is tried: they shall call on my name, and I will hear them: I will say, It is my people: and they shall say, The LORD is my God. (KJV)

Revelation 11:1-6

1 And there was given me a reed like unto a rod: and the angel stood, saying, Rise, and measure the temple of God, and the altar, and them that worship therein.

2 But the court which is without the temple leave out, and measure it not; for it is given unto the Gentiles: and the holy city shall they tread under foot forty and two months.

3 And I will give power unto my two witnesses, and they shall prophesy a thousand two hundred and threescore days, clothed in sackcloth.

4 These are the two olive trees, and the two candlesticks standing before the God of the earth.

5 And if any man will hurt them, fire proceedeth out of their mouth, and devoureth their enemies: and if any man will hurt them, he must in this manner be killed.

6 These have power to shut heaven, that it rain not in the days of their prophecy: and have power over waters to turn them to blood, and to smite the earth with all plagues, as often as they will. (KJV)

II Thess. 2:3-4

3 Let no man deceive you by any means: for that day shall not come, except there come a falling away first, and that man of sin be revealed, the sons of perdition;

4 Who opposeth and exalteth himself above all that is called God, or that is worshipped; so that he as God sitteth in the temple of God,

shewing himself that he is God. (KJV)

The obvious question is how the Antichrist could desecrate the Jewish Temple for three and one-half years and still find it necessary to implement a worldwide invasion of Jerusalem at the time of Armageddon? The answer lies in the fact that Satan encounters many unique and perplexing problems throughout his vast and difficult-to-manage world empire. There are the terrible plagues, as described in very vivid detail in Revelation; there are also the plagues performed by the Two Witnesses; and there is the constant turmoil created by Egypt and her confederacy of nations as they continually rebel against the rule of Antichrist, forcing him to destroy Egypt just before Armageddon (Dan. 11:40-45):

Daniel 11:40-45

40 And at the time of the end shall the king of the south push at him: and the king of the north shall come against him like a whirlwind, with chariots, and with horsemen, and with many ships; and he shall enter into the countries, and shall overflow and pass over.

41 He shall enter also into the glorious land, and many countries shall be overthrown: but these shall escape out of his hand, even Edom, and Moab, and the chief of the children of Ammon.

42 He shall stretch forth his hand also upon the countries: and the land of Egypt shall not escape.

43 But he shall have power over the treasures of gold and of silver, and over all the precious things of Egypt: and the Libyans and the Ethiopians shall be at his steps.

44 But tidings out of the east and out of the north shall trouble him: therefore he shall go forth with great fury to destroy, and utterly to make away many.

45 And he shall plant the tabernacles of his palace between the seas in the glorious holy mountain; yet he shall come to his end, and none shall help him. (KJV)

The "king of the north" is identified as the Antichrist in two ways. First, this prophecy concerns "the time of the end"; obviously that qualification alone narrows the possibilities considerably. Second, the verses immediately preceding this passage clearly identify this personage as none other than the Antichrist:

Daniel 11:35-39

35 And some of them of understanding shall fall, to try them, and to purge, and to make them white, even to the time of the end: because it is yet for a time appointed.

36 And the king shall do according to his will; and he shall exalt himself, and magnify himself above every god, and shall speak marvellous things against the God of gods, and shall prosper till the indignation be accomplished: for that that is determined shall be done.

37 Neither shall he regard the God of his fathers, nor the desire of women, nor regard any god: for he shall magnify himself above all.

38 But in his estate shall he honour the God of forces: and a god whom his fathers knew not shall he honour with gold, and silver, and with precious stones, and pleasant things.

39 Thus shall he do in the most strong holds with a strange god, whom he shall acknowledge and increase with glory: and he shall cause them to rule over many, and shall divide the land for gain. (KJV)

Verse 35 establishes the fact that this passage also involves "the time of the end." Daniel continues with his prophecy by describing the "king" as doing "according to his will"; as "exalting himself"; as "magnifying himself above every god"; as "speaking marvellous things against the God of gods"; and as "honouring the (g)od of forces." All of these attributes clearly find their ultimate fulfillment in the person of Antichrist. The fact that he also will "do in the most strong holds with a strange god" plainly suggests the extraordinary power and ability he will derive from Satan.

Daniel states in verse 40 that the "king of the south" attacks Antichrist (i.e., "the king of the north") who retaliates "like a whirlwind" in response. It is said that Antichrist enters into the "glorious land" (i.e., Israel), and many other countries, and that none of the countries in that part of the world, including Egypt, escape from his power and might (except for the land of Jordan). Accordingly, several intriguing points concerning this passage should be enumerated.

First, it is interesting that the king of the south would even dare to attack the Antichrist. After all, this is the man who will "come with all power and signs and lying wonders"; he also will be the man about whom the whole world will say, "who is able to make war with him?" Therefore, the fact that the "king of the south" will dare to attack the Antichrist would seem to indicate that the power and ability of the Antichrist is diminished somewhat when Satan physically possesses and indwells his body immediately after the Rapture, very possibly because Satan may lose some of his ability to influence events when he no longer has access to the heavenlies immediately after the Rapture.

A second observation concerns the identity of the "king of the south." Although we can not be for certain, the scriptural evidence seems to indicate that Egypt is the leader of this "end-time" confederacy of nations. Daniel makes reference to the gold and silver and all the "precious things" of Egypt, thereby hinting at the wealth and power she will enjoy at the "time of the end." Jeremiah also predicted a resurgence in power for her during the "latter years." (Jer. 46:26). Egypt also seems to be a primary military target for the Antichrist at this point in time. Finally, as mentioned previously, the first 35 verses of Daniel 11 focus primarily on historical military conflicts between Syria, the king of the north, and Egypt, the king of the south. (See *Dake's Annotated Reference Bible*.) On that basis, it seems logical to suppose that in subsequent verses of Daniel eleven these two "titles" continue to carry the same meaning. Therefore, it seems probable that the designation, "king of the south," represents Egypt at the "time of the end."

Third, Daniel states that Israel will be one of the countries attacked by Antichrist in this military campaign. Since we also are told that this happens just before his demise at Armageddon, it is very likely that this will be the time when he violates his seven year treaty with Israel, thereby ushering in "Jacob's Trouble."

Finally, Daniel states that Edom, Moab, and Ammon (i.e., modern Jordan) will "escape" the military destruction that will be wreaked by the Antichrist. The Hebrew word translated as "escape" is MALAT, meaning "to be smooth," i.e., (by implication) to "escape (as if by slipperiness); causatively to release or rescue." It is often translated as "deliver (self), escape, leap out, let alone, let go, preserve and save." Therefore, the implication is that the inhabitants of Jordan will utilize "trickery" to evade destruction by the Antichrist, or that the Antichrist will not want to attack them due to his friendship with the Palestinian Arabs who will be living there and most likely will comprise the majority of the Jordanian populace.

As we saw earlier, other Old Testament prophets also prophesied about this "end-time" destruction of Egypt. For instance:

Ezekiel 30:1-9

1 The word of the LORD came again unto me, saying,

2 Son of man, prophesy and say, Thus saith the Lord GOD; Howl ye, Woe worth the day!

3 For the day is near, even the day of the LORD is near, a cloudy day; it shall be the time of the heathen.

4 And the sword shall come upon Egypt, and great pain shall be in Ethiopia, when the slain shall fall in Egypt, and they shall take away her multitude, and her foundations shall be broken down.

5 Ethiopia, and Libya, and Lydia, and all the mingled people, and Chub, and the men of the land that is in league, shall fall with them by the sword.

6 Thus saith the LORD; They also that uphold Egypt shall fall; and the pride of her power shall come down: from the tower of Syene shall they fall in it by the sword, saith the Lord GOD.

7 And they shall be desolate in the midst of the countries that are desolate, and her cities shall be in the midst of the cities that are wasted.

8 And they shall know that I am the LORD, when I have set a fire in Egypt, and when all her helpers shall be destroyed.

9 In that day shall messengers go forth from me in ships to make the careless Ethiopians afraid, and great pain shall come upon them, as in the day of Egypt: for, lo, it cometh. (KJV)

"The day of the Lord is near." This phrase helps us to establish the time-element for this prophecy, just as it did in Obadiah. (This is not the case, however, for Jeremiah 46 which also mentions the "day of the Lord" in connection with a prophecy concerning the destruction of ancient Egypt. We know this to be true because, in that passage, verse 10 stipulates that the battle which is portrayed occurs "in the north country by the river Euphrates," an obvious reference to the historical battle of Carchemish along the Euphrates. This is where the rising Babylonian Empire decisively defeated Egypt. Armageddon, however, will be fought in Palestine. Furthermore, the name of Nebuchadnezzar, king of Babylon, is mentioned several times throughout this prophecy, thus establishing the time-element beyond dispute.)

"Ethiopia, and Libya, and Lydia, and all the mingled people, and Chub, and the men of the land that is in league." (Ezek. 30:5). "To make the careless Ethiopians afraid, and great pain shall come upon them, as in the day of Egypt." (Ezek. 30:9). Again, as in Daniel, there is a reference to these countries apparently being allied with Egypt.

Isaiah gives us additional information concerning this "end-time" destruction:

Isaiah 19:1-15

1 The burden of Egypt. Behold, the LORD rideth upon a swift cloud, and shall come into Egypt: and the idols of Egypt shall be moved at his presence, and the heart of Egypt shall melt in the midst of it.

2 And I will set the Egyptians against the Egyptians: and they shall fight every one against his brother, and every one against his neighbour; city against city, and kingdom against kingdom.

3 And the spirit of Egypt shall fail in the midst thereof; and I will destroy the counsel thereof: and they shall seek to the idols, and to the charmers, and to them that have familiar spirits, and to the wizards.

4 And the Egyptians will I give over into the hand of a cruel lord; and a fierce king shall rule over them, saith the Lord, the LORD of hosts.

5 And the waters shall fail from the sea, and the river shall be wasted and dried up.

6 And they shall turn the rivers far away; and the brooks of defence shall be emptied and dried up: the reeds and flags shall wither.

7 The paper reeds by the brooks, by the mouth of the brooks, and every thing sown by the brooks, shall wither, be driven away, and be no more.

8 The fishers also shall mourn, and ail they that cast angle into the brooks shall lament, and they that spread nets upon the waters shall languish.

9 Moreover they that work in fine flax, and they that weave networks, shall be confounded.

10 And they shall be broken in the purposes thereof, all that make sluices and ponds for fish.

11 Surely the princes of Zoan are fools, the counsel of the wise counsellors of Pharaoh is become brutish: how say ye unto Pharaoh, I am the son of the wise, the son of ancient kings?

12 Where are they? where are thy wise men? and let them tell thee now, and let them know what the LORD of hosts hath purposed upon Egypt.

13 The princes of Zoan are become fools, the princes of Noph are

deceived; they have also seduced Egypt, even they that are the stay of the tribes thereof.

14 The LORD hath mingled a perverse spirit in the midst thereof: and they have caused Egypt to err in every work thereof, as a drunken man staggereth in his vomit.

15 Neither shall there be any work for Egypt, which the head or tail, branch or rush, may do. (KJV)

"And I will set the Egyptians against the Egyptians." This sounds very similar to the type of fighting that will occur at the Battle of Armageddon. Since Egypt borders on Israel, it is very possible that the fighting that will take place at Armageddon will extend down into Egypt itself.

"A cruel lord; and a fierce king." This person could be none other than the Antichrist. Obviously this prophecy correlates with Daniel 11:40-45 perfectly.

"The heart of Egypt shall melt." The Hebrew word for "melt" is MACAC, and it means to "liquefy"; figuratively, to "waste" (with disease), to "faint" (with fatigue, fear or grief). Accordingly, this phrase means that the Egyptians "in that day" will be paralyzed with fear and panic. This sounds very much like the world conditions that will prevail at that time according to Luke 21: "distress of nations, with perplexity... Men's hearts failing them for fear." (Luke 21:25, 26). God also states that the idols and sorceries and witchcraft of the Egyptians will fail them completely — right when they are needed most.

"And they shall turn the rivers far away." Apparently the Egyptians will rely, in part, on the Nile River to aid in their defense, but the Antichrist will out-smart them. He will divert the water from the Nile River's two primary sources, Lake Victoria in Africa and Lake Tana in Ethiopia, and thereby cause the Nile to go dry.

Ezekiel 29:1-16

1 In the tenth year, in the tenth month, in the twelfth day of the month, the word of the LORD came unto me, saying,

2 Son of man, set thy face against Pharaoh king of Egypt, and prophesy against him, and against all Egypt:

3 Speak, and say, Thus saith the Lord GOD; Behold, I am against thee, Pharaoh king of Egypt, the great dragon that lieth in the midst of his rivers, which hath said, My river is mine own, and I have made it for

myself.

4 But I will put hooks in thy jaws, and I will cause the fish of thy rivers to stick unto thy scales, and I will bring thee up out of the midst of thy rivers, and all the fish of thy rivers shall stick unto thy scales.

5 And I will leave thee thrown into the wilderness, thee and all the fish of thy rivers: thou shalt fall upon the open fields; thou shalt not be brought together, nor gathered: I have given thee for meat to the beasts of the field and to the fowls of the heaven.

6 And all the inhabitants of Egypt shall know that I am the LORD, because they have been a staff of reed to the house of Israel.

7 When they took hold of thee by thy hand, thou didst break, and rend all their shoulder: and when they leaned upon thee, thou brakest, and madest all their loins to be at a stand.

8 Therefore thus saith the Lord GOD; Behold, I will bring a sword upon thee, and cut off man and beast out of thee.

9 And the land of Egypt shall be desolate and waste; and they shall know that I am the LORD: because he hath said, The river is mine, and I have made it.

10 Behold, therefore I am against thee, and against thy rivers, and I will make the land of Egypt utterly waste and desolate, from the tower of Syene even unto the border of Ethiopia.

11 No foot of man shall pass through it, nor foot of beast shall pass through it, neither shall it be inhabited forty years.

12 And I will make the land of Egypt desolate in the midst of the countries that are desolate, and her cities among the cities that are laid waste shall be desolate forty years: and I will scatter the Egyptians among the nations, and will disperse them through the countries.

13 Yet thus saith the Lord GOD; At the end of forty years will I gather the Egyptians from the people whither they were scattered:

14 And I will bring again the captivity of Egypt, and will cause them to return into the land of Pathros, into the land of their habitation; and they shall be there a base kingdom.

15 It shall be the basest of the kingdoms; neither shall it exalt itself any more above the nations: for I will diminish them, that they shall no more rule over the nations.

16 And it shall be no more the confidence of the house of Israel, which bringeth their iniquity to remembrance, when they shall look after them: but they shall know that I am the Lord GOD. (KJV)

It is possible that the first five verses of this scripture portray an ancient, fulfilled prophecy in 570 B.C. concerning Pharaoh Hophra of Egypt. If this is true, then in a move not without precedent, Ezekiel uses this "near-terem" prophecy as a springboard for launching into a prophecy about the "end-times." We can be certain, however, that the remainder of the prophecy is futuristic because consultation with an encyclopedia should confirm that the following predictions never have been fulfilled:

1. No man or beast is to be alive anywhere in Egypt after a time of destruction. (verse 8).
2. Egypt is to be in a state of complete desolation and waste. (verses 9 and 10). Not surprisingly, the Hebrew gives one a better understanding of the meaning intended in this passage. The Hebrew word for "desolate" is SHeMAMAH or SHIMAMAH, meaning "devastation"; figuratively "astonishment." Likewise, "waste" comes from the Hebrew word CHORBAH, meaning "drought," i.e., (by implication) a "desolation." Clearly, Egypt never has been completely devastated, perhaps even to the point of "astonishment."
3. Egypt is to be completely uninhabited for exactly 40 years. (verse 11).
4. No foot of man or beast is to touch the ground of Egypt for 40 years. (verse 11).
5. The Egyptians are to be scattered and dispersed throughout the countries of the world. (verse 12).
6. After the 40 years of waste and desolation, Egypt forevermore is to be the "basest" (Hebrew SHAPHAL, meaning "depressed," literally or figuratively) of the nations. (verses 13-15). Obviously an ancient fulfillment would make the "end-time" prophecy in Daniel 11:40-45 concerning the wealth and power of Egypt to be an impossibility.

Historically, Egypt has proven to be "a staff of reed" (i.e., not dependable) to the people of Israel during any time of trouble and distress; such will be the case also during Israel's Second Crisis.

To recapitulate: the Antichrist will find it necessary to mount a world-wide invasion of Jerusalem at the time of Armageddon for several reasons. There will be the plagues described in Revelation; the resistance of the Two Witnesses; and, of course, the instability caused by the rebellion of Egypt and her confederacy of nations. Because of all these circumstances, the Jews will manage to regain control of Jerusalem for 140 days just before the Battle of Armageddon. (Dan. 8:10-14). When Satan (who at this time will be in Africa) is informed that the Jews have regained control over Jerusalem and that the "kings of the east" are marching upon Palestine, he literally will be infuriated. (Dan. 11:44). It is then that the armies of Antichrist once AGAIN march upon Palestine, this time supported by all the armies and nations of the world.

Parenthetically, the above-mentioned 140 days as calculated from Daniel 8:10-14 are computed as follows. Although this passage states that the Sanctuary (rebuilt temple) will be desecrated for a period of "2300 days," a more accurate translation, as we saw earlier, reads "2300 evening-mornings." This is harmonious with Jewish Law which stipulated a morning sacrifice and an evening sacrifice each day. 2300 such sacrifices add up to 1150 days, which are 140 days short of the 1290 days mentioned in Daniel 12:11.

Likewise, it might be appropriate at this point to note that the Antichrist never would be able to persecute the Jews during Jacob's Trouble if they would retain the protection of God which they will gain during the Second Crisis. This protection will be lost when they (actually, only "many"; Dan. 9:27) negotiate a seven year treaty with Antichrist which supposedly will guarantee Palestine to the Jews. This action on their part will permit the Antichrist to assume the role of God as protector of the Jews.

After the armies of Antichrist reach their destination, a siege about the city of Jerusalem begins and the city quickly is taken. (Zech. 14:1, 2). Antichrist then kills the Two Witnesses in revenge for all of the problems they will have caused him, but three and one-half days later (after the dead bodies have been seen by people throughout the world via TV) they miraculously will be brought back to life by God. (Rev. 11:7-13). At that point, God audibly summons the Two Witnesses, who in turn ascend to Heaven within the sight of everyone. Within the hour of this stupendous event, the seventh and final trumpet is blown and the greatest earthquake in history will take place, completely destroying and demolishing all of the cities, islands, and mountains of the earth. (Rev.11).

The Battle Of Armageddon

The story continues in Revelation 19 where the scene of activity shifts to Heaven, and Christ, the "KING OF KINGS," is seen in preparation for His Second Coming to earth with His army of saints:

Revelation 19:1-9

1 And after these things I heard a great voice of much people in heaven, saying, Alleluia; Salvation, and glory, and honour, and power, unto the Lord our God:

2 For true and righteous are his judgments: for he hath judged the great whore, which did corrupt the earth with her fornication, and hath avenged the blood of his servants at her hand.

3 And again they said, Alleluia. And her smoke rose up for ever and ever.

4 And the four and twenty elders and the four beasts fell down and worshipped God that sat on the throne, saying, Amen; Alleluia.

5 And a voice came out of the throne, saying, Praise our God, all ye his servants, and ye that fear him, both small and great.

6 And I heard as it were the voice of a great multitude, and as the voice of many waters, and as the voice of mighty thunderings, saying, Alleluia: for the Lord God omnipotent reigneth.

7 Let us be glad and rejoice, and give honour to him: for the marriage of the Lamb is come, and his wife hath made herself ready.

8 And to her was granted that she should be arrayed in fine linen, clean and white: for the fine linen is the righteousness of saints.

9 And he saith unto me, Write, Blessed are they which are called unto the marriage supper of the Lamb. And he saith unto me, These are the true sayings of God. (KJV)

"Lamb is come." The Lamb, of course, is Jesus Christ, the "lamb slain" for our redemption.

"His wife...arrayed in fine linen, clean and white." The identity of His "wife" is clarified in the subsequent phrase of this same scripture: "...for the fine linen is the righteousness of saints." In other words, the bride of Jesus is all the saints (believers) from all the ages of history. (cf. Eph. 5:22-33) (cf. also: Hebrews 11; Rom. 8:17; Ps. 149:5-9; Heb. 9:15).

"Blessed are they which are called unto the marriage supper of the Lamb." This statement simply means that ALL saints are "blessed" because they are in the "First Resurrection." Some people use Matthew 22:1-14 to teach that other classes of saints will be in attendance at the "marriage supper of the Lamb." But that passage is a PARABLE, and the basic intent of a parable is to tell a story in order to illustrate a singular, basic truth. In that parable, the truth or lesson of the story intended is found in the last four verses:

"...The king came in to see the guests (at the wedding)...(and) saw there a man which had not on a wedding garment...Then said the king, Bind him hand and foot, and take him away, and cast him into outer darkness; there shall be weeping and gnashing of teeth." Obviously the truth of this story or parable is that only those who are wearing "fine linen" can attend the "marriage supper of the Lamb." As we saw earlier, to attend, wearing "fine linen," is the privilege of all saints from all ages.

Other people use Ps. 45 in a similar attempt to promote the idea that different classes of saints will be in attendance at the "marriage supper." But, only verses six and seven refer to God; the rest of that passage clearly narrates an earthly wedding of King Solomon and the daughter of the Pharaoh of Egypt. (I Kings 3). This view is supported by the following verses:

1. "King's daughters were among thy honorable women." (verse 9). This statement is a reference to the harem of King Solomon, and the fact that some of his wives were the daughters of kings. (I Kings 11).

2. "Upon thy right hand did stand the queen in gold of Ophir" (verse 9). The "church" is never called a queen anywhere in the Bible. Neither do saints wear clothing of gold; instead, they wear "fine linen, clean and white." Furthermore, the saints will not be restricted to standing ONLY on the right hand of God. (Matt. 20:20-22).

3. "Hearken, O daughter." (verse 10). "The king's daughter." (verse 13). The church is never called a daughter or a king's daughter.

4. "So shall the king greatly desire thy beauty." (verse 11). An obvious reference to King Solomon sexually desiring his new wife.

5. "Shall be thy children." (verse 16). Saints of God, after the Resurrection, do not have children to inherit the earth.

Revelation 19:10

10 And I fell at his feet to worship him. And he said unto me, See thou do it not: I am thy fellowservant, and of thy brethren that have the testimony of Jesus: worship God: for the testimony of Jesus is the spirit of prophecy. (KJV)

This happens again in Revelation 22:8, 9. Evidently, John was so overwhelmed by the Revelation shown to him that twice he began to worship the "angel" who was disclosing it to him.

"I am thy fellowservant, and of thy brethren." This angel, who identifies himself as a saint, is also identified as one of the angels who pours out the seven vials of plagues upon the earth. (Rev. 17:1). As noted before, this proves our interpretation concerning the identity of the angels throughout most of Revelation; it is the saints who will execute judgment upon the earth when it is being "redeemed." This also confirms that the saints must be Raptured to Heaven before the process of redemption begins.

Revelation 19:11-16

11 And I saw heaven opened, and behold a white horse; and he that sat upon him was called Faithful and True, and in righteousness he doth judge and make war.

12 His eyes were as a flame of fire, and on his head were many crowns; and he had a name written, that no man knew, but he himself.

13 And he was clothed with a vesture dipped in blood: and his name is called The Word of God.

14 And the armies which were in heaven followed him upon white horses, clothed in fine linen, white and clean.

15 And out of his mouth goeth a sharp sword, that with it he should smite the nations: and he shall rule them with a rod of iron: and he treadeth the winepress of the fierceness and wrath of Almighty God.

16 And he hath on his vesture and on his thigh a name written, KING OF KINGS, AND LORD OF LORDS. (KJV)

Once again the color "white" and white horses are associated with righteousness and the saints of God just as in Revelation 6:2.

"He was clothed with a vesture dipped in blood." Compare the following scripture:

Isaiah 63:1-4

1 Who is this that cometh from Edom, with dyed garments from Bozrah? this that is glorious in his apparel, travelling in the greatness of his strength? I that speak in righteousness, mighty to save.

2 Wherefore art thou red in thine apparel, and thy garments like him

that treadeth in the winefat?

3 I have trodden the winepress alone; and of the people there was none with me: for I will tread them in mine anger, and trample them in my fury; and their blood shall be sprinkled upon my garments, and I will stain all my raiment.

4 For the day of vengeance is in mine heart, and the year of my redeemed is come. (KJV)

"Out of his mouth goeth a sharp sword." Compare the following:

Isaiah 11:4

4 But with righteousness shall he judge the poor, and reprove with equity for the meek of the earth: and he shall smite the earth with the rod of his mouth, and with the breath of his lips shall he slay the wicked. (KJV)

Heb. 4:12

12 For the word of God is quick, and powerful, and sharper than any twoedged sword, piercing even to the dividing asunder of soul and spirit, and of the joints and marrow, and is a discerner of the thoughts and intents of the heart. (KJV)

Revelation 19:17-21

17 And I saw an angel standing in the sun; and he cried with a loud voice, saying to all the fowls that fly in the midst of heaven, Come and gather yourselves together unto the supper of the great God;

18 That ye may eat the flesh of kings, and the flesh of captains, and the flesh of mighty men, and the flesh of horses, and of them that sit on them, and the flesh of all men, both free and bond, both small and great.

19 And I saw the beast, and the kings of the earth, and their armies, gathered together to make war against him that sat on the horse, and against his army.

20 And the beast was taken, and with him the false prophet that wrought miracles before him, with which he deceived them that had received the mark of the beast, and them that worshipped his image. These both were cast alive into a lake of fire burning with brimstone.

21 And the remnant were slain with the sword of him that sat upon the horse, which sword proceeded out of his mouth: and all the fowls were

filled with their flesh. (KJV)

The Battle of Armageddon also is described in quite a few other scriptural passages. It is said that during this battle, God literally rains down "fire and brimstone" upon the armies of Antichrist which accomplishes much of the horrific destruction, and during the confusion of events, that the soldiers of Antichrist even turn upon each other and thereby add to the vast number of men slaughtered. Just before the visible Return of Christ, the sun and moon both are darkened, but during the battle itself the "sun stands still" for 24 hours so as to allow the complete destruction of the armies of Antichrist. This destruction is so vast and complete that Israel will require all of seven months to bury the dead and seven years to completely burn the weapons of wood. The blood from this fantastic battle actually will flow for a length of 170 miles and as high as a bridle on a horse. Near the conclusion of this battle, both Antichrist and the False Prophet are thrown into the "lake of fire," while Satan is chained in the "bottomless pit." (Dan. 7:11) (Rev. 19:20; 20) (Isa. 14:4-11).

Parenthetically, we should remember that before all of these events at the Battle of Armageddon begin to happen, there will be "signs" heralding the imminence of Christ's Return:

Luke 21:25-27

25 And there shall be signs in the sun, and in the moon, and in the stars; and upon the earth distress of nations, with perplexity; the sea and the waves roaring;

26 Men's hearts failing them for fear, and for looking after those things which are coming on the earth: for the powers of heaven shall be shaken.

27 And then shall they see the Son of man coming in a cloud with power and great glory. (KJV)

Matthew 24:27-31

27 For as the lightning cometh out of the east, and shineth even unto the west; so shall also the coming of the Son of man be.

28 For wheresoever the carcase is, there will the eagles be gathered together.

29 Immediately after the tribulation of those days shall the sun be

darkened, and the moon shall not give her light, and the stars shall fall from heaven, and the powers of the heavens shall be shaken:

30 And then shall appear the sign of the Son of man in heaven: and then shall all the tribes of the earth mourn, and they shall see the Son of man coming in the clouds of heaven with power and great glory.

31 And he shall send his angels with a great sound of a trumpet, and they shall gather together his elect from the four winds, from one end of heaven to the other. (KJV)

When Christ returns at His Second Coming with the saints, He first will execute judgment upon the Palestinian Arabs in Bozrah (i.e., southern Jordan):

Isaiah 34:1-17

1 Come near, ye nations, to hear; and hearken, ye people: let the earth hear, and all that is therein; the world, and all things that come forth of it.

2 For the indignation of the LORD is upon all nations, and his fury upon all their armies: he hath utterly destroyed them, he hath delivered them to the slaughter.

3 Their slain also shall be cast out, and their stink shall come up out of their carcases, and the mountains shall be melted with their blood.

4 And all the host of heaven shall be dissolved, and the heavens shall be rolled together as a scroll: and all their host shall fall down, as the leaf falleth off from the vine, and as a falling fig from the fig tree.

5 For my sword shall be bathed in heaven: behold, it shall come down upon Idumea, and upon the people of my curse, to judgment.

6 The sword of the LORD is filled with blood, it is made fat with fatness, and with the blood of lambs and goats, with the fat of the kidneys of rams: for the LORD hath a sacrifice in Bozrah, and a great slaughter in the land of Idumea.

7 And the unicorns shall come down with them, and the bullocks with the bulls; and their land shall be soaked with blood, and their dust made fat with fatness.

8 For it is the day of the LORD's vengeance, and the year of recompences for the controversy of Zion.

9 And the streams thereof shall be turned into pitch, and the dust thereof into brimstone, and the land thereof shall become burning pitch.

10 It shall not be quenched night nor day; the smoke thereof shall go

up for ever: from generation to generation it shall lie waste; none shall pass through it for ever and ever.

11 But the cormorant and the bittern shall possess it; the owl also and the raven shall dwell in it: and he shall stretch out upon it the line of confusion, and the stones of emptiness.

12 They shall call the nobles thereof to the kingdom, but none shall be there, and all her princes shall be nothing.

13 And thorns shall come up in her palaces, nettles and brambles in the fortresses thereof: and it shall be an habitation of dragons, and a court for owls.

14 The wild beasts of the desert shall also meet with the wild beasts of the island, and the satyr shall cry to his fellow; the screech owl also shall rest there, and find for herself a place of rest.

15 There shall the great owl make her nest, and lay, and hatch, and gather under her shadow: there shall the vultures also be gathered, every one with her mate.

16 Seek ye out of the book of the LORD, and read: no one of these shall fail, none shall want her mate: for my mouth it hath commanded, and his spirit it hath gathered them.

17 And he hath cast the lot for them, and his hand hath divided it unto them by line: they shall possess it for ever, from generation to generation shall they dwell therein. (KJV)

Isaiah 63:1-6

1 Who is this that cometh from Edom, with dyed garments from Bozrah? this that is glorious in his apparel, travelling in the greatness of his strength? I that speak in righteousness, mighty to save.

2 Wherefore art thou red in thine apparel, and thy garments like him that treadeth in the winefat?

3 I have trodden the winepress alone; and of the people there was none with me: for I will tread them in mine anger, and trample them in my fury; and their blood shall be sprinkled upon my garments, and I will stain all my raiment.

4 For the day of vengeance is in mine heart, and the year of my redeemed is come.

5 And I looked, and there was none to help; and I wondered that there was none to uphold: therefore mine own arm brought salvation unto me; and my fury, it upheld me.

6 And I will tread down the people in mine anger, and make them drunk in my fury, and I will bring down their strength to the earth. (KJV)

God will shake the heavens and the earth at His Coming, and will rescue Israel from the "northern army" (i.e., the army of Antichrist):

Joel 2:10-11, 18-21
10 The earth shall quake before them; the heavens shall tremble: the sun and the moon shall be dark, and the stars shall withdraw their shining:
11 And the LORD shall utter his voice before his army: for his camp is very great: for he is strong that executeth his word: for the day of the LORD is great and very terrible; and who can abide it?
18 Then will the LORD be jealous for his land, and pity his people.
19 Yea, the LORD will answer and say unto his people, Behold, I will send you corn, and wine, and oil, and ye shall be satisfied therewith: and I will no more make you a reproach among the heathen:
20 But I will remove far off from you the northern army, and will drive him into a land barren and desolate, with his face toward the east sea, and his hinder part toward the utmost sea, and his stink shall come up, and his ill savour shall come up, because he hath done great things.
21 Fear not, O land; be glad and rejoice: for the LORD will do great things. (KJV)

This final shaking of the earth and the heavens is the climax of the "shaking" that occurs throughout the judgments portrayed in Revelation:

Hag. 2:6-7, 20-23
6 For thus saith the LORD of hosts; Yet once, it is a little while, and I will shake the heavens, and the earth, and the sea, and the dry land;
7 And I will shake all nations, and the desire of all nations shall come: and I will fill this house with glory, saith the LORD of hosts.
20 And again the word of the LORD came unto Haggai in the four and twentieth day of the month, saying,
21 Speak to Zerubbabel, governor of Judah, saying, I will shake the heavens and the earth;
22 And I will overthrow the throne of kingdoms, and I will destroy the strength of the kingdoms of the heathen; and I will overthrow the chariots, and those that ride in them; and the horses and their riders shall come

down, every one by the sword of his brother.

23 In that day, saith the LORD of hosts, will I take thee, O Zerubbabel, my servant, the son of Shealtiel, saith the LORD, and will make thee as a signet: for I have chosen thee, saith the LORD of hosts. (KJV)

God will punish those people among the nations who will have sold some of the Jews into slavery; and again, we have the winepress symbolism illustrating the massive death and destruction at Armageddon:

Joel 3:1-21

1 For, behold, in those days, and in that time, when I shall bring again the captivity of Judah and Jerusalem,

2 I will also gather all nations, and will bring them down into the valley of Jehoshaphat, and will plead with them there for my people and for my heritage Israel, whom they have scattered among the nations, and parted my land.

3 And they have cast lots for my people; and have given a boy for an harlot, and sold a girl for wine, that they might drink.

4 Yea, and what have ye to do with me, O Tyre, and Zidon, and all the coasts of Palestine? will ye render me a recompence? and if ye recompence me, swiftly and speedily will I return your recompence upon your own head;

5 Because ye have taken my silver and my gold, and have carried into your temples my goodly pleasant things:

6 The children also of Judah and the children of Jerusalem have ye sold unto the Grecians, that ye might remove them far from their border.

7 Behold, I will raise them out of the place whither ye have sold them, and will return your recompence upon your own head:

8 And I will sell your sons and your daughters into the hand of the children of Judah, and they shall sell them to the Sabeans, to a people far off: for the LORD hath spoken it.

9 Proclaim ye this among the Gentiles; Prepare war, wake up the mighty men, let all the men of war draw near; let them come up:

10 Beat your plowshares into swords, and your pruninghooks into spears: let the weak say, I am strong.

11 Assemble yourselves, and come, all ye heathen, and gather yourselves together round about: thither cause thy mighty ones to come down, O LORD.

12 Let the heathen be wakened, and come up to the valley of Jehoshaphat: for there will I sit to judge all the heathen round about.

13 Put ye in the sickle, for the harvest is ripe: come, get you down; for the press is full, the fats overflow; for their wickedness is great.

14 Multitudes, multitudes in the valley of decision: for the day of the LORD is near in the valley of decision.

15 The sun and the moon shall be darkened, and the stars shall withdraw their shining.

16 The LORD also shall roar out of Zion, and utter his voice from Jerusalem; and the heavens and the earth shall shake: but the LORD will be the hope of his people, and the strength of the children of Israel.

17 So shall ye know that I am the LORD your God dwelling in Zion, my holy mountain: then shall Jerusalem be holy, and there shall no strangers pass through her any more.

18 And it shall come to pass in that day, that the mountains shall drop down new wine, and the hills shall flow with milk, and all the rivers of Judah shall flow with waters, and a fountain shall come forth of the house of the LORD, and shall water the valley of Shittim.

19 Egypt shall be a desolation, and Edom shall be a desolate wilderness, for the violence against the children of Judah, because they have shed innocent blood in their land.

20 But Judah shall dwell for ever, and Jerusalem from generation to generation.

21 For I will cleanse their blood that I have not cleansed: for the LORD dwelleth in Zion. (KJV)

The following passage in Zechariah 14 states that the city of Jerusalem is again captured by the forces of the Antichrist, and that half of the city's inhabitants go forth into captivity. Then the Lord God Jesus shall go forth to fight the Antichrist and his army. The feet of the Lord will touch down on the Mount of Olives, and it shall split in two, forming a great valley:

Zechariah 14:1-15

1 Behold, the day of the LORD cometh, and thy spoil shall be divided in the midst of thee.

2 For I will gather all nations against Jerusalem to battle; and the city shall be taken, and the houses rifled, and the women ravished; and half of the city shall go forth into captivity, and the residue of the people shall not

be cut off from the city.

3 Then shall the LORD go forth, and fight against those nations, as when he fought in the day of battle.

4 And his feet shall stand in that day upon the mount of Olives, which is before Jerusalem on the east, and the mount of Olives shall cleave in the midst thereof toward the east and toward the west, and there shall be a very great valley; and half of the mountain shall remove toward the north, and half of it toward the south.

5 And ye shall flee to the valley of the mountains; for the valley of the mountains shall reach unto Azal: yea, ye shall flee, like as ye fled from before the earthquake in the days of Uzziah king of Judah: and the LORD my God shall come, and all the saints with thee.

6 And it shall come to pass in that day, that the light shall not be clear, nor dark:

7 But it shall be one day which shall be known to the LORD, not day, nor night: but it shall come to pass, that at evening time it shall be light.

8 And it shall be in that day, that living waters shall go out from Jerusalem; half of them toward the former sea, and half of them toward the hinder sea: in summer and in winter shall it be.

9 And the LORD shall be king over all the earth: in that day shall there be one LORD, and his name one.

10 All the land shall be turned as a plain from Geba to Rimmon south of Jerusalem: and it shall be lifted up, and inhabited in her place, from Benjamin's gate unto the place of the first gate, unto the corner gate, and from the tower of Hananeel unto the king's winepresses.

11 And men shall dwell in it, and there shall be no more utter destruction; but Jerusalem shall be safely inhabited.

12 And this shall be the plague wherewith the LORD will smite all the people that have fought against Jerusalem; Their flesh shall consume away while they stand upon their feet, and their eyes shall consume away in their holes, and their tongue shall consume away in their mouth.

13 And it shall come to pass in that day, that a great tumult from the LORD shall be among them; and they shall lay hold every one on the hand of his neighbour, and his hand shall rise up against the hand of his neighbour.

14 And Judah also shall fight at Jerusalem; and the wealth of all the heathen round about shall be gathered together, gold, and silver, and apparel, in great abundance.

15 And so shall be the plague of the horse, of the mule, of the camel, and of the ass, and of all the beasts that shall be in these tents, as this plague. (KJV)

Geba is about 10 miles north of Jerusalem; Rimmon is in the southern part of Palestine, near Edom. All of the land between these two places, except for Jerusalem, will be turned into a plain. Zechariah gives us additional information in his twelfth chapter:

Zechariah 12:1-14

1 The burden of the word of the LORD for Israel, saith the LORD, which stretcheth forth the heavens, and layeth the foundation of the earth, and formeth the spirit of man within him.

2 Behold, I will make Jerusalem a cup of trembling unto all the people round about, when they shall be in the siege both against Judah and against Jerusalem.

3 And in that day will I make Jerusalem a burdensome stone for all people: all that burden themselves with it shall be cut in pieces, though all the people of the earth be gathered together against it.

4 In that day, saith the LORD, I will smite every horse with astonishment, and his rider with madness: and I will open mine eyes upon the house of Judah, and will smite every horse of the people with blindness.

5 And the governors of Judah shall say in their heart, The inhabitants of Jerusalem shall be my strength in the LORD of hosts their God.

6 In that day will I make the governors of Judah like an hearth of fire among the wood, and like a torch of fire in a sheaf; and they shall devour all the people round about, on the right hand and on the left: and Jerusalem shall be inhabited again in her own place, even in Jerusalem.

7 The LORD also shall save the tents of Judah first, that the glory of the house of David and the glory of the inhabitants of Jerusalem do not magnify themselves against Judah.

8 In that day shall the LORD defend the inhabitants of Jerusalem; and he that is feeble among them at that day shall be as David; and the house of David shall be as God, as the angel of the LORD before them.

9 And it shall come to pass in that day, that I will seek to destroy all the nations that come against Jerusalem.

10 And I will pour upon the house of David, and upon the inhabitants

of Jerusalem, the spirit of grace and of supplications: and they shall look upon me whom they have pierced, and they shall mourn for him, as one mourneth for his only son, and shall be in bitterness for him, as one that is in bitterness for his firstborn.

11 In that day shall there be a great mourning in Jerusalem, as the mourning of Hadadrimmon in the valley of Megiddon.

12 And the land shall mourn, every family apart; the family of the house of David apart, and their wives apart; the family of the house of Nathan apart, and their wives apart;

13 The family of the house of Levi apart, and their wives apart; the family of Shimei apart, and their wives apart;

14 All the families that remain, every family apart, and their wives apart. (KJV)

Ezekiel 38:18-23

18 And it shall come to pass at the same time when Gog shall come against the land of Israel, saith the Lord GOD, that my fury shall come up in my face.

19 For in my jealousy and in the fire of my wrath have I spoken, Surely in that day there shall be a great shaking in the land of Israel;

20 So that the fishes of the sea, and the fowls of the heaven, and the beasts of the field, and all creeping things that creep upon the earth, and all the men that are upon the face of the earth, shall shake at my presence, and the mountains shall be thrown down, and the steep places shall fall, and every wall shall fall to the ground.

21 And I will call for a sword against him throughout all my mountains, saith the Lord GOD: every man's sword shall be against his brother.

22 And I will plead against him with pestilence and with blood; and I will rain upon him, and upon his bands, and upon the many people that are with him, an overflowing rain, and great hailstones, fire, and brimstone.

23 Thus will I magnify myself, and sanctify myself; and I will be known in the eyes of many nations, and they shall know that I am the LORD. (KJV)

Ezekiel 39:1-29

1 Therefore, thou son of man, prophesy against Gog, and say, Thus saith the Lord GOD; Behold, I am against thee, O Gog, the chief prince of

Meshech and Tubal:

2 And I will turn thee back, and leave but the sixth part of thee, and will cause thee to come up from the north parts, and will bring thee upon the mountains of Israel:

3 And I will smite thy bow out of thy left hand, and will cause thine arrows to fall out of thy right hand.

4 Thou shalt fall upon the mountains of Israel, thou, and all thy bands, and the people that is with thee: I will give thee unto the ravenous birds of every sort, and to the beasts of the field to be devoured.

5 Thou shalt fall upon the open field: for I have spoken it, saith the Lord GOD.

6 And I will send a fire on Magog, and among them that dwell carelessly in the isles: and they shall know that I am the LORD.

7 So will I make my holy name known in the midst of my people Israel; and I will not let them pollute my holy name any more: and the heathen shall know that I am the LORD, the Holy One in Israel.

8 Behold, it is come, and it is done, saith the Lord GOD; this is the day whereof I have spoken.

9 And they that dwell in the cities of Israel shall go forth, and shall set on fire and burn the weapons, both the shields and the bucklers, the bows and the arrows, and the handstaves, and the spears, and they shall burn them with fire seven years:

10 So that they shall take no wood out of the field, neither cut down any out of the forests; for they shall burn the weapons with fire: and they shall spoil those that spoiled them, and rob those that robbed them, saith the Lord GOD.

11 And it shall come to pass in that day, that I will give unto Gog a place there of graves in Israel, the valley of the passengers on the east of the sea: and it shall stop the noses of the passengers: and there shall they bury Gog and all his multitude: and they shall call it The valley of Hamongog.

12 And seven months shall the house of Israel be burying of them, that they may cleanse the land.

13 Yea, all the people of the land shall bury them; and it shall be to them a renown the day that I shall be glorified, saith the Lord GOD.

14 And they shall sever out men of continual employment, passing through the land to bury with the passengers those that remain upon the face of the earth, to cleanse it: after the end of seven months shall they search.

15 And the passengers that pass through the land, when any seeth a man's bone, then shall he set up a sign by it, till the buriers have buried it in the valley of Hamongog.

16 And also the name of the city shall be Hamonah. Thus shall they cleanse the land.

17 And, thou son of man, thus saith the Lord GOD; Speak unto every feathered fowl, and to every beast of the field, Assemble yourselves, and come; gather yourselves on every side to my sacrifice that I do sacrifice for you, even a great sacrifice upon the mountains of Israel, that ye may eat flesh, and drink blood.

18 Ye shall eat the flesh of the mighty, and drink the blood of the princes of the earth, of rams, of lambs, and of goats, of bullocks, all of them fatlings of Bashan.

19 And ye shall eat fat till ye be full, and drink blood till ye be drunken, of my sacrifice which I have sacrificed for you.

20 Thus ye shall be filled at my table with horses and chariots, with mighty men, and with all men of war, saith the Lord GOD.

21 And I will set my glory among the heathen, and all the heathen shall see my judgment that I have executed, and my hand that I have laid upon them.

22 So the house of Israel shall know that I am the LORD their God from that day and forward.

23 And the heathen shall know that the house of Israel went into captivity for their iniquity: because they trespassed against me, therefore hid I my face from them, and gave them into the hand of their enemies: so fell they all by the sword.

24 According to their uncleanness and according to their transgressions have I done unto them, and hid my face from them.

25 Therefore thus saith the Lord GOD; Now will I bring again the captivity of Jacob, and have mercy upon the whole house of Israel, and will be jealous for my holy name;

26 After that they have borne their shame, and all their trespasses whereby they have trespassed against me, when they dwelt safely in their land, and none made them afraid.

27 When I have brought them again from the people, and gathered them out of their enemies' lands, and am sanctified in them in the sight of many nations;

28 Then shall they know that I am the LORD their God, which caused them to be led into captivity among the heathen: but I have gathered them

unto their own land, and have left none of them any more there.

29 Neither will I hide my face any more from them: for I have poured out my spirit upon the house of Israel, saith the Lord GOD. (KJV)

Ezekiel states that God "will send a fire on Magog (Russia) ...and...the isles (numerous countries of the world)." At that time, God also completes the destruction of Babylon which already will have been started by the soldiers of Antichrist (Rev. 17:16):

Isaiah 13:1-16

1 The burden of Babylon, which Isaiah the son of Amoz did see.

2 Lift ye up a banner upon the high mountain, exalt the voice unto them, shake the hand, that they may go into the gates of the nobles.

3 I have commanded my sanctified ones, I have also called my mighty ones for mine anger, even them that rejoice in my highness.

4 The noise of a multitude in the mountains, like as of a great people; a tumultuous noise of the kingdoms of nations gathered together: the LORD of hosts mustereth the host of the battle.

5 They come from a far country, from the end of heaven, even the LORD, and the weapons of his indignation, to destroy the whole land.

6 Howl ye; for the day of the LORD is at hand; it shall come as a destruction from the Almighty.

7 Therefore shall all hands be faint, and every man's heart shall melt:

8 And they shall be afraid: pangs and sorrows shall take hold of them; they shall be in pain as a woman that travaileth: they shall be amazed one at another; their faces shall be as flames.

9 Behold, the day of the LORD cometh, cruel both with wrath and fierce anger, to lay the land desolate: and he shall destroy the sinners thereof out of it.

10 For the stars of heaven and the constellations thereof shall not give their light: the sun shall be darkened in his going forth, and the moon shall not cause her light to shine.

11 And I will punish the world for their evil, and the wicked for their iniquity; and I will cause the arrogancy of the proud to cease, and will lay low the haughtiness of the terrible.

12 I will make a man more precious than fine gold; even a man than the golden wedge of Ophir.

13 Therefore I will shake the heavens, and the earth shall remove out

of her place, in the wrath of the LORD of hosts, and in the day of his fierce anger.

14 And it shall be as the chased roe, and as a sheep that no man taketh up: they shall every man turn to his own people, and flee every one into his own land.

15 Every one that is found shall be thrust through; and every one that is joined unto them shall fall by the sword.

16 Their children also shall be dashed to pieces before their eyes; their houses shall be spoiled, and their wives ravished. (KJV)

Isaiah 13:19-22

19 And Babylon, the glory of kingdoms, the beauty of the Chaldees' excellency, shall be as when God overthrew Sodom and Gomorrah.

20 It shall never be inhabited, neither shall it be dwelt in from generation to generation: neither shall the Arabian pitch tent there; neither shall the shepherds make their fold there.

21 But wild beasts of the desert shall lie there; and their houses shall be full of doleful creatures; and owls shall dwell there, and satyrs shall dance there.

22 And the wild beasts of the islands shall cry in their desolate houses, and dragons in their pleasant palaces: and her time is near to come, and her days shall not be prolonged. (KJV)

Revelation 18:1-3

1 And after these things I saw another angel come down from heaven, having great power; and the earth was lightened with his glory.

2 And he cried mightily with a strong voice, saying, Babylon the great is fallen, is fallen, and is become the habitation of devils, and the hold of every foul spirit, and a cage of every unclean and hateful bird.

3 For all nations have drunk of the wine of the wrath of her fornication, and the kings of the earth have committed fornication with her, and the merchants of the earth are waxed rich through the abundance of her delicacies. (KJV)

Revelation 18:7-11

7 How much she hath glorified herself, and lived deliciously, so much torment and sorrow give her: for she saith in her heart, I sit a queen, and am no widow, and shall see no sorrow.

8 Therefore shall her plagues come in one day, death, and mourning, and famine; and she shall be utterly burned with fire: for strong is the Lord God who judgeth her.

9 And the kings of the earth, who have committed fornication and lived deliciously with her, shall bewail her, and lament for her, when they shall see the smoke of her burning,

10 Standing afar off for the fear of her torment, saying, Alas, alas, that great city Babylon, that mighty city! for in one hour is thy judgment come.

11 And the merchants of the earth shall weep and mourn over her; for no man buyeth their merchandise any more: (KJV)

Revelation 18:17-23

17 For in one hour so great riches is come to nought. And every shipmaster, and all the company in ships, and sailors, and as many as trade by sea, stood afar off,

18 And cried when they saw the smoke of her burning, saying, What city is like unto this great city!

19 And they cast dust on their heads, and cried, weeping and wailing, saying, Alas, alas, that great city, wherein were made rich all that had ships in the sea by reason of her costliness! for in one hour is she made desolate.

20 Rejoice over her, thou heaven, and ye holy apostles and prophets; for God hath avenged you on her.

21 And a mighty angel took up a stone like a great millstone, and cast it into the sea, saying, Thus with violence shall that great city Babylon be thrown down, and shall be found no more at all.

22 And the voice of harpers, and musicians, and of pipers, and trumpeters, shall be heard no more at all in thee; and no craftsman, of whatsoever craft he be, shall be found any more in thee; and the sound of a millstone shall be heard no more at all in thee;

23 And the light of a candle shall shine no more at all in thee; and the voice of the bridegroom and of the bride shall be heard no more at all in thee: for thy merchants were the great men of the earth; for by thy sorceries were all nations deceived. (KJV)

Revelation 14:14-20

14 And I looked, and behold a white cloud, and upon the cloud one sat like unto the Son of man, having on his head a golden crown, and in his

hand a sharp sickle.

15 And another angel came out of the temple, crying with a loud voice to him that sat on the cloud, Thrust in thy sickle, and reap: for the time is come for thee to reap; for the harvest of the earth is ripe.

16 And he that sat on the cloud thrust in his sickle on the earth; and the earth was reaped.

17 And another angel came out of the temple which is in heaven, he also having a sharp sickle.

18 And another angel came out from the altar, which had power over fire; and cried with a loud cry to him that had the sharp sickle, saying, Thrust in thy sharp sickle, and gather the clusters of the vine of the earth; for her grapes are fully ripe.

19 And the angel thrust in his sickle into the earth, and gathered the vine of the earth, and cast it into the great winepress of the wrath of God.

20 And the winepress was trodden without the city, and blood came out of the winepress, even unto the horse bridles, by the space of a thousand and six hundred furlongs. (KJV)

Isaiah 24:1-23

1 Behold, the LORD maketh the earth empty, and maketh it waste, and turneth it upside down, and scattereth abroad the inhabitants thereof.

2 And it shall be, as with the people, so with the priest; as with the servant, so with his master; as with the maid, so with her mistress; as with the buyer, so with the seller; as with the lender, so with the borrower; as with the taker of usury, so with the giver of usury to him.

3 The land shall be utterly emptied, and utterly spoiled: for the LORD hath spoken this word.

4 The earth mourneth and fadeth away, the world languisheth and fadeth away, the haughty people of the earth do languish.

5 The earth also is defiled under the inhabitants thereof; because they have transgressed the laws, changed the ordinance, broken the everlasting covenant.

6 Therefore hath the curse devoured the earth, and they that dwell therein are desolate: therefore the inhabitants of the earth are burned, and few men left.

7 The new wine mourneth, the vine languisheth, all the merryhearted do sigh.

8 The mirth of tabrets ceaseth, the noise of them that rejoice endeth,

the joy of the harp ceaseth.

9 They shall not drink wine with a song; strong drink shall be bitter to them that drink it.

10 The city of confusion is broken down: every house is shut up, that no man may come in.

11 There is a crying for wine in the streets; all joy is darkened, the mirth of the land is gone.

12 In the city is left desolation, and the gate is smitten with destruction.

13 When thus it shall be in the midst of the land among the people, there shall be as the shaking of an olive tree, and as the gleaning grapes when the vintage is done.

14 They shall lift up their voice, they shall sing for the majesty of the LORD, they shall cry aloud from the sea.

15 Wherefore glorify ye the LORD in the fires, even the name of the LORD God of Israel in the isles of the sea.

16 From the uttermost part of the earth have we heard songs, even glory to the righteous. But I said, My leanness, my leanness, woe unto me! the treacherous dealers have dealt treacherously; yea, the treacherous dealers have dealt very treacherously.

17 Fear, and the pit, and the snare, are upon thee, O inhabitant of the earth.

18 And it shall come to pass, that he who fleeth from the noise of the fear shall fall into the pit; and he that cometh up out of the midst of the pit shall be taken in the snare: for the windows from on high are open, and the foundations of the earth do shake.

19 The earth is utterly broken down, the earth is clean dissolved, the earth is moved exceedingly.

20 The earth shall reel to and fro like a drunkard, and shall be removed like a cottage; and the transgression thereof shall be heavy upon it; and it shall fall, and not rise again.

21 And it shall come to pass in that day, that the LORD shall punish the host of the high ones that are on high, and the kings of the earth upon the earth.

22 And they shall be gathered together, as prisoners are gathered in the pit, and shall be shut up in the prison, and after many days shall they be visited.

23 Then the moon shall be confounded, and the sun ashamed, when the LORD of hosts shall reign in mount Zion, and in Jerusalem, and before his ancients gloriously. (KJV)

"Treacherous dealers." This is a reference to the foreign nations and leaders, especially Antichrist, who betray Israel at the "time of the end."

"Fear, and the pit, and the snare, are upon thee." This phrase simply means that no place will be safe for people during the judgments of Revelation. This is the same "snare" (i.e., trap) that Jesus said would engulf the whole world except for those accounted worthy to "escape" via the Rapture. (Luke 21:34-36).

"Lord shall punish the host of the high ones." The "high ones" represent Satan and his "fallen angels." (Eph. 2:2). Naturally, they also will be defeated at Armageddon, the day of reckoning for all evil in the world.

"They shall be gathered together...and shall be shut up in the prison, and after many days shall they be visited (or released)." When 1000 years have elapsed after Armageddon, Satan and his angels will be released from their prison (i.e., the bottomless pit) for one final tempting of mankind. (Rev. 20).

"Moon shall be confounded, and the sun ashamed, when the Lord of hosts shall reign." In other words, the light from both the sun and the moon will pale in comparison to the "glory" of God shining over Mount Zion and Jerusalem during the Millennium. Compare the following passages:

Isaiah 28:5-6

5 In that day shall the LORD of hosts be for a crown of glory, and for a diadem of beauty, unto the residue of his people,

6 And for a spirit of judgment to him that sitteth in judgment, and for strength to them that turn the battle to the gate. (KJV)

Isaiah 60:19-20

19 The sun shall be no more thy light by day; neither for brightness shall the moon give light unto thee: but the LORD shall be unto thee an everlasting light, and thy God thy glory.

20 Thy sun shall no more go down; neither shall thy moon withdraw itself: for the LORD shall be thine everlasting light, and the days of thy mourning shall be ended. (KJV)

Zeph. 1:7-18

7 Hold thy peace at the presence of the Lord GOD: for the day of the LORD

is at hand: for the LORD hath prepared a sacrifice, he hath bid his guests.

8 And it shall come to pass in the day of the LORD's sacrifice, that I will punish the princes, and the king's children, and all such as are clothed with strange apparel.

9 In the same day also will I punish all those that leap on the threshold, which fill their masters' houses with violence and deceit.

10 And it shall come to pass in that day, saith the LORD, that there shall be the noise of a cry from the fish gate, and an howling from the second, and a great crashing from the hills.

11 Howl, ye inhabitants of Maktesh, for all the merchant people are cut down; all they that bear silver are cut off.

12 And it shall come to pass at that time, that I will search Jerusalem with candles, and punish the men that are settled on their lees: that say in their heart, The LORD will not do good, neither will he do evil.

13 Therefore their goods shall become a booty, and their houses a desolation: they shall also build houses, but not inhabit them; and they shall plant vineyards, but not drink the wine thereof.

14 The great day of the LORD is near, it is near, and hasteth greatly, even the voice of the day of the LORD: the mighty man shall cry there bitterly.

15 That day is a day of wrath, a day of trouble and distress, a day of wasteness and desolation, a day of darkness and gloominess, a day of clouds and thick darkness,

16 A day of the trumpet and alarm against the fenced cities, and against the high towers.

17 And I will bring distress upon men, that they shall walk like blind men, because they have sinned against the LORD: and their blood shall be poured out as dust, and their flesh as the dung.

18 Neither their silver nor their gold shall be able to deliver them in the day of the LORD's wrath; but the whole land shall be devoured by the fire of his jealousy: for he shall make even a speedy riddance of all them that dwell in the land. (KJV)

Compare Zeph. 2:1-15; and Zeph. 3:1-20.

"Those that leap on the threshold." A reference to the superstitious practice of the ancient Philistines concerning the threshold of the temple of Dragon. (I Sam. 5:4, 5) (Ezek. 9:3; 10:4; 18; 46:2; 47:1). It means leaping over the threshold, instead of stepping on it; probably an allusion to the modern-day resurgence of sorcery and idolatry.

"Fish gate." It was located in the north wall of the city, the direction from which Antichrist will approach Jerusalem.

"They that bear silver." Silver gained through plundering.

"Men that are settled on their lees." A reference to the fact that wine would become strong if allowed to remain on the lees or dregs, thus causing men to become bitter and critical after drinking it. (Jer. 48:11) (Ps. 55:19).

Note what Micah has to say:

Micah 5:3-15

3 Therefore will he give them up, until the time that she which travaileth hath brought forth: then the remnant of his brethren shall return unto the children of Israel.

4 And he shall stand and feed in the strength of the LORD, in the majesty of the name of the LORD his God; and they shall abide: for now shall he be great unto the ends of the earth.

5 And this man shall be the peace, when the Assyrian shall come into our land: and when he shall tread in our palaces, then shall we raise against him seven shepherds, and eight principal men.

6 And they shall waste the land of Assyria with the sword, and the land of Nimrod in the entrances thereof: thus shall he deliver us from the Assyrian, when he cometh into our land, and when he treadeth within our borders.

7 And the remnant of Jacob shall be in the midst of many people as a dew from the LORD, as the showers upon the grass, that tarrieth not for man, nor waiteth for the sons of men.

8 And the remnant of Jacob shall be among the Gentiles in the midst of many people as a lion among the beasts of the forest, as a young lion among the flocks of sheep: who, if he go through, both treadeth down, and teareth in pieces, and none can deliver.

9 Thine hand shall be lifted up upon thine adversaries, and all thine enemies shall be cut off.

10 And it shall come to pass in that day, saith the LORD, that I will cut off thy horses out of the midst of thee, and I will destroy thy chariots:

11 And I will cut off the cities of thy land, and throw down all thy strong holds:

12 And I will cut off witchcrafts out of thine hand; and thou shalt

have no more soothsayers:

13 Thy graven images also will I cut off, and thy standing images out of the midst of thee; and thou shalt no more worship the work of thine hands.

14 And I will pluck up thy groves out of the midst of thee: so will I destroy thy cities.

15 And I will execute vengeance in anger and fury upon the heathen, such as they have not heard. (KJV)

"Until the time that she which travaileth hath brought forth." A reference to the nation of Israel going through severe persecution during the time of Jacob's Trouble, and then being reborn (i.e., saved or converted to salvation) in "one day" at the time of the Second Coming. This is analogous to the sun-clad woman in Revelation 12, representing the visible church on earth, travailing in birth as it suffers through incredible spiritual deception and apostasy until the manchild Christians are Raptured to Heaven.

"Remnant...shall return." After Christ rescues Israel at Armageddon, those Jews who will have been dispersed throughout the world will return.

"Seven shepherds, and eight principal men." Very possibly this could be a symbolic reference to seven spiritual leaders and eight prominent civic leaders in what is left of Israel at that point in time.

"The Assyrian" A reference to Antichrist, who will be confronted by the "true man of peace," i.e., Christ. Antichrist is called the Assyrian because he will originate from an area that once was ruled by the ancient Assyrian Empire. In like manner, the Antichrist is also called the "king of Babylon" (Isa. 14), the Syrian king of the north (Dan. 11:35-45), the Roman "prince that shall come" (Dan. 9:26-27) (Dan. 7), and the Grecian (Zech. 9:13) (Dan. 8:8-9). In the days of the prophets Micah and Isaiah, the Assyrians boasted the great and mighty empire within Bible lands, so it was only natural for them to use Assyria as a basis for comparison when prophesying about the future Antichrist. Compare the following:

Isaiah 10:5-8

5 O Assyrian, the rod of mine anger, and the staff in their hand is mine indignation.

6 I will send him against an hypocritical nation, and against the people of my wrath will I give him a charge, to take the spoil, and to take the

prey, and to tread them down like the mire of the streets.

7 Howbeit he meaneth not so, neither doth his heart think so; but it is in his heart to destroy and cut off nations not a few.

8 For he saith, Are not my princes altogether kings? (KJV)

Isaiah 14:24-27

24 The LORD of hosts hath sworn, saying, Surely as I have thought, so shall it come to pass; and as I have purposed, so shall it stand:

25 That I will break the Assyrian in my land, and upon my mountains tread him under foot: then shall his yoke depart from off them, and his burden depart from off their shoulders.

26 This is the purpose that is purposed upon the whole earth: and this is the hand that is stretched out upon all the nations.

27 For the LORD of hosts hath purposed, and who shall disannul it? and his hand is stretched out, and who shall turn it back? (KJV)

Isaiah 30:27-33

27 Behold, the name of the LORD cometh from far, burning with his anger, and the burden thereof is heavy: his lips are full of indignation, and his tongue as a devouring fire:

28 And his breath, as an overflowing stream, shall reach to the midst of the neck, to sift the nations with the sieve of vanity: and there shall be a bridle in the jaws of the people, causing them to err.

29 Ye shall have a song, as in the night when a holy solemnity is kept; and gladness of heart, as when one goeth with a pipe to come into the mountain of the LORD, to the mighty One of Israel.

30 And the LORD shall cause his glorious voice to be heard, and shall shew the lighting down of his arm, with the indignation of his anger, and with the flame of a devouring fire, with scattering, and tempest, and hailstones.

31 For through the voice of the LORD shall the Assyrian be beaten down, which smote with a rod.

32 And in every place where the grounded staff shall pass, which the LORD shall lay upon him, it shall be with tabrets and harps: and in battles of shaking will he fight with it.

33 For Tophet is ordained of old; yea, for the king it is prepared; he hath made it deep and large: the pile thereof is fire and much wood; the breath of the LORD, like a stream of brimstone, doth kindle it. (KJV)

"Tophet." The exact location where the Antichrist will be destroyed. It is an area in the valley of Hinnom which is just southeast of Jerusalem.

Isaiah 31:4-9

4 For thus hath the LORD spoken unto me, Like as the lion and the young lion roaring on his prey, when a multitude of shepherds is called forth against him, he will not be afraid of their voice, nor abase himself for the noise of them: so shall the LORD of hosts come down to fight for mount Zion, and for the hill thereof.

5 As birds flying, so will the LORD of hosts defend Jerusalem; defending also he will deliver it; and passing over he will preserve it.

6 Turn ye unto him from whom the children of Israel have deeply revolted.

7 For in that day every man shall cast away his idols of silver, and his idols of gold, which your own hands have made unto you for a sin.

8 Then shall the Assyrian fall with the sword, not of a mighty man; and the sword, not of a mean man, shall devour him: but he shall flee from the sword, and his young men shall be discomfited.

9 And he shall pass over to his strong hold for fear, and his princes shall be afraid of the ensign, saith the LORD, whose fire is in Zion, and his furnace in Jerusalem. (KJV)

Zechariah 9:1-8

1 The burden of the word of the LORD in the land of Hadrach, and Damascus shall be the rest thereof: when the eyes of man, as of all the tribes of Israel, shall be toward the LORD.

2 And Hamath also shall border thereby; Tyrus, and Zidon, though it be very wise.

3 And Tyrus did build herself a strong hold, and heaped up silver as the dust, and fine gold as the mire of the streets.

4 Behold, the Lord will cast her out, and he will smite her power in the sea; and she shall be devoured with fire.

5 Ashkelon shall see it, and fear; Gaza also shall see it, and be very sorrowful, and Ekron; for her expectation shall be ashamed; and the king shall perish from Gaza, and Ashkelon shall not be inhabited.

6 And a bastard shall dwell in Ashdod, and I will cut off the pride of the Philistines.

7 And I will take away his blood out of his mouth, and his

abominations from between his teeth: but he that remaineth, even he, shall be for our God, and he shall be as a governor in Judah, and Ekron as a Jebusite.

8 And I will encamp about mine house because of the army, because of him that passeth by, and because of him that returneth: and no oppressor shall pass through them any more: for now have I seen with mine eyes. (KJV)

In the above passage, please note that Tyre builds itself a strong hold, and heaps up huge amounts of gold and silver in its coffers. Yet, it is said that God smashes her into the sea, and destroys her with fire (at the time of Armageddon when the seventh Trumpet-Vial plague will unleash an incredibly horrific and cataclysmic earthquake that will destroy the mountains and islands and cities throughout the world). At that time, God will "encamp" about His "house" in Jerusalem because of the invading army of the Antichrist, i.e., "him that passeth by," and then no oppressor shall ever bother the land of Israel ever again. Obviously this passage requires a future fulfillment so that Tyre can gain the incredible degree of wealth and power mentioned in this scripture, and then be destroyed violently and suddenly as described.

Zechariah 10:9-11

9 And I will sow them among the people: and they shall remember me in far countries; and they shall live with their children, and turn again.

10 I will bring them again also out of the land of Egypt, and gather them out of Assyria; and I will bring them into the land of Gilead and Lebanon; and place shall not be found for them.

11 And he shall pass through the sea with affliction, and shall smite the waves in the sea, and all the deeps of the river shall dry up: and the pride of Assyria shall be brought down, and the sceptre of Egypt shall depart away. (KJV)

Mal. 3:1-6

1 Behold, I will send my messenger, and he shall prepare the way before me: and the Lord, whom ye seek, shall suddenly come to his temple, even the messenger of the covenant, whom ye delight in: behold, he shall come, saith the LORD of hosts.

2 But who may abide the day of his coming? and who shall stand when

he appeareth? for he is like a refiner's fire, and like fullers' soap:

3 And he shall sit as a refiner and purifier of silver: and he shall purify the sons of Levi, and purge them as gold and silver, that they may offer unto the LORD an offering in righteousness.

4 Then shall the offering of Judah and Jerusalem be pleasant unto the LORD, as in the days of old, and as in former years.

5 And I will come near to you to judgment; and I will be a swift witness against the sorcerers, and against the adulterers, and against false swearers, and against those that oppress the hireling in his wages, the widow, and the fatherless, and that turn aside the stranger from his right, and fear not me, saith the LORD of hosts.

6 For I am the LORD, I change not; therefore ye sons of Jacob are not consumed. (KJV)

Isaiah 29:1-8

1 Woe to Ariel, to Ariel, the city where David dwelt! add ye year to year; let them kill sacrifices.

2 Yet I will distress Ariel, and there shall be heaviness and sorrow: and it shall be unto me as Ariel.

3 And I will camp against thee round about, and will lay siege against thee with a mount, and I will raise forts against thee.

4 And thou shalt be brought down, and shalt speak out of the ground, and thy speech shall be low out of the dust, and thy voice shall be, as of one that hath a familiar spirit, out of the ground, and thy speech shall whisper out of the dust.

5 Moreover the multitude of thy strangers shall be like small dust, and the multitude of the terrible ones shall be as chaff that passeth away: yea, it shall be at an instant suddenly.

6 Thou shalt be visited of the LORD of hosts with thunder, and with earthquake, and great noise, with storm and tempest, and the flame of devouring fire.

7 And the multitude of all the nations that fight against Ariel, even all that fight against her and her munition, and that distress her, shall be as a dream of a night vision.

8 It shall even be as when an hungry man dreameth, and, behold, he eateth; but he awaketh, and his soul is empty: or as when a thirsty man dreameth, and, behold, he drinketh; but he awaketh, and, behold, he is faint, and his soul hath appetite: so shall the multitude of all the nations

be, that fight against mount Zion. (KJV)

"Ariel." Another name for Jerusalem.

"Add year to year; let them kill sacrifices." In other words, let years go by and sacrifices be killed, but this will not stop judgment.

Compare Amos 1:2; Zechariah 9:10-17; Micah 1:2-4; Micah 2:12-13; Isaiah 18:1-7; Zeph. 3:10; Isaiah 17:12-14; Micah 4:11-13; Jeremiah 10:10-11; Jeremiah 25:30-33; Jeremiah 49:13, 17-18, 33; Isaiah 66:15-19; Isaiah 3:16-26; Isaiah 10:20-27, 32-34; Isaiah 29:17-24; and Isaiah 33:1-12 with the scriptures above.

VIII. A New World

The Millennium

Revelation 20:1-6

1 And I saw an angel come down from heaven, having the key of the bottomless pit and a great chain in his hand.

2 And he laid hold on the dragon, that old serpent, which is the Devil, and Satan, and bound him a thousand years,

3 And cast him into the bottomless pit, and shut him up, and set a seal upon him, that he should deceive the nations no more, till the thousand years should be fulfilled: and after that he must be loosed a little season.

4 And I saw thrones, and they sat upon them, and judgment was given unto them: and I saw the souls of them that were beheaded for the witness of Jesus, and for the word of God, and which had not worshipped the beast, neither his image, neither had received his mark upon their foreheads, or in their hands; and they lived and reigned with Christ a thousand years.

5 But the rest of the dead lived not again until the thousand years were finished. This is the first resurrection.

6 Blessed and holy is he that hath part in the first resurrection: on such the second death hath no power, but they shall be priests of God and of Christ, and shall reign with him a thousand years. (KJV)

"I saw the souls of them that were beheaded." Quite interestingly, the very cruel and barbaric practice of beheading people apparently will come back into style under the rulership of the Antichrist — a perfect illustration of how many people will show their true colors whenever they gain a clear upper hand over others. Obviously when Satan achieves dictatorial rulership over the planet through Antichrist at a time when self-righteous "evildoers wax worse and worse," this will be just one of many atrocities and injustices they gladly will help to perpetrate.

"They lived and reigned with Christ a thousand years." Sometimes it is erroneously believed this passage teaches that the tribulation saints are not resurrected until after Armageddon when the Millennial Reign of Christ begins. However, as we saw earlier, the tribulation saints who are martyred by the Antichrist during the Great Tribulation are resurrected into Heaven immediately after the conclusion of the Great Tribulation because we saw them in Heaven in Revelation 7:9-17 just before the Trumpet-Vial plagues were unleashed on the earth. In this instance, John merely takes cognizance of the fact that they will be included with all of the other saints from all the ages who will be reigning with Christ on the earth as joint-heirs.

As a result of the final conflict at Armageddon, the earth is left literally in a shambles! However, since God's ultimate objective for the earth is redemption and complete restoration of the earth to its original state of perfection, a major reconstruction task of immense proportions awaits. Accordingly, Christ accomplishes this mission within one millennium of time. (Rev. 20:1-10). Quite naturally, Satan, arch enemy of all that is good and creative, is imprisoned in the "bottomless pit" for the duration of the millennium so as to prevent any interference with events on his part. At the conclusion of the Millennium, the final enemy of man, death, will be destroyed and God's Kingdom will then extend throughout all of the world as the following scriptures confirm:

Daniel 2:34-35

34 Thou sawest till that a stone was cut out without hands, which smote the image upon his feet that were of iron and clay, and brake them to pieces.

35 Then was the iron, the clay, the brass, the silver, and the gold, broken to pieces together, and became like the chaff of the summer threshingfloors; and the wind carried them away, that no place was found for them: and the stone that smote the image became a great mountain, and filled the whole earth. (KJV)

Daniel 2:42-45

42 And as the toes of the feet were part of iron, and part of clay, so the kingdom shall be partly strong, and partly broken.

43 And whereas thou sawest iron mixed with miry clay, they shall mingle themselves with the seed of men: but they shall not cleave one to another, even as iron is not mixed with clay.

44 And in the days of these kings shall the God of heaven set up a kingdom, which shall never be destroyed: and the kingdom shall not be left to other people, but it shall break in pieces and consume all these kingdoms, and it shall stand for ever.

45 Forasmuch as thou sawest that the stone was cut out of the mountain without hands, and that it brake in pieces the iron, the brass, the clay, the silver, and the gold; the great God hath made known to the king what shall come to pass hereafter: and the dream is certain, and the interpretation thereof sure. (KJV)

Daniel 7:24-27

24 And the ten horns out of this kingdom are ten kings that shall arise: and another shall rise after them; and he shall be diverse from the first, and he shall subdue three kings.

25 And he shall speak great words against the most High, and shall wear out the saints of the most High, and think to change times and laws: and they shall be given into his hand until a time and times and the dividing of time.

26 But the judgment shall sit, and they shall take away his dominion, to consume and to destroy it unto the end.

27 And the kingdom and dominion, and the greatness of the kingdom under the whole heaven, shall be given to the people of the saints of the most High, whose kingdom is an everlasting kingdom, and all dominions shall serve and obey him. (KJV)

Micah 4:1-5

1 But in the last days it shall come to pass, that the mountain of the house of the LORD shall be established in the top of the mountains, and it shall be exalted above the hills; and people shall flow unto it.

2 And many nations shall come, and say, Come, and let us go up to the mountain of the LORD, and to the house of the God of Jacob; and he will teach us of his ways, and we will walk in his paths: for the law shall go forth of Zion, and the word of the LORD from Jerusalem.

3 And he shall judge among many people, and rebuke strong nations afar off; and they shall beat their swords into plowshares, and their spears into pruninghooks: nation shall not lift up a sword against nation, neither shall they learn war any more.

4 But they shall sit every man under his vine and under his fig tree; and none shall make them afraid: for the mouth of the LORD of hosts hath spoken it.

5 For all people will walk every one in the name of his god, and we will walk in the name of the LORD our God for ever and ever. (KJV)

1 Cor. 15:24-28

24 Then cometh the end, when he shall have delivered up the kingdom to God, even the Father; when he shall have put down all rule and all authority and power.

25 For he must reign, till he hath put all enemies under his feet.

26 The last enemy that shall be destroyed is death.

27 For he hath put all things under his feet. But when he saith, all things are put under him, it is manifest that he is excepted, which did put all things under him.

28 And when all things shall be subdued unto him, then shall the Son also himself be subject unto him that put all things under him, that God may be all in all. (KJV)

Immediately after the events of Armageddon are concluded, Christ initiates a period of judgment for all people still alive on earth:

Matthew 25:31-46

31 When the Son of man shall come in his glory, and all the holy angels with him, then shall he sit upon the throne of his glory:

32 And before him shall be gathered all nations: and he shall separate them one from another, as a shepherd divideth his sheep from the goats:

33 And he shall set the sheep on his right hand, but the goats on the left.

34 Then shall the King say unto them on his right hand, Come, ye blessed of my Father, inherit the kingdom prepared for you from the foundation of the world:

35 For I was an hungred, and ye gave me meat: I was thirsty, and ye gave me drink: I was a stranger, and ye took me in:

36 Naked, and ye clothed me: I was sick, and ye visited me: I was in prison, and ye came unto me.

37 Then shall the righteous answer him, saying, Lord, when saw we thee an hungred, and fed thee? or thirsty, and gave thee drink?

38 When saw we thee a stranger, and took thee in? or naked, and clothed thee?

39 Or when saw we thee sick, or in prison, and came unto thee?

40 And the King shall answer and say unto them, Verily I say unto you, Inasmuch as ye have done it unto one of the least of these my brethren, ye have done it unto me.

41 Then shall he say also unto them on the left hand, Depart from me, ye cursed, into everlasting fire, prepared for the devil and his angels:

42 For I was an hungred, and ye gave me no meat: I was thirsty, and ye gave me no drink:

43 I was a stranger, and ye took me not in: naked, and ye clothed me not: sick, and in prison, and ye visited me not.

44 Then shall they also answer him, saying, Lord, when saw we thee an hungred, or athirst, or a stranger, or naked, or sick, or in prison, and did not minister unto thee?

45 Then shall he answer them, saying, Verily I say unto you, Inasmuch as ye did it not to one of the least of these, ye did it not to me.

46 And these shall go away into everlasting punishment: but the righteous into life eternal. (KJV)

Please note that Jesus did NOT indicate this narrative was a parable by beginning with a qualifying phrase such as: "is like unto," or "like," or "such as," etc. Instead, He very clearly said, "when the Son of Man shall come in his glory..." Therefore, the evidence quite obviously mandates we take Jesus at His Word literally, and apply this passage literally to the time of His Second Coming.

The purpose of this judgment will be to determine which individuals surviving after Armageddon are worthy enough to remain alive on the earth during the Millennial Reign of Christ. Each person will be judged strictly on his own individual merits since this would be the only fair method in judging. (The word for "nations" used in Matthew 25:31-46 is ETHNOS, which also means races, peoples, families, and individuals.) People will be classified as either "sheep" or "goat," depending upon their actions during the time-period between the Rapture and Armageddon. Those persons who help Jews or Christians during their time of tribulation if presented with an opportunity to do so, and never accept the "mark of the beast," will be classified as sheep. The others will be classified as goats and thrown into hell immediately.

Matthew 13:36-43, 47-50

36 Then Jesus sent the multitude away, and went into the house: and his disciples came unto him, saying, Declare unto us the parable of the tares of the field.

37 He answered and said unto them, He that soweth the good seed is

the Son of man;

38 The field is the world; the good seed are the children of the kingdom; but the tares are the children of the wicked one;

39 The enemy that sowed them is the devil; the harvest is the end of the world; and the reapers are the angels.

40 As therefore the tares are gathered and burned in the fire; so shall it be in the end of this world.

41 The Son of man shall send forth his angels, and they shall gather out of his kingdom all things that offend, and them which do iniquity;

42 And shall cast them into a furnace of fire: there shall be wailing and gnashing of teeth.

43 Then shall the righteous shine forth as the sun in the kingdom of their Father. Who hath ears to hear, let him hear.

47 Again, the kingdom of heaven is like unto a net, that was cast into the sea, and gathered of every kind:

48 Which, when it was full, they drew to shore, and sat down, and gathered the good into vessels, but cast the bad away.

49 So shall it be at the end of the world: the angels shall come forth, and sever the wicked from among the just,

50 And shall cast them into the furnace of fire: there shall be wailing and gnashing of teeth. (KJV)

Some people have thought perhaps this scripture teaches that the saints will be Raptured at the time of the Second Coming of Christ (i.e., a "post-tribulation" Rapture). But, as we saw earlier, the scriptural evidence overwhelmingly proves a "pre-tribulation" Rapture; an honest appraisal of all the evidence allows no other conclusion. The problem in understanding this passage comes from our limited view of the full scope and extent of God's Kingdom. We must realize there will be more than just Christians living in it; there also will be Jews living in the nation of Israel, and there also will be non-Jewish people living in all of the Gentile nations throughout the world. Accordingly, this passage parallels the passage which describes the judgment of the sheep and goats in Matthew 25:31-46.

Concerning the Gentile nations, consider the following passages:

Zechariah 14:16-21

16 And it shall come to pass, that every one that is left of all the

nations which came against Jerusalem shall even go up from year to year to worship the King, the LORD of hosts, and to keep the feast of tabernacles.

17 And it shall be, that whoso will not come up of all the families of the earth unto Jerusalem to worship the King, the LORD of hosts, even upon them shall be no rain.

18 And if the family of Egypt go not up, and come not, that have no rain; there shall be the plague, wherewith the LORD will smite the heathen that come not up to keep the feast of tabernacles.

19 This shall be the punishment of Egypt, and the punishment of all nations that come not up to keep the feast of tabernacles.

20 In that day shall there be upon the bells of the horses, HOLINESS UNTO THE LORD; and the pots in the LORD's house shall be like the bowls before the altar.

21 Yea, every pot in Jerusalem and in Judah shall be holiness unto the LORD of hosts: and all they that sacrifice shall come and take of them, and seethe therein: and in that day there shall be no more the Canaanite in the house of the LORD of hosts. (KJV)

This passage undoubtedly affirms there will be people from all the nations of the world who will live in God's Kingdom despite their non-Christian status. These people will be taught "the way of the Lord" so that they can live in the Kingdom as subjects who will be ruled by Christ and the saints. Note what Micah has to say in this regard:

Micah 4:1-2

1 But in the last days it shall come to pass, that the mountain of the house of the LORD shall be established in the top of the mountains, and it shall be exalted above the hills; and people shall flow unto it.

2 And many nations shall come, and say, Come, and let us go up to the mountain of the LORD, and to the house of the God of Jacob; and he will teach us of his ways, and we will walk in his paths: for the law shall go forth of Zion, and the word of the LORD from Jerusalem. (KJV)

This is why John wrote the following:

Revelation 21:23-24

23 And the city had no need of the sun, neither of the moon, to shine in

it: for the glory of God did lighten it, and the Lamb is the light thereof.

24 And the nations of them which are saved shall walk in the light of it: and the kings of the earth do bring their glory and honour into it. (KJV)

The nations are saved because they have accepted and learned "His ways" and "His paths." The fact that earthly nations are even present in God's eternal Kingdom also is supported by the following scriptures:

Ps. 2:7-11

7 I will declare the decree: the LORD hath said unto me, Thou art my Son; this day have I begotten thee.

8 Ask of me, and I shall give thee the heathen for thine inheritance, and the uttermost parts of the earth for thy possession.

9 Thou shalt break them with a rod of iron; thou shalt dash them in pieces like a potter's vessel.

10 Be wise now therefore, O ye kings: be instructed, ye judges of the earth.

11 Serve the LORD with fear, and rejoice with trembling. (KJV)

Revelation 2:26-27

26 And he that overcometh, and keepeth my works unto the end, to him will I give power over the nations:

27 And he shall rule them with a rod of iron; as the vessels of a potter shall they be broken to shivers: even as I received of my Father. (KJV)

Revelation 20:3

3 And cast him into the bottomless pit, and shut him up, and set a seal upon him, that he should deceive the nations no more, till the thousand years should be fulfilled: and after that he must be loosed a little season. (KJV)

Revelation 20:8-9

8 And shall go out to deceive the nations which are in the four quarters of the earth, Gog and Magog, to gather them together to battle: the number of whom is as the sand of the sea.

9 And they went up on the breadth of the earth, and compassed the camp of the saints about, and the beloved city: and fire came down from

God out of heaven, and devoured them. (KJV)

Please note that those people who are deceived by Satan after the Millennium are members of a group of people (i.e., nations) who are separate and distinct from the saints of God.

Revelation 22:1-2

1 And he shewed me a pure river of water of life, clear as crystal, proceeding out of the throne of God and of the Lamb.

2 In the midst of the street of it, and on either side of the river, was there the tree of life, which bare twelve manner of fruits, and yielded her fruit every month: and the leaves of the tree were for the healing of the nations. (KJV)

Daniel 7:27

27 And the kingdom and dominion, and the greatness of the kingdom under the whole heaven, shall be given to the people of the saints of the most High, whose kingdom is an everlasting kingdom, and all dominions shall serve and obey him. (KJV)

Isaiah 9:7

7 Of the increase of his government and peace there shall be no end, upon the throne of David, and upon his kingdom, to order it, and to establish it with judgment and with justice from henceforth even for ever. The zeal of the LORD of hosts will perform this. (KJV)

Naturally, a kingdom necessitates a king, a realm and a reign. Christ is the King, and the earth is part of His realm, and as we saw earlier, the reign will commence with the Second Coming of Christ. Since this kingdom will expand or "increase" forever, it is only sensical that the subjects of the Kingdom be ordinary men and women (i.e., the people of the nations). The saints, on the other hand, will be a fixed and unchanging number of individuals; they will not procreate offspring forever. Likewise, the saints will be "kings and priests" with Christ forever — not subjects of the Kingdom. Compare scriptures which state that both Jewish people and the Gentile nations will be present in God's eternal Kingdom:

Ezekiel 37:21-28

21 And say unto them, Thus saith the Lord GOD; Behold, I will take

the children of Israel from among the heathen, whither they be gone, and will gather them on every side, and bring them into their own land:

22 And I will make them one nation in the land upon the mountains of Israel; and one king shall be king to them all: and they shall be no more two nations, neither shall they be divided into two kingdoms any more at all:

23 Neither shall they defile themselves any more with their idols, nor with their detestable things, nor with any of their transgressions: but I will save them out of all their dwellingplaces, wherein they have sinned, and will cleanse them: so shall they be my people, and I will be their God.

24 And David my servant shall be king over them; and they all shall have one shepherd: they shall also walk in my judgments, and observe my statutes, and do them.

25 And they shall dwell in the land that I have given unto Jacob my servant, wherein your fathers have dwelt; and they shall dwell therein, even they, and their children, and their children's children for ever: and my servant David shall be their prince for ever.

26 Moreover I will make a covenant of peace with them; it shall be an everlasting covenant with them: and I will place them, and multiply them, and will set my sanctuary in the midst of them for evermore.

27 My tabernacle also shall be with them: yea, I will be their God, and they shall be my people.

28 And the heathen shall know that I the LORD do sanctify Israel, when my sanctuary shall be in the midst of them for evermore. (KJV)

It is interesting to note that King David of ancient biblical times will reign as prince and king with Christ, the "King of Kings," over the people of Israel. Some people have speculated that passages such as this one really mean "Christ" when they say "David." But this type of interpretation is a sure recipe for error, so it is imperative we consistently adhere to the common-sense rules of interpretation discussed earlier if we are to minimize our misunderstandings of biblical Scripture.

Ezekiel 36:22-38

22 Therefore say unto the house of Israel, Thus saith the Lord GOD; I do not this for your sakes, O house of Israel, but for mine holy name's sake, which ye have profaned among the heathen, whither ye went.

23 And I will sanctify my great name, which was profaned among the

heathen, which ye have profaned in the midst of them; and the heathen shall know that I am the LORD, saith the Lord GOD, when I shall be sanctified in you before their eyes.

24 For I will take you from among the heathen, and gather you out of all countries, and will bring you into your own land.

25 Then will I sprinkle clean water upon you, and ye shall be clean: from all your filthiness, and from all your idols, will I cleanse you.

26 A new heart also will I give you, and a new spirit will I put within you: and I will take away the stony heart out of your flesh, and I will give you an heart of flesh.

27 And I will put my spirit within you, and cause you to walk in my statutes, and ye shall keep my judgments, and do them.

28 And ye shall dwell in the land that I gave to your fathers; and ye shall be my people, and I will be your God.

29 I will also save you from all your uncleannesses: and I will call for the corn, and will increase it, and lay no famine upon you.

30 And I will multiply the fruit of the tree, and the increase of the field, that ye shall receive no more reproach of famine among the heathen.

31 Then shall ye remember your own evil ways, and your doings that were not good, and shall lothe yourselves in your own sight for your iniquities and for your abominations.

32 Not for your sakes do I this, saith the Lord GOD, be it known unto you: be ashamed and confounded for your own ways, O house of Israel.

33 Thus saith the Lord GOD; In the day that I shall have cleansed you from all your iniquities I will also cause you to dwell in the cities, and the wastes shall be builded.

34 And the desolate land shall be tilled, whereas it lay desolate in the sight of all that passed by.

35 And they shall say, This land that was desolate is become like the garden of Eden; and the waste and desolate and ruined cities are become fenced, and are inhabited.

36 Then the heathen that are left round about you shall know that I the LORD build the ruined places, and plant that that was desolate: I the LORD have spoken it, and I will do it.

37 Thus saith the Lord GOD; I will yet for this be inquired of by the house of Israel, to do it for them; I will increase them with men like a flock.

38 As the holy flock, as the flock of Jerusalem in her solemn feasts; so

shall the waste cities be filled with flocks of men: and they shall know that I am the LORD. (KJV)

God vows to put His Spirit into the hearts of the Jews, and cause them to keep His commandments. It will be a new day for Israel; one in which they will be reborn spiritually after their physical deliverance at the Battle of Armageddon. God then declares that "ye shall be my people, and I will be your God." (verse 28). Quite obviously the Jewish nation must endure forever as will the heathen or Gentile nations throughout the world who will bear witness to what God does for Israel. Accordingly, God promised that He would abolish the old covenant given through Moses and make a new and better covenant with Israel for all eternity — so the Law of Moses will not apply to Israel indefinitely:

Heb. 8:8-13

8 For finding fault with them, he saith, Behold, the days come, saith the Lord, when I will make a new covenant with the house of Israel and with the house of Judah:

9 Not according to the covenant that I made with their fathers in the day when I took them by the hand to lead them out of the land of Egypt; because they continued not in my covenant, and I regarded them not, saith the Lord.

10 For this is the covenant that I will make with the house of Israel after those days, saith the Lord; I will put my laws into their mind, and write them in their hearts: and I will be to them a God, and they shall be to me a people:

11 And they shall not teach every man his neighbour, and every man his brother, saying, Know the Lord: for all shall know me, from the least to the greatest.

12 For I will be merciful to their unrighteousness, and their sins and their iniquities will I remember no more.

13 In that he saith, A new covenant, he hath made the first old. Now that which decayeth and waxeth old is ready to vanish away. (KJV)

Heb. 10:14-19

14 For by one offering he hath perfected for ever them that are sanctified.

15 Whereof the Holy Ghost also is a witness to us: for after that he

had said before,

16 This is the covenant that I will make with them after those days, saith the Lord, I will put my laws into their hearts, and in their minds will I write them;

17 And their sins and iniquities will I remember no more.

18 Now where remission of these is, there is no more offering for sin.

19 Having therefore, brethren, boldness to enter into the holiest by the blood of Jesus, (KJV)

Rom. 11:25-27

25 For I would not, brethren, that ye should be ignorant of this mystery, lest ye should be wise in your own conceits; that blindness in part is happened to Israel, until the fulness of the Gentiles be come in.

26 And so all Israel shall be saved: as it is written, There shall come out of Sion the Deliverer, and shall turn away ungodliness from Jacob:

27 For this is my covenant unto them, when I shall take away their sins. (KJV)

Matthew 26:28

28 For this is my blood of the new testament, which is shed for many for the remission of sins. (KJV)

Isaiah 42:6

6 I the LORD have called thee in righteousness, and will hold thine hand, and will keep thee, and give thee for a covenant of the people, for a light of the Gentiles; (KJV)

Isaiah 59:19-21

19 So shall they fear the name of the LORD from the west, and his glory from the rising of the sun. When the enemy shall come in like a flood, the Spirit of the LORD shall lift up a standard against him.

20 And the Redeemer shall come to Zion, and unto them that turn from transgression in Jacob, saith the LORD.

21 As for me, this is my covenant with them, saith the LORD; My spirit that is upon thee, and my words which I have put in thy mouth, shall not depart out of thy mouth, nor out of the mouth of thy seed, nor out of the mouth of thy seed's seed, saith the LORD, from henceforth and for ever. (KJV)

Jeremiah 31:31-34

31 Behold, the days come, saith the LORD, that I will make a new covenant with the house of Israel, and with the house of Judah:

32 Not according to the covenant that I made with their fathers in the day that I took them by the hand to bring them out of the land of Egypt; which my covenant they brake, although I was an husband unto them, saith the LORD:

33 But this shall be the covenant that I will make with the house of Israel; After those days, saith the LORD, I will put my law in their inward parts, and write it in their hearts; and will be their God, and they shall be my people.

34 And they shall teach no more every man his neighbour, and every man his brother, saying, Know the LORD: for they shall all know me, from the least of them unto the greatest of them, saith the LORD: for I will forgive their iniquity, and I will remember their sin no more. (KJV)

Jeremiah 32:37-40

37 Behold, I will gather them out of all countries, whither I have driven them in mine anger, and in my fury, and in great wrath; and I will bring them again unto this place, and I will cause them to dwell safely:

38 And they shall be my people, and I will be their God:

39 And I will give them one heart, and one way, that they may fear me for ever, for the good of them, and of their children after them:

40 And I will make an everlasting covenant with them, that I will not turn away from them, to do them good; but I will put my fear in their hearts, that they shall not depart from me. (KJV)

Still other scriptures testify to the eternal nature of both Israel and the Gentile nations:

Isaiah 2:1-4

1 The word that Isaiah the son of Amoz saw concerning Judah and Jerusalem.

2 And it shall come to pass in the last days, that the mountain of the LORD's house shall be established in the top of the mountains, and shall be exalted above the hills; and all nations shall flow unto it.

3 And many people shall go and say, Come ye, and let us go up to the mountain of the LORD, to the house of the God of Jacob; and he will

teach us of his ways, and we will walk in his paths: for out of Zion shall go forth the law, and the word of the LORD from Jerusalem.

4 And he shall judge among the nations, and shall rebuke many people: and they shall beat their swords into plowshares, and their spears into pruninghooks: nation shall not lift up sword against nation, neither shall they learn war any more. (KJV)

Isaiah 66:18-24

18 For I know their works and their thoughts: it shall come, that I will gather all nations and tongues; and they shall come, and see my glory.

19 And I will set a sign among them, and I will send those that escape of them unto the nations, to Tarshish, Pul, and Lud, that draw the bow, to Tubal, and Javan, to the isles afar off, that have not heard my fame, neither have seen my glory; and they shall declare my glory among the Gentiles.

20 And they shall bring all your brethren for an offering unto the LORD out of all nations upon horses, and in chariots, and in litters, and upon mules, and upon swift beasts, to my holy mountain Jerusalem, saith the LORD, as the children of Israel bring an offering in a clean vessel into the house of the LORD.

21 And I will also take of them for priests and for Levites, saith the LORD.

22 For as the new heavens and the new earth, which I will make, shall remain before me, saith the LORD, so shall your seed and your name remain.

23 And it shall come to pass, that from one new moon to another, and from one sabbath to another, shall all flesh come to worship before me, saith the LORD.

24 And they shall go forth, and look upon the carcases of the men that have transgressed against me: for their worm shall not die, neither shall their fire be quenched; and they shall be an abhorring unto all flesh. (KJV)

Compare Isaiah 60:1-22; 61:1-11; and Zechariah 2:4-13. Still more scriptures attest to the fact that the nation Israel will last forever, and that she will be transformed through a spiritual cleansing and renewal:

Isaiah 4:1-6

1 And in that day seven women shall take hold of one man, saying, We

will eat our own bread, and wear our own apparel: only let us be called by thy name, to take away our reproach.

2 In that day shall the branch of the LORD be beautiful and glorious, and the fruit of the earth shall be excellent and comely for them that are escaped of Israel.

3 And it shall come to pass, that he that is left in Zion, and he that remaineth in Jerusalem, shall be called holy, even every one that is written among the living in Jerusalem:

4 When the Lord shall have washed away the filth of the daughters of Zion, and shall have purged the blood of Jerusalem from the midst thereof by the spirit of judgment, and by the spirit of burning.

5 And the LORD will create upon every dwelling place of mount Zion, and upon her assemblies, a cloud and smoke by day, and the shining of a flaming fire by night: for upon all the glory shall be a defence.

6 And there shall be a tabernacle for a shadow in the daytime from the heat, and for a place of refuge, and for a covert from storm and from rain. (KJV)

Isaiah 12:1-6

1 And in that day thou shalt say, O LORD, I will praise thee: though thou wast angry with me, thine anger is turned away, and thou comfortedst me.

2 Behold, God is my salvation; I will trust, and not be afraid: for the LORD JEHOVAH is my strength and my song; he also is become my salvation.

3 Therefore with joy shall ye draw water out of the wells of salvation.

4 And in that day shall ye say, Praise the LORD, call upon his name, declare his doings among the people, make mention that his name is exalted.

5 Sing unto the LORD; for he hath done excellent things: this is known in all the earth.

6 Cry out and shout, thou inhabitant of Zion: for great is the Holy One of Israel in the midst of thee. (KJV)

Ezekiel 11:17-21

17 Therefore say, Thus saith the Lord GOD; I will even gather you from the people, and assemble you out of the countries where ye have been scattered, and I will give you the land of Israel.

18 And they shall come thither, and they shall take away all the detestable things thereof and all the abominations thereof from thence.

19 And I will give them one heart, and I will put a new spirit within you; and I will take the stony heart out of their flesh, and will give them an heart of flesh:

20 That they may walk in my statutes, and keep mine ordinances, and do them: and they shall be my people, and I will be their God.

21 But as for them whose heart walketh after the heart of their detestable things and their abominations, I will recompense their way upon their own heads, saith the Lord GOD. (KJV)

Zechariah 12:10-14

10 And I will pour upon the house of David, and upon the inhabitants of Jerusalem, the spirit of grace and of supplications: and they shall look upon me whom they have pierced, and they shall mourn for him, as one mourneth for his only son, and shall be in bitterness for him, as one that is in bitterness for his firstborn.

11 In that day shall there be a great mourning in Jerusalem, as the mourning of Hadadrimmon in the valley of Megiddon.

12 And the land shall mourn, every family apart; the family of the house of David apart, and their wives apart; the family of the house of Nathan apart, and their wives apart;

13 The family of the house of Levi apart, and their wives apart; the family of Shimei apart, and their wives apart;

14 All the families that remain, every family apart, and their wives apart. (KJV)

Zechariah 13:1-5

1 In that day there shall be a fountain opened to the house of David and to the inhabitants of Jerusalem for sin and for uncleanness.

2 And it shall come to pass in that day, saith the LORD of hosts, that I will cut off the names of the idols out of the land, and they shall no more be remembered: and also I will cause the prophets and the unclean spirit to pass out of the land.

3 And it shall come to pass, that when any shall yet prophesy, then his father and his mother that begat him shall say unto him, Thou shalt not live; for thou speakest lies in the name of the LORD: and his father and his mother that begat him shall thrust him through when he prophesieth.

4 And it shall come to pass in that day, that the prophets shall be ashamed every one of his vision, when he hath prophesied; neither shall they wear a rough garment to deceive:

5 But he shall say, I am no prophet, I am an husbandman; for man taught me to keep cattle from my youth. (KJV)

"Neither shall they wear a rough garment to deceive." Ancient prophets wore rough camel skins for clothing. Accordingly, false prophets sometimes will wear such apparel in an effort to imply their prophetic authenticity.

Isaiah 45:14-18

14 Thus saith the LORD, The labour of Egypt, and merchandise of Ethiopia and of the Sabeans, men of stature, shall come over unto thee, and they shall be thine: they shall come after thee; in chains they shall come over, and they shall fall down unto thee, they shall make supplication unto thee, saying, Surely God is in thee; and there is none else, there is no God.

15 Verily thou art a God that hidest thyself, O God of Israel, the Saviour.

16 They shall be ashamed, and also confounded, all of them: they shall go to confusion together that are makers of idols.

17 But Israel shall be saved in the LORD with an everlasting salvation: ye shall not be ashamed nor confounded world without end.

18 For thus saith the LORD that created the heavens; God himself that formed the earth and made it; he hath established it, he created it not in vain, he formed it to be inhabited: I am the LORD; and there is none else. (KJV)

Isaiah 59:18-21

18 According to their deeds, accordingly he will repay, fury to his adversaries, recompence to his enemies; to the islands he will repay recompence.

19 So shall they fear the name of the LORD from the west, and his glory from the rising of the sun. When the enemy shall come in like a flood, the Spirit of the LORD shall lift up a standard against him.

20 And the Redeemer shall come to Zion, and unto them that turn from transgression in Jacob, saith the LORD.

21 As for me, this is my covenant with them, saith the LORD; My spirit that is upon thee, and my words which I have put in thy mouth, shall not depart out of thy mouth, nor out of the mouth of thy seed, nor out of the mouth of thy seed's seed, saith the LORD, from henceforth and for ever. (KJV)

Isaiah 60:1-7

1 Arise, shine; for thy light is come, and the glory of the LORD is risen upon thee.

2 For, behold, the darkness shall cover the earth, and gross darkness the people: but the LORD shall arise upon thee, and his glory shall be seen upon thee.

3 And the Gentiles shall come to thy light, and kings to the brightness of thy rising.

4 Lift up thine eyes round about, and see: all they gather themselves together, they come to thee: thy sons shall come from far, and thy daughters shall be nursed at thy side.

5 Then thou shalt see, and flow together, and thine heart shall fear, and be enlarged; because the abundance of the sea shall be converted unto thee, the forces of the Gentiles shall come unto thee.

6 The multitude of camels shall cover thee, the dromedaries of Midian and Ephah; all they from Sheba shall come: they shall bring gold and incense; and they shall shew forth the praises of the LORD.

7 All the flocks of Kedar shall be gathered together unto thee, the rams of Nebaioth shall minister unto thee: they shall come up with acceptance on mine altar, and I will glorify the house of my glory. (KJV)

Luke 1:31-33

31 And, behold, thou shalt conceive in thy womb, and bring forth a son, and shalt call his name JESUS.

32 He shall be great, and shall be called the Son of the Highest: and the Lord God shall give unto him the throne of his father David:

33 And he shall reign over the house of Jacob for ever; and of his kingdom there shall be no end. (KJV)

Compare Joel 2:12-27; Micah 7:7-20; Mal. 3:2-6, 17-18; Jer. 3:14-22.

Likewise, after the Battle of Armageddon, the nations of the earth will help the Jews return to Israel:

Isaiah 14:1-2

1 For the LORD will have mercy on Jacob, and will yet choose Israel, and set them in their own land: and the strangers shall be joined with them, and they shall cleave to the house of Jacob.

2 And the people shall take them, and bring them to their place: and the house of Israel shall possess them in the land of the LORD for servants and handmaids: and they shall take them captives, whose captives they were; and they shall rule over their oppressors. (KJV)

Isaiah 27:12-13

12 And it shall come to pass in that day, that the LORD shall beat off from the channel of the river unto the stream of Egypt, and ye shall be gathered one by one, O ye children of Israel.

13 And it shall come to pass in that day, that the great trumpet shall be blown, and they shall come which were ready to perish in the land of Assyria, and the outcasts in the land of Egypt, and shall worship the LORD in the holy mount at Jerusalem. (KJV)

Isaiah 49:22

22 Thus saith the Lord GOD, Behold, I will lift up mine hand to the Gentiles, and set up my standard to the people: and they shall bring thy sons in their arms, and thy daughters shall be carried upon their shoulders. (KJV)

Isaiah 66:20

20 And they shall bring all your brethren for an offering unto the LORD out of all nations upon horses, and in chariots, and in litters, and upon mules, and upon swift beasts, to my holy mountain Jerusalem, saith the LORD, as the children of Israel bring an offering in a clean vessel into the house of the LORD. (KJV)

Jeremiah 16:14-16

14 Therefore, behold, the days come, saith the LORD, that it shall no more be said, The LORD liveth, that brought up the children of Israel out of the land of Egypt;

15 But, The LORD liveth, that brought up the children of Israel from the land of the north, and from all the lands whither he had driven them: and I will bring them again into their land that I gave unto their fathers.

16 Behold, I will send for many fishers, saith the LORD, and they shall fish them; and after will I send for many hunters, and they shall hunt them from every mountain, and from every hill, and out of the holes of the rocks. (KJV) (Compare: Jeremiah 31:6-12.)

During the Millennium, the Jews not only will fulfill their original commission to be God's people, but even will preach the gospel to the nations of the earth:

Jeremiah 23:3-8
3 And I will gather the remnant of my flock out of all countries whither I have driven them, and will bring them again to their folds; and they shall be fruitful and increase.
4 And I will set up shepherds over them which shall feed them: and they shall fear no more, nor be dismayed, neither shall they be lacking, saith the LORD.
5 Behold, the days come, saith the LORD, that I will raise unto David a righteous Branch, and a King shall reign and prosper, and shall execute judgment and justice in the earth.
6 In his days Judah shall be saved, and Israel shall dwell safely: and this is his name whereby he shall be called, THE LORD OUR RIGHTEOUSNESS.
7 Therefore, behold, the days come, saith the LORD, that they shall no more say, The LORD liveth, which brought up the children of Israel out of the land of Egypt;
8 But, The LORD liveth, which brought up and which led the seed of the house of Israel out of the north country, and from all countries whither I had driven them; and they shall dwell in their own land. (KJV)

Isaiah 43:10
10 Ye are my witnesses, saith the LORD, and my servant whom I have chosen: that ye may know and believe me, and understand that I am he: before me there was no God formed, neither shall there be after me. (KJV)

Isaiah 52:6-10
6 Therefore my people shall know my name: therefore they shall know in that day that I am he that doth speak: behold, it is I.

7 How beautiful upon the mountains are the feet of him that bringeth good tidings, that publisheth peace; that bringeth good tidings of good, that publisheth salvation; that saith unto Zion, Thy God reigneth!

8 Thy watchmen shall lift up the voice; with the voice together shall they sing: for they shall see eye to eye, when the LORD shall bring again Zion.

9 Break forth into joy, sing together, ye waste places of Jerusalem: for the LORD hath comforted his people, he hath redeemed Jerusalem.

10 The LORD hath made bare his holy arm in the eyes of all the nations; and all the ends of the earth shall see the salvation of our God. (KJV)

Hosea 2:14-23

14 Therefore, behold, I will allure her, and bring her into the wilderness, and speak comfortably unto her.

15 And I will give her her vineyards from thence, and the valley of Achor for a door of hope: and she shall sing there, as in the days of her youth, and as in the day when she came up out of the land of Egypt.

16 And it shall be at that day, saith the LORD, that thou shalt call me Ishi; and shalt call me no more Baali.

17 For I will take away the names of Baalim out of her mouth, and they shall no more be remembered by their name.

18 And in that day will I make a covenant for them with the beasts of the field, and with the fowls of heaven, and with the creeping things of the ground: and I will break the bow and the sword and the battle out of the earth, and will make them to lie down safely.

19 And I will betroth thee unto me for ever; yea, I will betroth thee unto me in righteousness, and in judgment, and in lovingkindness, and in mercies.

20 I will even betroth thee unto me in faithfulness: and thou shalt know the LORD.

21 And it shall come to pass in that day, I will hear, saith the LORD, I will hear the heavens, and they shall hear the earth;

22 And the earth shall hear the corn, and the wine, and the oil; and they shall hear Jezreel.

23 And I will sow her unto me in the earth; and I will have mercy upon her that had not obtained mercy; and I will say to them which were not my people, Thou art my people; and they shall say, Thou art my God. (KJV)

"Ishi" means "my husband." Likewise, "Baali" means "my Lord."

The covenant between Israel and the animal kingdom is not the same as the "New Covenant" between Israel and God. The purpose of the animal covenant is to restore dominion over the earth to man.

Hosea 3:5

5 Afterward shall the children of Israel return, and seek the LORD their God, and David their king; and shall fear the LORD and his goodness in the latter days. (KJV)

Amos 9:11-15

11 In that day will I raise up the tabernacle of David that is fallen, and close up the breaches thereof; and I will raise up his ruins, and I will build it as in the days of old:

12 That they may possess the remnant of Edom, and of all the heathen, which are called by my name, saith the LORD that doeth this.

13 Behold, the days come, saith the LORD, that the plowman shall overtake the reaper, and the treader of grapes him that soweth seed; and the mountains shall drop sweet wine, and all the hills shall melt.

14 And I will bring again the captivity of my people of Israel, and they shall build the waste cities, and inhabit them; and they shall plant vineyards, and drink the wine thereof; they shall also make gardens, and eat the fruit of them.

15 And I will plant them upon their land, and they shall no more be pulled up out of their land which I have given them, saith the LORD thy God. (KJV)

"Tabernacle of David." This expression refers to the throne and kingdom of King David; he will become King over Israel again. (Isa. 9:6-7) (Isa. 16:5) (Jer. 30:9) (Ezek. 34:23, 24) (Ezek. 37:24, 25) (Hosea 3:5).

Isaiah 66:19

19 And I will set a sign among them, and I will send those that escape of them unto the nations, to Tarshish, Pul, and Lud, that draw the bow, to Tubal, and Javan, to the isles afar off, that have not heard my fame, neither have seen my glory; and they shall declare my glory among the Gentiles. (KJV)

Isaiah 27:6

6 He shall cause them that come of Jacob to take root: Israel shall blossom and bud, and fill the face of the world with fruit. (KJV)

Zechariah 8:20-23

20 Thus saith the LORD of hosts; It shall yet come to pass, that there shall come people, and the inhabitants of many cities:

21 And the inhabitants of one city shall go to another, saying, Let us go speedily to pray before the LORD, and to seek the LORD of hosts: I will go also.

22 Yea, many people and strong nations shall come to seek the LORD of hosts in Jerusalem, and to pray before the LORD.

23 Thus saith the LORD of hosts; In those days it shall come to pass, that ten men shall take hold out of all languages of the nations, even shall take hold of the skirt of him that is a Jew, saying, We will go with you: for we have heard that God is with you. (KJV)

Zechariah 3:9-10

9 For behold the stone that I have laid before Joshua; upon one stone shall be seven eyes: behold, I will engrave the graving thereof, saith the LORD of hosts, and I will remove the iniquity of that land in one day.

10 In that day, saith the LORD of hosts, shall ye call every man his neighbour under the vine and under the fig tree. (KJV)

Ezekiel 16:60-63

60 Nevertheless I will remember my covenant with thee in the days of thy youth, and I will establish unto thee an everlasting covenant.

61 Then thou shalt remember thy ways, and be ashamed, when thou shalt receive thy sisters, thine elder and thy younger: and I will give them unto thee for daughters, but not by thy covenant.

62 And I will establish my covenant with thee; and thou shalt know that I am the LORD:

63 That thou mayest remember, and be confounded, and never open thy mouth any more because of thy shame, when I am pacified toward thee for all that thou hast done, saith the Lord GOD. (KJV)

Ezekiel 20:40-44

40 For in mine holy mountain, in the mountain of the height of Israel,

saith the Lord GOD, there shall all the house of Israel, all of them in the land, serve me: there will I accept them, and there will I require your offerings, and the firstfruits of your oblations, with all your holy things.

41 I will accept you with your sweet savour, when I bring you out from the people, and gather you out of the countries wherein ye have been scattered; and I will be sanctified in you before the heathen.

42 And ye shall know that I am the LORD, when I shall bring you into the land of Israel, into the country for the which I lifted up mine hand to give it to your fathers.

43 And there shall ye remember your ways, and all your doings, wherein ye have been defiled; and ye shall lothe yourselves in your own sight for all your evils that ye have committed.

44 And ye shall know that I am the LORD, when I have wrought with you for my name's sake, not according to your wicked ways, nor according to your corrupt doings, O ye house of Israel, saith the Lord GOD. (KJV)

Ezekiel 28:25-26

25 Thus saith the Lord GOD; When I shall have gathered the house of Israel from the people among whom they are scattered, and shall be sanctified in them in the sight of the heathen, then shall they dwell in their land that I have given to my servant Jacob.

26 And they shall dwell safely therein, and shall build houses, and plant vineyards; yea, they shall dwell with confidence, when I have executed judgments upon all those that despise them round about them; and they shall know that I am the LORD their God. (KJV)

Joel 3:18-21

18 And it shall come to pass in that day, that the mountains shall drop down new wine, and the hills shall flow with milk, and all the rivers of Judah shall flow with waters, and a fountain shall come forth of the house of the LORD, and shall water the valley of Shittim.

19 Egypt shall be a desolation, and Edom shall be a desolate wilderness, for the violence against the children of Judah, because they have shed innocent blood in their land.

20 But Judah shall dwell for ever, and Jerusalem from generation to generation.

21 For I will cleanse their blood that I have not cleansed: for the

LORD dwelleth in Zion. (KJV)

For additional references, see the following scriptures: Isaiah 2:2-4; Isaiah 19:17-25; Isaiah 33:13-24; Isaiah 40:9; Isaiah 51; Isaiah 54:9-17; Isaiah 55:3-5; Isaiah 56:1-8; Jer. 16:14-21; Jer. 17:24-26; Jer. 24:5-7; Jer. 30:8-22; Jer. 31:27-40; Jer. 32:37-44; Jer. 33:6-26; Jer. 46:27-28; Hosea 1:10-11; Hosea 6:1-3. Likewise, Ezekiel 40-48 describes the visions in which Ezekiel "saw" millennial conditions on earth.

During the Millennium, people will enjoy a life span of hundreds of years. (Isa. 65:20-23). Likewise, they also will enjoy perfect health (Isa. 35), and after the Millennium will even become immortal (1 Cor. 15:24-26) (Rev. 21:4). Deserts of the world will suddenly bloom as a rose (Isa. 35:1-10) (Isa. 51:3) (Rev. 21:1), and the lamb and the wolf will once again feed together in complete peace and harmony (Isa. 11:6-9) (Isa. 65:25). Even stranger yet is the fact that night will seem as bright as day and day will seem seven times brighter than it does now (Isa. 30:26); this would appear to indicate that someday people will enjoy the privilege of greatly-heightened senses. This millennium of time also will offer a condition of unparalleled peace and security and prosperity throughout all of the world, a condition which will be enforced by the Lord. (Isa. 2:2-4) (Isa. 60:12) (Micah 4:1-8) (Zech. 14:16-21) (Isa. 11:1-10) (Isa. 14:1-8) (Isa. 32) (Isa. 57:13-19) (Zech. 3:8-10).

The following scriptures survey future millennial conditions on earth:

Isaiah 2:2-5

2 And it shall come to pass in the last days, that the mountain of the LORD's house shall be established in the top of the mountains, and shall be exalted above the hills; and all nations shall flow unto it.

3 And many people shall go and say, Come ye, and let us go up to the mountain of the LORD, to the house of the God of Jacob; and he will teach us of his ways, and we will walk in his paths: for out of Zion shall go forth the law, and the word of the LORD from Jerusalem.

4 And he shall judge among the nations, and shall rebuke many people: and they shall beat their swords into plowshares, and their spears into pruninghooks: nation shall not lift up sword against nation, neither shall they learn war any more.

5 O house of Jacob, come ye, and let us walk in the light of the LORD. (KJV)

Isaiah 35:1-10

1 The wilderness and the solitary place shall be glad for them; and the desert shall rejoice, and blossom as the rose.

2 It shall blossom abundantly, and rejoice even with joy and singing: the glory of Lebanon shall be given unto it, the excellency of Carmel and Sharon, they shall see the glory of the LORD, and the excellency of our God.

3 Strengthen ye the weak hands, and confirm the feeble knees.

4 Say to them that are of a fearful heart, Be strong, fear not: behold, your God will come with vengeance, even God with a recompence; he will come and save you.

5 Then the eyes of the blind shall be opened, and the ears of the deaf shall be unstopped.

6 Then shall the lame man leap as an hart, and the tongue of the dumb sing: for in the wilderness shall waters break out, and streams in the desert.

7 And the parched ground shall become a pool, and the thirsty land springs of water: in the habitation of dragons, where each lay, shall be grass with reeds and rushes.

8 And an highway shall be there, and a way, and it shall be called The way of holiness; the unclean shall not pass over it; but it shall be for those: the wayfaring men, though fools, shall not err therein.

9 No lion shall be there, nor any ravenous beast shall go up thereon, it shall not be found there; but the redeemed shall walk there:

10 And the ransomed of the LORD shall return, and come to Zion with songs and everlasting joy upon their heads: they shall obtain joy and gladness, and sorrow and sighing shall flee away. (KJV)

Isaiah 51:3

3 For the LORD shall comfort Zion: he will comfort all her waste places; and he will make her wilderness like Eden, and her desert like the garden of the LORD; joy and gladness shall be found therein, thanksgiving, and the voice of melody. (KJV)

Isaiah 11:6-8

6 The wolf also shall dwell with the lamb, and the leopard shall lie down with the kid; and the calf and the young lion and the fatling together; and a little child shall lead them.

7 And the cow and the bear shall feed; their young ones shall lie down together: and the lion shall eat straw like the ox.

8 And the sucking child shall play on the hole of the asp, and the weaned child shall put his hand on the cockatrice' den. (KJV)

Joel 3:18-21

18 And it shall come to pass in that day, that the mountains shall drop down new wine, and the hills shall flow with milk, and all the rivers of Judah shall flow with waters, and a fountain shall come forth of the house of the LORD, and shall water the valley of Shittim.

19 Egypt shall be a desolation, and Edom shall be a desolate wilderness, for the violence against the children of Judah, because they have shed innocent blood in their land.

20 But Judah shall dwell for ever, and Jerusalem from generation to generation.

21 For I will cleanse their blood that I have not cleansed: for the LORD dwelleth in Zion. (KJV)

Compare Isaiah 30:18-26; Isaiah 65:18-25; Isaiah 32:1-5; and Isaiah 32:15-20 with the preceding scriptures.

The Final Purging Of Evil

Revelation 20:7-10

7 And when the thousand years are expired, Satan shall be loosed out of his prison,

8 And shall go out to deceive the nations which are in the four quarters of the earth, Gog and Magog, to gather them together to battle: the number of whom is as the sand of the sea.

9 And they went up on the breadth of the earth, and compassed the camp of the saints about, and the beloved city: and fire came down from God out of heaven, and devoured them.

10 And the devil that deceived them was cast into the lake of fire and brimstone, where the beast and the false prophet are, and shall be tormented day and night for ever and ever. (KJV)

The final purging of sinful people living on the earth at the end of the

Millennial Reign of Christ is accomplished by freeing Satan from the "bottomless pit" and permitting him to "test" all individuals. Those persons who still are sinful in nature, despite having lived during the personal reign of Christ, will be "deceived" and will gather with Satan around the city of the saints, Jerusalem. God will then destroy them with fire from Heaven, after which Satan will be tossed into the "lake of fire and brimstone." (Rev. 20:7-10). After the Great White Throne Judgment is concluded, Hell also will be tossed into the Lake of Fire. (Rev. 20:14).

The Great White Throne Judgment

Revelation 20:11-15

11 And I saw a great white throne, and him that sat on it, from whose face the earth and the heaven fled away; and there was found no place for them.

12 And I saw the dead, small and great, stand before God; and the books were opened: and another book was opened, which is the book of life: and the dead were judged out of those things which were written in the books, according to their works.

13 And the sea gave up the dead which were in it; and death and hell delivered up the dead which were in them: and they were judged every man according to their works.

14 And death and hell were cast into the lake of fire. This is the second death.

15 And whosoever was not found written in the book of life was cast into the lake of fire. (KJV)

Only the unsaved dead will participate in this judgment. Those who knowingly rejected Christ as Savior will have no hope; they will go to the eternal lake of fire. However, those people who never receive a legitimate opportunity to accept Christ as Saviour will be judged according to their compliance with whatever amount of truth they did attain at every moment of their lives, resulting in eternal life for some, and eternal damnation for others. That is why this passage twice emphasizes that these people will be judged according to their works. Furthermore, such teaching does not contradict numerous other scriptures which state that Christ is the only mediator between God and man, and that eternal salvation is based solely upon faith in the finished, substitutionary work of Christ on the cross. (I Tim. 2:4-6) (Eph. 2:8-10) (Titus 3:4-8). But it does mean God takes cognizance of the stark reality that many people never will hear and understand the gospel message in their life-time. Accordingly, the only way for God to determine their true spiritual attitude will be to judge how they conduct their lives on earth.

Rom. 1:18-20

18 For the wrath of God is revealed from heaven against all ungodliness and unrighteousness of men, who hold the truth in unrighteousness;

19 Because that which may be known of God is manifest in them; for God hath shewed it unto them.

20 For the invisible things of him from the creation of the world are clearly seen, being understood by the things that are made, even his eternal power and Godhead; so that they are without excuse: (KJV)

Rom. 2:10-16

10 But glory, honour, and peace, to every man that worketh good, to the Jew first, and also to the Gentile:

11 For there is no respect of persons with God.

12 For as many as have sinned without law shall also perish without law: and as many as have sinned in the law shall be judged by the law;

13 (For not the hearers of the law are just before God, but the doers of the law shall be justified.

14 For when the Gentiles, which have not the law, do by nature the things contained in the law, these, having not the law, are a law unto themselves:

15 Which shew the work of the law written in their hearts, their conscience also bearing witness, and their thoughts the mean while accusing or else excusing one another;)

16 In the day when God shall judge the secrets of men by Jesus Christ according to my gospel. (KJV)

This passage reaffirms the previous passage. It states that every person, regardless of their time or place in history, will be without excuse to one degree or another on Judgment Day. Because of the testimony of the world and universe — the incredible organized complexity of the astronomical and biological worlds, and the extraordinary personality of man and his conscience — he will be without excuse. Every person will be judged according to their knowledge of, and consequential compliance with, the "truth"; no one will have any basis for complaint on Judgment Day concerning their adjudged fate for eternity.

Acts 17:30-31
30 And the times of this ignorance God winked at; but now commandeth all men every where to repent:
31 Because he hath appointed a day, in the which he will judge the world in righteousness by that man whom he hath ordained; whereof he hath given assurance unto all men, in that he hath raised him from the dead. (KJV)

Luke 12:47-48
And that servant, which knew his lord's will, and prepared not himself, neither did according to his will, shall be beaten with many stripes.
48 But he that knew not, and did commit things worthy of stripes, shall be beaten with few stripes. For unto whomsoever much is given, of him shall be much required: and to whom men have committed much, of him they will ask the more. (KJV)

John 9:41
41 Jesus said unto them, If ye were blind, ye should have no sin: but now ye say, We see; therefore your sin remaineth. (KJV)

Once again, these passages confirm that people will be adjudged according to their degree of conformity with whatever amount of truth they attain at every moment of their lives. Those individuals who live a "life of sin" despite their awareness of God's plan of salvation and His moral laws will be judged more harshly than those who live such a life without any specific knowledge of salvation. Likewise, it should be noted that everyone will be judged according to their "works" and "motives." This will be true of Christians as well as everyone else. Obviously there will be varying degrees of rewards and punishments for everyone:

II Cor. 5:10
10 For we must all appear before the judgment seat of Christ; that

every one may receive the things done in his body, according to that he hath done, whether it be good or bad. (KJV)

Gal. 6:7-10

7 Be not deceived; God is not mocked: for whatsoever a man soweth, that shall he also reap.

8 For he that soweth to his flesh shall of the flesh reap corruption; but he that soweth to the Spirit shall of the Spirit reap life everlasting.

9 And let us not be weary in well doing: for in due season we shall reap, if we faint not.

10 As we have therefore opportunity, let us do good unto all men, especially unto them who are of the household of faith. (KJV)

Revelation 22:12

12 And, behold, I come quickly; and my reward is with me, to give every man according as his work shall be. (KJV)

John 5:22

22 For the Father judgeth no man, but hath committed all judgment unto the Son: (KJV)

Matthew 12:35-37

35 A good man out of the good treasure of the heart bringeth forth good things: and an evil man out of the evil treasure bringeth forth evil things.

36 But I say unto you, That every idle word that men shall speak, they shall give account thereof in the day of judgment.

37 For by thy words thou shalt be justified, and by thy words thou shalt be condemned. (KJV)

Rom. 14:10-12

10 But why dost thou judge thy brother? or why dost thou set at nought thy brother? for we shall all stand before the judgment seat of Christ.

11 For it is written, As I live, saith the Lord, every knee shall bow to me, and every tongue shall confess to God.

12 So then every one of us shall give account of himself to God. (KJV)

I Cor. 4:5

5 Therefore judge nothing before the time, until the Lord come, who both will bring to light the hidden things of darkness, and will make manifest the counsels of the hearts: and then shall every man have praise of God. (KJV)

Luke 19:12-27

12 He said therefore, A certain nobleman went into a far country to receive for himself a kingdom, and to return.

13 And he called his ten servants, and delivered them ten pounds, and said unto them, Occupy till I come.

14 But his citizens hated him, and sent a message after him, saying, We will not have this man to reign over us.

15 And it came to pass, that when he was returned, having received the kingdom, then he commanded these servants to be called unto him, to whom he had given the money, that he might know how much every man had gained by trading.

16 Then came the first, saying, Lord, thy pound hath gained ten pounds.

17 And he said unto him, Well, thou good servant: because thou hast been faithful in a very little, have thou authority over ten cities.

18 And the second came, saying, Lord, thy pound hath gained five pounds.

19 And he said likewise to him, Be thou also over five cities.

20 And another came, saying, Lord, behold, here is thy pound, which I have kept laid up in a napkin:

21 For I feared thee, because thou art an austere man: thou takest up that thou layedst not down, and reapest that thou didst not sow.

22 And he saith unto him, Out of thine own mouth will I judge thee, thou wicked servant. Thou knewest that I was an austere man, taking up that I laid not down, and reaping that I did not sow:

23 Wherefore then gavest not thou my money into the bank, that at my coming I might have required mine own with usury?

24 And he said unto them that stood by, Take from him the pound, and give it to him that hath ten pounds.

25 (And they said unto him, Lord, he hath ten pounds.)

26 For I say unto you, That unto every one which hath shall be given; and from him that hath not, even that he hath shall be taken away

from him.

27 But those mine enemies, which would not that I should reign over them, bring hither, and slay them before me. (KJV)

This parable teaches that "worthy" individuals will be rewarded according to how much "good" they accomplish based upon ability and opportunity. In this example, the first two servants had the same amount of ability and range of opportunities because they both had "one pound" with which to work. Accordingly, the servant who gained "ten pounds" was rewarded with "ten cities"; likewise, the servant who gained only "five pounds" was rewarded with only "five cities." The unprofitable (i.e., wicked) servant was severely punished, and even had his "one pound" taken away.

Matthew 25:14-30

14 For the kingdom of heaven is as a man travelling into a far country, who called his own servants, and delivered unto them his goods.

15 And unto one he gave five talents, to another two, and to another one; to every man according to his several ability; and straightway took his journey.

16 Then he that had received the five talents went and traded with the same, and made them other five talents.

17 And likewise he that had received two, he also gained other two.

18 But he that had received one went and digged in the earth, and hid his lord's money.

19 After a long time the lord of those servants cometh, and reckoneth with them.

20 And so he that had received five talents came and brought other five talents, saying, Lord, thou deliveredst unto me five talents: behold, I have gained beside them five talents more.

21 His lord said unto him, Well done, thou good and faithful servant: thou hast been faithful over a few things, I will make thee ruler over many things: enter thou into the joy of thy lord.

22 He also that had received two talents came and said, Lord, thou deliveredst unto me two talents: behold, I have gained two other talents beside them.

23 His lord said unto him, Well done, good and faithful servant; thou hast been faithful over a few things, I will make thee ruler over many

things: enter thou into the joy of thy lord.

24 Then he which had received the one talent came and said, Lord, I knew thee that thou art an hard man, reaping where thou hast not sown, and gathering where thou hast not strawed:

25 And I was afraid, and went and hid thy talent in the earth: lo, there thou hast that is thine.

26 His lord answered and said unto him, Thou wicked and slothful servant, thou knewest that I reap where I sowed not, and gather where I have not strawed:

27 Thou oughtest therefore to have put my money to the exchangers, and then at my coming I should have received mine own with usury.

28 Take therefore the talent from him, and give it unto him which hath ten talents.

29 For unto every one that hath shall be given, and he shall have abundance: but from him that hath not shall be taken away even that which he hath.

30 And cast ye the unprofitable servant into outer darkness: there shall be weeping and gnashing of teeth. (KJV)

This parable approaches the issue from a different angle than the preceding parable did. In this parable, one servant "started" with "five talents" and "earned" an additional five talents; likewise, another servant "had" only "two talents" with which he earned two more talents. Obviously these two servants accomplished the same amount of good based upon ability and opportunity because they both doubled their number of "talents." That is why they received the exact same reward. The wicked servant, of course, was severely punished.

This parable also could illustrate that all people who will accept Christ as their Lord and Saviour will receive the same reward, namely eternal life with Christ. However, once Christians are in Heaven (after having been resurrected or translated during the Rapture), they also will be rewarded according to their "works":

1 Cor. 3:8-15

8 Now he that planteth and he that watereth are one: and every man shall receive his own reward according to his own labour.

9 For we are labourers together with God: ye are God's husbandry, ye are God's building.

10 According to the grace of God which is given unto me, as a wise masterbuilder, I have laid the foundation, and another buildeth thereon. But let every man take heed how he buildeth thereupon.

11 For other foundation can no man lay than that is laid, which is Jesus Christ.

12 Now if any man build upon this foundation gold, silver, precious stones, wood, hay, stubble;

13 Every man's work shall be made manifest: for the day shall declare it, because it shall be revealed by fire; and the fire shall try every man's work of what sort it is.

14 If any man's work abide which he hath built thereupon, he shall receive a reward.

15 If any man's work shall be burned, he shall suffer loss: but he himself shall be saved; yet so as by fire. (KJV)

So, in conclusion, everyone — without exception — will be judged at one time or another. Christians will be judged immediately after the Rapture; "tribulation saints" apparently will be judged immediately after the Second Coming of Christ (Rev. 20:3, 4) (Rev. 11:18) when Christians of all ages will be rewarded (Rev. 11:18). Those people who still are alive when Christ returns to establish His Kingdom on earth will be classified as "sheep" or "goats" and dealt with accordingly. Then finally, after the Millennium, all of the "unsaved" dead will be judged at the Great White Throne Judgment. These different times or occasions for judgment likewise are expounded in the following scriptures:

John 5:25-29

25 Verily, verily, I say unto you, The hour is coming, and now is, when the dead shall hear the voice of the Son of God: and they that hear shall live.

26 For as the Father hath life in himself; so hath he given to the Son to have life in himself;

27 And hath given him authority to execute judgment also, because he is the Son of man.

28 Marvel not at this: for the hour is coming, in the which all that are in the graves shall hear his voice,

29 And shall come forth; they that have done good, unto the resurrection of life; and they that have done evil, unto the resurrection of

damnation. (KJV)

In other words, there are two resurrections narrated in this passage. In the first resurrection portrayed, all who hear the voice of God will live; this is the Rapture. Then, the next resurrection describes a time when everyone (who is still in the grave after the Rapture) will hear the voice of Jesus Christ, our God and Saviour. Some of these people will be judged as having done "good" and will receive eternal life; others will be judged as having done "evil" and will be punished with eternal death and torment. This is the Great White Throne Judgment.

II Tim. 4:1
1 I charge thee therefore before God, and the Lord Jesus Christ, who shall judge the quick and the dead at his appearing and his kingdom; (KJV)

Another way of saying this would be "living ones will be judged by the appearance of Christ (i.e., the Rapture), and the dead will be judged after His Kingdom is established (which is when the Great White Throne Judgment commences)."

Daniel 12:1-2
1 And at that time shall Michael stand up, the great prince which standeth for the children of thy people: and there shall be a time of trouble, such as never was since there was a nation even to that same time: and at that time thy people shall be delivered, every one that shall be found written in the book.
2 And many of them that sleep in the dust of the earth shall awake, some to everlasting life, and some to shame and everlasting contempt. (KJV)

This passage is similar to the others. First, there is a time of trouble during which the saints of the New Testament era will be resurrected. Then, later, there is a resurrection in which some people will "awake" to eternal life, and others to "shame and everlasting contempt." So, obviously this scripture is yet another portrayal of both the Rapture and the Great White Throne Judgment.

We also should note that the term, "second death," is a reference to the fate of the "unsaved dead" who are judged to be evil at the Great White Throne Judgment. The others, judged as "good," apparently will have their names recorded in the "Book of Life" and will enjoy eternal life of an undisclosed nature somewhere within God's Kingdom. However, it is not likely that they will become a part of the saintly group who will be joint-heirs and rulers of the universe with Christ forever. Instead, it is more probable that they will become a part of the general populace consisting of ordinary men and women.

A New Earth

Revelation 21:1, 5

1 And I saw a new heaven and a new earth: for the first heaven and the first earth were passed away; and there was no more sea.

5 And he that sat upon the throne said, Behold, I make all things new. And he said unto me, Write: for these words are true and faithful. (KJV)

The context of this passage is immediately after the Millennium; it is here that John views the final results of the incredible reconstruction job accomplished by Christ during His Millennial Reign. Both earth and its inhabitants are now perfect, and this is the Kingdom which Christ will now deliver over to God. (I Cor. 15:24-28). A NEW WORLD; this is what John saw! Many people teach the world is destroyed at this point in time, but obviously this does NOT make any sense at all! If the earth was destroyed now, what even would have been the purpose of the Millennial Reign? Accordingly, it is not surprising to find that there are a number of scriptures which teach that the earth never is annihilated as many suppose:

1. "For the first heaven and the first earth were passed away." The Greek word for "pass away" is "aperchomai," meaning to pass or change from one condition to that of another. It never means total and absolute annihilation! Accordingly, here is how *Strong's Hebrew-Greek Dictionary* defines "aperchomai":

565 aperchomai (ap-erkh'-om-ahee);

from 575 and 2064; to go off (i.e. depart), aside (i.e. apart) or behind (i.e. follow), literally or figuratively:

KJV— come, depart, go (aside, away, back, out, ... ways), pass away, be past.

2. God said He will make "all things new," not all new things. (Rev. 21:1, 5). At first glance, this contrast in statements may seem to be a play on words, but actually they are entirely different in their meanings! The phrase "all new things" does, in fact, mean that all of the "former things" have been obliterated or annihilated and replaced by newly-created things. But, that is not what this passage says. Rather, God said He will take all things — and instead of annihilating them into complete extinction — will make them brand-new in appearance and condition. As *Young's Literal Translation* puts it: "'Lo, new I make all things."

3. Paul said that when one becomes converted, all "old things are passed away" and "all things are become new." (II Cor. 5:17). In like manner, neither will the earth be destroyed any more than a person is destroyed when converted to salvation and "all things...become new."

4. Paul said the Millennium is intended to provide Christ an opportunity to deliver over to God a PERFECT kingdom. This statement automatically precludes annihilation! Furthermore, why should anyone make the assumption that the reign of Christ on earth for a thousand years will culminate in a grand and glorious failure deserving complete and total destruction and obliteration?

5. Jesus said that the years immediately preceding Armageddon would involve the greatest "affliction" ever to be experienced by mankind! This certainly would not be true if the earth was destroyed after the Millennium:

Mark 13:19-20

19 For in those days shall be affliction, such as was not from the beginning of the creation which God created unto this time, neither shall be.

20 And except that the Lord had shortened those days, no flesh should be saved: but for the elect's sake, whom he hath chosen, he hath shortened the days. (KJV)

6. God promised Noah He would never "destroy" ALL "flesh" again. This covenant is valid for "PERPETUAL generations," and the rainbow, shown to Noah as a sign, is near God's throne during the events of Revelation, signifying God will NOT forget His promise. (Gen. 9:11-17)

(Rev. 4:3). Some people say God only promised never to destroy the world again with water; that His promise did not include other means such as fire. But, that would have been deceptive on God's part. Obviously God could destroy the world any number of ways, so adding this kind of condition to His promise would have made His promise essentially meaningless. Declaring a solemn covenant with Noah never to destroy the world again (and this is how Noah understood it), while mentally adding a reservation such as this would have been highly demeaning to God because it would have been a clear-cut case of outright deception and fraud. Therefore, it is certain that God never will destroy the earth again.

7. There are several scriptures which state emphatically that God's Kingdom will be established DURING the Millennium and that it never will be destroyed:

Daniel 2:34-35
34 Thou sawest till that a stone was cut out without hands, which smote the image upon his feet that were of iron and clay, and brake them to pieces.
35 Then was the iron, the clay, the brass, the silver, and the gold, broken to pieces together, and became like the chaff of the summer threshingfloors; and the wind carried them away, that no place was found for them: and the stone that smote the image became a great mountain, and filled the whole earth. (KJV)

Daniel 2:44-45
44 And in the days of these kings shall the God of heaven set up a kingdom, which shall never be destroyed: and the kingdom shall not be left to other people, but it shall break in pieces and consume all these kingdoms, and it shall stand for ever.
45 Forasmuch as thou sawest that the stone was cut out of the mountain without hands, and that it brake in pieces the iron, the brass, the clay, the silver, and the gold; the great God hath made known to the king what shall come to pass hereafter: and the dream is certain, and the interpretation thereof sure. (KJV)

Daniel 7:13-14
13 I saw in the night visions, and, behold, one like the Son of man came with the clouds of heaven, and came to the Ancient of days, and they

brought him near before him.

14 And there was given him dominion, and glory, and a kingdom, that all people, nations, and languages, should serve him: his dominion is an everlasting dominion, which shall not pass away, and his kingdom that which shall not be destroyed. (KJV)

Luke 1:32-33

32 He shall be great, and shall be called the Son of the Highest: and the Lord God shall give unto him the throne of his father David:

33 And he shall reign over the house of Jacob for ever; and of his kingdom there shall be no end. (KJV)

Ezekiel 37:21-28

21 And say unto them, Thus saith the Lord GOD; Behold, I will take the children of Israel from among the heathen, whither they be gone, and will gather them on every side, and bring them into their own land:

22 And I will make them one nation in the land upon the mountains of Israel; and one king shall be king to them all: and they shall be no more two nations, neither shall they be divided into two kingdoms any more at all:

23 Neither shall they defile themselves any more with their idols, nor with their detestable things, nor with any of their transgressions: but I will save them out of all their dwellingplaces, wherein they have sinned, and will cleanse them: so shall they be my people, and I will be their God.

24 And David my servant shall be king over them; and they all shall have one shepherd: they shall also walk in my judgments, and observe my statutes, and do them.

25 And they shall dwell in the land that I have given unto Jacob my servant, wherein your fathers have dwelt; and they shall dwell therein, even they, and their children, and their children's children for ever: and my servant David shall be their prince for ever.

26 Moreover I will make a covenant of peace with them; it shall be an everlasting covenant with them: and I will place them, and multiply them, and will set my sanctuary in the midst of them for evermore.

27 My tabernacle also shall be with them: yea, I will be their God, and they shall be my people.

28 And the heathen shall know that I the LORD do sanctify Israel, when my sanctuary shall be in the midst of them for evermore. (KJV)

Isaiah 45:17-18

17 But Israel shall be saved in the LORD with an everlasting salvation: ye shall not be ashamed nor confounded world without end.

18 For thus saith the LORD that created the heavens; God himself that formed the earth and made it; he hath established it, he created it not in vain, he formed it to be inhabited: I am the LORD; and there is none else. (KJV)

Isaiah 35:4-10

4 Say to them that are of a fearful heart, Be strong, fear not: behold, your God will come with vengeance, even God with a recompence; he will come and save you.

5 Then the eyes of the blind shall be opened, and the ears of the deaf shall be unstopped.

6 Then shall the lame man leap as an hart, and the tongue of the dumb sing: for in the wilderness shall waters break out, and streams in the desert.

7 And the parched ground shall become a pool, and the thirsty land springs of water: in the habitation of dragons, where each lay, shall be grass with reeds and rushes.

8 And an highway shall be there, and a way, and it shall be called The way of holiness; the unclean shall not pass over it; but it shall be for those: the wayfaring men, though fools, shall not err therein.

9 No lion shall be there, nor any ravenous beast shall go up thereon, it shall not be found there; but the redeemed shall walk there:

10 And the ransomed of the LORD shall return, and come to Zion with songs and everlasting joy upon their heads: they shall obtain joy and gladness, and sorrow and sighing shall flee away. (KJV)

Jeremiah 31:31-40

31 Behold, the days come, saith the LORD, that I will make a new covenant with the house of Israel, and with the house of Judah:

32 Not according to the covenant that I made with their fathers in the day that I took them by the hand to bring them out of the land of Egypt; which my covenant they brake, although I was an husband unto them, saith the LORD:

33 But this shall be the covenant that I will make with the house of Israel; After those days, saith the LORD, I will put my law in their inward

parts, and write it in their hearts; and will be their God, and they shall be my people.

34 And they shall teach no more every man his neighbour, and every man his brother, saying, Know the LORD: for they shall all know me, from the least of them unto the greatest of them, saith the LORD: for I will forgive their iniquity, and I will remember their sin no more.

35 Thus saith the LORD, which giveth the sun for a light by day, and the ordinances of the moon and of the stars for a light by night, which divideth the sea when the waves thereof roar; The LORD of hosts is his name:

36 If those ordinances depart from before me, saith the LORD, then the seed of Israel also shall cease from being a nation before me for ever.

37 Thus saith the LORD; If heaven above can be measured, and the foundations of the earth searched out beneath, I will also cast off all the seed of Israel for all that they have done, saith the LORD.

38 Behold, the days come, saith the LORD, that the city shall be built to the LORD from the tower of Hananeel unto the gate of the corner.

39 And the measuring line shall yet go forth over against it upon the hill Gareb, and shall compass about to Goath.

40 And the whole valley of the dead bodies, and of the ashes, and all the fields unto the brook of Kidron, unto the corner of the horse gate toward the east, shall be holy unto the LORD; it shall not be plucked up, nor thrown down any more for ever. (KJV)

8. The ultimate objective is redemption, not total annihilation:

Isaiah 45:17-18

17 But Israel shall be saved in the LORD with an everlasting salvation: ye shall not be ashamed nor confounded world without end.

18 For thus saith the LORD that created the heavens; God himself that formed the earth and made it; he hath established it, he created it not in vain, he formed it to be inhabited: I am the LORD; and there is none else. (KJV)

Daniel 2:44

44 And in the days of these kings shall the God of heaven set up a kingdom, which shall never be destroyed: and the kingdom shall not be left to other people....and it shall stand for ever. (KJV)

Daniel 7:13-14

13 I saw in the night visions, and, behold, one like the Son of man came with the clouds of heaven, and came to the Ancient of days, and they brought him near before him.

14 And there was given him dominion, and glory, and a kingdom, that all people, nations, and languages, should serve him: his dominion is an everlasting dominion, which shall not pass away, and his kingdom that which shall not be destroyed. (KJV)

Revelation 21:1, 5

1 And I saw a new heaven and a new earth: for the first heaven and the first earth were passed away; and there was no more sea.

5 And he that sat upon the throne said, Behold, I make all things new. And he said unto me, Write: for these words are true and faithful. (KJV)

Isaiah 11:6-9

6 The wolf also shall dwell with the lamb, and the leopard shall lie down with the kid; and the calf and the young lion and the fatling together; and a little child shall lead them.

7 And the cow and the bear shall feed; their young ones shall lie down together: and the lion shall eat straw like the ox.

8 And the sucking child shall play on the hole of the asp, and the weaned child shall put his hand on the cockatrice' den.

9 They shall not hurt nor destroy in all my holy mountain: for the earth shall be full of the knowledge of the LORD, as the waters cover the sea. (KJV)

1 Cor. 15:24-26

24 Then cometh the end, when he shall have delivered up the kingdom to God, even the Father; when he shall have put down all rule and all authority and power.

25 For he must reign, till he hath put all enemies under his feet.

26 The last enemy that shall be destroyed is death. (KJV)

Jeremiah 31:31-40

31 Behold, the days come, saith the LORD, that I will make a new covenant with the house of Israel, and with the house of Judah:

32 Not according to the covenant that I made with their fathers in the

day that I took them by the hand to bring them out of the land of Egypt; which my covenant they brake, although I was an husband unto them, saith the LORD:

33 But this shall be the covenant that I will make with the house of Israel; After those days, saith the LORD, I will put my law in their inward parts, and write it in their hearts; and will be their God, and they shall be my people.

34 And they shall teach no more every man his neighbour, and every man his brother, saying, Know the LORD: for they shall all know me, from the least of them unto the greatest of them, saith the LORD: for I will forgive their iniquity, and I will remember their sin no more.

35 Thus saith the LORD, which giveth the sun for a light by day, and the ordinances of the moon and of the stars for a light by night, which divideth the sea when the waves thereof roar; The LORD of hosts is his name:

36 If those ordinances depart from before me, saith the LORD, then the seed of Israel also shall cease from being a nation before me for ever.

37 Thus saith the LORD; If heaven above can be measured, and the foundations of the earth searched out beneath, I will also cast off all the seed of Israel for all that they have done, saith the LORD.

38 Behold, the days come, saith the LORD, that the city shall be built to the LORD from the tower of Hananeel unto the gate of the corner.

39 And the measuring line shall yet go forth over against it upon the hill Gareb, and shall compass about to Goath.

40 And the whole valley of the dead bodies, and of the ashes, and all the fields unto the brook of Kidron, unto the corner of the horse gate toward the east, shall be holy unto the LORD; it shall not be plucked up, nor thrown down any more for ever. (KJV)

9. Revelation goes into great detail concerning numerous events, many of them of minor importance. So why assume that an unrecorded catastrophe of fantastic proportions occurs?

10. A superficial reading of the following passages (Rev. 21:1) (II Peter 3:7-13) (Heb. 1:10-12) (Mal. 4:1) prompts many people to say that the earth will be annihilated after the Millennium or that it will be renovated by fire after the Millennium. However, a careful analysis of these scriptures will reveal they really refer to the results of the seven plagues of fire (Trumpet-Vial plagues) described in Chapter VI of this

book. Peter's passage even provides confirmation of this by stating that this fiery destruction of earth will occur DURING the "Day of the Lord" (previously defined as a period of wrath and judgment by God upon the earth, highlighted by the Trumpet-Vial plagues).

II Peter 3:7-13

7 But the heavens and the earth, which are now, by the same word are kept in store, reserved unto fire against the day of judgment and perdition of ungodly men.

8 But, beloved, be not ignorant of this one thing, that one day is with the Lord as a thousand years, and a thousand years as one day.

9 The Lord is not slack concerning his promise, as some men count slackness; but is longsuffering to us-ward, not willing that any should perish, but that all should come to repentance.

10 But the day of the Lord will come as a thief in the night; in the which the heavens shall pass away with a great noise, and the elements shall melt with fervent heat, the earth also and the works that are therein shall be burned up.

11 Seeing then that all these things shall be dissolved, what manner of persons ought ye to be in all holy conversation and godliness,

12 Looking for and hasting unto the coming of the day of God, wherein the heavens being on fire shall be dissolved, and the elements shall melt with fervent heat?

13 Nevertheless we, according to his promise, look for new heavens and a new earth, wherein dwelleth righteousness. (KJV)

The Greek word for "pass away" means "to go by or away from in the sense of changing from one condition to that of another; it never means annihilation." Likewise, the Greek word for "elements" is STOICHEION, and it means "element, principle, rudiment." It is used in Gal. 4:3, 9 and Col. 2:8, 20 in reference to the principle of sin and of the present world system, including the things which man has made that have to be destroyed before the earth can be purified. Finally, the Greek word for both "melt" and "dissolved" is LUO, and it means to "loosen" (literally or figuratively), except in verse 12 where the Greek word for "melt" is a different word, TEKO, meaning to "liquefy." Obviously none of these words imply an annihilation of the earth at any point in time; they simply indicate an episode of burning, melting, loosening and shaking for the earth. So, as confirmed previously, this period of burning and loosening must occur during the "Day of the Lord" — which is when the Trumpet-Vial Plagues of fire strike the earth.

Heb. 1:10-12
And, Thou, Lord, in the beginning hast laid the foundation of the earth; and the heavens are the works of thine hands; They shall PERISH (Gr. APOLLUMI; be destroyed or be ruined; but never annihilated)... and they shall be CHANGED (Gr. ALLASSO; changed or made different). (KJV)

Revelation 21:1
1 And I saw a new heaven and a new earth: for the first heaven and the first earth were passed away; and there was no more sea. (KJV)

The Greek word for "new" is KAINOS, which means "new or renewed," especially in freshness and character, but never new in existence; it is in direct contrast to the Greek word NEOS which means "new in existence." The Greek word for "passed away" is "aperchomai," and it is the same word we saw in II Peter 3:7-13. Clearly this scripture harmonizes with the preceding passages which we analyzed previously. Therefore, the earth never will be annihilated or obliterated to absolute extinction; instead, it will be redeemed and purged with fire during the Great and Terrible Day Of The Lord, a day of Wrath and Judgment!

Eternity

"And there was no more sea." (Rev. 21:1). This does not mean there will be no more water on the earth. The implication is that there will be no large bodies of water such as oceans and seas. Instead, there will be a more equitable distribution of land and water throughout the globe, very possibly as a result of the extraordinary earthquake that will happen during the seventh Trumpet-Vial plague (Rev. 16:17, 18, 20). The "surplus" water now on the earth very possibly could be restored to its original location in the sky. After all, the purpose of regeneration and redemption is the restoration of everything, including the earth itself, to the original condition:

Gen. 1:6-10

6 And God said, Let there be a firmament in the midst of the waters, and let it divide the waters from the waters.

7 And God made the firmament, and divided the waters which were under the firmament from the waters which were above the firmament: and it was so.

8 And God called the firmament Heaven. And the evening and the morning were the second day.

9 And God said, Let the waters under the heaven be gathered together unto one place, and let the dry land appear: and it was so.

10 And God called the dry land Earth; and the gathering together of the waters called he Seas: and God saw that it was good. (KJV)

Gen. 7:11

11 In the six hundredth year of Noah's life, in the second month, the seventeenth day of the month, the same day were all the fountains of the great deep broken up, and the windows of heaven were opened. (KJV)

This canopy of water in the sky might help to produce a "Garden-of-Eden" environment for the whole earth. It probably would help, at least, to shield the earth from certain harmful rays of the sun, including those that help cause decay. It might even act as an "air-conditioner" regulator, thereby creating a virtual paradise on earth. It is apparent, moreover, that the earth, in general, will be a much different place than it is now. A new world; this is what John saw in his vision.

Revelation 21:1-27

1 And I saw a new heaven and a new earth: for the first heaven and the first earth were passed away; and there was no more sea.

2 And I John saw the holy city, new Jerusalem, coming down from God out of heaven, prepared as a bride adorned for her husband.

3 And I heard a great voice out of heaven saying, Behold, the tabernacle of God is with men, and he will dwell with them, and they shall be his people, and God himself shall be with them, and be their God.

4 And God shall wipe away all tears from their eyes; and there shall be no more death, neither sorrow, nor crying, neither shall there be any more pain: for the former things are passed away.

5 And he that sat upon the throne said, Behold, I make all things new.

And he said unto me, Write: for these words are true and faithful.

6 And he said unto me, It is done. I am Alpha and Omega, the beginning and the end. I will give unto him that is athirst of the fountain of the water of life freely.

7 He that overcometh shall inherit all things; and I will be his God, and he shall be my son.

8 But the fearful, and unbelieving, and the abominable, and murderers, and whoremongers, and sorcerers, and idolaters, and all liars, shall have their part in the lake which burneth with fire and brimstone: which is the second death.

9 And there came unto me one of the seven angels which had the seven vials full of the seven last plagues, and talked with me, saying, Come hither, I will shew thee the bride, the Lamb's wife.

10 And he carried me away in the spirit to a great and high mountain, and shewed me that great city, the holy Jerusalem, descending out of heaven from God,

11 Having the glory of God: and her light was like unto a stone most precious, even like a jasper stone, clear as crystal;

12 And had a wall great and high, and had twelve gates, and at the gates twelve angels, and names written thereon, which are the names of the twelve tribes of the children of Israel:

13 On the east three gates; on the north three gates; on the south three gates; and on the west three gates.

14 And the wall of the city had twelve foundations, and in them the names of the twelve apostles of the Lamb.

15 And he that talked with me had a golden reed to measure the city, and the gates thereof, and the wall thereof.

16 And the city lieth foursquare, and the length is as large as the breadth: and he measured the city with the reed, twelve thousand furlongs. The length and the breadth and the height of it are equal.

17 And he measured the wall thereof, an hundred and forty and four cubits, according to the measure of a man, that is, of the angel.

18 And the building of the wall of it was of jasper: and the city was pure gold, like unto clear glass.

19 And the foundations of the wall of the city were garnished with all manner of precious stones. The first foundation was jasper; the second, sapphire; the third, a chalcedony; the fourth, an emerald;

20 The fifth, sardonyx; the sixth, sardius; the seventh, chrysolyte; the

eighth, beryl; the ninth, a topaz; the tenth, a chrysoprasus; the eleventh, a jacinth; the twelfth, an amethyst.

21 And the twelve gates were twelve pearls; every several gate was of one pearl: and the street of the city was pure gold, as it were transparent glass.

22 And I saw no temple therein: for the Lord God Almighty and the Lamb are the temple of it.

23 And the city had no need of the sun, neither of the moon, to shine in it: for the glory of God did lighten it, and the Lamb is the light thereof.

24 And the nations of them which are saved shall walk in the light of it: and the kings of the earth do bring their glory and honour into it.

25 And the gates of it shall not be shut at all by day: for there shall be no night there.

26 And they shall bring the glory and honour of the nations into it.

27 And there shall in no wise enter into it any thing that defileth, neither whatsoever worketh abomination, or maketh a lie: but they which are written in the Lamb's book of life. (KJV)

"New Jerusalem." (Rev. 3:12; Rev. 21:2). As noted in *Dake's Annotated Reference Bible*, New Jerusalem is called new because of its eternal freshness and newness of character and nature, not because it is brand-new in existence. Actually, it is as old as heaven itself, and was promised to the earliest saints on earth (Heb. 11:10-16; Ps. 93:2; Ps. 103:19).

"That great city." (Measuring about 1500 miles in its length, width, and height; with 216-foot-high walls surrounding it.) "New Jerusalem" is the "Lamb's wife" only in the sense that it is the home and dwelling-place of the saints. Thus, it is the saints who are the "bride of Christ" (Rev. 19:7-9), not an inanimate object such as the literal city, New Jerusalem. Obviously it would be erroneous to compare God's "relationship" to a literal city with the ideal marriage relationship portrayed in Ephesians 5:22-33. So, it will be the saints who enjoy a very special personal relationship with Christ, not the literal city itself.

Revelation 22:1-5

1 And he shewed me a pure river of water of life, clear as crystal, proceeding out of the throne of God and of the Lamb.

2 In the midst of the street of it, and on either side of the river, was

there the tree of life, which bare twelve manner of fruits, and yielded her fruit every month: and the leaves of the tree were for the healing of the nations.

3 And there shall be no more curse: but the throne of God and of the Lamb shall be in it; and his servants shall serve him:

4 And they shall see his face; and his name shall be in their foreheads.

5 And there shall be no night there; and they need no candle, neither light of the sun; for the Lord God giveth them light: and they shall reign for ever and ever. (KJV)

The prophet Isaiah "saw" this marvelous and radiant city existing near the earth during the eternal age to come. Watching its inhabitants come and go prompted him to ask, with wonderment and amazement:

Isaiah 60:8

8 Who are these that fly as a cloud, and as the doves to their windows? (KJV)

"And the leaves of the tree were for the healing of the nations." This does not mean there will be any sickness or disease in God's eternal Kingdom; only a simple recognition that accidents can happen even to people in a perfect, sin-free environment so long as they are free-will in nature. This probably does not mean, either, that the leaves give immortality to people because death is abolished by Christ at the end of the Millennium. Also, apparently there are huge numbers of these trees because they are in the middle of the streets and on both sides of the river (probably rivers) of this incredibly-large city where rolling foothills near the walls gradually become mountains until they reach the very center of the city where the highest mountain reaches 1500 miles into the sky on which the temple of God is located.

"Shall reign for ever and ever." Some people have said that time and causality will cease in Heaven, thus implying a static and boring existence for the saints throughout eternity. This erroneous concept probably stems from the *King James Translation* of Revelation 10:6, which reads: "There should be time no more." A more accurate rendering of this passage would say something to the effect that the fulfillment of the "mystery of God" will not be delayed any longer. (The Greek word for "time" is CHRONOS, and it means a space of "time"; by implication, "delay.")

Therefore, eternity is not the indefinite cessation of time itself, but the infinity of time.

Revelation 22:6-21

6 And he said unto me, These sayings are faithful and true: and the Lord God of the holy prophets sent his angel to shew unto his servants the things which must shortly be done.

7 Behold, I come quickly: blessed is he that keepeth the sayings of the prophecy of this book.

8 And I John saw these things, and heard them. And when I had heard and seen, I fell down to worship before the feet of the angel which shewed me these things.

9 Then saith he unto me, See thou do it not: for I am thy fellowservant, and of thy brethren the prophets, and of them which keep the sayings of this book: worship God.

10 And he saith unto me, Seal not the sayings of the prophecy of this book: for the time is at hand.

11 He that is unjust, let him be unjust still: and he which is filthy, let him be filthy still: and he that is righteous, let him be righteous still: and he that is holy, let him be holy still.

12 And, behold, I come quickly; and my reward is with me, to give every man according as his work shall be.

13 I am Alpha and Omega, the beginning and the end, the first and the last.

14 Blessed are they that do his commandments, that they may have right to the tree of life, and may enter in through the gates into the city.

15 For without are dogs, and sorcerers, and whoremongers, and murderers, and idolaters, and whosoever loveth and maketh a lie.

16 I Jesus have sent mine angel to testify unto you these things in the churches. I am the root and the offspring of David, and the bright and morning star.

17 And the Spirit and the bride say, Come. And let him that heareth say, Come. And let him that is athirst come. And whosoever will, let him take the water of life freely.

18 For I testify unto every man that heareth the words of the prophecy of this book, If any man shall add unto these things, God shall add unto him the plagues that are written in this book:

19 And if any man shall take away from the words of the book of this

prophecy, God shall take away his part out of the book of life, and out of the holy city, and from the things which are written in this book.

20 He which testifieth these things saith, Surely I come quickly. Amen. Even so, come, Lord Jesus.

21 The grace of our Lord Jesus Christ be with you all. Amen. (KJV)

Actually, we know very little about the fantastic conditions that will prevail for eternity in the future, perfect Kingdom of God. But, it is very exciting to realize that we (Christians) will actually acquire such an amazing inheritance! Thus, we shall be both "kings" and "priests" with Christ forever! (Dan. 7:27) (Rev. 2:26) (Rev. 21:7-10) (Rev. 22:5) (Isa. 32:1) (Isa. 56:5) (Isa. 60:8). Although ordinary people will not possess the incredible supernatural abilities of the saints, some of which Christ demonstrated after His resurrection, they will enjoy greatly-enhanced mental and physical attributes as well as over-all perfection and immortality. Additionally, they will procreate offspring forever, an ever-expanding kingdom (Isa. 9:7) (Isa. 60:22) in which people will populate planets of the universe forever. Moreover, rest assured that God never again will allow sin to blot the perfection of His creation; the absence of Satan will make it very easy to rear children so that they never will sin, while everyone will be free to look down into the Lake of Fire anytime they wish to observe the fate of transgressors (Isa. 34:8-15) (Isa. 66:24) (Rev. 14:10, 11).

Appendix: Special Acknowledgements

The late Arthur E. Bloomfield, theologian and prophecy commentator extraordinaire, author of several books on prophecy which I found to be very enlightening on numerous issues in Bible prophecy. His prophecy books, published by Bethany Fellowship, included the following: *The End Of The Days* (Daniel); *A Survey Of Bible Prophecy*; *All Things New* (Revelation); *Signs Of His Coming* (Olivet Discourse).

The late Finis Jennings Dake, theologian, whose works provided useful insights to my research and studies. His published works (available at: http://www.dake.com) included *Dake's Annotated Reference Bible* and *Revelation Expounded.*

Guy Cramer, whose research paper entitled "Ezekiel Prophesied The 1967 Recapture Of Jerusalem," offered a complete and precise explanation for the 2520 year prophecy portrayed in Ezekiel 4. His research paper is available at: http://www.direct.ca/trinity/jerusalem.html.

Jack Shelton, whose research paper entitled "Prophetic Events Before The Rapture," provided valuable insight regarding Greek textual considerations in Revelation 12.

Frank L. Caw, Jr.
10/30/01

About the Author

Since 1974, Frank Caw has devoted enormous amounts of time to research and study in the fields of biblical prophecy and related philosophical and theological issues. While always insisting on a plain, literal and sensible approach to scriptural exegesis, he has pieced together many new scriptural insights regarding a number of astounding prophetic developments that are poised to be fulfilled in our very immediate future! Thus, it is safe to say that things are not going to happen the way most people think they will happen. That is why the Antichrist will be so successful in foisting a future final great deception on people that will surprise even Christians in many respects! But, this book gives you the scriptural keys for truly understanding what God has said will happen and how you can survive the incredible scenario of events about to unfold!

Printed in the United States
735000002B